UNITED STATES

30°N

MEXICO

HAWAII

15°N

Mexico City ⊙

North Pacific Ocean

Clipperton .

. Kiritimati

I

Line Islands

ls

0°   equator

C O O K

Marquesas
Islands

F R E N C H

RICAN
MOA

I
S
L
A
N
D
S

Tuamotu Archipélago

P O L Y N E S I A

15°S

. Tahiti

Society Islands

Rarotonga .

Austral Islands

Gambier Islands

Pitcairn
Islands

Pacific Ocean

30°S

Easter .

THE PACIFIC ISLANDS

Prepared for the Center for Pacific Islands Studies
University of Hawai`i at Manoa
by Manoa Mapworks, Inc.
Revised 1997.

155°W

140°W

W — E

125°W

45°S

110°W

THE PEOPLE TRADE

PACIFIC ISLANDS MONOGRAPH SERIES 16

The People Trade

Pacific Island Laborers and
New Caledonia, 1865–1930

Dorothy Shineberg

CENTER FOR PACIFIC ISLANDS STUDIES
School of Hawaiian, Asian, and Pacific Studies
University of Hawai‘i
UNIVERSITY OF HAWAI‘I PRESS
Honolulu

04 03 02 01 00 99   5 4 3 2 1

Library of Congress Cataloging-in-Publication Data
Shineberg, Dorothy
    The people trade : Pacific Island laborers and New Caledonia, 1865–1930 /
Dorothy Shineberg
        p.   cm. — (Pacific islands monograph series ; 16)
    Includes bibliographical references and index.
    ISBN 0-8248-2101-7 (alk. paper)
    1. Indentured servants—Vanuatu—History.   2. Pacific Islanders—Vanuatu—
History.   I. Title.   II. Title: Pacific Island laborers and New Caledonia, 1865–1930.
III. Series: Pacific islands monograph series ; no. 16.
HD4875.V36S55   1999
306.3′63′099595—dc21   98–47371

                                                                                    CIP

Maps by Manoa Mapworks, Inc

Design by Kenneth Miyamoto

Printed by the Maple-Vail Book Manufacturing Group

Editor's Note

Dorothy Shineberg's *The People Trade: Pacific Island Laborers and New Caledonia, 1865–1930*, the sixteenth volume in the Pacific Islands Monograph Series (PIMS), is a most welcome addition to the scholarly literature on Pacific history in general and on the indentured labor trade in the Pacific Islands in particular. For reasons not easily explained, anthropologists have generally neglected the traffic in human cargo, and historians have largely focused on the trade in areas within the British sphere of influence. Shineberg is the first scholar to address the topic for New Caledonia in a comprehensive manner, and her work fills a major gap in the literature.

As Shineberg informs us, the labor trade in New Caledonia was the longest lasting and the third largest in the Pacific. It began in 1865 and lasted well into the 1930s. While official records are far less comprehensive than those available for Fiji and Queensland, Shineberg's exhaustive and innovative research strategies have allowed her to calculate that approximately fifteen thousand laborers were eventually involved. About 90 percent of them were from what is now Vanuatu, and impressively, Shineberg's computer files have details on over six thousand individuals.

The experience of indentured laborers in New Caledonia was unique in the Pacific, and a number of ironies were involved. On the one hand, they provided a buffer group between French settlers and those whom they feared, the indigenous Kanaks and escaped and released convicts. They were commonly used as domestics, providers of childcare, and watchmen and had a reputation for dependability and trustworthiness. Settlers of the time observed that the laborers "constitute for us a sort of natural gendarmerie" and "the fidelity and honesty of these blacks is a most extraordinary thing" (207).

At the same time, and except for two periods when the French government exercised stringent control over the labor trade, among Islanders New Caledonia had the reputation of being the least favored destination for indentured laborers. New Caledonia's climate was unaccustomably cold. The clothing provided for laborers was often as not inadequate, food rations were in many cases lacking in quantity and nutritional value, and corporal punishment was commonplace. Death rates were high, particularly during the initial year of indenture and for those who were put to work in New Caledonia's mines. Workers were frequently cheated out of their meager wages, and children were recruited at a much younger age than elsewhere, often as young as six years old. New Caledonia was the darkest spot on an already dark enterprise.

Shineberg provides useful comparisons with the indentured labor trade in Fiji and Queensland. Approximately 10 percent of the laborers were women, and Shineberg's analysis of her material on female recruits adds a new dimension to earlier works on the labor trade. One of the main contributions of her book is Shineberg's insights into the debate about the recruitment of laborers: volunteerism versus kidnapping.

Shineberg's volume also represents a turning point in the history of PIMS. The series began with Francis Hezel's *The First Taint of Civilization* in 1983. At the outset, the intention was to publish the best of scholarship in the humanities and social sciences focusing on the Pacific Islands, but otherwise, it was not possible to project the directions that PIMS might take. A decade and a half later, and with the publication of this sixteenth PIMS title, some reflection about the series and the Center for Pacific Islands Studies' larger publishing program is appropriate.

It was not anticipated that 11 of the 16 volumes would be works of history. Judith Bennett's *Wealth of the Solomons,* David Hanlon's *Upon a Stone Altar,* Kerry Howe's *Where the Waves Fall,* August Kituai's *My Gun, My Brother,* Brij Lal's *Broken Waves,* Diane Langmore's *Missionary Lives,* Klaus Neumann's *Not the Way It Really Was,* Mark Peattie's *Nan'yō,* and Dorothy Shineberg's *The People Trade* are the works of professionally trained historians. Ironically, only the self-taught historian, Jesuit scholar Father Francis Hezel, has authored two PIMS volumes, *The First Taint of Civilization* and *Strangers in Their Own Land.*

While these eleven volumes represent a contribution to Pacific history and scholarship in general, several warrant special comment. In his editorial in the second volume of *The Journal of Pacific History,* H E Maude observed that Micronesia's "varied and often exciting history has been ignored as if by some tacit agreement," and he pondered why "American historians have apparently no contribution to make to the historical study of an American Trust Territory." The four volumes by Hanlon, Hezel, and Peattie have put Micronesian history firmly on the map and should set Maude's worries to rest.

August Kitaui's work is the first of its kind for a scholar from Papua New Guinea. Howe's is a significant and oft-quoted regional history focused on the last century. Bennett's contribution is the definitive history of the Solomons, and Lal's work has a similar distinction as a twentieth-century history for his own native land of Fiji. The volumes by Hanlon and Neumann represent innovative approaches to historical scholarship.

I expected that my own discipline of anthropology would have been better represented, but only four PIMS volumes are the work of anthropologists. Of these, Edvard Hviding's *Guardians of Marovo Lagoon* is an outstanding work that combines several strands of contemporary social and cultural anthropology, and it is acquiring recognition as a notable work in Pacific anthropology. The work of Sir Arthur Grimble, *Tungaru Traditions* as edited by H E Maude, and Torben Monberg's *Bellona Island Beliefs and Rituals* are rich in valuable ethnographic data and represent a descriptive anthropology of an earlier era. The multi-authored *The Pacific Theater,* edited by Geoffrey White and Lamont Lindstrom and written by a number of anthropologists and a historian, is largely anthropological in viewpoint but with strong historical dimensions.

Lastly, *Woven Gods* by the Rotuman playwright Vilsoni Hereniko is the most innovative work of all the PIMS volumes, combining as it does perspectives from anthropology with the imagination of a creative writer.

Concerning the geographical distribution of PIMS, seven volumes (Bennett, Hviding, Kituai, Lal, Langmore, Neumann, and Shineberg) are focused on Melanesia, five are concerned with Micronesia (Grimble-Maude, Hanlon, Hezel's two volumes, and Peattie), only two are on Polynesian cultures (Hereniko and Monberg), and two are more general works (Howe, and White and Lindstrom).

Early in the development of PIMS, it became apparent that certain manuscripts were more appropriate for an audience of lay readers with an interest in the Pacific. The first of these was Daniel Peacock's *Lee Boo of Belau,* published in 1987 as the initial volume in South Sea Books, a series title suggested by Stuart Inder, former editor of *Pacific Islands Monthly*. Four other titles have subsequently appeared in that series: Stewart Firth's *Nuclear Playground,* Stephen Henningham's *France and the South Pacific,* Lamont Lindstrom's *Cargo Cult,* and Joël Bonnemaison's *The Tree and the Canoe.* All five South Sea Books have found appreciative audiences, but I am now convinced that *The Tree and the Canoe* would have been more appropriately published as a PIMS volume. Bonnemaison thought of this work as one intended for a broad lay audience, but it is actually a more serious piece of scholarship than he himself acknowledged.

Contributors to PIMS and South Sea Books come from nine different nations of the world: Australia, Denmark, Fiji, Germany, New Zealand, Norway, Papua New Guinea, the United Kingdom, and the United States.

Collectively, the PIMS and South Sea Books volumes are 21 in number, and after more than a decade and a half as general editor of both series, I feel that the time has come to have someone else take over. At the unanimous invitation of the editorial board, David Hanlon, Department of History, University of Hawai'i, has agreed to assume the editorship upon the publication of the volume at hand. Hanlon's *Upon a Stone Altar* won the Erminie Wheeler-Voegelin Prize for Ethnohistory in 1988, and he is well known as a distinguished scholar in his own right. Hanlon turned in a superb performance as the editor of *The Contemporary Pacific: A Journal of Island Affairs* over the six-year period 1993–1998, and I am personally very pleased that he is willing to take on this new task.

I wish to recognize the many contributions of Linley Chapman, Manager of Publications and Manuscript Editor, Center for Pacific Islands Studies. Chapman has edited all of the PIMS and South Sea Books volumes, *The Contemporary Pacific* since its inception in 1989, and Ratu Sir Kamisese Mara's *The Pacific Way: A Memoir,* which was copublished as a special publication with the Pacific Islands Development Program, East-West Center. In addition, Chapman also copyedited *Tides of History: The Pacific Islands in the Twentieth Century,* which I coedited with Kerry Howe and Brij Lal and which was copublished by Allen & Unwin, Australia, and the University of Hawai'i Press. Chapman's efforts have given our publishing program a touch of quality that would not have been achieved without her, and I wish to express my deepest gratitude and appreciation.

Beginning with PIMS 5, we have been fortunate to have had the cartographic services of Jane Eckelman of Manoa Mapworks, Inc. The maps and figures that have since appeared are the products of her labor, and Eckelman's talents and superb craftsmanship have contributed immeasurably to the high quality of our Center's publication program. I sincerely thank Eckelman for her efforts on our behalf.

Lastly, from the outset, our publication program has been a joint effort with the University of Hawai'i Press. William Hamilton, Director, and Pamela Kelley, Acquisitions Editor, have always been supportive, helpful, and constructive in their advice. Without fail, the UH Press's oversight of the production process has resulted in well-designed volumes of the highest quality. I could not have asked for a better collaborative relationship, and I have valued my work with the UH Press.

ROBERT C KISTE

Contents

Illustrations

Appendix: Tables

Acknowledgments

My thanks are due to many people for their cooperation during the long period of research for this book. I am grateful to the staff of libraries and archives who helped me gather material: in Sydney the Mitchell Library; in Canberra the Australian National Library, the Menzies Library at the Australian National University, and the Australian Archives; in Noumea the Service Territorial des Archives, the Bibliothèque Bernheim, the Bibliothèque de la Chambre de Commerce, and the Archives de l'Archevêché; and in France the Archives Nationales d'Outre-Mer, the Archives de la Marine, the Archives des Affaires Etrangères, and the Bibliothèque Nationale.

I owe very special thanks to Bruno Corre, *conservateur-en-chef* of the Noumea Archives, for his assistance and kindness well beyond the call of duty; his help, skill, and support made this a better book. At the *Etat-civil* section of the Palais de Justice in Noumea, Madame Jeudi and Madame Tartavel were extremely helpful to me. The librarian at the Noumea Chamber of Commerce, Madame Péguilhan, deserves particular thanks for her cooperation. Max Shekleton, Louis-José Barbançon, Jacques and Geneviève Boengkih, and Denyse-Anne Pentecost encouraged and helped me during my stays in Noumea. I thank David Becker of Noumea and Bob Cooper of the Australian National University for their skill in making excellent photographs from old postcards, books, and newspapers, and Serge Kakou for allowing me to include two precious old photographs. I am indebted to Anne-Gabrielle Thompson for her assistance in the early stages of gathering material and for continuing friendship and support afterwards.

I owe thanks to several people who read my manuscript and improved it with their comments: Stephen Henningham, Judy Bennett, Donald Denoon, and Barry Shineberg. I am indebted to my editor, Linley Chapman, for her skill and patience. Many thanks to Daniel

Fritsch, Jude Shanahan, and Dorothy McIntosh for solving my computer problems. Thanks also to Bronwen Douglas for her encouragement and for access to her expertise in New Caledonian history. Finally, I wish to acknowledge support by an Australian Research Council grant during the first three years of this research, and by the Division of Pacific and Asian History at the Australian National University for enabling me to use its facilities through a Visiting Fellowship.

Conventions

Currency

Unless otherwise stated, sums of money are expressed in French francs. The United States dollar was worth about 5.26 francs and the pound sterling about 25 francs (or 1 franc = US 19 cents or 9.6 British pence) for most of the period studied. After the First World War, the French franc depreciated sharply in relation to both the US dollar and the pound sterling. By 1926 the franc had fallen to less than a quarter of its prewar value in both American and British currencies. It was then devalued and stabilized at 122.25 francs per pound sterling (about 25 francs per US dollar.) The market value thereafter appreciated somewhat in relation to British and American currencies. After devaluation, sums were sometimes expressed in "gold francs" (old French francs) as well as in the new standard francs.

Place-Names

The names of islands in Vanuatu (New Hebrides) are spelled in accordance with the *Official Gazeteer of Place Names (Nomenclature Officielle des Noms Géographiques)* 1979, except for the island formerly known as Aoba. After independence (1980) it was decided in the Parliament of Vanuatu that Aoba would henceforth be known as Ambae, which spelling is used universally today. Place-names in New Caledonia are spelled according to modern French spelling, except for those commonly used in English, such as Noumea, Lifu, Uvea and New Caledonia itself.

Translation

Annotations from French sources have been translated into English, along with French titles and institutions where there are appropriate English counterparts. Unless otherwise noted all translations are my own.

Weights

Metric weights are used: 454 grams = approximately 1 imperial pound; 28 grams = approximately 1 imperial ounce.

Shipping weights are expressed in metric tonnes: 1 tonne = 0.984 imperial tons.

Note on Sources

Systematic records relating to immigrant labor are extant for the British colonies of Queensland and Fiji but not for the French colony of New Caledonia. It seems important therefore to begin by describing the sources and the methods used to establish the basic framework of this book.

Estimating the number of Islanders who went abroad to work in New Caledonia presented the first major task. Statistics were quoted in official or other sources for occasional years, but those years are few. On the other hand, the French colony has always been rich in newspapers. The official weekly paper, *Le Moniteur de la Nouvelle-Calédonie*, first appeared in 1859 (changing its name to *Le Journal Officiel de la Nouvelle-Calédonie* in 1886), and was soon joined by a large number of independent papers. Intermittent publications appeared from as early as 1874, and after 1880 always at least one private newspaper, sometimes two, and occasionally three or four. The newspapers carried shipping information in almost every issue, as ships were the lifeline that linked the colony to the outside world. The numbers of recruits carried by the labor vessels arriving in port was almost invariably reported in the newspapers, because cheap labor was the most sought-after commodity in the colony and the arrival notice was an advertisement for the trader.

Where possible, I checked the newspaper figures against other extant documents (such as a government agent's journal, or an official report), and in each case found them reliable. The numbers of recruits reported on each ship were then added for each year, and eventually a total for the whole period was calculated. The resulting estimate must be considered a minimum, because a few numbers of several newspapers are missing, and because up to 1882, ships carrying laborers sometimes berthed at ports other than Noumea, escaping the attention of the reporter. In the latter case, figures from official reports were available for the years 1873, 1877, 1879, and 1880; these had to be accepted at face value for those years, but in the knowledge that such figures were usually below the real annual totals. It is not clear why official annual totals were lower. Perhaps they were drawn up before the end of the year, failing to include the last arrivals, or perhaps the arrival of small vessels carrying laborers was overlooked. However, the discrepancy is very general and raises the question whether the ready-to-hand statistics in Queensland official papers should be treated more critically.

The newspapers are less reliable in the case of departures, for shippers no longer had the incentive of advertising their cargo, and occasionally just said "a number of natives to be repatriated" in reply to the reporter's inquiry. On the other hand, since repatriation had to be organized through the administration, which paid the shipper a set amount for repatriating each worker, the official figures for departures, for the years where they exist, were helpful, and sometimes higher than those collectible from the newspaper columns. The result of all these calculations is set out in appendix table 1.

The total number of recruits—more than 15,000—is very much larger than earlier estimates, and in itself warrants more attention to the subject. Although this total would include any who might have recruited for a second time, New Caledonia was for most of the period not the preferred destination of New Hebridean workers, so the number of "second-timers" there was small, unlike Queensland. Because the estimated figure is in any case a minimum, it probably gives a reasonable sense of the number of individuals recruited.

The period for which there was systematic recruitment of foreign Oceanian labor for New Caledonia (1865–1930) had also to be calculated. It is derived partly from official documents and partly, once again, from the shipping columns in the newspapers.

Another large source of information was the *état civil,* the French equivalent of a registry of births, marriages, and deaths for all the districts, which I searched for the entire period. Although far from all the imported Oceanians had these stages of their lives recorded in the registry when relevant, a great many did. Their names always had the tag *néo-hébridais* or *salomonien* after them. I fed these names into a computer, allowing space for twenty-four selected attributes that I might eventually be able to find, such as island of origin, date of arrival, occupation, name of employer, age at death, and so forth. Some entries in the *état civil* had no detail apart from the one registered plus the group of origin, but most of the death registrations also gave the island of origin of the workers, their estimated age at death, and often their occupation and the name of their employer. More rarely, the workers' registration numbers appeared—a clue to the year when they arrived—and sometimes the precise date of their arrival in the colony and the name of the ship that brought them. Very occasionally, the cause of death was given. Birth notices gave the names of the mother and father, if the latter was also an Oceanian, their estimated age, often their island of origin, occupation, and the name of their employers.

Details turned up fortuitously as I searched other sources. The reports of court cases gave names, and sometimes ages, origins, and other details about imported Oceanian workers: if some of these later died in the colony or had children, this information could be supplemented by that in the *état civil* and vice versa. Similar information from the few ships' journals that are extant, inspectors' reports, official correspondence, proceedings of assemblies and commissions, newspaper pieces, and literary sources were added to the computer file, which now contains details of 6,124 individuals with varying degrees of documentation.

Missing from this history—except for isolated instances—is the oral history of participants or descendants that so enlivened Peter Corris's story of the Solomon Islanders abroad. A few attempts in New Caledonia convinced me that it would be another long job of research even to track down such people, not least because many pointed out as descendants of *hébridais* proved to be those of a more recent wave of immigrant workers, the New Hebrideans who came over to work in the processing and mining of nickel in the boom of the 1960s and early 1970s. Not many people in New Caledonia were aware that a large number of New Hebridean workers had been introduced a hundred years earlier than these. It would take a long residence in New Caledonia and Vanuatu to find descendants and to collect and analyze their stories. In the meantime, the publication of this version, overwhelmingly from written sources, might assist the task by prompting the remembrance of stories told in the islands and by providing a few pegs to hang them on. I look forward to a New Caledonian or ni-Vanuatu scholar supplementing or taking issue with this study by the addition of oral evidence.

Part One

Recruiting for New Caledonia

Chapter 1
The Pacific Island Labor Trade and New Caledonia

> People were born and they died, she was thinking,
> but they had never been simply taken away.
>
> FAITH BANDLER, *Wacvie*

In the travelers' tales of the nineteenth century, visitors to New Caledonia mentioned the New Hebridean laborers who carried their luggage, rowed them ashore, waited at table, dressed up on Sundays to parade in the Place des Cocotiers, or worked in plantations or mines. Nowadays their place in the history of migrant labor has slipped from the collective memory of New Caledonians, overshadowed by a later large influx of Asian workers. Yet the number of Pacific Island workers introduced was considerable; more than fifteen thousand, most of them from the New Hebrides (now Vanuatu), came to work in the French colony before the Second World War.

A demand for cheap labor was a consequence of European expansion in the Pacific partly to exploit its agricultural and mining resources and partly for complex reasons of state. The settlement of Europeans in tropical colonies of the Pacific in the last half of the nineteenth century occurred too late for the introduction of slaves, forbidden everywhere in European colonies by 1848 and in the United States of America by 1865. But Pacific entrepreneurs were allowed to introduce colored labor under a system of indenture already prevailing in several colonies following the demise of slavery.

The régime of indenture—that is, being bound to serve a master for a fixed term and for fixed wages under a contract with penal sanctions—was borrowed ultimately from the notion of apprenticeship, but it was used as a system of controlling workers emigrating from Europe to the Americas and the West Indies in the seventeenth and eighteenth centuries. From the 1830s it was revived as a substitute for slavery, this time involving the labor of *non*-white races. In the process it became a more oppressive form of servitude than before. The humanitarian societies set up during the campaign to abolish slavery continued to monitor what they saw as slavery under another name, particularly the efforts to introduce African labor into the West In-

dian colonies and into Réunion and Mozambique under an indenture system, as well as the contracting of Indian laborers for work in
Mauritius and the West Indies. Therefore, when traders began to ship
Pacific Islanders to foreign places as cheap labor for European enterprises, an immense controversy erupted. The Anti-Slavery Society
and the Aborigines' Protection Society in England and the *Société
française de protection des indigènes* in France turned their attention to
the so-called "kanaka traffic" or the "labor trade" in the Pacific as
soon as it began. Whether or not the indenture of Pacific Island labor
was simply "disguised slavery" was argued as soon as the first shipload
arrived in Queensland in 1863. The argument has not stopped since.

Opposition to the indenture of Oceanians was particularly fervent
because of popular notions about life in the Pacific Islands. South Sea
Islanders were supposed to live in a state of childlike innocence in a
Garden of Eden, without the curse of work. Why would they want to
leave paradise to toil on a plantation? They must have been forced to
go. And, given a widespread belief that island populations were dying
out, it could not be said that migration was a boon to poor, over-
crowded communities, as it might have been for the Indians (and was
later argued in the case of the Indochinese and Javanese). It seemed
obvious to many contemporaries, therefore, that taking Islanders from
their homes was nothing but a revival of the slave trade. The fact that
most recruits came from the then New Hebrides, the Solomon Islands,
and the former Gilbert Islands (now most of Kiribati), none of them
under the control of European governments until thirty to forty
years after the labor trade began, increased the suspicion that foul
deeds were being committed with impunity in the islands. Opponents
cast the slavery epithet at both the manner of recruiting workers and
at the régime under which they lived and worked in foreign lands.
A large polemic literature reflects these concerns and the counter-
arguments of the supporters of the system during its entire lifetime.

Early historians of the labor trade[1] took up the same controversy
in their work, perhaps, as one writer suggests, because it dominated
their main sources, British official papers.[2] But the next generation of
Pacific historians tried to reflect on the significance of the labor trade
as part of the history of the islands, rather than as part of imperial
history. Instead of a moral problem for the European powers, they
began to see it as a major migration: the movement of a large proportion of the adolescents and young adults from small communities
over two or three generations.

The sustained recruiting of Pacific Island labor began in 1863.
The first destination was Queensland, joined soon after by Fiji, New
Caledonia, Tahiti, Hawai'i, and Western Sāmoa. By 1900, more than
a hundred thousand Pacific Islanders had been taken from their

homes to work for European employers in foreign lands. On some islands, entire villages were stripped of their adult male populations
except for old men. From most of the islands of the New Hebrides,
the Solomon Islands, and the Gilbert Islands, young people went
abroad for a period of labor. In the year 1882, for example, there
were about 14,000 New Hebrideans working abroad, out of a population of 100,000 or so (to take the upper limit of the informed estimates of the time).[3] About 7,000 of these were in Queensland,
about 3,000 in Fiji, 2,800 in New Caledonia, 1,000 or so in Sāmoa and
Hawai'i,[4] plus an unknown number working as sailors or boat crew
on European ships. Chevillard, a French settler established in Efaté,
estimated a total population of 125,000 in the New Hebrides, and
that "16 to 17,000" were absent working abroad in 1882. Captain
Bridge thought his figures too high,[5] and I agree, but his estimate of
the proportion abroad is roughly the same. Considering that most
were young men in the prime of life, 14 percent represented a very
high proportion of active males in these societies. In regularly recruited areas, most of the men had been to one or other labor destination, some more than once. The Reverend R Steel claimed this for
Efaté before 1880,[6] and it is very likely. It was probably equally true of
Tanna at that date, and later for several northern islands in the New
Hebrides group. By 1871, according to Bishop Patteson, many villages
in the Banks Islands were depopulated, while in Emae he counted
forty-eight people in a village where there had certainly been three
hundred a few years before.[7] A social upheaval was taking place in the
islands, for small communities were losing a very large proportion of
their most active members. Although in absolute figures the number
of Asians who came to work in the Pacific colonies was much larger,
their movement was not of comparable significance in terms of their
home populations.

In the island groups supplying these laborers, there would have
been few villages where no one had gone abroad for a period of at
least three years. The total impact of the event in these places was
considerable, either directly on the laborers who spent from one to
five or more years in a wholly foreign environment, or indirectly on
the small communities left behind, who had to adjust their lives to the
absence of their fittest members, about a quarter to a half of whom
never returned. As well, the access to trade goods that the labor traffic
brought to these areas had repercussions on the local economies and,
since one of the main items traded was a supply of breech-loading
firearms, on the balance of power between rival groups.

When they began to look for it, historians of the labor trade to
Queensland and Fiji found a wider range of documentary evidence
throwing light on some of these issues. The old controversy about

kidnapping still loomed large in research, in part because popular literature had accepted and even exaggerated the stories of kidnapping to the exclusion of all else. Since print and television journalists continue that emphasis to this day—probably because of its inherent drama and its simple plot of good versus evil—scholars felt an imperative to show that the business of recruiting was far more complex. They retrieved valuable evidence that Melanesian societies often actively participated in the labor trade rather than being simply the victims of it.[8] It was clear that when Islanders became aware of possible advantages to themselves or their community, they were willing to offer recruits. While confirming that kidnapping undoubtedly formed a part of the business, historians began to look for the local agenda behind cooperation. As one historian put it, the inquiry "broadened to include the reasons why Pacific Islanders recruited, the part played by indigenous middlemen, the extent to which Islanders were changed by their overseas experience, and to a lesser extent the social change brought about by returned labourers."[9]

There was another difference in focus. Earlier historians tended to dwell on the action of European governments in regulating the labor trade as a means of eliminating abuses, or, as Doug Munro put it, viewed it as "part and parcel of the question of law and order on the frontier,"[10] whereas the so-called revisionists of the last thirty years again stressed the agency of the Islanders themselves in forcing change. In the latter scenario, after the people became experienced in the ways of the traders, the control of abuses owed more to the constraints imposed by the Islanders, through witholding cooperation or through violent retribution, than to European regulations. I argue that this misses the point that the Islanders' awareness also included an assessment of how well the trade was regulated: the two approaches are complementary. Just enforcement of the bargain added to the reputation of recruiters and employers and their place of origin, and its converse diminished it. As I shall elaborate, material benefits were sought from cooperation with the labor trade, but the good name of recruiters or employers was also an important element in Islanders' choice of destination, leading to distinct preferences at different times. Moreover, their knowledge of the current situation at any given place and time was very good.

Earlier depictions of the trade have also been simplified. Writers and historians may have spoken as if all recruits were kidnapped, but far from all contemporary critics did. Some were well aware that a relatively small proportion of recruits was forcibly taken. Their condemnation of the traffic as "disguised slavery" was based on the belief that many recruits were influenced by their sponsors to enlist. The Reverend R H Codrington even considered that the situation deteriorated after kidnapping largely gave way to trading for workers, since it was then possible to enlist more recruits when youths, as he believed, were traded by their seniors for their own gain.[11] F A Campbell in 1873 believed that only about ten percent of recruits were kidnapped, but that the traffic was an "unmixed evil"[12] for the same reason. Nearly ten years on, the Russian explorer Nikolai Miklouho-Maclay reckoned that only five percent were kidnapped—a disparity quite reasonably accounted for by the change in conditions over the period—but he too was aware that a power relationship between recruits and their sponsors on the beach was often also at issue.[13] Most revisionists have simplified the controversy as one between voluntary enlistment and European coercion. Clive Moore has asked, "Were they kidnapped and used as slaves to establish the sugar industry? Or were they willing participants, protected by contracts and gaining substantially from their participation in the labour trade?"[14] There are many different questions here, not just two, and I try to distinguish them in the chapters that follow. An important one is whether volunteering recruits were necessarily "willing participants," or whether the decision was made by others in their community. Sometimes this distinction is raised, but summarily dismissed or treated superficially. The question is not easy to answer, but it should be asked more seriously.

Although the accusation of slavery, as Moore implied, was also applied to conditions at the workplace, less work has been done on the life led by indentured Islanders abroad than on the recruiting process. Good studies have nevertheless emerged, most concerning Queensland.[15] The effects of the experience on those who were repatriated after their term of service—"returns" in labor trade parlance—proved very difficult for historians to trace, partly because so far as written records were concerned, the story ended with repatriation. In effect, historians were dependent on incidental references to the history of returns by missionaries, local traders, and naval visitors, and had limited opportunity for fieldwork to collect oral evidence. Peter Corris was able to point to some consequences for the Solomon Islanders he studied: the varying ability to be absorbed back into village life, the effect of the diffusion of goods they brought with them, and how acquired ideas—especially for those who had been converted to Christianity during their stay abroad—made a difference to their new life in the islands.[16] Those who stayed in Queensland, avoiding forced repatriation in the early years of the twentieth century, have been studied in the admirable work of Patricia Mercer and Clive Moore,[17] while descendants surviving in Sāmoa have also received some attention.[18] On the other hand, little has been discovered about how the home communities managed without the many who went abroad, for this question centered on those who stayed home, especially women, who were virtually absent in the documentary evidence. In her novel *Wacvie,* based on the memories of her father, who was taken to Queensland in 1883, Faith Bandler has tried to recreate the ambience of the depleted village. As for direct evidence from participants, even in the 1960s there were few left to be consulted, although Corris was able to talk to some very old men who had recruited in the first years of the twentieth century. Oral evidence from descendants still offers some possibility for reconstruction, but so far it has proved difficult to interpret.[19] There may still be an opportunity here for anthropologists to incorporate some of these questions into their investigations, as one of them has suggested,[20] given that extended periods of fieldwork in a single cultural area are a normal part of their research.

Although the labor trade to Fiji and Queensland has been much studied,[21] other segments of the islands labor trade have not. Judith Bennett's research into recruiting to Hawai'i[22] was a beginning that has not been followed up. Stewart Firth has published articles on the life of workers on plantations in Sāmoa and New Guinea,[23] but his thesis on the recruiting and employment of island laborers in those areas remains unpublished.[24] The history of the New Caledonian sector, although it was the longest lasting and the third largest, is virtually untold. Apart from the work of Pierre Gascher,[25] which contains a chapter on the labor problems of New Caledonia with a useful outline of the importation of New Hebridean labor up to 1894, historians have either ignored it or made only brief allusions to it. This book should fill that gap. Workers imported from other islands, mainly from the New Hebrides, formed the backbone of the workforce in nineteenth-century New Caledonia, so their story is important in its own right. It is a missing piece of the history of New Caledonia, as well as of the Pacific Island labor trade. However, I hope to throw light also on some of the general issues of the labor trade, especially the recruiting process and the life of recruits at their workplace, enabling scholars to make comparisons with evidence already collected. Based on this study and a brief review of the work of others, I add my own contribution to the general analysis. While data on questions concerning returns and stayers are even more sparse for New Caledonia than for Queensland and Fiji, I hope to lay the groundwork for further investigation of these subjects.

                              *   *   *

Systematic recruiting of Oceanian workers for New Caledonia started in 1865, and the trade continued, with two interruptions, well into the twentieth century. The metropolitan government twice suspended the trade in Oceanian labor, first from June 1882 to February 1884, and second from March 1885 to March 1890. But recruiting ships continued to bring laborers during the last three years of the second suspension, despite the prohibition. In the twentieth century, the average annual intake was smaller—a little more than a hundred a year—up to the onset of the great depression of 1929–1931. My study ends there, but New Hebrideans continued to arrive in decreasing numbers, and there was apparently no formal end to the indenture of these workers before the end of the Second World War.

When the difficulties of researching the story became clear, I understood one important reason why the subject had received scant attention. The existing official documentation is so poor that it does not even provide an accessible framework of basic facts, such as the number of Islanders who served in New Caledonia and precisely when. It was necessary to assemble a jigsaw of a large number of fragments in order even to sketch an outline of the episode, as I discussed in the Note on Sources.

Memories of the labor trade now play an important part in the collective identity of the peoples of the independent nations of Vanuatu and the Solomon Islands. One of the aims of this work is to add some account, however inadequate, of what happened to those who were the "disappeared" of their time, whether because they stayed in New Caledonia or died there during their term of indenture. For the descendants of those who made it back, I hope that I may enlarge the context of stories passed down to them, and contribute to an understanding of their ancestors' experience.

This book deals with both ends of the labor trade, at the islands of origin and at the workplace, and consists of three parts. The first sketches the background of the demand for labor and follows the story of recruiting in the islands over the period. The second considers the recruits themselves: their age and gender, island provenance, and the reasons for their enlistment, if they were not kidnapped. The third part is a description, from many fragments, of the circumstances of the life of foreign indentured laborers in the colony, and the outcome—whether death, staying in the colony, or return to their homeland. In the conclusion I address some of the questions raised here, and suggest ways in which the New Caledonian experience sheds light on this chapter in Pacific Islands history.

The imported Pacific Island laborers were commonly known to settlers as *néo-hébridais* or simply *hébridais*, whatever their origin. This label reflected the fact that more than 90 percent of them came from the then New Hebrides, Banks, and Torres Islands (together now Vanuatu), but it also arose from a vagueness in island geography. The origin of some workers was occasionally given as "Malaita, New

Hebrides," and in one case, "Solomon Islands, New Hebrides." To cover the whole group more exactly would be difficult without a long-winded rubric. "Melanesian" will not do, even if one is prepared to overlook the few Gilbertese and Wallisians, for the local indigenes are also Melanesian, and were also to be indentured before the end of the period. I have therefore often followed the expression of the times and used the catchall term "New Hebridean" to refer to imported Oceanian labor. This term must be understood to include about a thousand Solomon Islanders, perhaps a hundred Gilbertese, and even fewer Wallisians. I hope that this work will soon be followed by a study of indigenous Melanesian workers in New Caledonia, whom the administration was eventually to succeed in coercing into the labor force, for their story also remains to be written.

Chapter 2
The Colony Established

At the beginning of September 1774, Captain Cook sailed southwest from Espiritu Santo in the New Hebrides on a return visit to New Zealand. On his way he encountered the northern end of a large uncharted island surrounded by a reef. Nobody knows why he named it New Caledonia. It bears little resemblance to Scotland—called Caledonia by the Romans—which Cook, in any case, had probably never seen.[1]

He penetrated the reef at a northeastern pass and anchored at Balade, spending a week exploring the neighboring country and bartering with the people. Unlike the colonial dreamers who followed him, Cook was impressed by the people but not by the prospects of the land: "From this little excursion, I found that we were to expect nothing from these people but the privilege of exploring their country undisturbed for it was easy to see they had little else but good Nature to spare us. In this they exceeded all the nation[s] we had yet met with, and although it did not fill our bellies it left our minds at ease."[2] He sailed down the eastern side outside the reef and found an island to the south, which he called the Isle of Pines. Cook was followed nineteen years later by a French expedition under Bruni d'Entrecasteaux, whose crew, by contrast, was on bad terms with the same people for the nineteen days of their stay at Balade.

The accounts of these voyages awakened the interest of both France and England in this part of the Pacific. Cook had taken possession of the land for the king of England, a claim that was never pursued by His Majesty's government. After the Napoleonic wars, however, British traders and missionaries followed in Cook's tracks. A thriving trade in sandalwood and bêche-de-mer from the Australian colonies provided the earliest regular contacts between Europeans and both the New Hebrides and the New Caledonian groups.[3] Christian teachers chosen by the London Missionary Society from their converts in the Polynesian islands of Sāmoa and Rarotonga were left on several islands of the New Hebrides, as well as the southeast of the mainland of New Caledonia, the Isle of Pines, and also the Loyalty Islands, not seen by Cook (back endpaper). The teachers were followed by European missionaries of the London Missionary Society. Although French Marist missionaries arrived at Balade in 1843, the southwest Pacific was for the most part a region of exclusively British interest.

However, the French government felt in serious want of a naval base in the area, a need that pressed more strongly after Britain acquired New Zealand in 1840. France annexed the Marquesas in 1842 and proclaimed a protectorate over Tahiti in 1844, but a base in the western Pacific was still lacking. Moreover, since the disasters of the Napoleonic wars, France felt the need to regain its position as a world power.[4] Like Britain, France also had a problem of overpopulated prisons and decided to emulate the British solution of the convict colony of New South Wales. Guyane was the colony of first choice for this purpose, but the French government decided to annex New Caledonia in 1853 in case it should be needed as a place of exile for malefactors as well as a naval base and a claim to an imperial presence in the region.

Only when the murderous climate of Guyane had taken severe toll of the lives of the convicts and their guardians, did thoughts return to New Caledonia as a place of transportation. In 1863, ten years after annexation, the decision was taken to transport convicts to the new Pacific colony, because it was free of malaria and had a more temperate climate. The first of the more than 22,000 convicts who were to come to New Caledonia arrived in 1864. These *transportés,* sentenced to hard labor, were joined in 1872 by about 4,000 *déportés,* political prisoners, most of them from the repression of the 1871 Communard uprising in Paris, but some from the defeat of the Kabylie rebellion in Algeria at almost the same time. Finally, after 1885, almost another 4,000 recidivists were exiled to the colony.[5] After the model of New South Wales, free settlers were also to be encouraged to emigrate, profiting from the works of infrastructure of the *transportés,* and developing the country in tandem with the *libérés,* or freed convicts. Little, however, was known about the productivity of the soil that was basic to this colonial project, and even less about the 30,000 or so Kanaks or indigenous people on the mainland (Grande Terre) engaged in subsistence agriculture, who were unlikely to give up their land without a struggle.

By the time of the arrival of the convicts, very little development had occurred. The colony had languished for nine years as a near-forgotten naval outpost, an adjunct to the establishment at Tahiti. Until 1860 it was administered in theory by the governor of Tahiti, who made occasional visits, but in practice it was governed by subordinate navy officials. When Rear-Admiral Charles Guillain arrived in 1862, the first real governor of the separate colony of New Caledonia, the state controlled only the southern third of the island and the military post of Napoléonville (later Canala). Sporadic expeditions into the northeast were merely containing operations, inadequate to fully protect settlers and missionaries.[6] Occasional punitive expeditions in response to attacks absorbed the remainder of French power on the island.

At this time the only considerable European landholder was the Marist Mission. It had large properties at Conception and St Louis in the southern district that it populated from 1856 with about four hundred converts from its outposts in the northeast, Balade, Pouébo, and Touho. In the 1850s a private settler, ex-naval officer Louis-Théodore Bérard, had established a plantation, also in the south, at Mont Dore, but was killed in the first Kanak uprising of 1856, along with many of his workers.[7] As a report from the colonial secretariat pointed out, up to 1862 the effect of the administration on the indigenous population was minimal: within fifty kilometers north or south of the capital, and outside the environs of each military post, the indigenous people were either not aware or barely aware of the invading power.[8] Local warfare, which the administration was powerless to control, continued in the north and the west.

The Need for Imported Labor

The new colony was starved for funds, a veritable orphan child of the empire. Such public works as were undertaken were achieved mainly by the labor of the troops, further limiting the ability of the colonial administration to extend its control.[9] When Guillain arrived to give the colony some direction, he was able to undertake only the minimum of public works and the minimum extension of control.[10] His extreme anticlerical attitudes and favoritism toward the so-called pagan tribes caused a breakdown in the mission–administration alliance on which his predecessors had depended. He experimented with local Melanesian laborers, whom he dragooned by pressure on "pacified" chiefs. Contingents of men were sent to Port-de-France (later Noumea) to work for a year, but as they had to be fed, clothed, sheltered, and paid a small wage, the scheme failed within two years for lack of funds.[11]

On 2 September 1863, Guillain was charged with the organization of the penal establishment. As well, the governor vigorously encouraged more private settlement, offering grants of land and other concessions to attract free migrants, in the usual forlorn hope of colonizers that private capitalism would eventually enable the colony to pay its own way. In fact, the penitentiary was the major pivot of the economy until the end of the century. However, the hope of fortune inspired a number of settlers to take up the challenge, and both public and private ventures intensified the demand for labor.

The arrival of the convicts in 1864 increased the demand for labor rather than meeting it. Buildings had to be erected to receive them; rowers had to be employed to row them from Ile Nou, where they were stationed, to their place of work in Port-de-France; and convicts had to be guarded. Moreover, Guillain's policy of penal colonization limited the use of convict labor for public works.[12] The free settlers who occupied the region near the Dumbea River just north of the capital, as well as Canala, and the northeastern area around Pouébo, all required labor for their plantations of sugar, coffee, and rice. Guillain began releasing convicts on private assignment as soon as practicable, but settlers generally found the costs of employing them too high.[13] After the administration became involved in more conflicts with the Kanaks before the end of the decade — in Wagap (1865), Pouébo and the northeast (1867–1868), and Canala-Bourail (1868)[14]—the prospect of employing indigenous labor became more remote, for both the administration and the settlers.

To meet the demand for cheap, unthreatening labor it was clear that workers would have to be imported on contract. The British government would not allow the French to recruit in India, although settlers from Réunion brought out a number of Indians already in that colony on five-year contracts. More than another twenty years would pass before France controlled Indochina, later a source of labor for New Caledonia and the New Hebrides. It was not surprising, therefore, that Guillain followed the lead of Queensland and decided to introduce Melanesian workers from neighboring islands.[15]

From time to time the Ministry for the Navy and Colonies in Paris questioned the need to import labor, pointing out that New Caledonia was inhabited by thousands of Melanesians who could be employed, not to mention the several shiploads of French convicts that arrived every year from 1864 to 1897. The ministry was never entirely happy with the answers it received from the colonial administration, which were usually expressed in terms of the inherent unsuitability and unreliability of the local Kanaks, who were represented as by nature lazy and treacherous. However, it would have been more to the point to say that they were feared, and that to control them sufficiently to turn them into a workforce would have required more resources than were at the disposal of the administration for many years to come.

The Beginnings of the Labor Trade

Traders and whalers already knew that away from their homes, Islanders were capable and reliable workers. They had become accustomed to hiring them as ship hands, boat crew, and rouseabouts since the end of the eighteenth century. During the 1840s and 1850s, Islanders had been recruited for months at a time for work at sandalwood, bêche-de-mer, and copra stations, preparing the product for the carrier ships that collected it.[16] In the southern islands of the New Hebrides and in the northern island of Espiritu Santo many people already spoke "sandalwood English," the forerunner of Bislama; in other islands, many had at least heard of the goods and ways of the Europeans and were ready to receive them.

In New Caledonia, a few employers had been using New Hebridean labor before the administration organized regular importations. A planter, Louis-Théodore Bérard, had about forty people working his newly granted lands at the foot of Mont Dore, just east of Noumea, in 1856.[17] James Paddon brought his workers with him when he settled on Ile Nou in 1855. Bêche-de-mer and sandalwood traders like J C Lewis and Andrew Henry employed New Hebrideans almost exclusively as sailors and boat crew on their ships trading around the Grande Terre, and as laborers at the trading station on the Isle of Pines.

The experience of one of these men was used to recruit workers for the emerging plantations in the Pacific. Henry provided the New Caledonian administration with its link to this labor reserve, just as another, James Paddon, had provided a connection to the general trade of the region and the beginnings of free colonization. Henry had performed the same service for the Queensland labor trade, when, on request from his then employer, Robert Towns, he sent the first contingent of indentured laborers to Queensland in 1863 from his sandalwood station on Erromango,[18] where he had about two hundred fifty New Hebrideans working.[19]

Henry had lived with his wife and children in the New Hebrides since 1848, first under contract to Paddon and later to Robert Towns. For seventeen years the Henrys lived at various stations in danger and in penury, never managing to get out of debt despite the hard work of the whole family.[20] Sandalwood was becoming scarce in the group in the early 1860s, and in 1864 Henry suffered the crowning blow of losing his schooner *Ariel;* little wonder that he began to look to the new French colony for the prosperity and comfort that had so far been denied him. In May 1865, he left his station on Erromango to enter into negotiations with the New Caledonian administration to import laborers from the New Hebrides. A contract was successfully concluded. He was to receive a land grant and a concession to exploit sandalwood and bêche-de-mer in the colony, plus 25 francs (then about £1 sterling or us$4.75) for each recruit landed in New Caledonia, a payment known as "passage money" in labor trade parlance.[21] This money covered not only the cost of the journey, but also gifts to the relatives of recruits and other expenses, plus a profit margin.

While Henry was away, hostile Erromangans attacked his station, killing his associate, Captain Fletcher, and several of his employees. The Henrys decided to quit the New Hebrides and in November 1865 they moved everything they owned to their new home at Oubatche, near Pouébo on the northeast coast of the colony, bringing thirty of their New Hebridean workers with them.[22]

Henry's *La Lionne* left Noumea for Erromango early in July 1865, returning with 33 recruits indentured for one year only.[23] Most of these were employed by Henry himself. In April of the following year he brought 57, mostly from Tanna and Efaté, who were distributed among other employers requiring labor (photo 1). Within a year there were 239 New Hebrideans under indenture in the colony.[24] Figure 1 indicates as nearly as possible how the recruitment waxed and waned over the next seventeen years (see also appendix table 1).

The number of imported New Hebrideans increased slowly at first. By the end of the decade, over a thousand had arrived; with regular repatriations, this brought the number present in the colony in 1870 to 720.[25] Other brokers had begun to compete with Henry, and passage money rose. When in December 1868 John Higginson entered the business—the origin of his significant involvement with New Hebridean history—his contract with the government allowed him 75 francs per head as passage money, three times the original rate.

In islands familiar with Europeans, a procedure evolved that was recognized as legitimate by both recruiters and recruits. Two boats were sent from a recruiting ship to a "passage"—a landing-place on the coast, often near a passage through a surrounding reef. One boat would back in, ready to head out in case of trouble, and the other stood off to cover the first in case of an attack. The recruiter in the first boat often gained the attention of the local people by distributing "small trade" on the beach, such as sticks of tobacco, matches, fishhooks, and colored beads (photo 2). When trade in labor became routine, people who wished to offer recruits would attract the boats by making a fire on the beach. After some socializing, which might include a trip to the ship to see more wonders, have something to eat, or examine it for comforts, traders offered a substantial gift for each person who would "touch the pen," that is, enlist to go with the ship to a foreign land to work for a stated period, reckoned in years or

Photo 1 A laborer from Tanna, at Paita in 1868. Photograph by E Robin. Collection of S Kakou, Brignoles, France.

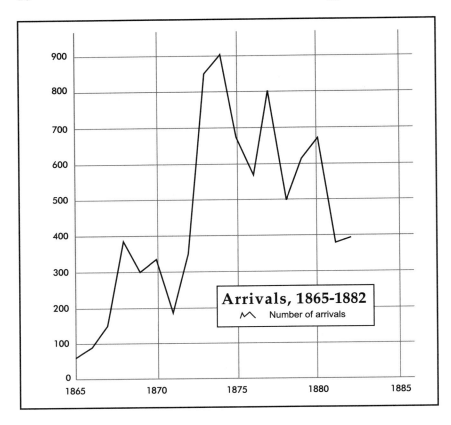

Figure 1

"yams" (an annual crop). This gift, or "beach payment," was given to
a recruit's sponsor, a person who claimed to have control over the recruit—a parent, senior kinsman, or chief. The acceptance of the gift
signified agreement to the deal. If a recruit left without a gift having
been accepted, the arrangement was illegitimate. Such recruits would,
in the eyes of their kin, have been "stolen," no matter how willingly
they left, and vengeance could follow. The recruits themselves would
be rewarded by money wages, converted at the end of their term into
a box full of goods of their own choice to take home. The recruits'
original sponsors, and their kin, would claim a share of it.

It took time for this routine to spread to less familiar areas. Encounters with inexperienced Islanders were fraught with difficulty,
increasing the temptation to resort to kidnapping. The familiar southern islands of Efaté and Tanna were becoming used up as sources as
a result of extreme competition, with traders out of Fiji and Queens-

Photo 2 Recruiting in the New Hebrides. Mitchell Library, State Library of New South Wales.

land as well as New Caledonia. A slight decline in intake in the early 1870s was probably due to problems in supply. Traders went farther north to islands of little experience in trading with Europeans. Increasing hostility from the Islanders, as some recruiters resorted to sharp practice or brutal methods to reach their quota, in turn magnified the problem of supply.

By 1873, however, there was such a hunger for cheap labor that all obstacles were overcome. Exciting prospects had opened up in New Caledonia: as a result of the discovery of important mineral deposits, there was a considerable mining boom. Agriculture was still in the market for New Hebridean workers, but found itself competing with the mining sector. The annual intake of New Hebridean labor leapt from 349 in 1872 to 847 in 1873, and nearly 900 in 1874, the highest figure for the whole period.[26] The boom continued until the end of the first quarter of 1875. After that, although a variety of local circumstances created dips and surges, the number of recruits averaged 600 a year until mid-1882, when the labor traffic was suspended for two years (see figure 1 and appendix table 1).

The boom period coincided with a relaxation of state control. In the 1870s passage money was no longer fixed, and it rose quickly in response to higher demand. It shot up to 135 francs per man in 1870[27] and "rising with every ship,"[28] reached 250 to 300 francs by 1874,[29] and 400 francs by the beginning of 1882.[30] This price—which was to go higher later—was comparable to the Queensland price at the time, reckoning the franc at the current rate of 25 francs to the pound sterling (US$4.75), but after the controlled prices of the Guillain administration, the higher price would have come as a severe blow to small employers, who now had to compete at market rates with the new mining companies and large merchants.

With passage money now determined by demand, the venture became attractive to numerous entrepreneurs. New recruiting ships joined the old, and the inexperience of their crews plus the hope of a quick return on their outlay increased the risk of abuses. With the boom in the market in 1873, laborers were rushed in from the New Hebrides in anything that would sail. Small vessels from the Fiji trade were attracted to Noumea, and coastal shipping was pressed into service. At least one of the Fiji ships—the *Lapwing*—was fleeing the consequences of a kidnapping report by a British warship.[31] No regard was paid to the comfort and health of the human cargo; on practically no voyage in 1874–1875 was the working rule of one passenger per tonne[32] observed. In 1875, for example, the *Reine Hortense,* of only 15 tonnes, arrived in Noumea with 40 recruits after a long return passage—and therefore undoubtedly a rough one—of thirteen days, and at the end of 1874 the *Viti,* of 13 tonnes, carried 46, after a return passage of six days. The overcrowding was especially serious in 1875, when the colony was hit by an epidemic of measles, with high loss of life among indentured laborers in particular.

Recruiting and State Control

During the administration of Governor Guillain (1862–1870), state involvement covered more than the control of passage money. The initial cost of recruiting was borne by the administration—in effect an advance to the settlers, who were obliged to repay it at an unstated time. When the ship arrived, it was boarded by a medical officer to check that the so-called immigrants were healthy and physically able to do the work required of them, and by an immigration officer to verify—as well as he was able—that recruits had come of their own free will (photo 3). In addition to bearing the cost of this procedure, the administration also housed and fed the laborers until they were assigned to employers. The government provided a model contract setting out basic provisions for rations, medical care, and burial. Hours of work and wages were left open for negotiation, but in practice, the working day was generally around twelve hours, including two hours for meals and rest, and monthly wages settled at around 12 francs for

Photo 3 Arrival of new recruits aboard a schooner. Mitchell Library, State Library of New South Wales.

a man (about 10 shillings in British currency or US\$2.40), and 9 francs for a woman or child. At first the contract was to be signed before the clerk of court, but after 1867 by the immigration commissioner. Repatriation was also overseen by the administration. The close commitment of the government during this period is evident in its use in 1867 of a warship, the *Bonite,* to repatriate 45 New Hebrideans from three ports, Noumea, Canala, and Pouébo, and to recruit another 61 workers for its return journey.[33]

Under Henry's first contract with the administration, New Hebridean "immigrants" were returned to their islands after a one-year engagement. Gradually the indenture period was extended. By 1869, the norm was a two-year contract, but by 1874 workers could be engaged for periods of from two to five years,[34] the most common engagement toward the end of the seventies being for three years, the period prevailing in Queensland and Fiji. Under a peculiarity of the New Caledonian regulations, minors could be engaged for much longer, a provision that lent itself to abuse, as is later elaborated.

That there was a degree of cooperation with island societies was shown early by the emergence of definite choices of destination. The advantages of Queensland over Fiji were soon known all round the islands. The money wages were twice what was paid in Fiji, and goods available to be bought with them were more varied, of better quality, and cheaper than anywhere else. Queensland absorbed by far the largest number of recruits, providing more opportunity for comradeship and more information from returns about the things they did there. While New Caledonia paid about the same rates as Queensland, goods were more expensive and not as reliable. But there were clearly other considerations affecting the reputation of a destination. New Caledonia had no trouble getting recruits in the 1860s, and that seemed to be because the administration's involvement offered some guarantee of protection to the Islanders. This was certainly the opinion of Captain George Palmer, RN, when he described the New Caledonian system to the New South Wales Royal Commission into the Kidnapping of Islanders in 1869.[35] A British cotton planter, James Row, living on Efaté at the time, also testified to the strict supervision of conditions and the preference of the people on his island to work in New Caledonia rather than in Queensland or Fiji,[36] a preference that was reversed within a few years. This short-lived preference may also be related to the shorter term of indenture and strictly regimented repatriation at the end of that time, as Henry believed;[37] he too was of the view that the "French are very particular to see that the natives understand their agreements," as well as being on the whole well paid, and paid in cash,[38] a state of affairs that, if it were indeed the case, also quickly changed.

If recruiting for New Caledonia was relatively free of abuses in the

1860s, it was probably because of direct supervision by an energetic administration, for no special régime had been created to deal with it. Recruiting was still carried on under imperial legislation of 1852 (predating the annexation of the colony) that was an explicit response to the problem of a covert revival of the slave trade following the emancipation of slaves in Réunion and the Caribbean colonies. Under the terms of the legislation, the consent of the imported laborer was to be guaranteed by a government agent at the place of recruitment,[39] a provision that was impracticable in Oceania unless such an agent was on board ship, and that reform did not occur until 1875. Preoccupied with the establishment of a penal settlement and operating with shrinking resources, the colonial administration contented itself with piecemeal regulations modifying the 1852 legislation. Up to 1875, recruiting ships carried no government agents and did not need a license to recruit. A medical inspection and routine questions concerning consent to engage were all that was required on arrival in New Caledonia, apart from formal registration and small payments by the employer. As time would prove, even such meager regulations were of little avail, for the personnel of British ships— which New Caledonian labor vessels were, almost without exception— turned out to be immune from French law.

The period of close government control came to an end with the departure of Governor Guillain in March 1870. His successor, Gaultier de la Richerie, had to preside over a different scene in New Caledonia. The hopes for a varied agriculture—so strong in the sixties— had been dashed by a series of disasters, including a severe drought in 1868–1869 and plagues of locusts. But mining soon took its place as the staple of the free economy. Gold mining on the Diahot River in the northeast began in 1871, and although it petered out, copper mining in Ouégoa took its place in 1873, followed soon afterward by the mining of nickel throughout the Grande Terre. In France, defeat in the Franco-Prussian War was succeeded by the uprising and overthrow of the Paris Commune in 1871. One large consequence for New Caledonia was the exile of nearly four thousand political prisoners to the colony, reinforcing the central place of the penitentiary in the local economy, but putting a new strain on labor and financial resources. Cohorts of convicts of the ordinary sort continued to arrive several times a year. Free white settlement also expanded, though slowly, notably through a group of settlers from Alsace, unwilling to accept the cession of their province to the new nation of Germany. And there were by now a couple of hundred *libérés* to be settled on land concessions or otherwise accommodated.

All these developments had to be dealt with on an even more miserable budget. The defeat and the Communard uprising resulted in a financial crisis in France, quickly felt in New Caledonia through a substantial cut to its grant in 1870–71 that was ascribed to the *"malheurs de la patrie."* One of the effects of the diminished funds was the withdrawal of military posts on the northeast coast, so that colonial control actually shrank in these years,[40] making it even more difficult than before to extract corvée labor. Once again the need for imported labor increased as the means of controlling local labor diminished.

Probably out of financial necessity as well as its new responsibilities, the colonial administration opted out of its role as labor broker, leaving it entirely to private enterprise. While it retained responsibility for the conduct of the labor trade, the government was slow to provide a legal framework for it. If it had managed to supervise labor recruiting with minimal legislation in the 1860s, its policing powers proved totally inadequate to the changed situation of the 1870s. Gradually a body of regulations emerged to deal with the upsurge in the recruitment of immigrant labor, but it always limped hopelessly behind the events it was supposed to control. The effect of each measure lasted only as long as it took interested parties to devise a way of subverting it.

A commission had been set up in 1869 to draft a code of laws to deal with the introduction of immigrant labor. It did not begin its deliberations until 1871. The five-member commission—three of whom were local property owners—then took two years to produce recommendations that were the basis of an *arrêté* (local edict) of 26 March 1874. This law, which provided the framework for all immigrant labor regulation until replaced by a *décret* (metropolitan decree) in 1893, is sometimes assumed to have been the equivalent of the British Pacific Islanders' Protection Act of 1872, but the whole tenor was different. The British act concentrated on the recruitment process, aiming at guarantees of voluntary enlistment and humane treatment during the voyage, at the termination of which its responsibilities ceased and those of the colony took over. The New Caledonian *arrêté* had the opposite slant, confining itself almost exclusively to the management of labor once in the territory: for the regulation of recruiting it continued to rely on the 1852 decree, except where introduced workers were covered by later international conventions. While the minister had recommended in 1870 that traveling government agents should go with recruiters in Oceania, as required under the international convention covering the import of Indian laborers,[41] an inspector in 1873 found that no such agent traveled on ships recruiting in Oceania from Noumea. He confidently believed that this lacuna would be filled by the regulations about to be promulgated,[42] but in the event the 1874 *arrêté* did not provide for traveling government agents.

Chapter 3
Entrepreneurial Recruiting in the 1870s

A number of factors came together in the 1870s to increase the like-lihood of malpractice in the New Caledonian labor trade. Not only had passage money risen substantially, attracting greedy as well as in-experienced operators, and not only had control decreased, but at the same time recruiters were seeking new reserves of labor. Like their counterparts from Queensland and Fiji, they found that they had ex-hausted the old beats and had to go farther north for their workers. These new areas were, inevitably, islands with less contact with Euro-peans than the southern New Hebrides. They went to islands north of Efaté in the New Hebrides and as far as the Solomon group (map 1). With the exception of Espiritu Santo, all these islands had less expe-rience of doing regular business with Europeans. As one recruiter pointed out, with the best will in the world it would have been diffi-cult to communicate what it might be like to go away and work on a plantation or a mine for a couple of years to people who spoke no Bislama, had no relatives who had been abroad, and had little or no contact with Europeans.

There was small reason to suspect most labor recruiters of having the best will in the world, and it is not surprising that the earliest ex-ample of malpractice to come to the attention of the authorities was committed by a recruiter in a new area—the case of the *Volunteer* in the Solomon Islands. Without a government agent, in a place where the experience of the local population was minimal, the conduct of the master and crew depended only on their own temerity and their own conscience. At stake was the going rate of 110 francs per head against very little overhead if the "recruits" were abducted. Because the es-capades of the master of the *Volunteer,* Captain H McKenzie, provide an excellent example of the attractions of New Caledonian labor trading in this period, the inadequacy of the law to cope with it, the increased opportunities for malpractice in a newly opened area, and

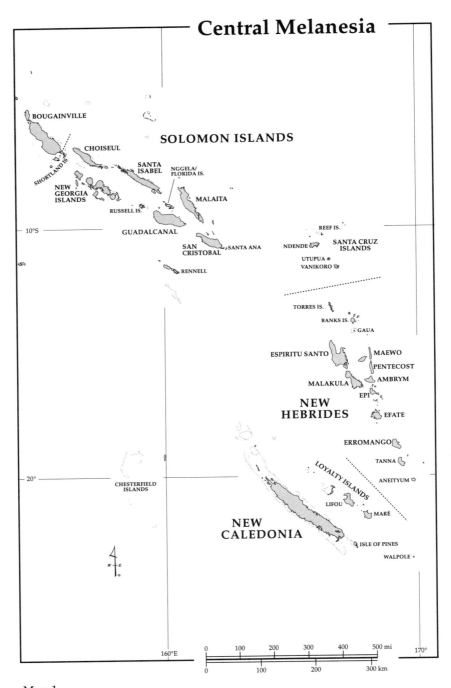

Central Melanesia

BOUGAINVILLE

SOLOMON ISLANDS

CHOISEUL

SHORTLAND IS.

SANTA
ISABEL

NGGELA/
FLORIDA IS.

NEW
GEORGIA
ISLANDS

MALAITA

RUSSELL IS.

10°S

GUADALCANAL

SAN
CRISTOBAL

SANTA ANA

RENNELL

REEF IS.

NDENDE

SANTA CRUZ
ISLANDS

UTUPUA
VANIKORO

TORRES IS.

BANKS IS.

GAUA

ESPIRITU SANTO

MAEWO

PENTECOST

AMBRYM

MALAKULA

EPI

NEW
HEBRIDES

EFATE

ERROMANGO

TANNA

LOYALTY ISLANDS

20°

CHESTERFIELD
ISLANDS

ANEITYUM

LIFOU

MARÉ

NEW
CALEDONIA

ISLE OF PINES

WALPOLE

160°E

170°

| 0 | 100 | 200 | 300 | 400 | 500 mi |

| 0 | 100 | 200 | 300 km |

Map 1

the way in which rivalry between the French and the English could hinder the implementation of the regulation that existed, I present them in some detail.

McKenzie was apparently attracted out of the coastal trade of New Zealand by the surge in passage money in New Caledonia together with the easing of controls. In May 1870, he cleared from Noumea "for the New Hebrides" in the *Volunteer,* a small British-registered vessel of twenty-two tonnes. He returned three months later, not from the New Hebrides but from the eastern Solomons, with thirty-two recruits from Ugi, Ulawa, and "Ehoua" (probably Santa Ana), small islands between San Cristobal and Malaita.

The recruits appeared bewildered and reluctant to follow their employers when engaged. Nearly all of them, in the bush as well as in Noumea, deserted forthwith, arousing suspicions as to the manner of their recruitment. Another labor trader, Captain Donald McLeod, passed on testimony from an Ugi man in his crew that his countrymen claimed to have been taken by force. An inquiry was begun, and with this man interpreting, it emerged that the men had gone on board to sell shells and other curios, whereupon they were seized and put into the hold and forced to remain there until the ship was well away from their shores. Others who refused to board had been shot at.[1]

Governor Gaultier de la Richerie wrote to the head of the Department of Justice for legal advice on the means of prosecuting the captain. The answer illustrates one of the thorniest problems in the history of policing the Pacific, the limitation of jurisdiction over ships carrying foreign flags. The *Volunteer,* said the judge in reply, was clearly in breach of the Anti-Slavery Act, but as had been shown in a precedent at Martinique some forty years before, could not be prosecuted by the French government because it sailed under foreign colors. Nothing could be done in the present case apart from referring the matter to the British authorities.[2]

It was a bad beginning for the regulation of private ventures in labor trading, for virtually all the ships in the trade at this time were British and were now deemed unanswerable to French law. This incident began turning the wheels that were to produce the process of "francisation" of such ships—giving them French registry and obliging them to fly the French flag, thus restoring French jurisdiction over them. On the other hand, this process made them immune to British law at sea. After the British government passed the Pacific Islanders Protection Act in 1872, French law was less strict in the matter of recruiting than British law, which was also better policed, for British warships operating in the sphere of the Western Pacific High Commission were patrolling the region in numbers. New Caledonian labor traders moved at once to request francisation when it became available, suggesting that they saw more benefits than costs in flying French colors.

But in 1871 Captain McKenzie was still free to command a British ship recruiting to a French port. In spite of his record of kidnapping the year before, he was allowed to clear out of Noumea on a recruiting voyage in the *Helen* in June 1871, ostensibly for the New Hebrides. However, the Reverend Joseph Aitkin in the Melanesian Mission vessel *Southern Cross* saw him at San Cristobal, in the Solomon Islands, the following month, and noted in his journal: "A small Auckland vessel [the *Helen*], Captain M'Kenzie, came to an anchor at Wono. He is after labour, and from his own account is not particular how he gets it. He says he is not going to Fiji. Someone on board told Stephen [Tariniaro, mission assistant] it was to New Caledonia."[3] The next day, the *Helen* went down the coast of San Cristobal and a few days later was seen again by the mission ship at Sa'a, at the southern tip of Malaita. This time McKenzie claimed that he was recruiting for his own two-thousand-acre plantation at Tanna, but said that he had not picked up any labor since leaving San Cristobal. The mission learned shortly afterward that he was lying, for he had picked up people from Ulawa at least, five of whom had managed to swim ashore at Sa'a— fairly convincing evidence that they were not volunteers.[4] On 13 August the Reverend Charles Hyde Brooke of the Melanesian Mission at Nggela reported that Malaita people from a vessel at anchor there said that a "kill kill" vessel was in the offing. The next day the schooner they signalled arrived: it was the *Helen*, Captain McKenzie, of New Zealand. "[T]here were two or three Ambrym lads on board. Captain M'Kenzie said honestly, 'If I got a chance to carry off a lot of 'em I'd do it, I don't deny, but killing is not in my creed'." Soon after, on seeing a fine canoe with some twenty men in it, he exclaimed, "Ah what a nice haul you'd make, just a nice day's work; if your friend was not here (meaning me [Brooke]) I'd have the lot of you."[5]

Brooke's suspicions were confirmed by the government agent of the Queensland recruiter *Isabella*, which met the *Helen* at Nggela two days before Brooke had seen him.

> The master of the *Helen* came on board this morning. He does not conceal in the least that he takes men when he cannot get them otherwise. He volunteered the information to me; he said he had come a long way for men and meant to get them, and considered he was conferring favours on them by taking them. We picked up a canoe with a hole in it floating about shortly afterwards. It certainly looked as if he had been conferring favours on some natives in his way. Afterwards a canoe came close to us with a number of natives in it, who seemed greatly excited by something but we could

not make out what it was. The *Helen* has 30 islanders on board, 25 being from this group [Nggela]. They keep their laborers under hatches to prevent them jumping overboard, 30 in so small a vessel in this weather must be miserable.[6]

Captain Markham of HMS *Rosario* met the *Helen* at Santo on 18 December 1871. McKenzie claimed to be out of Levuka, Fiji, recruiting labor for that colony. Markham found that McKenzie had no clearance from the British consul at Fiji, no labor license, and no log of the ship's proceedings "since leaving Levuka," all of which was not surprising, as he had in reality cleared from Noumea. Not yet armed with the Pacific Islanders Protection Act, Markham felt that the most he could legally do was to make McKenzie sign a paper stating that he was carrying labor to Fiji without any official papers whatever.[7] He apparently did not conceive that even in making such an affidavit McKenzie was prepared to lie. When Markham arrived in Noumea a few weeks later, he was mortified to find that McKenzie had already unloaded his labor there, not at Fiji as he had affirmed, and had again cleared out of Noumea. When the commander raised questions in Noumea about the legitimacy of his last voyage, he was referred to the report of the delegation that had boarded the *Helen* on its arrival, consisting of a doctor, the port captain, a delegate of the colonial secretary, and an English interpreter assisted by two "kanaka" interpreters in "the dialects of the New Hebrides." The delegation found that all the recruits had engaged voluntarily for a term of three years' service in New Caledonia. "Being thus assured of the free consenting of the immigrants to come to be indentured in the Colony," and upon the doctor finding them fit to perform the work for which they were engaged, the report recommended their introduction.[8]

Challenged by the British, Gaultier de la Richerie was happy to take this report at face value, in spite of his efforts to prosecute McKenzie for kidnapping only the year before, for French honor was now at stake. He replied that the operations of the *Helen* had been found to be "*très régulières,*" and that he had taken the opportunity of having the captain questioned since his return to Noumea (which on past record would not have added much by way of the truth). For good measure, the governor included a countercharge of kidnapping at the Isle of Pines by a Fiji-bound British ship.[9] Whether or not the charge was well founded, countercharging became, regrettably, a standard way of answering allegations. Franco-British rivalry diverted the powers from an opportunity to cooperate in suppressing abuses.

It is unlikely that McKenzie's illegal operations were unique or even unusual in the period. A report received by the Foreign Office

in 1875 accurately claimed that in this period the New Caledonian
trade "was conducted chiefly not by Frenchmen, but by foreigners,
including Englishmen who could not ply the same trade so easily at
Fiji on account of English ships of war." The informant stated that a
friend of his in Noumea believed that the laborers were generally kidnapped, and that he had seen many of them arrive in wretched condition, some dying soon after they were landed.[10]

That regulations dealing with the Oceanian labor trade were not
adequate to control abuses was recognized by the new governor of
New Caledonia, Léopold de Pritzbuer, who arrived to take up his commission in Noumea in February 1875. He immediately announced
significant new measures in an *arrêté* of March 1875, imposing stricter
conditions on francised ships, prefaced by the explanation that "it is
a matter of public notoriety that the majority of such francised ships
engage in a trade in recruiting native workers in the New Hebrides
and neighbouring islands, a trade of which one has reason to suspect
the morality."[11]

The *arrêté* ruled that francised vessels would now be confined to
the coastal trade, unless they received special authorization. This they
could only obtain from the governor, under certain conditions, including the necessity of having a French captain, to ensure that he
was answerable to French law. The governor could withdraw the privilege immediately should there be due cause. It was in effect a licens-
ing system. Apart from ensuring that the activities of the ship fell
within French jurisdiction, it was also a device to fill several lacunae
in the 1874 regulations. When the first vessel was authorized under
this law, the terms included an obligation to carry a government agent,
whose functions were to ensure that recruitment was voluntary and
to supervise the conditions of the recruits on the voyage. The overcrowding and neglect of the preceding years was clearly another of
Pritzbuer's targets: the ship was to be boarded before each departure
from the colony to check that it was over forty tonnes and in good
condition, to set a quota of recruits appropriate to its size, and to ensure that the provision of food and medical supplies was adequate for
that number.[12]

These measures were applied separately to each such authorization that followed. In short, the edict introduced the main protection
provisions of the British act of 1872, and, since almost all the vessels
currently engaged in the labor trade were francised British vessels,
the coverage was sufficiently wide, although a German ketch, the *Laura
Lind,* seems to have slipped the net. The new régime effectively eliminated at least seven or eight small vessels—the worst, though not the
only, offenders in serious overcrowding. Only the *Donald MacLean,* the
Tanna, and the *Esperance* were accorded the authorization needed in

1875. When the governor authorized the repatriation of laborers on the *Tanna* in September 1875 he gave orders that the returning workers ("returns" in labor trade parlance) were to be repatriated strictly only to their own communities,[13] suggesting that this had not been the practice hitherto.

The Pritzbuer reforms were part of a surge in official interest in the colonization of the New Hebrides. What the governor did not say in his *arrêté* was that the new government agents on recruiting ships were also to act as informants to the French government, giving details about the islands' port facilities, economic production, and the attitude of the indigenes to the French, with a view to the annexation of at least the southern half of the archipelago.[14] Pritzbuer believed that an improvement of the image of the French through stricter control of recruiting and repatriation would further national ambitions in the islands. The reports of the government agents were later put at the disposal of Rear-Admiral Du Petit-Thouars when he went on his fact-finding tour of the group in 1879, and, as it happened, reported against annexation. This kind of information continued to form part of government agents' journals until at least 1885; it appeared thereafter in the reports of warships.

As happened with every piece of legislation regulating the labor trade, rumor had preceded the enactment of Pritzbuer's reforms, with a rush to beat the gun. Just before the March 1875 *arrêté* came into effect there was a flurry of small ships going out on recruiting voyages: no fewer than 446 recruits were introduced in the three months preceding the application of this legislation. Business slowed somewhat for the rest of the year, due to the elimination of the very small ships as well as the new restrictions. It was to become clear, however, that the measures did not put a stop to abuses, which remained endemic until the trade was suspended by the colonial administration in 1882.

By contrast with the preferences of the 1860s, New Caledonia was no longer a favored destination for recruits. Adding to the pressure on recruiters to fill their ships, the predilection of recruits was for Queensland, and for Fiji as second option, observed as early as 1875.[15] Choices had changed decidedly since the beginning of the trade, evidence of a rapid diffusion of information. Fiji vessels had been shunned in the past, the result of a sorry record of kidnapping and poor conditions at the workplace, as well as the well-circulated fact that wages were only half those offered in Queensland and New Caledonia; but in his tour of the New Hebrides in 1879, Du Petit-Thouars observed that the reputation of Fiji had greatly improved since the new colonial government had taken serious steps to improve the lot of recruits: "Every time I asked the savages which they preferred out of Queensland, Fiji or Noumea, without the least hesitation all said that they preferred the first two destinations because they brought back almost nothing from Noumea."[16]

Although money wages were roughly comparable to those in Queensland (12 francs a month, quite close to the 10 shillings of Queensland), trade goods were nearly twice as expensive in New Caledonia. Time after time, French officials heard the same story in the islands.[17] Lieutenant d'Arbel saw the high price of goods as "one of the great difficulties for the Caledonian recruiter." As an example, "the price of a much-required item, guns, can be quoted. For carbines of recent model the going price in Maryborough is 5fr 50, whereas in Noumea old guns cost 8 fr. There is a similar difference for lengths of cloth, matches, tobacco, in a word, for all trade articles." He noted that the "natives are adept in spreading the news, to explain why they refuse to enlist, that fewer goods are brought back from Caledonia than from Queensland."[18] The theme had hardly changed in 1892, when Commander Gadaud wrote to the governor that "it is unfortunately true that the New Hebrideans have a great repugnance to enlisting for Noumea. The reason that they give for it is that those natives who do [go to Noumea] bring back very few goods and almost no money. It is not the same, they say, with those who return from Queensland or Fiji." Like others, he wondered whether the failure of the colony's employers to pay wages and their propensity to inflict fines on their workers may have also had something to do with this state of affairs.[19] As well, New Caledonia was the only place where they could be sent to work at the mines, universally detested,[20] and known in the islands (rightly) for a high death rate.[21] Only when Islanders were unable to get firearms from any other source, did the New Caledonian market regain its early favor. Where consent was lacking, the odds tipped in favor of ruse and force. Recruiters often falsely claimed that their ship's destination was the more popular one of Queensland, and the fact that most of them at this time were British, and spoke Pidgin or Bislama, was used to support this deception. Some dispensed with such stratagems and relied on brute force. It was a vicious circle, for the use of fraud and kidnapping only worsened the reputation of "Noumea" recruiters.

Although no further cases of kidnapping reached the level of a government inquiry until 1880, abuses were still rife despite Pritzbuer's reforms. The lack of competitive inducements increased the temptation to use force and fraud to get the numbers of recruits required, and the absence of effective policing made it possible to get away with it. It was only a matter of time before a full-scale scandal erupted.

In the last half of the 1870s, stories of kidnapping were common in Noumea. Some, from several independent sources, surrounded the ship *Aoba,* given special authorization in 1876, and the chief recruiter of labor in the period 1876–1879, during which it made fifteen round trips to the New Hebrides without being challenged by the authorities. Yet people in Noumea were aware that the ship was engaged in kidnapping, including Léon Moncelon (a man not opposed to the labor trade, later the first New Caledonian delegate to the Conseil Supérieur des Colonies in Paris) who described in detail the abduction by the *Aoba* of a group of Maewo people in about 1878: the story was told to him by Louai, his child servant, one of the victims.[22] Albert Picquié, Doctor of Law, assistant supply officer to the navy and later acting governor of the colony—hardly a radical—wrote to the famous humanitarian Victor Schoelcher about the "disguised slave trade" in New Caledonia, also citing the case of the *Aoba:* "It is true," he said, "that there is on board a government agent (a citizen who is in other respects perfectly honest) but this agent is as much a slaver as the Captain himself."[23] A passenger on the British recruiter *Bobtail Nag* related that they met the *Aoba* at Vila, Efaté, in May 1877, fresh from Noumea, with as yet no recruits: when they met the same ship nineteen days later, at Merelava in the Banks group, he was surprised to find it had 94 recruits on board, "so that I think at this rate, the French system of recruiting must be near akin to kidnapping."[24] The *Aoba*'s success on this occasion was not due to exceptional luck, for a six-week round trip over September–October 1877, another in November–December 1877, and yet another in June–July 1878 yielded 79, 102, and 81 recruits respectively.[25] One's confidence in the proper conduct of these rapid voyages is not enhanced by the knowledge that three out of four of them were under the titular command of Napoléon Le Vigoureux, a year later described by a settler as a drunkard who was not the real master of the vessel. And the *Aurora*'s voyages were almost equally opportune in those years—one lasting only one month, yet signing on 50 recruits.

It seemed at first that the problem might be overcome by a change in procedures. The manner of the appointment of the government agent left much to be desired. Until 1878 he was appointed and paid directly by the shipowner, a system obviously open to abuse, as the director of the Interior Department later admitted.[26] A settler, Ludovic Marchand, told Schoelcher that the owner's practice was not to pay the government agent the required 500 francs a month, but instead to give him 150 or 200 francs as retainer plus a bonus for each recruit taken. While government agents signed on for 500 francs at the Marine Registry, "they give the difference to the middleman from whom they got the position. You see that there was, in reality, no more moral guarantee than when they sailed under the British flag, since the government agent had an interest in the operation bringing in as much profit as possible. All means to that end appeared proper to him."[27] Marchand cited examples of abuse, including one of an assistant supply agent to the navy, who traveled as government agent on the *Donald MacLean,* which he owned himself, having bought it from Donald MacLeod. He was recruiting labor on his own account and at the same time acting as government agent, overseeing the morality of his own operation![28] Marchand believed that outrageous cases of corruption in the appointment of government agents led to the reform of May 1878, whereby these officials were to be appointed directly by the director of the Interior Department.[29] Certainly the preamble to this *arrêté,* beginning "Considering that the government agents on board ships authorized to recruit New Hebrideans do not enjoy all the independence necessary to the delicate functions with which they are entrusted,"[30] appears to confirm that opinion.

According to Marchand, a lack of integrity among officials was also to blame. The first two government agents appointed by the director, M Littaye, did their job as they should, but when Littaye left for France, things deteriorated under his successor, M Dufrénil. Marchand had his own experience to recount. When he applied for a post as government agent on the *Venus* in July 1879, he received no reply. He tried in vain to speak to the director, being put off with one excuse after another by his underlings. When he finally confronted Dufrénil, he was told, in flagrant breach of the 1878 edict, to apply to the shipowners, Joubert & Carter! He forbore to do that, having already heard that Joubert had two nominees prepared to take cut rates. The man eventually appointed was Félix-Aristide Russeil, a man of 65 years suffering mental impairment as a result of typhoid fever.

Marchand then applied to be government agent on the *Aurora.* The department clerks succeeded in concealing his application from the director, and the *Aurora* left Noumea carrying as government agent a young man just arrived from France, without any experience. Clearly, neither of these voyages would be properly supervised by the appointee. Marchand heard that the first—the *Venus* voyage of 1879— was conducted in anything but a regular manner. The only two white sailors on board told him that there was a "dummy" captain—since the 1875 reform required a Frenchman—the aforesaid Napoléon Le Vigoureux, who was kept in a state of blissful inebriation throughout the voyage, while an Englishman, McCarthey, was the real master. Russeil, the government agent, was paid at only half the rate laid down in the 1878 *arrêté.* At Epi, "fifteen little darkies," in the words of the sailors, were grabbed by the wrist and thrown into the boat, and the *Venus* finally returned to Noumea with 52 New Hebrideans, "nearly all children."[31]

These voyages of the *Venus* and the *Aurora* went unchallenged. Their next two voyages, later exposed as kidnapping voyages of the grossest kind, might also have escaped attention but for outside complaints, for as Governor Courbet was to protest, there was a conspiracy of silence in the colony itself, these escapades being "inevitably known in New Caledonia."[32]

During the 1860s, although operating under archaic laws, the labor trade was under relatively strict supervision. Compared with the next decade it was limited in extent, and New Caledonia was said to be a favored destination for New Hebridean recruits. In the 1870s, demand increased, but conditions worsened, due to the withdrawal of state control. By 1880 the situation had become a scandal, and the Noumea administration was forced to deal with it as a result of complaints from outside the colony. An inquiry held later in the year is discussed in detail in the next chapter for the light it threw on the general conduct of the trade.

Chapter 4

The Kidnapping Inquiries and the Suspension of the Labor Trade, 1880–1882

Abuses came to light in 1880 through a complaint of Commodore Wilson of the Royal Navy to the British consul in Noumea. Wilson enclosed extracts from journals of British labor ships, a letter from the missionary Daniel Macdonald, and an article in the *Sydney Evening News* describing incidents in the northern New Hebrides involving two French labor vessels, the *Aurora* and a "green ship" thought to be the *Lulu*. Governor Courbet ordered an inquiry into the charges and into the "general facts relative to immigration," little knowing that he was opening a Pandora's box. The *Lulu* was rapidly exonerated from blame, but serious allegations of kidnapping were made against the *Aurora* and the *Venus*. The immediate charges related to the recent voyage of the *Aurora* of July–August 1880 (which I call *Aurora*-2), carrying as captain Gabriel Madézo and as government agent Paul Dufrénil. However, evidence alleged kidnapping on an earlier voyage of the *Aurora* of March–June 1880 (which I call *Aurora*-1), with the same captain but a different government agent, Jullion. The "green ship" proved to be the *Venus* instead of the *Lulu*. Wilson's charges implicated the March–June voyage of the *Venus* (which I call *Venus*-2), carrying a dummy French captain and Government Agent Perrot, but again, an earlier voyage of the *Venus* of December 1879 to March 1880 (which I call *Venus*-1), carrying Government Agent Simard, became involved in accusations of kidnapping.

The Charges

Wilson's complaint concerned a number of incidents at the islands of Pentecost, Ambae, Malo, and Epi, involving two vessels recruiting for New Caledonia, one painted green, name unknown, the other the *Aurora*. Government Agent Gaggin, of the Queensland labor ship *Stanley*, had noted in his journal three accounts of kidnapping, apparently by the same ship. At Pentecost, the people had shown signs of fear at his approach. When he pursued the matter he was told that a "green ship" belonging to "man oui-oui" (Frenchman) had been there the day before and when canoes had gone out to it they had been smashed and their occupants captured. The next day the *Stanley* was at Ambae, where the people also complained about a "green ship that stole men." A canoe from Santo visiting Ambae was seized on its return journey, and all its occupants taken away. Off Malo the following day, Gaggin was told that the week before a green ship had fired on a canoe, smashed it to pieces, and carried off the nine men who were in it. The "green ship" was supposed to be the *Lulu* "or some such name."

A second report from the missionary Daniel Macdonald implicated the *Aurora* in kidnapping activities at Epi. Macdonald made a declaration on behalf of a chief called Baua, who claimed that two men had been "stolen," one of them the young son of a chief. The chief demanded the release of his son, threatening the recruiter with his tomahawk, whereupon the recruiter shot him dead. Another man was also shot but had recovered. The story was apparently confirmed by an extract from the journal of a Fiji recruiting vessel, the *Winifred,* dated 22 July. The government agent recorded that while at Pentecost he had met the master and government agent of *Aurora*-2, who had told him of a misadventure at Epi. They claimed that their recruiter had narrowly escaped a blow from a tomahawk and that he had shot the attacker in self-defense. The local people then fired on the boat, and they returned fire, probably wounding three or four of them before getting back to the ship.[1]

As soon as *Aurora*-2 arrived in Noumea, on 25 August 1880, Governor Courbet nominated his commission of inquiry: M Poittevin, inspector of administrative and financial services; Arthur Pelletier, a privy councillor and president of the Chamber of Commerce; Lieutenant Vincent, of the navy; M Hubert, administrator of the Maritime Registry *(commissaire de l'inscription maritime);* and M Verignon, deputy chief of the Department of the Interior. At the outset, Pelletier expressed the hope that if, as he presently believed, the accusations were found to be unjustified, the inquiry might "give the lie to rumors that people, perhaps interested parties, are spreading so ostentatiously."[2]

The Inquiry

The question of the *Lulu*'s voyage was quickly eliminated. As a preliminary inquiry had already found, the *Lulu* had not been in the labor trade for years. It turned out later that the incidents involving the "green ship" were real; only the identity of the vessel—in fact, the *Venus*—was mistaken. The commission then turned its attention to the voyage of *Aurora*-2 (July–August 1880).[3]

Captain Madézo, all the crew, and Paul Dufrénil, the government agent, gave evidence of conflict at Epi and Pentecost.[4] They claimed that the Epi affair had occurred just as they had recounted it to the crew of the *Winifred* when they met them at Pentecost. Soon after the departure of the *Winifred*, they had been attacked without provocation by the Pentecost people. Dufrénil testified that the *Aurora*'s voyage had been entirely regular and that all ninety-one recruits had volunteered. Most of the recruits had been landed at Houailou on the east coast for work at the nickel mine Bel-Air. One who had gone on with the ship to Noumea was questioned by the commission: he agreed that he had consented to recruit. It seemed as if this matter would be disposed of as summarily as the question of the *Lulu*, and that Pelletier's hope would be gratified. Yet an anomaly had passed without comment. When Dufrénil was asked about the incidents at Epi and Pentecost, it emerged that he had not accompanied the recruiting boats at either place. In his evidence he was quoting from the report of the recruiter and his boat crew—the interested parties whom he was supposed to oversee—to justify his opinion that they had given no provocation for the attack! Why did the commission allow such evidence? Would it have done so if the government agent had not been the son of F Dufrénil, director of the Department of the Interior, the official responsible for policing the labor trade regulations, whose deputy was a member of the commission?

Passing from the voyage of *Aurora*-2, the commission, now in its eighth session, agreed to hear the complaints of some New Hebrideans in Noumea who had been recruited on the *previous* trip of the *Aurora*. Boob, of Ambrym, recounted that he had come on board *Aurora*-1 to buy tobacco but was kept against his will. The government agent had said nothing about it. Then came the lengthy and confident testimony of Feufeu, also of Ambrym, who had previously served a term in New Caledonia for which he had been legitimately recruited. His contribution proved to be the turning point of the investigation. He said: "I was on the beach when a boat from the *Aurora* landed and a white[5] 'bourbonnais' offered me tobacco to recruit. I told him several times that I did not want to come to Noumea; we exchanged tobacco and yams. My canoe was beside the boat of the *Aurora;* all at once it was set adrift and swept out by the sea, and I was grabbed by the arm, put in the boat and taken aboard the ship."[6] The questioning proceeded:

Q Who grabbed you?
A It was Peter [Charles Petersen Stuart, the recruiter of *Aurora*-1].
   I wanted to go away but Peter aimed his gun at me; I was afraid
   and I stayed.
Q Did you receive any trade goods?

A No; I said to them: "I don't want to accept anything, I don't want to go away to Noumea."

Q Why didn't you jump into the water?

A Because I was afraid of the gun.

Q Once on board the *Aurora* did you make any protests?

A Once aboard, I said to the captain, "I don't want to go to Noumea, I want to go back to land." I insist [sic] again, weeping, and the captain did not listen to my protest.

Q Did you protest to anyone else?

A No, the government agent was in his room, and I insisted to the captain that I did not want to leave, saying to him: "I have worked at Koé, at Joubert's place, where I cut sugar-cane, and I don't want to go back."

Q Do you know the government agent?

A Yes, he's a little man who works in the offices where *canaques* go [ie, a clerk at the Immigration Office, Department of the Interior].[7]

Q What happened after that?

A The ship weighed anchor, went to Pentecost, where it stayed a day, and from there made sail for Paama and Epi. During this time I was on board, and nobody said they were going to land me at my place.

Q Didn't the captain offer to let you off at an island next to yours?

A No.

Q Do you know if many natives were recruited like you?

A Yes, there were many who were recruited in the same way and without any payment.

Q Do you know any natives in this category?

A Yes; there are two at the Port [Authority], one at M Rolland's place, one at M Cheval's place, three at M Rataboul's place.

This cogent evidence then took a new turn, when, after repeating what he had been told by other men of their being recruited against their will, Feufeu was asked: "But have you seen people recruited by violence?" and replied, "Yes, I have seen it, and at Malakula a *canaque* recruited in this fashion jumped into the water; the captain killed him with a shot to the head; it was aboard the *Aurora* that the thing happened." Feufeu went on to describe a kidnapping at Pentecost, in which "Tom," the other recruiter on *Aurora*-1, took a man by the feet and someone else took him by the head; they laid him down in the boat and punched him. "This man," he said, "is with Nicolas, the fisherman [in Noumea]." In response to questions he added that the government agent had seen these events, and afterward he had seen him having an animated conversation with the captain.[8]

The commissioners now had some well-described incidents around which they could frame questions to other possible eyewitnesses. They were not lacking. There were three other young men who had previously spent a term in New Caledonia: Oussa and Jounhy of Ambrym, and Misdino of Malakula. Oussa, who first described his own kidnapping, had also seen the murder at Malakula and the kidnapping at Pentecost. Misdino recounted his own seizure, which had occurred after the murder; he had not been an eyewitness to it, but he had heard it talked about by the other recruits on *Aurora*-1. Jounhy impressed the commissioners with the idiomatic French he had learned on his previous stay.[9] He said that Petersen had invited him aboard to chat with the Islanders being repatriated; he came, and the captain forced him to stay. "I didn't want to come to Noumea. I was conned [*J'ai été couillonné*]."[10] He told Government Agent Jullion that he wanted to go ashore, but Jullion replied that the captain had said he was to stay, so he would go to Noumea. Jounhy also gave a vivid account of the murder at Malakula.

Government Agent Jullion was then called. At first he maintained that nothing in particular had occurred at Malakula, but confronted with Feufeu's detailed description of the murder, he finally broke down and confessed that he had himself witnessed it. He had yielded to the pleas of Captain Madézo not to "take the bread out of his children's mouths"[11] by recording the incident in his journal. Eight other New Hebrideans on this voyage were then questioned. Only one said he had come willingly. One could not be made to understand, one was too ill to reply, although others had seen him seized, and the rest described their abduction, either by ruse or by force, by one or other of the two recruiters, "Tom" ("Black Tom") or "Peter."

These revelations prompted the commission to hear evidence from "immigrants" selected at random, who had recently arrived on the ships *Orion* and *Venus*. They began with members of the convoy by *Venus*-2 which had arrived in June 1880, who were now working in Noumea. Four of these were questioned: one, a woman, was unable to comprehend the questions, but the other three told of their being kidnapped by the breaking of their canoes after they had come alongside to trade for tobacco. One incident took place at Malakula, another at Pentecost.

The commission then requested permission to send a delegation to Houailou to question recruits who had recently arrived by *Aurora*-2 and *Venus*-2 and were working at the Bel-Air nickel mine. On receiving the assent of the governor, the delegation began its sessions at Houailou, on 5 November 1880, by interviewing recruits taken at random from the list of immigrants landed at Houailou by *Aurora*-2, the ship carrying Dufrénil as government agent. Of the eighteen members

of this convoy questioned, ten claimed to have been kidnapped, describing in detail how they were taken. The delegation also heard a
witness from the convoy of *Venus*-1, who had a story to tell about
canoe-smashing and kidnapping at Santo and Pentecost, virtually the
same procedure as that described in Noumea in relation to *Venus*-2.
The events, he said, took place in view of the government agent,
Simard. Finally, a recruit who came by *Venus*-2, carrying Government
Agent Perrot, described incidents of kidnapping at Pentecost, the
details of which tallied closely with the accounts of the witnesses in
Noumea from the same voyage.

The commission then went to Thio, another mining center more
than a hundred kilometers down the coast from Houailou, having
heard that many New Hebrideans from recent convoys were employed
there. Eleven witnesses were heard, all from *Venus*-2 (the Perrot voyage). With the exception of one who was too frightened to speak,
all told of violent kidnapping, mostly from canoes, at Santo, Malakula, Epi, and Pentecost. Their evidence corroborated in detail the
evidence heard in Houailou and Noumea. The three centers were far
apart, accessible to each other only by sea: the witnesses could not
possibly have colluded.

With four voyages now inculpated—two of the *Venus* and two of
the *Aurora*—the commission sat again in Noumea, chiefly to confront
Perrot, the government agent of *Venus*-2, with the evidence taken from
New Hebrideans from the three different centers. Although it was
strongly put to Perrot that the evidence of many witnesses from three
different locations was consistent, he held fast to his position that
there had been no illegality in recruiting by the *Venus* on this voyage.

In its report, the commission accepted entirely Paul Dufrénil's
account of the incidents at Epi and Pentecost. The recruiting on
Aurora-2 had been carried out "with probity."[12] The commissioners
were forced to address the awkward testimony of the ten New Hebrideans on this voyage who had related in detail the manner of their
kidnapping. The commission concluded that the evidence of the recruits on this voyage was contradictory, since some declared that they
had volunteered and some that they had been kidnapped[13]—a circumstance that a judge later saw as an indication that witnesses were
telling the truth.[14] Dufrénil and the crew of *Aurora*-2 were exonerated
of all charges.

The commissioners were more impressed by the testimony of recruits taken by *Aurora*-1 and *Venus*-2. They confronted Government
Agents Jullion and Perrot with this evidence, something they had not
done in the case of Dufrénil. There was a difference, for in the first
two cases, the evidence was taken in three different places and found
to be consistent, while nearly all the witnesses from Dufrénil's ship,

Aurora-2, were at Houailou. It is hard to escape the conclusion, however, that the commissioners were relieved to find a reason to clear the son of the director of the Department of the Interior. Although they seemed to be convinced that kidnapping had taken place on *Aurora*-1 and *Venus*-2, they found the case unproven, depending as it did on "native evidence."[15]

Such was not the case with the act of murder by Madézo and acts of violence by Tom. Since Government Agent Jullion had confessed to witnessing these, the commission recognized them as criminal acts. As a result of the evidence given by the recruits, members were also brought to the opinion that the recruiting of New Hebrideans was frequently carried out by threats, trickery, and surprise attacks. The appointment of government agents from the staff of the Department of the Interior had not had the intended effect. While he insisted that ships of other nationalities had to share the blame, the president of the commission advised the governor that "the manner of recruiting New Hebrideans [for New Caledonia] left much to be desired" and recommended a tightening of the regulations.[16]

Madézo was eventually tried in May 1882 and condemned to four years' jail. Tom ("Black Tom") got eighteen months.[17] Madézo did not serve the whole term, however, for he turned up again as captain of the *Ernestine* for the Compagnie Calédonienne des Nouvelles Hébrides in 1885. In October of that year an explosion in the ship's cabin — apparently a suicide by the captain — killed him and two others.[18]

The *Aurora* commission recommended several measures to modify recruiting procedures: a warship should be sent to supervise labor recruiting; not only the captain but also half the crew should be French and therefore able to understand each other; there should be better provision for language interpretation between recruiter and potential recruit; government agents should be supplied with badges in order to be recognizable to recruits.[19] A warship was unavailable, but otherwise the path of reform was duly followed. Soon after, a body of instructions was issued to government agents spelling out their responsibilities. They were reminded that they were supposed to be present at negotiations between recruiters and potential recruits, to ensure that conditions of employment such as duration and wages were explicitly stated, that "the chief's consent" was secured, and that repatriations were properly conducted so that returns were landed at their place of origin with all their possessions.[20]

The *Venus*-1 Inquiry

The scandals aired in 1880 continued unabated as a result of another external complaint. The Anglican Bishop of Melanesia received pre-

cise accusations from Christian converts of kidnapping activities by
Venus-1 in the Torres group. These were conveyed to the administration through the British consul, and a fresh administrative investigation was held in December 1880. The details taken in the islands accorded admirably with evidence from recruits already heard in three
different centers of New Caledonia during the *Aurora* inquiry. Two
Torres Islanders, Lagoro and Houinéama, testified that they and eighteen others had come out in a canoe and had gone aboard *Venus*-1.
They had been seized, tied up, and put in the hold. They recognized
Government Agent Simard as the man who had taken their names,
but said that he had not asked them whether or not they wished to recruit, nor had he given them any payment. Simard at first denied that
there had been anything illegal in the transactions, but when Lagoro
and Houinéama testified in his presence, he was challenged again,
and "with obvious despondency," replied that "the evidence that those
two natives have just given is the exact truth. I was a witness of the
event that took place at Torres." [21]

The report was passed to the Department of Justice. Its head, Paul
Cordeil, feared that prosecution might only result in an acquittal by
the jury, "knowing the entirely favorable feeling of the population
towards New Hebridean immigration," so at first he advised that the
matter would be best dealt with by administrative penalties. However, on examining the facts of *both* voyages of the *Venus* in 1880, as
revealed in the preliminary instruction, he concluded that the case
involved common law crimes of such an odious nature that they had
to come before the Criminal Court. [22]

The Trial of the Personnel of *Venus*-1 and *Venus*-2

The trial did not take place until September 1882, a lapse of time that
permitted Simard, the government agent of *Venus*-1, and Thomas
Davis, one of the recruiters of *Venus*-2, to skip the country. By then,
too, the administration had already suspended all "immigration"
from the New Hebrides.

On trial were the dummy captain, Eugène Duret, of *Venus*-1, his
nominal supercargo but real captain, Walter Champion, a British subject, and Perrot, government agent of *Venus*-2, who had already survived the interrogation of the *Aurora* inquiry. The public prosecutor
pointed out that the evidence of thirty-nine recruits corresponded in
detail despite the untraversable distance between the witnesses, and
that it had now survived unchanged during four administrative inquiries since the events. [23]

It emerged [24] that on the first voyage in question, from December
1879 to March 1880 (*Venus*-1), fifteen to twenty local people swam out

or came by canoe to the ship in order to trade, or out of pure curiosity. Seeing his chance for a large haul of recruits, Walter Champion asked them to help him move a large barrel of water in the hold. Once they were in the hold, the hatches were immediately battened down, except for one that was broken, where his brother Joseph stood sentinel with his gun. However, out of fear that the kidnapping would be denounced in Noumea, three of the captured who spoke English were put ashore and given presents of guns and powder, presumably to buy their silence. A fourth English speaker refused to leave his comrades; he was kept, but menaced with terrible threats to prevent him from speaking.

On the second voyage, many incidents of the same sort took place. At Santo, local people were invited on board to trade or to chat with those already recruited, and then detained by force. Off Santo, nine men were returning in a canoe from a voyage to Ambae to trade for pigs when the *Venus*-2 crew fired shots at them to frighten them, attached the canoe to the ship, and while towing it, first made the men hand over their ninety pigs, their guns and other arms, then broke their canoe, fishing them from the sea. The concurrence of this story with that told to Government Agent Gaggin of the *Stanley* at Ambae was remarkable. The canoe-smashing technique, perfected in the old Queensland and Fiji trades before 1872, was also used at Epi, Pentecost, and Malakula on this voyage, as had been briefly related in the *Aurora* inquiry. The president of the court, Lafarge, estimated that 70 out of 107 of the New Hebrideans recruited on this voyage had been kidnapped.[25]

Despite the strong evidence against them, conclusive in the view of the judge and of Cordeil himself, of confessions made by Simard, Duret, and the Champion brothers at the preliminary hearing (but denied at the trial), and of the best efforts of the prosecuting counsel, the accused were acquitted by the jury. Cordeil explained, "But this was not long after the decision of the Governor . . . suspending the recruitment of New Hebridean workers. Had not the memory of that decision, which had brought on so many protests and provoked so much anger, passed through the minds of the jurors at the time of their decision? One might also suppose that the impression caused by the recent murder of M. Zaepfeld and his companions, massacred by the natives of Spiritu Santo, was not without influence on the verdict of the criminal court."[26] In his report, Lafarge agreed that "vested interests" had affected the jury, but added another factor, the effect of the national rivalry between France and Britain. The president of the court had a mild criticism of the counsel for the prosecution: he had been badly advised to base his argument on the "denunciations of the priests, bishop and English authorities," thus allowing the defense to enter a political area full of traps. "I hasten to add," he said, "that the most unerring eloquence would have failed in the face of the predisposition of the assessors to acquit the three accused."[27] Two months before, Governor Courbet also had predicted that the "emotion produced by the suspension of Hebridean immigration will not be without influence on the opinion of the assessors" in the *Venus* trial.[28]

Recruiting in the islands for New Caledonia had drastically changed course since the end of the 1860s. Beginning as the most controlled in the South Pacific, it had become the most lawless, except, perhaps, for German recruiting to Sāmoa, where there appeared to be no rules at all. Recognizing the unsavory state of the colony's labor trade when he arrived as governor in 1875, Pritzbuer had introduced the appointment of government agents and other reforms similar to those in the British régime at the time. Neither his administration nor the two following it, however, had the means of policing them. Such safeguards as the administration had introduced had failed for lack of the ability to detect abuses through an independent source. Government agents—even those appointed from the staff of the Department of the Interior—were too prone to pressure from the owner or commander of the recruiting ship. As Courbet pointed out, even after the *Aurora* and *Venus* incidents, and the issue of stricter instructions, government agents complained that the "traditions were bad" aboard recruiting ships, admitting that they had the greatest difficulty in asserting their authority to prevent irregularities.[29]

A warship patrolling the islands would have been a useful supplement to their efforts. This had been the first recommendation of the 1880 commission of inquiry, supported by the director of the Department of the Interior, who pointed out that "numerous cruisers of the English Navy" supervised recruiting for Queensland and Fiji.[30] The governor was forced to reply that the Naval Division was not in a position to organize a régime of surveillance in the islands. He proposed to send a warship there from time to time, but had not so far been able to do so, for the division had recently had urgent business to attend to on its coastal voyages, and one of its cruisers had been damaged. He was hopeful that as soon as a private coastal service had been organized, a surveillance ship might be sent to the islands every four months.[31]

With the Australian squadron to call on, and five schooners built for the purpose, surveillance by the navy was far easier for the British, but the New Caledonian administration still relied on its navy for transport all round the coast of the Grande Terre, to the Loyalty Islands, and to Tahiti, and could hardly ever spare it for other duty. Only when the Joint Naval Commission of the New Hebrides came into be-

ing (1887–1888) did the patrolling of the New Hebrides become fea-
sible for the New Caledonian administration, and then it operated
under many handicaps by comparison with its British analogue.

Kidnapping and the Awareness of the Islanders

Recent historians have concluded that "the growth in the awareness
of the islanders themselves . . . made kidnapping at once unnecessary
and impossible."[32] This must be qualified. While Oceanians in many
places were by 1880 more aware of their rights, of the nature of the
work and its possible rewards in the European colonies, such awareness did not necessarily lead either to a wish to enlist or to immunity
to kidnapping. At the *Aurora* inquiry, at least seven witnesses who described their kidnapping were about as experienced as they could be,
having already served a term abroad, four in New Caledonia and three
in Queensland.

Feufeu had approached the boat crew to trade for tobacco, and
had been seized. He refused to accept any trade goods, knowing that
this would be taken as a sign of consent, pointing out that he had
already worked in New Caledonia and had no desire to repeat the experience. He was thereupon threatened with a gun. Of what use was
his experience in this situation? It would have made him aware of
what the gun could do, and probably also that the recruiter would not
hesitate to use it since they were far from any authority. When asked
why he did not jump into the water he answered, "Because I was
afraid of the gun." Events soon demonstrated how well informed he
was, for shortly afterward at Malakula he saw Captain Madézo, as a
warning to others, shoot dead an escapee swimming off to shore.
Once on board ship, Feufeu protested vainly to the captain that he
was being held against his will. He never saw the government agent.

Oussa, not long returned from service in Noumea, had gone on
board to try to get his friend Feufeu back. He was thereupon seized
himself. He did succeed in protesting to the government agent, who,
he said, replied in the same way as he had to Jounhy: "The captain
wants you to go to Noumea, so go you will."[33] Misdino had also served
a term at Noumea, and had only been back three months when he
was seized by the boat crew while trading yams and coconuts for tobacco. The ship that kidnapped him, the *Aurora,* Captain Madézo,
was the very ship that had repatriated him. Jounhy, another "old
hand" from New Caledonia who spoke fluent French, had been invited to visit Islanders on board but was kept there against his will.
Telei, of Pentecost, was not long back from a stint in Rockhampton
(Queensland). He went out to the *Venus* to trade for tobacco and was
kidnapped after his canoe had been sunk, as in the earliest days of

the Queensland trade.[34] Durane, also from Pentecost, and an "English" (probably Pidgin) speaker, had worked for three years in Maryborough (Queensland). He had approached the *Aurora*'s boat to get tobacco, when he was seized. He did not try to escape because he would have been fired on. He knew enough to complain to the government agent (Dufrénil) that not only he but his comrades had been "stolen," but Dufrénil (who probably could not understand him) had only written down his name. Tomlabo, from Epi, had also served a term at Maryborough. He went on board the *Venus* to buy tobacco and was kept by force, put into the hold, and guarded by a man with a gun. He too protested to the government agent (Perrot), "but he did not understand my language."[35]

In these cases, familiarity with Europeans appears to have lowered the guard of these returns, so that they readily contacted the ship. It also made them realize that, once taken aboard, resistance would only make matters worse. While historians have taken into account the difficulty, for recruiters, of physically abducting unwilling young men, they do not seem to have considered the difficulty, for the recruits, of getting off the ship, once on board. Instead of physical force, the abduction was sometimes done by trickery and sometimes by threatening with a gun, a threat probably *more* effective with experienced Islanders than with the uninitiated. At all events, these cases prove that the kidnapping of experienced young men was certainly not impossible. Nor, from the standpoint of the recruiter, was it unnecessary, insofar as the prospect of another term of indenture failed to attract them. These stories are not peculiar to French recruiting. Exactly the same tactics have been described by Deryck Scarr in the Queensland trade in 1884, although he called them "petty acts of duress" rather than kidnapping.[36] Moore described similar events told him by the descendants of laborers in Queensland, which he said are "typical of oral testimony about the recruiting methods."[37] Puzzled that this oral testimony is so much "at odds with the conclusions of modern historians,"[38] he discussed four very plausible reasons,[39] but they did not include the possibility that historians had underestimated the extent of kidnapping. Faith Bandler's story that her father was kidnapped from Ambrym in 1883 was seriously doubted by one of them, on the grounds that this was too late a date for the use of force,[40] and that she did not describe the actual kidnapping. But a number of kidnapping incidents were recorded after 1883 and even into the next decade. Moore's own oral evidence from a Queenslander (Len McGann) whose father worked on the recruiting ship *Sybil* relates a tale of kidnapping that occurred in the 1890s.[41] However, it is odd that Bandler gave no account of the kidnapping, if that were part of her father's story.

The return of laborers for a second period of indenture is often used as evidence that they were making a free and informed choice. It is a sobering thought that but for the accident of the true account of their second enlistment seeing the light of day, the cases of the abducted men Feufeu, Misdino, Oussa, Jounhy, Telei, Durane, and Tomlabo would have formed part of that evidence.

The Suspension of Recruiting (1882)

Several voyages went out in 1881–1882 on the basis of the new ground rules laid down after the *Aurora* inquiry's report, but there was no time for the effect of these to be evaluated before the sudden order from Paris to cease all recruiting. A ministerial order to suppress Oceanian "immigration" was issued on 5 May 1882, becoming operative in the colony from 30 June 1882.[42] In promulgating the decree, Courbet changed the "suppression" of the trade to a "suspension," in an attempt to placate the enormous furore that arose when it was learned that the ban was about to be introduced.[43] Business would be ruined, the settlers argued, agriculture and mining would go to the wall. Colonists in the bush, unprotected by their Hebridean servants, would be attacked by escaped convicts, or *libérés*. Worse, they could be massacred by Kanaks, whose rebellion of 1878, only four years before, was still vividly remembered.[44] Petitions were got up by the Chamber of Commerce and the so-called Committee of Caledonian Interests arguing for an adjournment of the measure until a full inquiry into the matter could be held. Courbet saw this as a delaying tactic, and "the signal for fitting out numerous recruiting ventures"[45]—another rush to the islands for labor during the time they had gained, as there had been in 1874–1875 with the rumor of Pritzbuer's impending reforms. While making no practical difference to the immediate cessation of the trade, by changing the order from a suppression to a suspension he hoped to attenuate the "alarms of the inhabitants."[46]

It was too late for those who had been kidnapped. No attempt was made to return them to their homes. Many died within a few years, among them Feufeu, whose eloquent testimony had changed the course of the inquiry. He had been convicted of violently resisting a policeman in the execution of his duty during a street brawl and given the maximum sentence of two years.[47] He died in jail, seven years after his abduction and return to New Caledonia. His friend Oussa, who had come on board to rescue him, died a year before him.[48]

Courbet's lengthy description of abuses in his report of February 1882,[49] along with the revelations of the inquiries and trials, no doubt influenced the French government to ban the trade on humanitarian grounds, but the sorry record of kidnapping was only one reason for the ban. The ministerial correspondence makes it clear that other factors were involved. One was the desire that the vast pool of labor represented by the convicts and freed convicts, both a charge on the French state, should "bring about a fusion between penal and free colonization," as the British had achieved in Australia, to the benefit of developing "our colonial wealth." Another was the hope of encouraging the employment of local Kanaks, whose "idleness" was a real danger to security: "our interest is thus in accord with that of civilization" in the cessation of the labor trade.[50]

Chapter 5

Settlers Triumphant: The Labor Trade Revived

> It is . . . cheap labor, and without exaggerating in the least,
> one can say that the future of the colony is intimately tied
> to the re-establishment of this immigration. Everyone uses
> the New Hebridean; the public servant and the settler for his
> household, the merchant for his shop, the farmer for his fields,
> the cattleman for his herd, the mine-owner for his claim.
>
> IMMIGRATION COMMISSION, 1883

Governor Courbet and the minister for the Navy and Colonies underestimated the outrage of the settlers in being denied the labor of their choice. Persistent efforts to regain access to New Hebridean workers twice successfully overcame government policy. Notwithstanding considerable efforts to meet colonists' labor needs in alternate ways, the administration was obliged to resume the Oceanian labor trade in 1884. When Paris imposed a new ban in 1885, employers found a device to evade it. The government was forced to restore the trade in 1890 in order to have some control over it. No further attempt was made to forbid it; when fresh sources of labor were found and changing circumstances made it less important, it was allowed to wither away.

"New Hebridean Immigration" Suspended, 1882–1884

When he banned "New Hebridean immigration" in 1882, Governor Courbet was convinced that greater efforts to employ the indigenous people through pressure on their chiefs—particularly in the Loyalty Islands—would produce a satisfactory outcome for the labor market.[1] But the plan yielded indifferent results. A number of Loyalty Islanders were introduced for work on the mainland—the beginning of a stream of migration that continues to this day—and while they were regarded as more controllable than mainland Kanaks, being farther from home, they were not considered an adequate substitute for imported Oceanians. The cost of employing them was about twice as

50

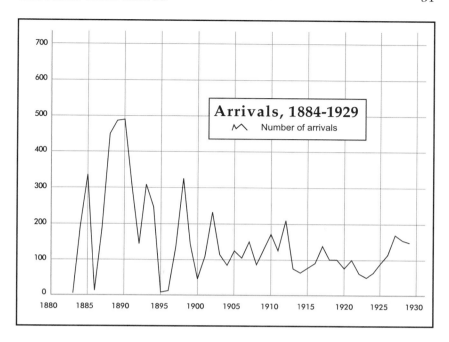

Figure 2

high, and they were considered too independent: they would only be employed for short periods and were unwilling to go to the country.[2] The "New Hebrideans"—a term which by now covered a good sprinkling of Solomon Islanders—were the preferred workers.

The metropolitan government authorized the renewal of the Oceanian labor trade in November 1883, on condition that the local administration introduced stricter regulation of recruiting practices. Governor Pallu de la Barrière lifted the ban in January 1884 and nominated yet another commission to draw up a more rigorous code to control recruiting. In the meantime, he reminded labor traders that they had to observe the most recent regulations, drafted immediately before the suspension, including the set of strict instructions given to government agents, and that they would shortly have to conform to a revised code.[3] From mid-February 1884, recruiting expeditions to the islands were allowed to resume. As shown in figure 2, the intake of Oceanians was sporadic over the rest of the period, not only because of a renewed ban and another resumption, but also because of fluctuating conditions in the economy and, later, more satisfactory alternative sources of labor.

Resumption and a Second Ban, 1884–1890

Things began well for the resumption of recruiting. In 1884, "Noumea" ships held an important advantage over their British rivals, the first time they had been in this position since the end of the 1860s. After considerable pressure from the British government over seven years, early in 1884 the colonial governments of Fiji and Queensland prohibited the offer of firearms either as an inducement to enlist, or as part of the trade goods purchased by laborers from their wages at the end of their term.[4] The breech-loading Snider rifles entering the New Hebrides and the Solomon Islands at this time were the most highly prized of all European goods, so much so that they sometimes enabled recruiters to penetrate difficult new areas or to restimulate recruiting in places long since considered defunct. They were even effective in overcoming the predilection for recruiting for Queensland and Fiji rather than New Caledonia. Queensland Government Agent Douglas Rannie felt the disadvantage immediately. In 1884, his ship met the French schooner *Marie* trading at Santo in brand new Snider rifles. They could not compete.[5] Firearms were still sold in Queensland and smuggled back to the islands, but returns risked a large part of their earnings if their guns were discovered on board and thrown into the sea. The firearms ban continued to benefit French and German recruiters to the end of the trade,[6] except in a few of the recruiting centers of the central and northern islands of the New Hebrides, where the Compagnie Calédonienne des Nouvelles Hébrides was established. Here sponsors and returns found their way around the prohibition by demanding cash from British traders and employers and buying their guns at the company's stores.[7]

In 1884–1885, the voyage of the *Annette* and the first two voyages of the *Marie* were very successful. But it was not long before new troubles broke out. Despite being able to trade in Sniders, the third voyage of the *Marie* in 1885 took six months to recruit its complement of ninety-three men and twenty women. It is clear that the supervision of an unusually energetic and honest government agent on this voyage was a factor in slowing down the rate of recruiting. F G Petit was the first government agent to discern, or at least to complain about, the nefarious activities of Charles Petersen Stuart, the recruiter on this voyage. "Peterson," or "Peter" as he was known in the islands, had never been held accountable for his actions although many Melanesians had testified in the *Aurora* inquiry of 1880 that he had brutally abducted them and held them by force. On the contrary, he was permitted to sail as skipper on the *Havannah* the year after the inquiry. This voyage was also the object of complaints by English recruiters, but it was cleared by the administration.[8] After the resumption of the labor trade, Petersen Stuart went out as recruiter on two voyages of the *Marie* in 1884. On the second of these he, along with Government Agent Dangeville, was charged with recruiting women without the permission of their menfolk. Dangeville was given a *blâme sévère*, a very bad mark in the civil service, but Petersen Stuart escaped without punishment. However, the director of the Department of the Interior wrote to Governor Le Boucher, "It is well understood . . . that we will refuse in future to authorise M. Petterson [sic] as a recruiting agent," an embargo confirmed by the governor in a letter to the minister.[9] Yet Petersen Stuart went out as recruiter on the third voyage of the *Marie* in the very next month, February 1885. The reappearance of known villains was a recurring problem in New Caledonia, diminishing every gain in reputation the traders might have made.

"Peter" had such a good name in Noumea as a recruiter that Petit was at first surprised to find that he had a "detestable reputation in the various islands where the *Marie* had to recruit." He reported that Petersen Stuart was so notorious that the minute the local people caught sight of him in the boat they ran away into the bush. "It did not take me long to perceive that he was naturally irascible and brutal. Left to his own initiative, he could perhaps have succeeded in engaging natives by intimidation; but under the administrative surveillance of the Government Agent continually going in the boats and therefore not permitting any pressure, the so-called recruiting talents of the recruiter amounted to nothing." When Petit proposed certain places well known to him as good sources of recruits, Petersen Stuart always declined going there on one pretext or another. "I concluded from that that he must have had an interest in not showing himself there."[10] Petersen Stuart thereafter pursued his career in the New Hebrides, although he undertook one more stint as recruiter for New Caledonia in 1889.

The latest commission to draw up new labor regulations had not yet completed its task by September 1884, when Governor Le Boucher spoke to the Privy Council of "rumors" circulating in the town about irregularities committed in the islands by the *Ferdinand de Lesseps*. He had initiated an inquiry, "the results of which showed the recklessness of accusations spread about by prejudiced detractors of immigration, among whom, unhappily, must be counted an officer of the Administration." This was, he continued, not to say that the regulations could not be improved. The committee was preparing a new code, but he decided to frame a provisional code to give effect to items already agreed upon.[11] The code emerged in an *arrêté* of 4 September: some of the provisions had already appeared among the instructions to government agents, and some were borrowed from British regulations. The main clauses relating to recruiting practices concerned the clear identification of labor vessels. They had to fly a special flag during recruiting operations and to carry an individual striped border painted around the ship. The recruiter had to be a French speaker as well as the captain a French citizen. An interpreter had to be carried who could speak the "language used in relations between the natives and Europeans who frequent these shores," in other words, Bislama. Recruitment could only be carried out for New Caledonia or its dependencies. It could only be done by one boat (so that the government agent could always be present); a second boat could only be used as support and cover for the first. The government agent's journal should record not only recruiting operations but also "all the facts that could be interesting to the colony in any way whatever," an instruction similar to Pritzbuer's more covert direction that useful information be collected to assist possible later colonization. To allow more space for each person, the number of recruits taken would be at the rate of one per 1.1 tonnes of the ship instead of one for each tonne. A concession to the settlers was that the minimum term of contract was to be three years instead of two.[12]

The same day that Le Boucher spoke to the Privy Council about the *Ferdinand de Lesseps* incident, he wrote his own account of it to the minister for the Navy and Colonies.[13] The vessel, with nine Tannese recruits aboard, had been wrecked near Tanna. The warship *Bruat* picked up the crew, the recruits, being near their own shores, having deserted. The dissident "officer of the administration" of whom he spoke to the Privy Council, was M Chassaniol, deputy administrator of the Maritime Registry, who had gone to the scene with the *Bruat*. Chassaniol reported stories from the crew that they had got the Tannese recruits drunk aboard ship then kept them against their will, as well as other anomalies in recruiting procedures. According to the governor, Chassaniol encouraged the crew to make critical comments about the labor trade in general. He was also suspected of being the source of a story in *Le Progrès,* which used the incident in one of its attacks on "the trade in human flesh." The publicity was a severe blow for Governor Le Boucher, the first civilian governor of New Caledonia, a settler of twenty-one years' standing who had risen from the rank of clerk in the Department of the Interior.

His commission of inquiry concluded—apparently on the basis of the government agent's own testimony!—that the men were recruited of their own free will. However, the inquiry found breaches of the regulations. It seemed that the crew had been told to say they were going to Honolulu, a more popular destination, and that a young boy had been taken from Aneityum to one of the Banks Islands as a servant to an English settler. Moreover, an English recruiter, Kilgour, who could not speak French, had been picked up at the Loyalty Islands en route to the New Hebrides—another breach of the regulations (but also, it would seem, having an English-speaking recruiter was part of the plot to pretend that the vessel was going to Honolulu).[14] Chassaniol—an ex officio member of the commission—refused to sign the report. He was given a *blâme sévère* and lost his job for his part in the affair. As the governor wrote to the minister: "We will have enough to do to defend New Hebridean immigration against the systematic attacks of detractors of that immigration, without having those detractors find declared allies within our ranks."[15] The government agent, Russeil—the same man judged by Marchand, five years before, to be mentally impaired and too old for the job—had seen nothing wrong with pretending that the ship was bound for Honolulu, and had expressly given permission for the enlistment of Kilgour. He was found guilty of "culpable weakness" and also received a *blâme sévère*.[16]

The minister clearly took the *Ferdinand de Lesseps* incident more seriously than did the local administration. He asked that Russeil and Cornu, the captain of the ship, be relieved of their commissions, but Le Boucher replied that Captain Cornu had left for France, while Government Agent Russeil, whose function had ended with the return of the ship, would not be trusted with such a post again.[17] Yet Russeil sailed as nominal captain of the *Dauphin* in 1889, a ship recruiting during the period of an official ban. He died during the voyage, aged seventy-three.[18]

Paris used the episode, together with the illegal recruitment of women by the *Marie* and the *Annette,* as a pretext for another ban. The resumed labor trade was brought to an abrupt end in 1885. The new ban was telegraphed from Paris on 16 March 1885 and confirmed by *arrêté* a week later.[19] There is little doubt that a situation of severe unemployment arising from a closure of the nickel mines had a good deal more to do with the decision than simply one more case of abuse in recruiting. The position of jobless *libérés*, in particular, had become critical. Governor Le Boucher had telegraphed the minister about the nickel crisis, asking for extra funds to pay for public works to create employment. The telegram in reply ordered him instead to cease the intake of Oceanian laborers forthwith.[20] British Consul Layard remarked: "A flourish of trumpets announced that it was a *philanthropic measure!* but it was well understood that it was to compel the Colonists to employ the Libérés, who were a heavy charge on the government."[21]

Free Immigration, 1887–1889

Officially, the second suspension of the trade lasted five years, from 1885 to 1890. For most of 1885 and 1886 no Oceanian laborers came in, and given the recession they would not have been much missed,

Photo 4 Noumea (rue Alma) about 1890. Drawing by Jouas, engraved by Bazin. From A Hagen, "Voyage aux Nouvelles-Hébrides et aux Iles Salomon," *Le Tour du Monde* 65 (1893): 337. Mitchell Library, State Library of New South Wales.

despite the continual clamor for the revival of the trade. But toward the end of 1886 the rumor got about that the local administration had no objection to "free immigration" by private arrangement.[22] And so it proved. British Consul Layard had every justification for believing that officials looked the other way while the usual brokers brought in "passengers" from the New Hebrides, allegedly paying their own fare in order to seek work in New Caledonia. There was little attempt to disguise the subterfuge, and anyone who wished to employ any of these "tourists" would be asked for passage money of about 500 francs or £20 (us$95).[23]

The only difference between "free immigration" and the indenture system was that the first was now subject to no control, either in recruiting or at the workplace. Recruiting ships did not now even have to carry government agents, and small ships recruiting for plantations within the New Hebrides—not yet subject to surveillance—could and did combine their business with the New Caledonian trade, bringing the surplus of their recruits to New Caledonia. The English journalist "Julian Thomas" (Stanley James, who also used the pseudonym The Vagabond) reported that the *Marie* and the *Lulu* were recruiting in the islands in 1887 without government agents and without supervision. He said they were taking recruits to the plantations of the New Hebrides Company,[24] but in fact both ships brought back recruits to Noumea in 1887, the *Lulu* on three occasions.[25] They had no need to carry government agents in this year. According to Thomas, these ships made their task easier by employing English-speaking re-

Photo 5 Group of New Hebridean recruits in Noumea. From J Durand, "Bois d'Ebène," *La Revue des Revues,* 1900. Bibliothèque Bernheim, Noumea.

cruiters who were more likely to persuade Islanders that they were being recruited for work in the favored places of Queensland or Fiji.[26] Free of the restrictions imposed by the regulations of 1875–1876, hastily francised English and American ships reentered the New Caledonian trade.

Between January 1887 and March 1890, 1,221 "free" laborers from the New Hebrides or the Solomon Islands arrived in the colony.[27] These workers were not registered on the Immigration Office's lists, and no charges were paid to the government. The administration had no control over conditions of work, payment of wages, the issue of rations and clothing, or repatriation. Private contracts were sometimes signed before a justice of the peace where the laborers were employed. Documents covering 73 workers engaged by three employers have been found, indicating that 15 men and 4 women were to work at Bernheim's mines in Thio, 40 men and 9 boys aged eight to ten were destined for Laurie's coffee plantation near Canala, and 5 adolescent boys were to work for Descot at Thio. All contracts mentioned the obligation of paying wages and providing maintenance according to the 1874 regulations, but only Descot's and Laurie's agreements mentioned repatriation.[28] Other documents were "signed" before the employer alone; in all cases workers were absolutely unprotected by the administration.[29] The "free immigration" period did further harm to the reputation of New Caledonian ships and employers.

In times of high demand, the "free" workers had at least the advantage that the tie to their first master was not enforceable by the administration, and, judging by the number of desertions, not a few used their feet to exercise this freedom. In 1907, in a register of unclaimed estates, 61 out of 138 New Hebrideans were listed as being "without trace" since the 1890s.[30]

Governor Pardon, who arrived early in 1889, was concerned by the lack of supervision of workers privately engaged, as well as by the shortage of labor for agriculture. He was sympathetic to the continual demands of the *Conseil général* (an advisory body elected since 1885 by free citizens) for the official resumption of indentured labor, provided that new measures were taken to regulate recruiting. He found a willing ear in France—that of Eugène Etienne, undersecretary of state for the colonies and ardent colonialist. Etienne conferred with the Department of Foreign Affairs, which had no objection to a resumption provided that it did not create a problem with arrangements with Britain in their Joint Naval Commission for the New Hebrides.[31]

The Joint Naval Commission and the Labor Trade

The first regular patrolling of New Hebridean waters by French warships coincided with the "free immigration" period. The naval presence was the result of the territorial claims of France in the New Hebrides, its stationing of troops there in 1886 (withdrawn after protests from the British), and its eventual agreement to set up an Anglo-French Joint Naval Commission in the group at the end of the following year. A by-product of this activity was that the mandatory French naval vessel would also be able to provide regular surveillance over the conduct of French labor-recruiting ships in the region, a control that Governor Courbet had earnestly but vainly sought for the New Caledonian administration. In September 1889, the French part of the Joint Naval Commission was consulted about the advisability of an official resumption of the labor trade under a new régime, which would include the appointment of a better class of government agents by requiring a medical officer to fill the office.

Commander Bigant gave a mixed response.[32] The commission was not opposed in principle to the "immigration," but if there were abuses, as before, it would cause trouble and create enemies for them in the New Hebrides. The proposal to enlist medical officers as government agents was all very well, but ships in the French trade were generally too small to provide a cabin and the appropriate comforts for such an officer, and he believed the rule would be "inapplicable." He considered that proper guarantees would rest on strengthening the policing powers of the French navy, at the moment virtually nil. They needed the power, already held by British commanders, to board and inspect labor vessels and to bring them to justice if they were transgressing. "The French commission thinks that the only remedy . . . is to give French warships all the powers given to English captains in their instructions on the suppression of the slave-trade in the Pacific, not only vis-à-vis French ships concerned with the migration of the New Hebrides natives to New Caledonia, but also all French ships having on board immigrants coming from any island whatever in the Pacific." In the absence of these powers, he thought the government should renounce recruiting: "Every day the natives have new grievances to raise against Europeans and above all against the French, they become more and more alienated from us, and there is no longer any course remaining but to employ force against the poor creatures whose only crime is to defend themselves against thieves and murderers."

He pointed out also that in order to facilitate their own mission in the New Hebrides, it was important that New Hebrideans were well treated in New Caledonia. And if they were taught French there, instead of Bislama "composed of 8 English words out of 10," French-speaking repatriates who bore goodwill toward the French could be very useful to the Naval Commission. Above all, recruits should not be given Snider rifles "which they can then turn against us."[33]

This was hardly the answer that Etienne and the governor wanted. They were satisfied that the observance of improved regulations was all that was required. Moreover, as any recruiter could tell them, without Sniders there would be no recruits. In his report, the director of the Department of the Interior quoted Bigant's lack of opposition "in principle," but ignored everything else he said.[34] The introduction of free labor was formally forbidden from mid-December 1889, and the official indenture of Oceanians recommenced in March 1890.[35] In an effort to bring the conditions of surviving "free immigrants" under its control, the administration demanded that employers regularize their position by registering them retrospectively. The frequent appearance thereafter of a warning that settlers who continued to employ unregistered laborers would be prosecuted suggests that these efforts were not very successful.

No new regulation accompanied the renewal of indenture, except that the government agent was to be an officer of the naval health service,[36] the proposal that Bigant had slighted. Consideration of a new régime was under way, however, including some canvassing of the idea that the labor market be again put under the direct control of the colonial government, as in its earliest days.

The Resumption, 1890–1900

Merchants complained that the appointment of doctors as government agents (although they were allowed to get away with the appointment of pharmacists on at least two occasions) raised the cost of equipping a labor voyage to the islands to an unacceptable level, as Bigant had foreseen. Some predicted that such voyages would soon cease as a result of increased costs.[37] As well, recruiters believed that they now had to go farther for their labor than the New Hebrides, where the labor reserve was being thoroughly tapped by local plantation owners. In 1892 the recruiting ship *Lady Saint Aubyn* reported that the number of labor vessels in the New Hebrides was now out of proportion to the number of recruits available. On its last cruise the crew counted ten Queensland and German ships working the area, apart from numerous small vessels recruiting for local plantations.[38] The captain also complained that Protestant missions—often represented by Islanders known as "teachers"—were now well entrenched in most places in the New Hebrides. They actively tried to stop the local people from leaving on labor ships, "so that it is almost impossible to recruit wherever Protestant missionaries are to be found."[39] There followed a pronounced shift to recruiting in the Solomon Islands in the 1890s, where only occasional visits had been made by New Caledonian recruiting ships, although Queensland and Fiji ships had been thoroughly exploiting this source for twenty years.

In the Solomons, the advantage of Snider rifles as recruiting "presents" to relatives gave Noumea recruiters, as elsewhere, a competitive edge. British traders were strictly forbidden to dispense firearms, and, although guns were still sold by non-British traders, there were no French stores to fill this gap. At east Malaita in 1888, the British recruiter Wawn found that he could no longer get recruits, or even wood and water, as French and German vessels had freely given Snider rifles there: "Recruits to be had for firearms but their friends won't let them go without. It is a mistake for a Queensland vessel to anchor here."[40] In a group where in some areas, particularly in densely populated Malaita, warring was frequent and there were no resident traders, the offer of firearms by visiting ships was almost impossible to refuse. After 1893, when the British extended a protectorate over most of the Solomons, the French as well as the British were forbidden to trade in guns. Both continued to do so, but it was easier for French vessels to get away with it.

Photo 6 The *Lady Saint Aubyn* landing to recruit at Makira Bay, San Cristo-bal, Solomon Islands. Drawing by Jouas, engraved by Devos. From A Hagen, "Voyage aux Nouvelles-Hébrides et aux Iles Salomon," *Le Tour du Monde* 65 (1893): 373. Mitchell Library, State Library of New South Wales.

Renewed Success in Tanna

Against the trend to go farther afield, good business was done in Tanna, in the southern New Hebrides, between 1892 and 1912. The return to Tanna in this period is as pronounced as it is surprising. As the oldest and most prized source of labor in the first decade of the labor trade to Queensland and Fiji as well as New Caledonia, Tanna had yielded recruits in ever-diminishing numbers after the mid 1870s. Considered "old hands," having experienced European contact since the sandalwooding days, and well versed in Pidgin as well as white men's ways, Tannese were sometimes hired as intermediaries or boat crew for short periods and higher wages, but fewer and fewer enlisted for long periods of indenture in the 1880s.[41] Of these, most went to Queensland. New Caledonian recruiters in the 1880s expected no more than the odd recruit from Tanna, the large majority of their New Hebrideans coming from the northern islands. Yet in 1893 Tanna be-came a favorite haunt for Noumea recruiters, and remained so for nearly twenty years. Throughout the 1890s and into the twentieth century, recruiters from Noumea competed well in Tanna with both internal and other foreign traders, and best of all, their ships were filled quickly.

The renewed importance of Tanna as a source of labor seems to have occurred as a result of the ability of French recruiters to peddle firearms during a state of intermittent warfare on the island from the 1890s to 1912. When the *Lady Saint Aubyn* made its second hugely successful trip in 1893—securing forty-six recruits "of both sexes" in fifteen days—it reported that it could have filled the ship to its maximum quota of one hundred recruits "if it had not run out of big Snider rifles, the only object of trade accepted by the natives of this island."[42] Tanna had no resident French traders or stores, so the only source of firearms was French recruiters. An "extensive war" on the east side of Tanna in 1892[43] guaranteed a high demand for firearms and munitions. A British labor vessel reported being offered a £1 note for ten cartridges at Tanna that year.[44] French recruiters were then freely dispensing Snider rifles and ammunition, so continual fighting in the 1890s ensured that business remained good.

The Labor Market and Its Regulation

In New Caledonia itself, the market for Oceanian labor slackened temporarily in the 1890s. The higher cost of recruiting it, together with the arrival of several large convoys of Asian labor, made it less desirable, while depressed economic conditions, especially in 1895–1896 when there was a severe recession compounded by a drought, diminished the demand.

A metropolitan decree governing indentured labor was eventually issued in 1893, the first since 1852, the first to apply specifically to the colony of New Caledonia, and the first directed solely at the introduction of Oceanian labor. Most of its provisions were in the same year applied to Asian indentured labor for lack of other relevant legislation.[45] This new code, superseding all others, gathered together all the previous measures, covering not only the management of the workers in the colony but also recruitment at the islands and conditions on board ship. It added a few provisions relating mainly to the payment of wages. It is difficult to say whether the new legislation had much effect in controlling abuses. In the New Caledonian trade— as distinct from the internal New Hebridean trade—no further acts of wholesale kidnapping were reported. Possibly the very presence of a French warship in these waters, despite being restricted in its operations, was a deterrent. But the "Snider factor" probably made kidnapping less necessary. In areas where there was no alternate supply, it was an expensive but seemingly irresistible inducement. On the other hand, violent and piratical episodes continued to accompany the trade.

Lawlessness in the Labor Trade in the 1890s

Recruiting was renewed in 1890 without the safeguards sought by the navy, so when in the same year Commander Bigant was asked to inquire into a report that a vessel under French colors, the *Mary Anderson*, was recruiting without a government agent, he wrote somewhat testily to the governor that there was nothing he could do about it. Unless the vessel was in breach of the merchant marine laws, the only laws he was empowered to police, "I cannot prevent the *Mary Anderson* from taking passengers or emigrants where she likes. . . . We have not, in France, like the English, either a Kidnapping Act or a Western Pacific Order in Council. . . . I have already had the honor of pointing out to you this lacuna in our laws."[46] He was particularly concerned with the burgeoning internal labor traffic in the New Hebrides itself, where not even the regulations for New Caledonia existed to control the recruiters: "I have long ago brought this state of affairs to the attention of the Minister for the Navy."[47] He was also far from impressed with the cooperation of the administration in Noumea. In August 1890 he complained to the governor that he had had to learn of the resumption of the labor trade in March from the *Journal Officiel,* and that he had never received a copy of the decree with its new guidelines, so was unaware of the precise provisions. "I doubt, however, that it makes any change to the general rules on policing ships. The *arrêté* or *décret* of the Minister for Colonies has validity only in New Caledonia itself."[48] Little had changed, in his opinion, and the upgrading of the government agent proved no solution. Bigant was exasperated to find a whole raft of villains in 1890 still recruiting labor for the New Hebrides, New Caledonia, or both.

> For a long time no-one has spoken of serious acts of violence committed by English recruiters, whereas sailing still on French ships among these islands are M. Gaspard, well-known in Noumea for the numerous ill-deeds that he has committed in the New Hebrides, M. Villedieu, who last year burnt a village at Santa Cruz, M. Fraser, a very cruel German, and finally on the *Ika Vuka,* a ship just become French, they have embarked as recruiter M. Proctor, an American subject, legendary in the whole archipelago for his acts of barbarity.[49]

Governor Pardon had already complained about Villedieu to the undersecretary of state for Colonies, saying that although it was only too true that Villedieu had committed "cruel and inhuman acts," he was powerless to do anything except prevent him from commanding a voyage in the future.[50] But a few months later Bigant found Villedieu sailing as "recruiter or supercargo" on the *Mary Anderson* and in his opinion evidently in command.[51]

Bigant's misgivings about Proctor were soon vindicated. Three months later, he received a report from Lieutenant Grossin, who had held an inquiry, following complaints from the Loyalty Islands crew of the *Ika Vuka,* about the conduct of Proctor, the other recruiter Joe Tunbridge, and the government agent Dubois. Grossin found that barbarities had been committed by all three while recruiting on the west coast of Malaita. Tunbridge hit a man with a piece of wood when he protested against the engagement of two sons of the chief, and Proctor shot at the same man as he fled. A few days later, the boats were called ashore by local people who then ran away at their approach—probably recognizing unwelcome faces. Proctor, Dubois, and Tunbridge all fired at them as they fled, and ordered the boat crews to do the same. Proctor and Tunbridge shot holes into their hats to support a story that they had been attacked, and the boat crews were threatened with severe consequences if they said a word about the affair. In spite of this, Billy, a Lifu sailor who spoke French better than the others, told the captain what had happened, whereupon Proctor twice tried to shoot him during the voyage. Another sailor threatened by Proctor had to hide in the hold.[52] Proctor continued his career in the New Hebrides, where in December 1892, he abducted a woman, and when her husband came to free her, shot him dead.[53]

Bigant pointed out to his commander-in-chief that a ship might have to be sent to the Solomons, because two outrages had now been committed there in short order. He had passed all the information on to the governor. He said he would have asked the minister to take action against Government Agent Dubois—a pharmacist—if he had belonged to the metropolitan health service, but since he belonged to the colonial one he would not even bother to inform him.[54]

If he had still been sailing in South Pacific waters a few years later, Bigant could have added to his list of miscreants enjoying immunity from a feeble or partisan administration. In 1885, the commander of the warship *Bruat* had held an inquiry into the conduct of Captain Briault of the *Idaho* and Captain Déniel of the *Ambroua* while trading in the New Hebrides. They were subsequently tried in the Criminal Court at Noumea, along with other members of their crews, for kidnapping, acts of piracy, rape, and aggravated assault at Ambrym, Aore, Pentecost, and Ambae. Despite a strong plea from the procureur of the Republic, all had been acquitted except Briault, who failed to appear, having absconded to Malakula. In his absence he was condemned to five years' hard labor.[55] Fresh accusations of kidnapping and firing on people followed him around the New Hebrides for the next few years.[56] In 1893 Briault eventually returned to Noumea, where he was retried and, after an eloquent speech by the counsel for the defense that brought tears to the eyes of "old Caledonians" in the courtroom, acquitted of all charges.[57] (The acquittal, however, owed more to the intervention of President Carnot at the request of Briault's family and friends.) [58] Six months later, Briault sailed as captain of the *Lady Saint Aubyn* on a recruiting cruise to the Solomons and the New Hebrides. As recruiter he carried Dick Pentecost, whose buccaneering acts in the islands had been described by Lieutenant Doze, of the warship *Dives,* seven years before.[59] Déniel, unhindered, landed recruits in New Caledonia in 1888, and carried on recruiting for the New Hebridean trade. Others who had also escaped sentence—like Walter Champion (of the *Venus* affair), described to Doze by "ex-captain Briault, who should be an expert in these affairs" as a slaver of the first rank[60]—were recruiting for both the New Hebrides and New Caledonia a few years later.

Given a bonus by the British law banning firearms, New Caledonian recruiters were unable to make the most of it because of further blows to their reputation. The local administration was much to blame. It showed remarkable weakness in allowing captains and recruiters known to be brutal, and government agents censured as tolerant of abuses, to reenter the business. It allowed an unofficial trade, with no regulation, for three years during a so-called banned period. It was lax in enforcing regulations protecting conditions of employment. Officials were generally drawn from the settlers themselves, and were loath to swim against the tide of local opinion. The governor and high officials from France, who could have been expected to exercise control over local bureaucrats, were never entirely aware of the circumstances that preceded their appointment, nor entirely independent of the goodwill of the settlers during it. Many were tempted to avoid trouble for the sake of their next posting. Those who acted firmly were not there long enough to oversee the pursuit of their policy.

For its part, the metropolitan government never gave its naval commanders the necessary powers to board and investigate suspect ships. The New Caledonian labor trade was small, by comparison with its British rivals, and did not seem to justify the expense of naval patrols. In retrospect, it is clear that there was an excellent opportunity for the two great powers to cooperate in eliminating recruiting abuses, to the advantage of both in the long term. Unfortunately, national rivalry was so great at the time that this was out of the question.

Chapter 6
The New Century

In 1901, the number of imported Oceanian laborers still exceeded the combined totals of Asian workers, but local Kanaks—most of them from the Loyalty Islands—had begun to outnumber them both.[1] A mix of Asian, Hebridean, and Kanak labor, especially in agriculture, became common early in the century (photo 7). With the extension of its control in New Caledonia, the colonial administration was able to enforce the head tax on increasing numbers of the indigenous population, forcing more and more Kanaks to work to find the cash. As this policy produced results, and as the importation of Indochinese and Javanese workers was stepped up, New Hebrideans became just an auxiliary source of labor. They were nevertheless imported steadily to the end of the 1920s in lots of around a hundred per year, and by then as well a number of them had foregone their right to repatriation and were working as "free residents," mainly as domestic servants or laborers.

The new century saw many changes in recruiting foreign Oceanians for New Caledonia. The most visible was the disappearance of the old recruiting voyage—the long expedition in a sailing ship equipped solely for enlisting and repatriating large convoys of workers. The *Jeannette* made the last such trip in 1899. When it was wrecked in the last month of the nineteenth century, the steamer *La Perouse* brought back its recruits and crew. Thereafter, Noumea merchants used the regular steamer service to the New Hebrides to bring smaller batches of recruits, assembled at the ship's regular ports of call. In 1911, for example, 125 recruits came in by steamer in thirteen batches, the largest of which was twenty-two and the smallest three.[2] If a less romantic business, it was no doubt a more comfortable journey for the recruits, lasting only a few days.

Administrative changes early in the twentieth century also affected the trade. First, in 1901, the French government created a post (sim-

Photo 7 Mixed labor on a coffee plantation, early in the twentieth century: New Hebrideans, Kanaks, and Javanese (in the coolie hats). From H Russier, *Le Partage de l'Océanie*, Paris, 1905. Archives Territoriales, Noumea.

ilar to, and in emulation of, that of the British Western Pacific high commissioner) with judicial and administrative responsibility over French nationals in areas where no formal European annexation had taken place. The governor of New Caledonia was given this authority, receiving the title of General Commissioner for the Republic in the Pacific Ocean.[3] He could appoint a special commissioner as his delegate for each island or group of islands, in whose absence an officer commanding a French warship would exercise the powers of a delegate, the authority that Bigant had vainly sought. This arrangement took more than a year to come into effect, through a local *arrêté* (October 1902).[4] The new structure made it possible, at last, to attempt some control of the island-to-island labor trade within the New Hebrides. Governor Picanon, now also the general commissioner, was able to introduce regulations and procedures aimed primarily at this lawless trade. But the regulations were extended to *all* French recruiters, regardless of their destination. All recruiting ships were henceforth to obtain an annual permit from the general commissioner or his delegate, leaving a bond of 2,000 francs as a guarantee of good behavior. All recruiting ships, including those going to Noumea, were to call at Port Vila on their return journey, where the French resident delegate would be responsible for ascertaining that their *engagés* had enlisted willingly. The new arrangement superseded recruiting procedures imposed by the 1893 law, making the old-style government agent superfluous.

Photo 8 At Barrau's store, Noumea. Max Shekleton collection, Noumea.

Finally, the New Hebrides came under formal—if not very effective—colonial control with the establishment of the Anglo-French Condominium in 1906. The procedures for French recruiting for destinations inside and outside the group were formalized in the Anglo-French Convention, along with a few more rules and some changes of name for the administering officers.

The new regulations had little effect in controlling the appalling conditions of the internal labor trade, but they brought a windfall for Noumea traders. Not having to carry high-priced government agents on recruiting ships considerably diminished the costs that had beset labor brokers in the nineties.[5] The newspaper *La France Australe* rejoiced at the disappearance of the government agent, a change they reckoned to be worth about 1,200 francs a month to recruiting ships—750 francs a month in salary, plus board. "M. Picanon's *arrêté* was one of the wisest and most sensible. At the same time he preserved the laws of humanity and the interests of the recruiters."[6]

Large merchant houses in Noumea quickly adapted to the new arrangements. Their agents recruited legally in the New Hebrides, then had their recruits immediately "transferred" (*cédés*) to third parties in New Caledonia for the usual passage money. Recruiting in this fashion netted a profit of at least three hundred percent, according to calculations made in 1907, an advance on the return of two hundred percent estimated for the previous system.[7] And there was nothing to stop individual employers in New Caledonia arranging for New Hebrides settlers to engage workers on their own account, then transfer them immediately to themselves, or even traveling to the New Hebrides to engage employees directly. In 1919, the British resident commissioner in the New Hebrides, Merton King, explained that the official number of recruits going to Noumea was unreliable. He wrote that he had reason to believe that "every year many natives, male and female, recruited nominally for service in this Group, are, soon after engagement, transferred, or to use the term commonly employed, 'sold,' with or without their consent, and, I believe, without reference to the French Residency, to people in New Caledonia. The natives concerned rarely return to their homes."[8] As he thought they were mostly employed in domestic duties and usually well treated, King believed that little hardship was involved, since "as a rule their lot may, I think, be regarded as far happier with the New Caledonian employer than it would be as indentured laborers in this Group."[9]

As Asian labor gradually supplanted New Hebridean labor in the fields and in the mines, the tendency to employ imported Oceanians as domestics encouraged the trend for settlers to find their own Hebridean servants. Information in the shipping columns bears out King's observation about the transfer of indentured workers from the New Hebrides to New Caledonia. In the 1920s the list of passengers going by the mail steamer to or from the New Hebrides each month is remarkable for the number of servants, "popinées" and "boys," apparently accompanying their employers. Of 66 New Hebrideans arriving in 1925, for example, 44 were designated as servants to named Europeans, some of whom were persons traveling on the same ship, and some not.[10] The first impression is that some settlers could not do without the services of their domestics when traveling; however, when the same ship made its longer Sydney trip, no servants appeared in the passenger list, and they also seem to have been considered unnecessary to travelers on almost all other voyages for which there are passenger lists. Nor did domestic servants figure on the New Caledonia–New Hebrides route until 1921, suggesting that the device of acquiring servants directly in the New Hebrides might have also been an attempt to evade a tax imposed in 1920 in New Caledonia on the engagement of indentured labor. It was possible to enlist workers as "free labor" in the New Hebrides, and the cost of an agent's fee and the fare to pick up and return the laborer probably compared favorably with the price of passage money, the *livret*, and the tax, not to mention the vexation of having to conform to labor regulations. To 1930, and possibly later (as there seems to have been no formal abolition of the indenture of Oceanians before the end of the Second World War), servants appear to have been engaged from the New Hebrides in this fashion.

The new and cheaper method of recruiting appeared to come at a propitious time, because Queensland had by then stopped its labor trade. In 1906, the French consul-general in Australia alerted Governor Liotard to the fact that Queensland was about to repatriate its Melanesian workers en masse (worrying that the returns would extend British influence in the New Hebrides!). Liotard asked the French resident delegate in Vila to try to get the returns placed with French nationals or to encourage them to get employment in New Caledonia, in order to prevent them from becoming "active agents of English influence" in the group.[11] However, there was no great influx to New Caledonia, although there was a small rise in the number recruited over the next few years. A few ex-Queensland repatriates may have preferred going to Noumea to returning to their villages, and the French colony did become more attractive as the reputation of the main alternative, the internal trade, continued to worsen, but the increase in recruits is more consistent with a mild improvement in economic conditions in New Caledonia. As the New Caledonian economy slowly picked up in 1907–1908, the demand for labor gradually rose, with a noticeable acceleration around 1910, when the Société Le Nickel established a smelter at Thio, and still more after the inauguration of the Ballande works at Doniambo the following year (the two were combined in 1912). Those gains remained fairly stable over the period 1903–1912 (figure 2). Rather more had been expected from Queensland's withdrawal from the business.

While Queensland was no longer a threat, pressure from planters in the New Hebrides intensified. Settlers of both English and French nationality combined, for once, to oppose the export of local labor, and occasionally had some success. In 1902 the agents of New Caledonian business houses were simply told that they were forbidden to recruit labor in the New Hebrides for the moment,[12] but they fought the directive and eventually prevailed. When the Condominium was declared, British government representatives (now called resident commissioners) urged their French colleagues to act jointly with them to ban recruiting for external destinations. Such a ban would have involved no sacrifice of the interests of British citizens in other colonies, because Queensland had already abolished the trade, while Fiji—in the market for Oceanian labor until 1911—concentrated on its Solomon Islands source and after 1907 took very few recruits from the New Hebrides. However, a ban would have involved a conflict between the interests of French employers in New Caledonia and those in New Hebrides, causing the French government to hold back. Time after time it rejected a ban on recruiting for service outside the New Hebrides, pointing out that the numbers going to Noumea were now small.[13] At the New Hebrides Conference in 1914, Governor Picanon again refused to insert a provision in the Anglo-French Convention forbidding the export of labor to New Caledonia, saying that it had almost ceased and would very soon stop altogether, being now of very small importance to the French colony.[14] After that, the British government seemed to drop the proposal, its representatives limiting themselves to noting each year the official number who went to work in New Caledonia, and sometimes commenting that the real number was probably much greater.[15] From time to time the French authorities did make efforts to discourage the traffic in the interest of their planters in the New Hebrides.[16] Finally, in October 1920, a tax was levied in New Caledonia on the employment of any labor originating in the New Hebrides, Banks, or Torres Islands, consisting of 5 francs for a six-month engagement and 10 francs for a longer period.[17]

Under the Condominium régime, the offer of alcohol and firearms to New Hebrideans was forbidden, but only the British (who introduced the regulation) seriously enforced it on their nationals.[18] It did not affect the recent success of French recruiting in Tanna, where French labor traders were the only reliable suppliers of both these sought-after commodities. Missionaries complained that French recruiters were making "good hauls" by the free offer of grog as well as guns.[19] Their most successful year was 1912, when more than a hundred Tannese recruits left home for New Caledonia; by then there was no longer any competition from Queensland or Fiji.[20] Late in 1912, however, when the Presbyterian mission had achieved dominance in the island, recruiting again became difficult. A French ship recruiting in Tanna in September and October reported that it was unable to obtain a single recruit. The mission was blamed: "The Presbyterians who seem to be all-powerful in that island are absolutely opposed to the recruiting of natives."[21] But the mission believed that the decline in recruiting was due to the peace produced through their influence, through the resolution of disputes in their "native courts," for warfare meant that rifles were in demand from labor traders, and that refugees from the defeated sought safety on labor ships.[22]

French recruiters continued their trade in the recently colonized Solomon Islands, in competition with Fiji ships. They were consistently reported trading firearms for labor by the Royal Navy until 1912. The Solomon Islands was thereafter closed to recruiting for external destinations,[23] mainly because local plantations in the new colony required all the available labor. About this time a small experiment was tried with a new source of Oceanian labor that was destined to become a vast reserve after the Second World War. In 1912 Nicolas ("Tiby") Hagen brought in 31 Wallisians. By 1919 there were 57 under contract, but in the 1921 census only 27 were counted, and by 1929 only 9.[24]

In his report of 1929, Inspector Gayet noted that the numbers of New Hebridean laborers in New Caledonia were regularly diminishing as colonization and plantations developed in the New Hebrides. In that year 403 New Hebrideans were still under engagement— as against 563 ten years before—but all current contracts were re-engagements. In addition, he noted, there were known to be "a good number of indentured Hebrideans" who for several years had eluded the system: "Nobody knows what has happened to them. Thus for Tobeul, [no.] 1400, and Mouna, [no.] 1819, there is no payment of wages since 1922 and 1920, when this payment is supposed to take place every three months." Only a very small percentage had opted for repatriation over the past six years and Gayet thought that most of those present were fixtures in New Caledonia, "if not without hope, at least without envisaging a return to the Hebrides." He thought they were tending to melt into the local Melanesian population.[25] In the 1936 census, the only foreign Oceanians counted were 157 New Hebrideans and 11 Wallisians.[26]

As Gayet rightly said, the old-time recruitments by special ships equipped for the purpose were now only a "memory of adventurous expeditions on the seas." His final prediction, however, was somewhat astray: "In brief, New Hebridean and Wallisian labor is a relic of the past and it appears that it will never resume any appreciable significance in New Caledonia."[27] The new nickel boom of the 1960s and 1970s brought about a large inflow of both these peoples, this time under more equitable conditions.

Part Two

Profile of Recruits

Chapter 7
Men and Motives

As in Fiji and Queensland, settlers in New Caledonia hoped that recruiting ships would bring them strong young men. But different conditions and regulations in the French colony ensured that female and child workers were also in demand there. Because both the recruitment and the experience at the workplace of women and child workers differed from that of young men, I treat them separately in the next two chapters.

The prize recruit, attracting the highest beach payment, was a fit young man aged about eighteen to twenty-five years. But why would he want to enlist for hard work in an unknown country? Evidence of clear cases of kidnapping support the simple answer that he was taken by force, so for many years historians did not concern themselves with motivation. Modern historians have a more complex answer. Finding evidence that, after the labor trade became familiar, Islanders were often waiting on the beach and even swimming out to recruiting boats to enlist,[1] they began to look for reasons why they might want to sign on.

On the Beach: The Local Agenda

In 1882, Governor Courbet recognized that Islanders were keenly involved in the labor trade. After reading his government agents' reports, he informed the minister for the navy and colonies that although the ways of obtaining recruits varied a great deal, he was convinced that:

> [m]ost often, and above all in the most frequented islands, it is the natives who present themselves on the shore in view of the boats. The interpreter or the recruiter distributes tobacco and trifling objects, shows them knives and guns that he will give in exchange

for engagements, the natives parley and some of them decide to go aboard. At other times, natives come out in canoes to visit the ship. The sight of trade goods, some timely gifts made to them, decide them to stay.[2]

Although indigenous communities reacted violently to wrongs committed against them by labor traders, there also evolved a kind of collaboration between ships recruiting for New Caledonia and the island people they visited, as in the British trade. It became common for recruiters to see the smoke of fires, or to hear the boats hailed, signaling that recruits were waiting on the shore. Even on voyages where the grossest acts of kidnapping had occurred, such as those of the *Venus* and the *Aurora,* a number of young men were also legitimately recruited. Given that communities in the same region had already adapted sandalwood and bêche-de-mer trading to suit their needs, it should not be surprising that labor trading was soon fitted into their requirements.

In the northern New Hebrides, the main recruiting ground for New Caledonia, the structure of many societies favored this development. Most were characterized by a competitive quest for status among adult males, a status ultimately depending on the acquisition of wealth, for which the labor vessels provided a fresh opportunity. Despite many variations, some societies having more elaborate grading systems than others, the general path to achieving a higher grade was through rites revolving around pig-killing ceremonies accompanied by great feasts—the culmination of much wealth accumulation—and particularly the raising and killing of special boars, whose carefully enhanced tusks were later worn as a mark of rank. As the ethnographer Robert L Rubinstein said of one of these societies, although status was achieved rather than ascribed, the society was highly stratified, and "younger men were held in check by their seniors," who held the important control of access to women.[3]

Social life in these communities—which normally had no problem in feeding themselves—revolved around the accretion of wealth for the purpose of achieving status in these rank-taking ceremonies. One writer, Takeo Funabiki, referred to the "pig complex" of the society he studied in Malakula, where the main topic of conversation was pig raising and pig trading and where pig metaphors ran all through the language. The first thing a field-worker is asked about, he reported, is the pigs in his homeland.[4] In his study of Malo, Rubinstein referred to the top-graded people as "wheelers and dealers in pigs," importing them from neighboring islands. They achieved status through patron–client relationships, building up followers among the young men whose services they could use to add to their wealth.[5]

In the Solomon Islands, hereditary chiefs and warrior chiefs were more common, especially in coastal areas, while leaders in bush areas tended to acquire authority through the accumulation of wealth and a consequent following of indebted clansmen, in the same way as New Hebridean big-men. In Tanna, while ascriptive power was very little, competition for status also depended on wealth accumulation. By the time of the labor trade, the people had an established conduit to European goods through earlier trading, but used the labor trade in a more sophisticated way than in the later-contacted north, trading their service as interpreters, suppliers, and boat crew for the desired commodities, as well as going abroad to work. Their special demand for firearms has already been discussed.

It is not difficult to see how the labor trade could be incorporated into these systems, and there is evidence that it was.[6] In the northern islands European trade goods were soon worked into the process of wealth accumulation for the purpose of achieving status and acquiring a wife. According to missionary anthropologist and linguist W G Ivens, in south Malaita foreign goods or money could not form part of bride-price, "even if he [the prospective groom] was allowed to retain them,"[7] but they could be traded as payment for local valuables or to create obligation in a sponsor to collect them for him. The "wheeling and dealing in pigs" was sometimes done directly with recruiting ships. The labor trade was a potential source of trade goods in three ways: from the increased trade in vegetables, wood, and water to labor vessels, whether or not recruits were forthcoming; from the "beach payment" for whoever successfully claimed control over the recruit; and from the box of goods brought back by a recruit who survived the term of labor and was repatriated.

The goods required by sponsors as beach payment for recruits varied considerably with place and time, as they had in earlier trade. Almost everywhere and throughout the period, Islanders were particularly interested in acquiring guns and ammunition, and this became the strongest reason to cooperate in the labor traffic, for both individuals and communities. However, certain other goods were required at certain places and certain times, defying ready explanation. In these cases one can only record the demands, leaving the interpretation to those who know the particular community more intimately, especially the descendants of that society. In general, the goods most in demand were firearms, cloth, steel axes, hatchets and knives, tobacco, and pigs.

Pigs were often demanded, just as they were in Santo toward the end of the sandalwood trade.[8] Usually the ships picked them up at one island and traded them at another, but early in 1885, the *Annette* brought pigs from Noumea specifically for beach payments. At Epi

Photo 9 Solomon Islanders recruited to New Caledonia. From J Durand, "Bois d'Ebène," *La Revue des Revues,* 1900. Bibliothèque Bernheim, Noumea.

they were preferred to Snider rifles on at least two occasions.[9] Pigs were also demanded at Malaita in 1890.[10] An excerpt from the journal of the *Marie* in 1885 illustrates the necessity for the labor traders to accommodate a demand for pigs in the northern New Hebrides. The government agent related that at Ambae

> we lost a whole month in the following circumstances. The chief Tamby of Boat-Cove had put a taboo on his *canaques;* consequently none of them were permitted to enlist on a recruiting ship. This prohibition of the chief arose from the fact that an English ship had landed a *canaque* who was one of his subjects in a neighboring tribe. Naturally his trade-box was stripped and the poor unfortunate man half killed. Tamby however consented to raise the taboo in favour of the *Marie* on the express condition that he would be presented with three boars. We had only one on board; it was necessary at all costs to complete the number required by the chief in order to get recruits. . . . For a month we visited the various tribes of Walurigi, Labouty, Allaii, Water-comban, Launay, Duindue, Walaa and Naboutriqui. Finally after many refusals on the part of the natives and even armed attacks, we succeeded in finding the two animals.
>
> The taboo was raised! But they only furnished us with a few workers. It was a lost month.[11]

Demands could quickly change. In 1888, the government agent of the British labor vessel *Ariel* told the recruiter William Wawn that the last time he was at Maramasike Passage, at Malaita, the only thing wanted was "Pigs! Pigs!" Wawn was glad he did not take the agent's advice "to fill up the ship with grunters," for this time pigs were not asked for at all.[12]

Firearms, however, were by far the most sought-after goods. They were given as beach payment right from the beginning of the trade to New Caledonia. In 1871 one ship—the *Donald MacLean,* clearing for "Tanna and the New Hebrides"—carried nothing but muskets, powder, and lead.[13] As competition heightened, Snider rifles were given at the rate of one for each adult male recruit.[14] Recruiters to New Caledonia had an advantage, after 1884, in being able to give firearms as payment, especially in times of local warfare, though the desire for firearms had to be balanced against the need for warriors. In 1885, on the west coast of Paama, the *Annette* was besieged with demands for guns and ammunition, for which the people offered large sums of cash but no recruits. They were at war with the people of the opposite coast and needed all their young men.[15]

Sometimes guns were sought from labor traders by those defeated in battle, in order to restore the status quo. In 1900, the commander of a British warship in the Santa Cruz group reported that a strong tribe from the Reef Islands had come over to Carlisle Bay, Ndeni, bullying and killing the neighboring Vena people, who subsequently had obtained fifteen rifles from a French labor vessel in exchange for recruits "and now turn the tables in retaliation on the Carlisle Bay people."[16] Possibly the conflict went back one stage further, for in July 1899 the Melanesian Mission found that a French labor vessel had, within the previous few weeks, given rifles in exchange for forty recruits at a village in Ndeni.[17]

Occasionally firearms were refused, at least in the New Hebrides, for reasons impossible to infer from the information given. They could have included highly specific circumstances or even personal grounds. At two places in Pentecost during one recruiting trip, all trade was refused by the sponsor. One canoe brought "a fine young man," for whom his uncle would not accept anything, even a Snider, asking that payment be made directly to the recruit, partly in cash.[18] Another man brought two sons but gave the guns to the elder brother, keeping only a few trade articles for himself.[19] At east Ambae in 1884, people asked for tomahawks for a female recruit from "the Launay tribe," refusing both muskets and a Snider rifle, while at the same passage on the same day the relatives of a male recruit from "the Coromoné tribe" required a gun and ammunition.[20] Cloth was said to be most in demand in 1890 at "Navutiriki near Walaha" in west Ambae.[21] At Pentecost in 1885, a man said to be a "chief from the bush," refused guns in favor of general trade articles, including a large amount of tobacco, for the two young men he offered.[22] Possibly he had been warned against accepting firearms by the shore dwellers who gave him passage. Coastal people, often in conflict with inland communities, jealously guarded their advantage in acquiring firearms. At Tanna the year before, a coastal community threatened to fire on the boats of the *Marie* should they trade arms for recruits from the interior.[23]

Wealth in firearms and other trade goods was not the only thing sought through the trade in labor. The hope of medical treatment for relatives was a reason for some of those offering recruits, just as it was in the Queensland trade. A report on recruiting in the New Hebrides in 1882 mentioned that at Santo there was a great deal of poverty and sickness, and consequently people freely offered themselves as "migrants." It frequently happened, it said, that those who present themselves "àre all sick, and ask only to be cured."[24] More than ten years later a pharmacist acting as government agent on the *Ika Vuka* remarked that at Malaita "skin diseases are quite extensive and when one recruits here the people propose first of all those who have skin complaints that they cannot or don't know how to cure."[25] At Nguna, Efaté, the chief and the parents of a boy with an injured finger offered him as a recruit, in the hope of his being cured in Noumea. On the same voyage, two other young men, one at Epi and one at Ambrym, enlisted in expectation of treatment for injured limbs.[26]

Sometimes the motive was not the lure of perceived advantage but desperation. Compulsion of a different kind occurred at times of famine in the islands, from the failure of food crops through natural disasters such as droughts, hurricanes, and floods.[27] Recruiters were aware that they would get a windfall of recruits under these circumstances. In 1893, for example, the *Lady Saint Aubyn* found much devastation from a hurricane, especially in the island of Ambrym. There, on the west coast alone, they recruited more than twenty people without difficulty. They lamented that the high seas made it impossible to anchor on the east coast, where the damage was so bad that they could probably have completed their quota on the spot. "The natives of the east coast, whose plantations had been ravaged by the hurricane, are in a very critical situation and a great many of them would have been delighted to enlist for Noumea."[28]

Another class of refugees rather than migrants resulted from warfare, which was useful to labor traders apart from the sale of guns. In the Solomon Islands, the function of labor vessels as a refuge for the defeated in war and those taken captive in raids has been noted as a well-known means of obtaining recruits in the British labor trade.[29] A Presbyterian missionary declared that warfare on Tanna was good for labor traders from Noumea for the same reason, "because recruiting was much more free when war was waged, natives being driven on board their schooners for safety. Sometimes the remnant of a beaten tribe would all be carried away at one time, a most profitable haul at £15 or £20 a head in Noumea."[30] Commander Bigant also spoke of "poor unfortunates wanting to flee from their enemies," as well as others escaping the anger of a father or a husband, who were enlisting as a means of getting away.[31]

No doubt others took refuge in New Caledonia for the same reasons as they did in Queensland and Fiji, including a surprising number who enlisted to avoid punishment for crimes committed at home.[32] Peter Corris also found several examples of recruiting to flee naval retribution for attacks on labor vessels, ironical in view of the alleged purpose of the Royal Navy patrols to protect them.[33]

The Role of Chiefs, Big-Men, and Seniors

Naturally the "seniors"—elders, big-men, aspiring big-men, or chiefs—sought to control the changes brought by the labor trade, particularly the new flow of trade goods. The conditions under which a community offered its young men as recruits would have varied greatly according to the social structure of the community and the circumstances of the time, especially times of war—when the need for men was weighed against the need for guns—but also times of planting and harvest and times of ceremonies and feasts. Except in the case of runaways, chiefs, big-men, or older relatives were always present to conduct negotiations when prospective recruits were awaiting the recruiter. It was certainly worth while for recruiters to enlist the support of local authorities. Those involved in recruiting believed that either the beach payment or the prospect of the repatriated workers' boxes of trade goods at the end of their term sometimes inspired the elders to impel youths to recruit. As one said, "All, or part of what a young native brings back into his tribe is generally to the profit of the chief who made him enlist. One has to be adult to keep one's possessions, buy pigs, find a wife etc. in a word to be responsible only to oneself."[34]

Contemporaries who favored the labor trade and those who were against it agreed that the role of elders, big-men, and so-called chiefs was crucial in a well-ordered recruiting operation. If they opposed it, an experienced recruiter would be worried about the consequences of accepting the recruits; if they offered the recruits, the deal was peacefully done. Whether this control was exercised in favor of recruitment or against it could be a matter of local circumstance or the value of the reward. One government agent lamented the necessity to get the consent of elders, believing that recruitment would be "more considerable if, among the islanders, the individual will was more independent of the authority of the chief of the tribe or the family. Indeed, either by threats or persuasion, the latter often hold back and restrain on shore men who had decided to leave."[35]

On the other hand, especially as the material rewards of the trade became first more familiar, then more valuable, authority could be exerted to induce young men to recruit. As in the Queensland trade,[36] many New Caledonian recruiters and government agents believed that this was the way things were generally done.[37] After reading the journals of his government agents, Governor Courbet reported that "it must frankly be said, in the majority of cases, that it is the parents who bring their sons to the recruiter. The 'boy' is traded against objects that arouse the avarice of the father; the latter withdraws and the deal is done."[38] In answer to a question from the commissioners in the *Aurora* affair in 1880, Douglas Carter, with experience both in Queensland and New Caledonia, concluded that "most often they are constrained by their families to go abroad. . . . Chiefs very often make their people recruit in exchange for trade goods."[39] Commander Bigant also believed that some recruits were delivered at the order of a "chief."[40]

While scholars have given due weight to the pressure exerted by figures of authority to stop young men from enlisting,[41] most of them[42] have fairly lightly dismissed the possibility that such influence was used to cause them to enlist. Corris recognized the common view of Europeans involved in recruiting that young men were often induced to get into the recruiters' boats by those who stood to gain from beach payments or those who were entitled to claim a share of the returned recruit's box.[43] The recruiter William Wawn made few bones about this, confiding to his journal that two Solomon Islands "chiefs," Foulanger and Kwaisulia, "have been made much of by Queensland Labour vessels' Captains—receiving large presents & being entertained in the cabin. These men are simply crimps, who sell recruits to the highest bidder and I firmly believe that masters and G.A.'s know this."[44] Corris gave no weight to his testimony, however, quoting Scarr's judgment that Wawn was prejudiced against uppity "passage masters"—local men who specialized in energetic cooperation with recruiters—whom captains had to invite to their table. But Wawn was, as well, one of the most experienced of the labor traders; moreover, five years after he wrote this, Kwaisulia was caught in the act, forcing two men and four women to go in the boats of the Queensland recruiting ship *William Manson*. Ivens was told by one of the participants in this incident that other people from the interior were also forced to recruit on this ship by a *ramo* or fighting man called Fuli namo, who was to be paid by Kwaisulia. "A message was sent to him [Fuli namo] from the shore people that men were wanted, and that he was to share in the purchase money. His reputation for killing was well known among his people, and he obtained recruits for the ship by saying to this man and that, 'I can't stand your face; get out of this or I will kill you.'"[45] The government agent would have no inkling that such recruits were other than willing volunteers, as, in a sense, they were.

In other situations, however, recruiting crews would not be in doubt. On his first labor voyage in 1884, Douglas Rannie met Gorai, the "king" of the Shortland Islands, who offered him full cooperation. "We wanted about eighty recruits and Ghorai undertook to put them on board ship provided he was paid at the rate of one pound in gold or silver per head in advance." Gorai intended to get the recruits by a raid on the coast of Bougainville. Rannie indignantly refused the offer, but as Gorai lived very well, his house provided with luxuries ordered from Australia, it was evident that other recruiters had not.[46] At Malaita, Rannie was convinced that there were many "free-booters" who, knowing that there was a labor ship in the offing, would go out and kidnap for it and sell to the boats.[47]

Powerful chiefs and warriors were more common in the Solomon Islands, and Corris granted that "[i]t is likely . . . that the chiefs and passage master sometimes intimidated men into migrating. They may also have forced to enlist—as a means of discharging the debt—people who were under an obligation to them."[48] Corris's conclusion was, however, that "[t]his is unlikely to have been done often," because his eighteen informants, who recruited in the early twentieth century, dismissed the idea that they had been forced to leave. He concluded, "The chiefs and passage masters did not compel people to engage. . . . Chiefs did not place people under restraint and deliver them bodily to the boats. Informants deny that this was done, and it would not, in any case, have been possible after the 1870s, for even the most complaisant of government agents could not have countenanced it."[49] Yet apart from the fact that government agents *did* conspire in the use of brutal means, as shown earlier, overt force might not have been a necessary part of coercion. While leaders in most Melanesian societies were rarely in a position to order others to work for themselves or for others, the repayment of an obligation may have worked equally well to induce men to enter the boats.

The power of indebtedness could have worked the same way for ambitious relatives and big-men in the New Hebrides as for Solomon Islands chiefs. The system of reciprocal payments inevitably involved the indebtedness of one family to another, resulting sometimes in severe pressure to repay. A debtor might well have been forced to discharge that debt by enlisting himself or a relative, especially if that were suggested by a "creditor." A "volunteering" recruit could have been responding to pressures from within his own society without attracting the notice of a government agent. As Adrian Graves pointed out, confusing the motive of the recruit with the "corporate" motive "overlooks coercive mechanisms of clientage and control" within the society. But Graves disabled his argument by linking it to his thesis that villagers were, in any case, inevitably drawn into the international workforce through the disruptive effects of European capitalism on their home economies,[50] for, in the New Hebrides and the Solomon Islands, the system of subsistence agriculture was largely undisturbed then and, except in a few places, the disruption is not overwhelming even now. There is no correlation between places where there was cash cropping and places where there was success in recruiting. On the contrary, where European penetration into the local economy was greatest, enlistment in the labor trade was least.[51]

Free will on the part of those enlisting is too simple to account for the participation of Islanders in the labor trade. The cooperation of island communities and the free choice of individual recruits must be differentiated, and at least a possible conflict of interest investigated. Not only passage masters, but also big-men, elders, and successful clansmen had influence over young men, especially those of declining clans.

Munro has distinguished between an individual and a "corporate" act and recognized that "recruits need not have been kidnapped in order to be effectively compelled to enlist" for the purpose of acquiring wealth for their seniors,[52] but he did not explore the point. Instead he equated it with Moore's argument that the Europeans had an unfair advantage in these transactions because of their "more global outlook" and, he might have added, an enormous superiority of wealth. Moore used the rather awkward notion of "cultural kidnapping"[53] to encapsulate this advantage. With some elaboration it might cover the use of wealth to entice senior clansmen, causing them to pressure young men into signing on, but Moore did not distinguish between the interest of recruits and that of their sponsors.

Practical help for the recruiter was sometimes forthcoming from a person of rank. At Port Olry in Santo, the "chief" Bai aided the work of the *Marie* on its voyage of 1884, going in the boats with the recruiter. This cooperation brought the *Marie* ten recruits, and Bai was rewarded with a gift of two pigs, tobacco, and pipes.[54] To maintain the French connection, with its certain supply of arms and liquor, pagan big-men on Tanna may have exercised their influence to urge young men into the recruiting boats. Certainly the cooperation of a "chief" for the renewed trade to Tanna seems to have been sought and achieved. The ship that had previously reported the difficulty of recruiting in the New Hebrides in 1892—the *Lady Saint Aubyn*—went to Tanna a few months later and brought back, after only three weeks, thirty-one Tannese, including "one of the principal chiefs of the island to find out for himself how the natives recruited from his tribe were treated."[55] The "chief" Ongaré (or Okaré) of White Sands (if influential probably a big-man, given that so many Tannese were apt to claim chiefly titles)[56] had been present at all the recruiting operations.[57] He and some companions paid a visit of two months to Noumea, where one imagines they were well looked after. Ongaré returned to Tanna on the same ship at the end of March 1893. On its next voyage in July, the *Lady Saint Aubyn* sailed directly for Tanna. This trip was even more successful. *La Calédonie* enthusiastically congratulated the recruiter, Dick Pentecost, and the government agent, Dr St Germain, on "the quickest recruiting voyage that has ever been made," bringing back, moreover, "robust and healthy recruits who would make excellent workers. Everyone knows that Tanna natives are the most sought-after."[58] The ship continued to have remarkable success at Tanna, trading only Snider rifles for recruits.

A young man who *wanted* to go abroad certainly might persuade a relative to sponsor him by touting the prospect of the beach payment or reminding him that he would share his box when he returned, but there was also clearly room for a sponsor's influence on less willing individuals. Unless one agrees with Corris that "the majority" of recruits were in any case eager to leave, his contention that the beach payment merely "broke down the reluctance that men felt about their kinsman's departure"[59] is surely only another way of saying inducement.

How did a European tell when recruits waiting on the beach with their sponsors were eager to recruit or not? With great difficulty, one would think. One government agent affirmed that he was sure of the consent of those on the beach when he enlisted his recruits, but admitted that "as for knowing if the natives they present as their relatives really are such, it is impossible to be sure."[60] In another instance, a government agent was totally convinced that two recruits were enthusiastic volunteers. At the southeast point of Sukau Island, near Santo, the *Annette* was offered "two fine young men, for whom a payment out of the ordinary was demanded." Despite the exorbitant price, the recruiter acquiesced, "considering the pressing desire of these two recruits to see Noumea." Alas for his judgment, it was a set-up. Three days later the new recruits jumped ship a little farther down the coast. His pride and his credibility no doubt hurt, the recruiter set in train elaborate measures to recover the young men, and they eventually saw Noumea whether they liked it or not.[61]

The Runaways

The indubitable volunteers were the runaways who left without the consent of the community. Sometimes they were forcibly held back or pursued by family heads or leaders who opposed their wish to recruit. As one government agent said, after pleas and threats failed to move those determined to leave, "It is not rare to see the most courageous and determined of the latter put an end to these departure scenes by saying sharply to us: 'Go, go quickly, let's go'."[62]

Lieutenant d'Arbel, overtly sent to the New Hebrides by Governor Pallu in 1882 to report on labor recruiting (although his secret mission was to buy land for the purpose of sending convicts there),[63] observed, "It sometimes happens that natives throw themselves into the recruiters' boats and ask them to leave, while their chiefs or parents wish to keep them on shore. If the recruiter takes no notice, and takes the *canaques,* he does good business, but on shore the natives will complain that he has stolen people, and there will be problems for the next ship even if there was some payment given."[64] Sometimes the recruiter suffered on the spot, a blow from an axe being the reward of one recruiter who allowed the son of a chief to leave in spite of the protest of his father.[65] Nevertheless, recruiters often ignored such protests, because the consent of the individual—very clear in such cases—was all that was required by the law.[66]

Young men sometimes even jumped into the boats of *non-recruiting* ships. An ardent volunteer who had come aboard the non-recruiter *Grace Dent* at Ambae had to be forced ashore to rejoin his comrades, who were already showing their disapproval by firing on the ship.[67] D'Arbel observed a similar case. At Malakula he saw a dozen men get into the boats of his ship, the *Calédonien;* when told that the ship was not recruiting, they "looked very disappointed."[68] The lure of travel was certainly strong, as most missionaries attested, and a voyage abroad brought (and can still bring) the traveler much prestige.[69] On the other hand, as early as 1882 French recruiters found that the appeal of enlisting for foreign parts was diminishing in places where island communities found they could obtain the desired trade goods by selling copra or bêche-de-mer to resident traders.[70] For this reason a refusal to offer recruits occurred twice on the same voyage of the *Lady Saint Aubyn* in 1890.[71] Such refusals reinforce the primacy of the economic motive, but tend to weaken the "attractiveness of travel"[72] as a stimulus to recruiting, or again raise the question of whose decision it was that a young man should or should not go.

Recruiters or government agents sometimes tried to infer the motives of runaways from their actions. Dr Hagen, government agent of the *Lady Saint Aubyn,* praised the courage of five "fine young people, aged from eighteen to twenty-two years." He attributed their leaving to a sense of adventure, to their imagining unknown marvels and perils in the new land,[73] but one is not told on what grounds. It is quite likely that young men keen to board recruiters' boats were curious about foreign lands, attracted by the possibility of gaining wealth, wanting to emulate comrades who boasted of their adventures, or had some reason to escape punishment, shame, or pressure from their own society. A missionary claimed in 1912 that some fled the rule of their elders, who kept them "back from the worship."[74] At this time something of the sort might well have occurred among returns who had converted to Christianity in Queensland. If they were faced with severe opposition, New Caledonia was then the only recruiting colony left where they could take refuge.

In the case of recruits accompanied by young women, the motive of runaways was somewhat clearer. A young man with little prospect of accumulating the necessary wealth and sponsorship to obtain a wife, or not for many years, found it an attractive option to persuade a young woman to flee with him on a recruiting ship as his "wife"; the proposal was often more appealing to many young women than an arranged marriage with an older man. Elopements were as common in French recruiting ships as they were in British, confirming the reputation of the labor trade as the "Gretna Green, nay the divorce court of the islands."[75] Recruiters often not only knew about but also connived in such intrigues by claiming them as a married couple, or performing shipboard "marriages." If elopement was not possible, an alternative solution for a young man might be the prospect of finding a woman on board ship or at the place of work. Recruiters liked to have women aboard the ship to lure men to sign on, as missionaries

were well aware.[76] And women were not the only ones to flee an unwanted spouse in an arranged marriage. The Reverend J C Rae reported that one of his deacons, a "true and worthy Christian native,"
having returned from Queensland with his trunk of goods, was to be
settled with a wife; however, the choice of the "Chief and men of his
village" did not please him. He was to be married to a very old woman
who was nearly blind. "Much against his will he consented, and at the
first opportunity he recruited in a French vessel to New Caledonia,
and remained there for years until the woman died, and then, to be
on the safe side, he brought back a woman from Pentecost Island."[77]

The Coconut Wireless

Information filtering from the workplace formed a most important
part in the decision to enlist and the choice of destination. Recruiters
and government agents were surprised by how much the people on
the beach knew about events in New Caledonia. News was dissemi-
nated from returned laborers and from others sent to find out how
recruits were faring, and a good account was kept of the time already
served by departed countrymen. At Pentecost, men from a bush community came down to the passage to see the government agent of
the *Marie* to demand the return of their compatriots Rokman and
Bouléwara, who had engaged for Noumea three years earlier, threatening to fire on the boats if they did not hand them over.[78] Government Agent Rouzaud, in the *Donald MacLean,* reported that a "chief"
on the west coast of Malakula demanded the return of "two of his warriors," quoting their names, the names of their employers, and their
place of work. They were Babartanobe, working for Sould [or Fould]
at Bouloupari, and Nabar, employed by Metzger at Paita. According
to the chief, they had left for two years only, and they had by then
been absent for four. He would not accept the idea of a voluntary
reengagement.[79] Rouzaud also heard frequent complaints in the islands about insufficient food rations, nonpayment of wages, too much
"carabousse" [prison], and workers being kept beyond their time. He
recommended more inspection of conditions at the workplace, being
convinced that the failure to supervise the terms of the contract led
to the choice of Queensland above New Caledonia, for, he remarked,
"The state of savagery does not exclude among these peoples of the
archipelago, the memory of the treatment undergone in our colony
and the reports of those of them who are sent to the normal places of
immigration as visitors."[80]

Lieutenant d'Arbel also found that people in the islands made an
informed choice of destination, being well aware not only of the
going rates of pay in the various colonies, but also that the price of

the trade goods they put in their boxes was much higher in New Caledonia than in Queensland. Certain workplaces were specified as more desirable than others in New Caledonia. Mine work had a bad reputation, but it was recognized that workers were well fed at the mines. Most wanted to go only to Noumea, where there were more interesting things to do. The fact that the trade was officially suspended at the time of d'Arbel's visit (late in 1882) was known in the islands, and some men asked to go as free labor.[81]

One of the ways such information was spread was graphically related by the government agent of the *Lady Saint Aubyn* at the beginning of 1891. When his ship met the *Sandfly* at San Cristobal, where it was returning some workers, the returns came aboard to talk to the *Lady Saint Aubyn* recruits. The returns had been recruited to New Caledonia as "free laborers" about 1887, during the second ban on the trade, and sent to work at the mines. Many of their comrades had died, and they gave such a horrific description of the life they had endured that the *Lady Saint Aubyn* not only had no success recruiting there, but also felt it necessary to take extra precautions to prevent the escape of the recruits they already had.[82] There was a tragic outcome, for at the next harbor, one of these returns was delegated to kill a totally innocent member of the crew of the *Sandfly* by way of revenge. He did so, and some months later was himself executed for the deed by a commander of the Royal Navy.[83]

The notion of ingenuous Islanders rudely snatched by slavers from an idyllic habitat certainly has to give way to a complex mix of pressures. Calculation, internal coercion, attraction, and the exigencies of a harsh environment must also enter the picture. It is, as well, a matter involving more than recruiters, recruits, and European regulations. Diverse conditions existed on the island side as well as the European side, varying with the structure of authority in particular islands and the circumstances of the time. Nevertheless, outright kidnapping did occur from time to time in the 1880s and 1890s, even where Islanders were experienced in the trade. Moreover, while recent historians have pointed to various "push and pull" factors stimulating island societies to offer recruits independent of European persuasion and coercion, they have been less diligent in distinguishing between the will of the recruit and the interest of the sponsor. Further, discussion of the question of coercion is often limited to the manner of recruitment. The next stage of the cycle, involving the dependence of workers on their employers, was productive of oppression and should not be left out of the account. The situation of female and child recruits was even more dependent than that of the young men.

Chapter 8
The Women

Arrived from the New Hebrides in the Effie-Meikle
Two New Hebridean women to be indentured
Inquire at Hagen's
ADVERTISEMENT IN *Le Néo-Calédonien,*
14 OCTOBER 1881

Even ordinary shipping notices recording the arrival of a recruiting ship from Oceania rarely neglected to report the number of women among its recruits as a form of advertisement. Some variation in the demand for female workers over the period related to the kind of service required, but the main problem was one of supply.

As in Queensland and Fiji, the percentage of women recruited from the Pacific Islands[1] was always small. However, according to my calculations it was larger than that in the British colonies, where it is generally reckoned at between 6 and 8 percent.[2] No systematic figures exist in the documentation for New Caledonia, but only references for isolated years, and the number working at any one time varied greatly. In 1865, the first year of systematic recruiting, only 7 out of 239 foreign Oceanians were women. The proportion varied from 1 to 3 percent until 1877, after which it rose rapidly. Women made up from 5 to 12 percent of the convoys of 1877–1880, and by April 1881 they formed 6 percent of the total migrant workforce.[3] The intake of women workers continued to increase. In the 1880s and 1890s some convoys contained 10 to 20 percent of female recruits, and sometimes more, depending largely on which islands the ships visited.[4] According to the censuses, the proportion of females among adult Oceanian *engagés* was 7 percent in 1887 and 1891, but rose to between 16 and 27 percent in the years 1901–1921. The relatively higher presence of females in the later period partly reflects a tendency to replace mine and field workers with Asians, while continuing to employ Oceanians in domestic work that could be done as well or better by women. However the *total* intake of Oceanians was much smaller in the twentieth century, so the proportion is less significant than it may seem. Adjusting for the decline in intake in the later period, the overall proportion of female recruits appears to be about 10 percent. The figure must remain conjectural, given the lack of complete

Photo 10 Recruits from the New Hebrides. Mitchell Library, State Library of
New South Wales.

documentation. However, it is roughly consistent with the gender breakdown of registered deaths of indentured New Hebrideans over the whole period—slightly more than 10 percent were female deaths.[5] As there is no reason so far to believe there was a significant disparity in the death rates of men and women workers, this figure is probably a reasonable indication of the average presence of female recruits in the colony.[6]

Much less is written about female than male workers in all the colonies, perhaps because they formed only a small part of the imported workforce. But piecing together the fragments of evidence about them richly repays the effort, as recent historians have shown.[7] Differences in their recruitment and their life in the colony illuminate the whole story as well as their place in it.

Although women workers were in demand in New Caledonia, they were difficult to recruit in the New Hebrides and the Solomon Islands, because, in general, their menfolk would not allow them to leave. It followed that, as in the Queensland and Fiji labor trade, many female recruits were runaways. Some, however, recruited in company with their husbands and still others, in societies where women had a degree of independence, recruited as single persons with the consent of their community. Women were also among the kidnapped. In the lawless period of the 1870s there were no doubt many women among those who were abducted for work in New Caledonia. In 1877 the *Aurora* returned from Vanikoro, a small island in the Santa Cruz group, with a convoy of 51 recruits of whom almost a third were female—an improbably high proportion of women for a legitimate recruiting operation. In 1880, 77 women (11.5 percent) were among the New Hebrideans brought to Noumea in a year when six out of seven cohorts came in the *Venus* or the *Aurora*, both shown to have been kidnapping ships.[8]

Administration Policy on Female Recruitment

For the first sixteen years of its Oceanian labor trade there was no legal bar to accepting runaway female recruits in New Caledonia; the consent of the women themselves, as for the men, was all that was legally required. The French administration's policy on the recruitment of women took some time to emerge. Nothing was said about it in the first general regulation of indentured labor—the *arrêté* of 1874—but that legislation scarcely dealt with recruitment at all, as has been noted. It acknowledged the existence of female recruits only in Article 38, dealing with the garments to be issued them by their employers. In 1875 Government Agent Rouzaud mentioned that the immigration commissioner had recommended to him "the value of recruiting a certain number of women." Not only, he suggested, would they be useful as domestic servants, but they would also establish a more even ratio between the sexes "of the same race," and hopefully "keep the immigrant islander for a longer period in the colony." Rouzaud remarked that the attitude of island men toward the emigration of their women gave little room for optimism on that score.[9]

Special regulations on the recruitment of women were first set out in the "General Instructions to Government Agents" of 1881. The document began by encouraging the recruitment of women: "If you can, you will see that a certain number of women are engaged; this recruitment may extend to one quarter of the immigrants that your ship is licensed to recruit." But it went on to add a clear statement of restrictions: "In no case, may women be engaged without the consent of persons on whom they depend and the consent of the chiefs. This last injunction must be scrupulously observed."[10]

After some flagrant breaches of the instructions had been discovered, the policy was more emphatically stated in 1885, when the government agent was urged to strenuously oppose "every attempt made to recruit native women in the absence or refusal of their husbands to let them leave. Each time, then, that a woman is brought aboard, your first duty will be to ensure that she comes free of all family ties or indeed authorized by her husband or by those who have authority over her according to local custom."[11] A version of this rule was incorporated in the metropolitan decree of 1893 governing indentured labor. When in 1906 the New Hebrides became a Condominium, a similar clause became Article 33 of the Anglo-French Convention governing the labor regulations of the New Hebrides.

In pre-Condominium days, the New Caledonian rule was more permissive than the Queensland regulations, which allowed females to leave only when accompanied by their husbands. Both colonies were in agreement that bringing in island women would keep the male workers there longer, but as Queensland was opposed to a permanent settlement of colored labor it was a reason for *dis*couraging the arrival of single female recruits there, in contrast with New Caledonia.[12] Single women could be recruited to Fiji "if the circumstances be such that it appears probable that the rejection of any fugitive woman would entail her death."[13]

The French regulations, like the British ones, were no stronger than the judgment or conscience of the government agent who was supposed to police them. Enforcement of the law was particularly difficult in the case of runaway women. Regardless of the laws of either the British or the French, numbers of women were taken aboard recruiting ships without the consent of their menfolk. A typical way of evading the law was to "marry" a woman on the beach or on the ship to a willing young male recruit who was ready to swear to an inspecting officer that the woman in question was his wife before recruiting.[14] Those who recruited as a married couple, and were possibly eloping, were rarely asked too many questions by the recruiter. Merton King, British resident commissioner of the New Hebrides, went so far as to say that in nearly every case of illegally recruited women "they are recruited with men who pose as their husbands, at all events for the time being."[15] However, marriages of convenience were not considered binding by the recruiter when the couple arrived at their destination: the man and woman could be and often were indentured to different employers at different places.[16]

Runaway Women

Missionaries, traders, and recruiters all recognized that labor vessels, whatever their destination, offered an opportunity to women "anxious to get away."[17] As Margaret Jolly has pointed out, these observers, all of them male, always interpreted this desire in terms of the women's relations with men, never imputing to them the same motivation that inspired the male recruits.[18] In most cases, one might rule out the specific male ambition of acquiring wealth to take home and be converted into obligations leading to the acquisition of bride-price or status or both. The desire to acquire goods, however, was no doubt present among women as well as men, just as curiosity and the desire for adventure and independence were not limited to the male gender. One Ambae woman decided to recruit for her own distinctly personal reasons, as discussed later. There may have been many more like her.

Escaping marital obligations was nevertheless an important motive. Sometimes it was a question of fleeing from an unwanted marriage partner. Elopement with a preferred partner was certainly a common cause for women to leave. At Boat Cove, Ambae, Government Agent Dangeville recruited Jimmy ["Djemi"] along with Metayalla, whom Jimmy declared was his wife, a claim disputed by the Anglican missionary Bice. As the couple demanded the beach payment for themselves in cash, rather than a gift to their relatives—often a sign that they were not likely to return—Bice was probably right.[19] In one case of a woman who fled an unwanted fiancé, another man simply turned up to recruit on the same ship asking "if she wanted to have the same master as he, this woman replied affirmatively."[20] In 1911, a woman was said to have recruited with a "so-called husband" while her real husband was in jail for murdering her former husband.[21]

The attachment of illicit couples was often strong. In one of the instances where the Reverend Daniel Macdonald succeeded in persuading the government agent to send an absconding wife ashore, she refused to leave and "clung to her lover."[22] At Santo, Dangeville recruited a couple, Wartibly and Warguet, who came only on condition that they would not be separated.[23] They arrived in January 1885 and began working for the same employer in Noumea. Five months later they committed suicide together; they were found hanging in an abandoned hut.[24] Had there been talk of their being separated? In any case, the strength of their feeling for each other could not be doubted. Such elopements in a recruiting ship were very common, but some women claimed that they had fled ill-treatment from a husband rather than followed a lover.

Whatever the reasons, the sources are full of stories about women escaping to labor ships and men's efforts to prevent them from leaving or to bring them back. There is even a description of a posse of male vigilantes patrolling the beach when a labor vessel docked at Lenakel in Tanna: "There she [the ship] remained; and every night along the shore I could see little points of light piercing the darkness. They were the torches and fires kindled by the men of the different villages, who were there on guard to prevent the escape to the schooner of any of their women!"[25]

Wronged husbands and fathers freely appealed to a local white resident—often a missionary, but sometimes a trader—to assist in cases of runaway women. Sometimes the case was well known to the missionary. Among converts he may have performed the marriage from which the woman was fleeing. But even when the aggrieved male was a pagan, he might try to enlist the support of the missionary to retrieve the woman. In one instance, Macdonald was asked by some inland pagans to board a labor vessel to get back a runaway wife "saying they would give pigs if she were obtained." Macdonald said he would go "if they would undertake *to listen* to the gospel should any preacher thereof visit them in their district, but if they would not undertake to do this I would not go." The pagans declined this bargain.[26]

European residents usually cooperated with such requests. On the part of the missionary it was often a matter of principle, but on the part of both missionaries and traders it was also a question of personal safety, as a refusal might incur reprisals from the people among whom they lived and whose support was necessary to their work. Their intervention was often successful. Captains often took the view that it was hardly worth while having a missionary on their tail. When, for example, the Reverend Frank Paton received a complaint from a Tanna "chief" that three of his brother's daughters had run away on a French labor schooner, the captain was intimidated by the missionary's persistence. "I warned him," said Paton, "in the presence of these witnesses, that it was illegal for him to take these women, as both the

Chief and the father objected, and that I would leave no stone un-
turned to bring him to justice. This brought about a fierce argument
between the Captain and the Recruiter, the final upshot being that
the women were returned."[27]

Others tended to resist what they saw as missionary interference in
the matter,[28] feeling that they could appeal to popular anti-British
sentiment in Noumea, where Presbyterian missionaries were routinely
characterized as covert agents of British imperialism. For the most
part, of course, there was no missionary or trader on the spot to support a claim of recruitment without the consent of a male guardian,
or to dispute that the man with whom a woman recruited was indeed
her husband, and then attempts by men to get their women back met
with no success, and sometimes with gunfire from the ship. In one
case at least, at Tanna, the men took their own measures to retrieve
their women, holding three crew members hostage until a woman was
given back.[29]

Official Policy toward Women

Cases of the illegal recruitment of women that reached the level of official complaint were very few by comparison either with those in which
recruiters successfully evaded the law, or with those in which they
gave way to pressure for the return of the women. But cases in official
papers are particularly interesting for the detail they contain. They
throw light on the human dilemmas involved in recruiting women,
the attitudes of officials toward it, and the way in which action taken
related to various phases in official policy.

Three such cases occurred at a testing time for the colonial administration in Noumea. After the bad international publicity of the
Aurora inquiry and the *Venus* trials, the metropolitan government was
concerned to avoid any further problems from abuses in the labor
trade. In 1884, having finally consented to lifting the suspension on
recruiting, Paris made it clear that it had done so only on condition
that the regulations were strictly enforced. Yet in the very year that recruiting resumed, there were complaints of the illegal recruitment of
women. The missionary Macdonald claimed that three Efaté women
had been signed on by the government agent of the *Marie,* who was
well aware that they had run off against the wishes of their male
guardians. An embarrassed colonial government promptly dealt with
the complaint by administrative inquiry. Government Agent Dangeville, who seemed to have trouble understanding his instructions,
pointed out that the women had come off to the ship of their own accord: "Lakoro had lost her son, she brought with her her daughter-
in-law Leideva and her friend or follower Leibele."[30] The consent of

the women was, of course, no defense: the report of the inquiry concluded that they had left of their own free will but without the permission of their husbands, who had refused payment for them. They had deserted to follow Charley, recruited the same day. "They seem to be very fond of [Charley]; he is said to have put them up to running away."[31]

On the same voyage of the *Marie,* Dangeville, in clear breach of the regulations, had felt justified in recruiting a young woman, Woubdehari, who was brought down to the passage by her mother from a village (called by him Wanélogot) three miles inland from Nduindui, west Ambae, in order to escape a marriage that both mother and daughter opposed. Dangeville received an official reprimand, and all four women were returned on the next voyage of the *Marie.* The new government agent on this voyage, Petit, said that Woubdehari's discarded husband was "highly satisfied" at the outcome, but it was only with great difficulty that he extracted a promise from the "chief of the tribe" that the Efaté women would be well received.[32]

In the same year the *Annette* was forced to return the woman Hessy, also of Efaté, who had been allowed to recruit on the previous voyage, as the director of the Interior Department explained to the government agent, in order "to escape the pursuit of [her husband], from whom, they say, she was fleeing, 'wishing to put the sea between her and him'."[33] At the insistence of Macdonald, she was returned not to her husband, who had since left for Queensland, but to his younger brother, much to the disgust of the government agent.[34]

These incidents, added to charges of kidnapping against the *Ferdinand de Lesseps* in the same year, gave the French government the pretext it needed to close outside labor recruiting once more in 1885. During the next five years there was officially no labor trade to New Caledonia, although it continued without supervision during the years 1887–1889, so recruiters could then enlist women without even the notional problem of consulting their menfolk. In that period a woman fleeing her husband was refused by the government agent of the British recruiter *Winifred,* who then saw her taken into the boats of the *Lulu,* going to Noumea. He remarked indignantly that the *Lulu* did not even carry a government agent,[35] but in this year (1887) labor ships had no need to, and the woman would have been classed as a "free laborer" with no regulations governing her recruitment.

When the government resumed its supervisory role, in 1890, there was immediate trouble over the illegal recruitment of women. The Reverend Joseph Annand of Tangoa, an islet just south of Santo, complained that the *Marie* had taken two women aboard as recruits against the wishes of their husbands. Annand declared that the next night two young men decided to go with the women "as they can now obtain them as wives without payment."[36] The government agent, Dr Legendre, argued that he had asked the women, Beriri and Venata, to go ashore but that they had "refused energetically, saying that they were tired of the ill-treatment to which their husbands subjected them. In fact they bear on their bodies numerous traces of harsh treatment, and are covered with scars."[37] Beriri's husband eventually accepted payment for her. Legendre did not feel justified in forcing Venata ashore because she said she had made previous attempts to escape and her husband had threatened her with death if she tried again, so "humanity" forbade him from sending her to that fate. He spoke grandly of "the right which every creature has to dispose of itself,"[38] but that was then no more a legal right for women in France and Britain than for women in Melanesia. Beriri died in Noumea soon after arrival, at the age of sixteen;[39] Venata's case dragged on for more than a year, but it seems she was eventually repatriated.[40] Two other cases of runaway women—two women at Malo and one at Tanna—were reported to the authorities in the same year,[41] but the outcome of these is not known.

Cases of illicit recruitment of women after the Condominium was established in 1906 took longer to pursue, partly because of the cumbersome structure of the joint government, and partly because of the rivalry between the two administrations (particularly shown in the British claim to moral superiority in attitudes to native peoples, something that naturally provoked French resistance). Under the Condominium régime, French recruiters were responsible to the labor regulations of the Anglo-French Convention of 1906, whether recruiting for the interisland labor trade of the New Hebrides or for New Caledonia. French ships were free to do mixed business for either destination, and missionaries claimed that this ambiguity encouraged recruiters to ship illegally recruited women to New Caledonia in order to be beyond the control of the administration at Vila.[42] It certainly increased the opportunity to deceive recruits into thinking they were going to a neighboring island when they ended up in New Caledonia, or more commonly—since New Caledonia by this time had a better reputation than the infamous local labor market—enlisting recruits for New Caledonia who soon found themselves on a plantation on another island of the New Hebrides. An Erromango woman, Taval, was apparently expecting to join her husband in Efaté, but was taken to Noumea where she was employed in a white settler's household. Given that a missionary had performed and registered her marriage and the husband was absent when she was embarked, there was no doubt that a married woman had been recruited without her husband's permission. On the representation of British Resident Commissioner Mahaffy to his French counterpart, Taval was returned.[43]

On the other hand, two Tanna women, Namaké and Yatéhé, ostensibly to be taken to neighboring islands, went to service in New Caledonia, a situation that contented them but caused a long war of words between the British and French governments. Namaké's case was first dealt with by the Joint Court of the New Hebrides sitting in Vila. In 1911 Louis Macé was convicted of illegally recruiting her and fined 50 francs plus costs of 279.80 francs for the offense, but instead of being returned, Namaké was shipped on to New Caledonia. When British Resident Commissioner King asked his French counterpart, Repiquet, to arrange her repatriation, he was informed that Namaké was now employed by a Dr Collard, "a very respectable person," and as she had been properly engaged by the Immigration Office at Noumea it was not possible to order her repatriation.[44] King persisted and had the matter referred to the French general commissioner (Governor Brunet) in Noumea. At Brunet's behest, the head of the Immigration Office had Namaké questioned and assured his superiors that Namaké wished to remain in her employment and was unwilling to be returned to Tanna. The paper battle continued for another year, but finally Brunet ordered Namaké's repatriation in January 1913. She was landed on Tanna in mid-March, to what reception was not related.[45]

The case of Yatéhé ran even longer, because it was pursued by the young lawyer and missionaries' friend Edward Jacomb. Yatéhé had been married in a Christian ceremony to Néai, a servant of the Reverend William Watt in Tanna. In July or August 1910, Yatéhé lit a fire on the beach near the mission station at Port Resolution to attract the attention of a passing French labor vessel, the *Jean B Charcot,* recruiting for the large firm of De Béchade, with interests in both New Caledonia and the New Hebrides. When the boat came ashore for her, she asked to be recruited quickly while her husband slept. Next morning when her husband demanded that she be landed, Yatéhé refused to leave the ship. Néai complained to a local trader, who sent a letter to the captain on the subject. The missionary Thomas Macmillan became involved in the effort to retrieve Yatéhé, but was told by the captain that she was only being taken to Vila as a witness in an inquiry.[46]

Another version of the event was recorded from the recruiter's standpoint. According to Marc Cariou, the first mate of the *Jean B Charcot,* when Yatéhé came out to the ship she said she was a widow, working for Macmillan at White Sands; the mission teachers had forced her, by ill-treatment of which she still bore the marks, to marry a "man bush" she did not want, in order to attract him to the mission. She had consequently fled and asked to be taken to Noumea as a recruit. Because they were forbidden to take a woman without the permission of her husband or a chief, they were about to return her, but received such an intemperate letter from the missionary, containing "outrageous insinuations," that they decided to take the woman to Port Vila so that the two resident commissioners could decide her case against the teachers. Having heard her grievances, both residents agreed that she could go on to Noumea with the other recruits.[47] It was not quite the truth. In fact, the case was referred to the Joint Court, which declined jurisdiction because the incident had occurred before its opening, on 15 November 1910.[48]

When Yatéhé failed to return to Tanna from Vila, Edward Jacomb took up Néai's case. He raised the matter in Vila as Native Advocate, and then wrote to French General Commissioner Richard (governor of New Caledonia), all to no avail. In October 1911, more than a year after Yatéhé's departure, he visited Richard in Noumea, who promised to forward his written complaint to the Immigration Office. Jacomb then visited the office of that department, where he found that his letter had duly arrived but had already been filed away as too vexatious; it was explained to him that any interference would displease De Béchade, who might sue the administration if they took up the matter.[49] In this letter, Jacomb had again set out the circumstances of the case, recalling that he had had no replies to his letters on the subject for fifteen months. He added, "I would further point out that even though it should on enquiry appear that the woman left Tanna of her own free will and with the express intention of deserting her husband, such intention can in no way modify the rights of my client [Néai] to challenge the legality of his wife's alleged engagement."[50] More than two years after the original incident, British Resident Commissioner Mahaffy again raised the matter with his French counterpart, Repiquet, who discovered that Yatéhé had been on board the *Koné*, which had recently visited Port Resolution. She had been taken on to Fiji and Wallis Island and "was probably now in Noumea." One can only surmise what her employment aboard ship might have been. Repiquet added that she was very sick, "falling to pieces."[51] Alas for Yatéhé's hopes of a better life, she was returned to Tanna toward the end of 1912 "full of syphilis," according to the report.[52]

Melanesian or European Mores?

These cases are remarkable for the persistence of the inquiries, often through circuitous channels. They are even more remarkable for the fact that in all known outcomes, except those of death in New Caledonia, the runaway women were repatriated. This is highly significant because even those male recruits known by the administration to have been kidnapped were not returned. They had to serve their term first. The only cases I know of male recruits being sent back from New Caledonia were those rejected at the medical inspection on arrival. Paradoxically, kidnapped men who wanted to go back had to stay, while volunteering women who wanted to remain were sent back, although they might face a hostile or even dangerous reception. At Tongoa, a government agent saw a returned woman hanged on a tree, still dressed in her Queensland clothes; she had been killed as punishment for leaving without consent.[53]

The French administration's concern was, like that of the British, largely inspired by the belief that vengeance for recruiting such women was a potent source of trouble. They were on firm ground. In most parts of Melanesia, taking away a woman without the consent of her menfolk was certain to produce an aggressive reaction. Governments had a need to placate indigenous authorities, if only to avoid conflicts and keep the labor supply open, yet the administrators showed a sensitivity to Melanesian concerns on this subject that was not evident in relation to other problems.

Both British and French officials went so far as to say, independently, that the "woman question" was at the bottom of all conflicts— it was *cherchez la femme* pure and simple. In 1894 a Queensland immigration official asked that the recruitment of women be stopped altogether because "almost every complaint against the trade owes its origin to a woman."[54] This was outrageously untrue. Innumerable complaints originated from all kinds of abuses, and the recruiting of women played a small role in the labor trade anyway. Yet such a statement has its echo in the French official instructions to a government agent in 1885: "The recruitment of women is quite certainly the reef on which this kind of operation can founder"[55]—an odd perspective when it was only one of many causes of trouble.

It seems that the problem was a conflict with European as much as Melanesian mores. The regulations aimed at ensuring that the consent of the individual male laborer was paramount when he was recruited, a policy that was in keeping with the nineteenth-century liberal view that, in law at least, an adult male was at liberty to travel wherever he liked and employ himself howsoever he wished. However, this notion was generally in conflict with Melanesian custom, for a young man's desire to recruit without community consent was seldom recognized, and recruitment under those conditions could produce a crisis. But there was no such conflict in relation to the movement of women. In nineteenth-century European law, as in nineteenth-century Melanesian custom, a woman was deemed to be under the control of her male guardian—husband or father—and needed his consent for travel or employment. In other words, while there was a conflict of cultural attitudes over the recruiting of men with their consent but without the consent of the community, the cultural attitude of both societies toward dissident women was similar.

An element of cross-cultural male solidarity underlies some official responses to flighty women. A director of the Interior Department in the New Caledonian administration admitted that most women came of their own free will, although against the wishes of their husbands, adding that this was understandable because they were often ill-treated. He explained that he took his stand on a point of principle: "But whatever our judgment on the brutalities which are, over there, the lot of the native woman, we cannot allow our flag to protect a rebellion against marital or paternal authority legitimated by local custom."[56] That it was also legitimated by *European* custom and law was no doubt also relevant. A completely independent statement of a similar principle by a British official contains just such a comparison. Answering the proposition that a woman recruit named Remering had left her husband of her own free will, and might suffer reprisals if returned, he said,

> If we admit the right of every native woman to discard her husband, and ally herself with another man simply for the purpose of recruiting, we shall give our authority and sanction to all the illegal engagements of women that take place. . . . As far as my experience goes, all Remering has to fear if she is returned, is, possibly, some degree of personal chastisement, which is what she might expect under similar circumstances, were the colour of her skin and that of her husband's white instead of black.[57]

Some, however, felt uncomfortable with the requirement to enforce marital authority in all cases. French Resident Commissioner Repiquet, for example, was distinctly uneasy about the return of Namaké to her husband. He finally agreed that "the prescriptions of Article XXXIII of the New Hebrides Convention would doubtless be satisfied to the letter" by the enforced repatriation of Namaké but, he asked, "would equity?"[58]

Provenance and Community Attitudes

Community consent to the recruitment of women tended to increase over the years as the labor trade became more familiar, but it varied also with the culture of the area from which the recruit was sought. Such consent occurred first, it seems, in cultures where women enjoyed more independence in general. In the New Hebrides, that seemed to be more often in the northern islands.[59] A favorite spot for recruiting women was the island of Ambae, which was the chief sup-

plier of female recruits in relation to the total number of female recruits, at about 19 percent. Significantly, Ambae women contributed
about the same high proportion of female recruits to Fiji.[60] (The
figures for the origins of laborers to Queensland are not broken
down by gender.)

The ratio of Ambae women to all Ambae recruits in New Caledonia, sampled from the figures of registered deaths where provenance
is known, is 26.7 percent, more than double that of Santo (the largest
island and the largest absolute supplier of recruits) where the corresponding figure for women is 12.8 percent; for Pentecost women it
is 9.0 percent; for Malakula women, 4.4 percent; and for Epi women,
1.7 percent. From another perspective, using the same sample (from
the death registers), the proportion of Ambae women of all female
recruits whose provenance is known is nearly 19 percent, whereas Ambae supplied only 8.1 percent of all recruits of known provenance.[61]

The fragmentary literary evidence supports the impression that a
relatively high proportion of Ambae women recruited, and that they
formed a substantial proportion of all women recruited. After the
Marie's first recruiting voyage, a list of 107 of its 135 recruits was published in the Moniteur;[62] of the 7 women listed, 6 were from Ambae
and 1 from Pentecost. The next voyage of the Marie is described in a
full journal kept by the government agent, so that the manner of recruitment can be followed more closely. On this trip, the Marie recruited 27 women, of whom 16 were from Ambae. The others were 3
from Nguna, near Efaté (who had to be repatriated on the grounds
of being recruited illegally); 4 from Malakula, one of whom appears
to have eloped; 2 from Pentecost, one of whom recruited with her
husband; and 1 from Hog Harbour, Santo, also accompanying her
husband. Of the 16 Ambae women, 12 recruited singly with the consent of their kin and community, 1 recruited singly with the con-
nivance of her mother but without the consent of her male kin, and
only 3 recruited in company with men said to be their husbands.
Single Ambae women sometimes recruited with their friends, as the
young men commonly did, whereas women from other islands very
rarely recruited in this way.[63] It probably proved advantageous for
them, for as Kay Saunders pointed out, enlisting with friends—a
much more common pattern of male recruiting—was likely to lead to
mutual support once they arrived at their destination, whereas women
usually found themselves in an isolated position.[64]

On the third voyage of the Marie, in 1885, Ambae provided 13
women as well as 13 men—a proportion of the sexes seldom seen
outside Kiribati, where the normal method of recruitment was by
married couple—and Ambae women constituted nearly two-thirds
of the Marie's total of 20 female recruits.[65] On the Annette in 1885,

only 4 women were recruited out of a total cohort of 58: all were from Ambae.[66]

The island of Ambae always figured in travel literature when the subject of Melanesian women came up. One traveler linked Malo with Ambae as the islands where the least male resistance to access to their women was to be found.[67] A French naval officer, sent by the governor to report on recruiting in the New Hebrides in 1882, observed that it was easier to recruit women from Ambae and Santo, his explanation being that New Caledonia was an attractive destination for them because there they were employed in "women's work." "Frequently they come forward themselves. In general a tribe offers several of them. This is not the case when they are recruited for Australia and above all for Fiji where they are used for plantation work."[68] It was true that women could be employed as house servants in New Caledonia, which was less likely in the other colonies (and in Queensland was illegal after 1884), but the inference was wide of the mark, for the records show that women from Ambae and Santo went in roughly similar proportions to Fiji as they did to New Caledonia.[69] As well, the supposed allure of New Caledonia for women workers did not result in the same ratios of female to male recruits from other islands in the New Hebrides, including Santo, where they recruited at only half the rate of Ambae women in relation to the number of male recruits.

The relatively high intake of women from Ambae can be seen purely as a function of demand, in that European men considered Ambae women attractive. The point was crudely made by a plantation manager on Epi who had an Ambae concubine: "I should not call the [Ambae] women classically beautiful, but they are very pleasing and petite. Also they are worshippers of bodily cleanliness, spending the whole day in the sea. They are quite established in the N.H., and in a good many other groups, as white men's 'keeps'."[70] But such a preference by Europeans would not have prevailed over the objections of the women's menfolk. It seems clear that recruiters were simply more able to sign on Ambae women—even singly, as French law permitted. It would be interesting to know whether this was related to the greater autonomy of women in east Ambae described by Margaret Rodman.[71] In these communities, females had their own status-making ceremonies, which, although subject to the overall male power structure, were not just auxiliary to the male gradings.[72] This was not the only community on Ambae with a reputation for the higher status of its women. An anthropologist of the western district of Nduindui considered that the women there probably held the highest status in the northern islands.[73] Several traders also referred to the greater assertiveness of Ambae women, unfortunately seldom specifying the particular community concerned. Douglas Rannie, an experienced government agent in the Queensland trade, quaintly set this observation against his own predilection:

> Although the women of Aoba [Ambae] enjoy far more liberty, and seem to be much more independent, than the women of any other island in the New Hebrides, they certainly are much more comely, and many of them are very pretty, and they appear to be most decided coquettes. The women frequently danced in groups by themselves, and at times indulged in some extraordinary and fantastic antics.[74]

Dr A Hagen, government agent of the French recruiter *Lady Saint Aubyn,* when visiting Ambae at Navutiriki, remarked that the local men did not "have the same scruples" as at other islands in relation to trading their women, and that the women were "not timid and do not flee at the approach of a stranger," ascribing both traits to their being Polynesian by "race."[75]

Details from a recruiting journal seem to accord with the view of the greater independence of some Ambae women. At Longana, on the east coast, a woman called Teremoli conducted her own business negotiations with the *Marie* in 1884, explaining to the government agent "in English" (probably Bislama) that she had already completed a term of work in Queensland. She sponsored the recruitment of another woman, demanding in exchange a cash payment of 20 francs, then finally agreed to sign on herself, asking for a gun for her brother as beach payment. She said she had a sister already in Noumea and had decided to join her.[76] This was a degree of female independence that recruiters did not find common in Melanesia, nor would it have been widely prevalent in European countries. The *Marie* was also carrying another Ambae woman, known as Lisa, returning home with no qualms after a period of service in Noumea, who agreed to be employed by the recruiter to help care for female recruits.[77] In 1888 a British recruiter spoke of signing on a very experienced Ambae woman who had been "for some years" in Noumea and "speaks French as well as English fluently."[78] Recruiters were familiar with the adventurous male labor "tourist" who signed on for one colony after another to see the world,[79] but it was most unusual to find a woman doing the same.

There were limits, however. In Woubdehari's case, for example, a case of a betrothed woman fleeing an unwanted marriage, the men were so angry that they threatened the life of the resident European trader. And on the 1885 trip of the *Marie,* the recruiter was unable to sign on anyone at Nduindui. The reason given was that the people had heard from returns from New Caledonia that female recruits had paired up with other Islanders at the workplace. The government agent was told that "women from our islands do not marry natives from other islands." This grievance prevented him from recruiting *either* sex in that area, but on the eastern side of the island he was able to recruit, as mentioned earlier, thirteen women as well as thirteen men.[80]

When the Solomon Islands began to be regularly combed for recruits, after 1890, the same variations appeared—due apparently to local mores—in the ease with which women were recruited. In Malaita, recruiters had the same difficulties as they had experienced in Tanna in the early days. Although the island was a rich source of male recruits, women were not available. Almost no women were recruited in Malaita, but a number of women from San Cristobal made the voyage to New Caledonia.

The remarkable return to Tanna as a recruiting source in the 1890s and 1900s was accompanied by the even more remarkable ability to recruit Tanna women, for Tanna was a place where women were strictly controlled. My computer file records only 2 female recruits before 1890 whose known origin is Tanna, compared with 91 between 1890 and 1912. Because recruiters found the experienced and well-armed Tanna men impossible to bully even in the 1870s,[81] it appears that in the later period the leading males were induced to permit the recruitment of women for a consideration, at least from one part of Tanna, confirming the extraordinary influence exercised, for a period, by the suppliers of firearms and alcohol. Even then, these Tanna women seem to have been generally recruited in company with their husbands rather than singly.[82]

The Proportion of Women and Economic Theory

It has been argued elsewhere that the relatively low ratio of female to male workers was the outcome of employer preference for unattached males as the most cost-efficient units. Saunders, for example, argued that "Queensland masters . . . desired a highly mobile, unencumbered and expendable labor force. Indentured service of young unattached males . . . possessed these criteria; for masters envisaged the individuals within the system being exploited as a temporary and expendable commodity."[83] In the case of New Caledonia, at least, the high proportion of males was by no means wholly the result of demand factors. Of course, the prime labor demand was for physically strong workers for the fields, and especially for the mines after 1873 and until the end of the century, after which Asian males began to predominate in the mining workforce. But a free choice by white settlers would have resulted in a higher ratio of women among imported laborers. Female workers were always in strong demand in New Caledonia for service

Photo 11 Copra making at Hienghène, 1885. Mitchell Library, State Library of New South Wales.

not only as domestics or field laborers or both, but also as consorts for employers, overseers, or male workers, in a society with more than the usual preponderance of unattached males. Finally, women were paid at a lower rate, and when minimum wage rates were fixed in 1893, the rate for men and children rose, but the women's remained the same, so that women were paid at the same rate as male children. From almost every point of view, then, the recruitment of women was attractive to brokers and employers. Nor were serious limits put on the intake of women by the authorities, unlike the Queensland case.[84] The quota eventually set by the French colonial government (up to one quarter of each convoy) was hardly ever attainable by recruiting ships. In brief, New Caledonia could never recruit as many women as its European community would have wished.

The main constraints on female labor migration came from the supply side. Recruiters were in no doubt that the chief impediment to recruiting island women was the opposition of their menfolk. European observers explained this on the grounds that Oceanian women did all the drudgery for their men, who were not about to lose this convenience. The most explicit statement came from Rear Admiral Du Petit-Thouars in his 1879 report on the New Hebrides: "As for the native women, if the men do not want them to leave it is because in the New Hebrides, as in New Caledonia, they are their servants, their beasts of burden, their laborers."[85] Forty years later, while involved in a campaign to secure the return of a female runaway, the Reverend

J C Rae thought he understood the reason for her flight: "custom" was too hard on women in Tanna. "She is really a slave, a beast of burden with no will to call her own."[86]

The women were no slaves, but in most communities a young woman's labor was less dispensable than a young man's. Whether for the garden work for daily food, surplus production for trade, or the special tasks of pig raising for status-making feasts, women were the core of the routine workforce, while men's input was more sporadic, in such tasks as heavy clearing and canoe building. As Corris argued in the case of the Solomon Islands, in most societies there was "no great pressure on young [male] people to work" and, as a general rule, before marriage "young men lacked a defined and demanding social role."[87] In a sense there was a surplus of male labor at the disposal of the local communities. It could be tapped by elders engaged in entrepreneurial activities aimed at increased status, or for cash cropping, or for fighting, or it could be passed to the labor recruiter in exchange for the beach payment—especially when that became a gun—and the promise of a trunkful of trade goods on the recruit's return. The withdrawal of female labor, however, could not be recompensed in the same way.

More important, keeping the women at home was seen by Melanesians, like the Queensland government, as a means of motivating their menfolk to return. The main concern of the island community was to preserve and reproduce itself without disruption. As a missionary report pointed out, "Any woman of an age fit for the labor traffic is almost certain to be betrothed, if not married."[88] The dislocation of exchange networks and alliances, in which the exchange of women was crucial, would have represented a major social upheaval. One can imagine the consequences for the father, for example, of a daughter promised to a man of a neighboring community, if he allowed her to leave the island with no guarantee of her return. As in European society of the period, the mobility of women was strictly controlled by their male guardians. To delve further into the structural factor, what was also at stake was the very reproduction of the society. For the same reasons, most societies have not allowed their women to go to the front line of battle, for the concern of ensuring future progeny is paramount everywhere. Melanesian communities were above all safeguarding the continuity of their society by keeping their women home.

Life for Female Laborers in New Caledonia

Whatever their expectations, women who left their village for work in New Caledonia were embarking on a hazardous future. Most were employed as house servants in Noumea. In the bush they served as field hands as well as domestics, often doing double duty as both, and

some worked at the mines, as women in both France and French Indochina still did at this time. They would have had very different
experiences in their new life. Some, like the experienced Teremoli of
Ambae, probably put their term of service to maximum profit. The
women earned their own money as individuals, if at a lesser rate than
the men, thus exercising a degree of independence they had not previously known. Beyond the supervision of kinsfolk, like most migrants
they may also have relished a greater freedom in personal behavior.

On the other hand, the absence of kinsfolk and taboos, particularly in a convict colony like New Caledonia with a huge disproportion of males to females, made women employees extremely vulnerable to sexual exploitation. In encouraging the recruitment of island
women in 1875, the immigration commissioner had implicitly referred to the sexual role of female workers. Women recruits would be
"very useful," he said, in domestic service, and would also help repair
the sex imbalance in "the same race," thus offering an incentive to the
male migrant laborer to remain in the colony. That the women played
their part as sexual partners is incontrovertible, given the number of
births to New Hebridean women in the colonial register, let alone the
many births that were not registered.[89]

The women were entering a colony with a very large preponderance of men. They were a small minority of the imported workforce,
as they were in Fiji and Queensland, and the engagement of a female
worker was certainly considered a lure for male workers, as the commissioner had anticipated. It seems clear that valued Melanesian
workers were allotted "wives" to induce them to work for longer periods, just as the procedure was described on New Hebrides plantations
by a manager who claimed to have performed seven "marriage" ceremonies of this sort, which consisted of writing on a piece of paper
that M was married to F for the term of the engagement.[90]

The white population, however, was also overwhelmingly male,
and it is less clear that indentured women were partners only for men
"of the same race." Among the free whites, there were more than
twice as many men as women until the end of the nineteenth century,
and women were still only 38 percent of the total free white population in 1921. More significant, a much higher proportion of the white
women were married, so that the ratio of single white men to single
white women among the free settlers was 4.5 to 1 in 1887, and in 1901,
when males were not counted as adults until over eighteen, while females were counted as adults when over fifteen, the ratio was still
2.4 single male adults to 1 single female adult. The freed convicts or
libérés (never counted in the free white population) were far more
predominantly male, and in this case the disproportion increased
every year as more convicts were liberated. The gender ratio was 15:1
in 1887, 29:1 in 1891, and 36:1 in 1901, after which the figures for

Photo 12 A woman and her baby, recruited at Ambrym by the *Lady Saint Aubyn*. Engraving of Thiriat, after a photograph. From A Hagen, "Voyage aux Nouvelles-Hébrides et aux Iles Salomon," *Le Tour du Monde* 65 (1893): 373. Mitchell Library, State Library of New South Wales.

libérés were not broken down by gender. An overall ratio for the adult white population (always excepting convicts still serving their time) was between 2.7:1 and 3.5:1 until 1901, and although the figures for *libérés* were not broken down by gender after that, the free and freed white males together would still have been well over twice the female numbers by 1911.

The gender disparity was seen as posing a moral problem. In 1879 Camille Hoff wrote to the newspaper *La Nouvelle Calédonie* urging, among other things, that the government should ship two or three thousand white women out to the colony, commenting cryptically, "There were perhaps fewer abominations committed in the towns of the Dead Sea, destroyed by fire from heaven, than are committed almost openly and with impunity in our unfortunate colony. Ah! if one were to make a study of the illnesses from which the New Hebrideans die!"[91]

The most common response to the paucity of women among both free and freed white males in the bush was to take a concubine from the local Melanesian communities, as evidenced by the numerous births to indigenous women not living in their tribal situation.[92] Often fraught with difficulties even in the interior, this course was much less an option in Noumea. In both the city and the bush, however, a female imported laborer might be engaged by Europeans as a domestic servant, her most common employment in New Caledonia. Because she worked in the confines of her employer's own house, far removed from her own kin or any other support, a New Hebridean housemaid was scarcely in a position to resist sexual advances by her employer. In this atmosphere, it would hardly be surprising if she were expected to fulfill the role of concubine as well, or even if this were the primary purpose of her being engaged.

Of the immigrant Oceanian women who gave birth in the colony, 279 appear in the records.[93] Nearly a half of the 389 children born to them were registered as unrecognized by the father. The named fathers were almost all immigrant Oceanians themselves, sometimes casual co-workers, sometimes stable partners, and occasionally spouses; two, however, were local Kanaks from Houailou who were working in Noumea. Nineteen non-Oceanians recognized their paternity, but only seven employers recognized the children of New Hebridean employees as their own, and all of these were in the bush. In Noumea, two French soldiers and one English sailor recognized the children of their liaisons with New Hebridean women, as did an Indochinese worker in Canala. Two non-Oceanians formally married the New Hebridean mother of their children, one a Frenchman in Noumea and one an Indian who lived near Koné. It seems fair to assume that the large majority of unrecognizing fathers were white, those alone with the power and the motive to deny paternity. Some very late recognitions (some when the child wished to marry, some in old age perhaps making their peace with heaven), are with one exception by white fathers. On one occasion in Canala, the recorder of the birth of a baby girl ingenuously referred to her as "métisse," even though her father was officially "unknown."

The editor of the liberal newspaper *Le Progrès, déporté* Eugène Mourot, a vigorous opponent of the labor trade which he saw as a form of slavery, spoke in no uncertain terms about the concubinage of New Hebridean women. In 1884 he opposed the reintroduction of the labor trade, asking, among other things, "must we recall the memories of the native girls [*popinées*] paraded in the yards and under the verandahs of our estimable merchants: 500 francs, the young ones of fifteen years, 400 francs, those approaching 20 yams [years] and 300, those unfortunates whose charms have faded?" He referred to the "big shots" who were sometimes sellers of *popineés*.[94] Mourot's opinions could be viewed as exaggerated and partisan, but the *Néo-Calédonien,* defender of the resumption of the labor trade, did not answer this point, although it took issue with Mourot on most others. Indeed, three months later Mourot repeated, without challenge, the assertion that very young women formerly brought more than twice as much in passage money as young robust men, reiterating that the "prices" varied inversely with the age of the women.[95]

At the beginning of 1880, Albert Picquié wrote of New Hebridean girls carried off "for what purpose you can imagine," and quoted the "price" in Noumea of a girl of thirteen to sixteen as double the rate of a young man.[96] Julian Thomas—a supporter of the labor trade—made exactly the same observation, if in more guarded terms: "The owner of a vessel brings in his cargo, and by private contract these are disposed of; £4 for a likely boy, £10 to £15 for a good household servant, £30 *for a young girl.*"[97] The emphasis is his, and readers are left to draw their own conclusions. Miklouho-Maclay made a similar remark in relation to the Queensland trade that seems to have escaped the notice of its historians. Speaking of the variation of passage money with market requirements, he wrote, "In one case, in Rockhampton in 1876, the 'passage money' of four Polynesian [= island] women rose to £25 each, while the ordinary rate was about £12 at the time: it is almost needless to add that they were all young and nice looking."[98] This suggests an area of research as yet lightly touched in the Queensland and Fiji labor trades. Saunders alluded to sexual exploitation of women by male recruits in Queensland, and the collusion of their employers in this. She found, however, that documentation of relations between island women and white men was "extremely sparse" in the records. As she said, it was very likely that Melanesian women were constrained to provide sexual services for their masters in Queensland, as indigenous women were.[99] This was especially true when Melanesian women worked as house servants there, before 1884, for in every culture and time, women in domestic service were and are vulnerable to this abuse. Paucity of evidence would be due partly to the reticence of Victorian convention on a subject on which the French were more candid. However, a search of the Registry of Births for the indenture period, apparently not yet done in Fiji and Queensland, should put the matter beyond doubt.

Mourot argued that the high price of young women in Noumea was really an investment, for the "owner" could traffic with the "merchandise." "And when the said *popinée* rebels and flees from the embraces to which she is legally constrained to prostitute herself, the gendarmerie brings her back, with handcuffs on, to her legitimate owner, and the accomplice who gave her sanctuary and refuge will be remanded in custody for sixty days."[100]

Moncelon, another proponent of the labor trade, although a critic of the inhumanity that sometimes accompanied it, is hardly less clear on this question. On going down to a ship to "buy" New Hebrideans ("one never uses any other expression," he explained, "as the alleged cost of passage is in reality considered the price of the black"), and having completed the "purchase," he noticed that a female recruit was upset at being parted from one of the men he had chosen. In disgust, he reported that the captain, laughing, said that he could very well take the man and leave the woman behind, since he would find plenty to take *her*. Moncelon refused to separate the couple, and felt strongly that recruits should be able to choose their employers, instead of the reverse. If a man is contracted to work for a settler in the north for three years, he wrote, while his wife is snatched from him to be delivered to a bar owner in the town, "who will make me believe that this poor unfortunate is a voluntary employee?"[101] Again, although saying that it did not always agree with the author's opinions, *Le Néo-Caledonien* did not react as if this complaint were a misrepresentation.

In general, the administration took no interest in the *ménages* of the indentured workers and their employers, or possibly approved of them as conducive to stability, as they did in the Dutch East Indies and in French Indochina up to the early twentieth century.[102] Because there were no on-the-spot labor inspectors to question the degree of exploitation involved, as there were in the case of the Indian women in Fiji, one has to rely on casual allusions to the sexual services rendered by New Hebridean women that take the situation for granted. The normally liberal-minded Le Goupils considered a gendarme prurient for objecting to "X," a neighboring employer, "living conjugally with one of his female New Hebridean employees,

officially a ward of the Administration. The Brigadier of the Gendarmerie, Immigration *syndic* [administrator], claimed to have the
right to inspect even the bed of his ward." Le Goupils added, probably correctly, "I doubt that in France X . . . would interest even the
League of the Rights of Man in these abuses of power. On the contrary this would be *la droite balle,* as Montaigne said, of a colonial
Courteline . . . , if such a one existed."[103]

In a court case in 1882, a New Hebridean woman was asked whether
she had "had relations" with the *libéré* foreman de Rios. Perhaps not
understanding the question, she replied in the negative, whereupon
her employer, plantation owner de Gimel, broke in, "This woman was
bought by M. Shiel[104] expressly for de Rios. For at least a fortnight
she inevitably had relations with de Rios since she was only there for
that. De Rios was not happy with her services. That's why he kicked
her out."[105] The same question was put to the other female New
Hebrideans in his service. One said she had not only cohabited with
de Rios but had also borne him a child.[106] Later de Gimel added that
eight male New Hebridean employees on his property, recently repatriated, had been the lovers of the four women appearing in court.[107]
Although the reporter was in the habit of observing interesting reac-
tions in the courtroom, these remarks evoked no comment; presumably the relations described were not considered abnormal or unusual.

Without direct evidence, it is difficult to know how a female recruit
viewed her own situation as a sexual partner. As there can be little
doubt that the news of an indentured woman's life in New Caledonia
would have gone back to the home islands on the coconut wireless,
this part of it must have been known, yet it did not deter some women
from trying to recruit. Commenting on the likely life of a female
recruit, an Anglican mission report seemed to imply that to her, becoming a white man's concubine was a superior outcome: "She may
be employed as a house-servant; she may work as a field-hand from
6 A.M. to 5 P.M. and then live with the field hands; she may, especially
if she goes to Noumea, aspire to be the mistress of some white man."[108]

It was possibly a better fate than others, for at the very least she
would most likely have had plenty to eat, reasonable sleeping quarters, the run of the house, and protection from the advances of other
males. However, the fact remains that she would have had no real
choice in the matter. Possibly she achieved some power when able to
play off one Melanesian partner against another, as one employer described,[109] but it was a dangerous game, resulting in quarrels and in
at least one case her own death at the hands of a jealous man.[110] It was
probably in her own interest to form as soon as possible a relationship
with one man for the duration of the engagement.

The alternative—also dangerous, but more lucrative—was to sell her favors in town. A settler described the temptation to take this course: "As for the New Hebridean girls, they are domestic servants in Noumea; there are many intelligent girls who quickly adapt to things they never dreamt of in their own land: cookery, washing and ironing linen. Unfortunately they soon lose their good qualities and are easily led into prostitution, egged on by our amiable soldiers and sailors."[111]

Childbirth was, of course, a major hazard for Oceanian women workers. It was still a considerable danger for their white sisters in the colony, as the melancholy record in the death register shows, but one that was increased for the foreign Oceanian by poorer living conditions, the absence of kin to care for her and the child, the absence of taboos, common in Melanesia, that enforced the spacing of children,[112] and possibly a too-early return to work after parturition.[113] It is impossible to arrive at statistics of the death rate from this cause, given the irregularity in the registration of Oceanian births in the first place, and the absence of a statement of the causes of death in the records. A series of entries in the *état civil* often told its own story:

> *12th May 1879:* The birth of DOUGUINA, Amélie, is reported by M. Jean Newland, landowner, the child of DOUGUINA, native woman of Santo, engaged in his household, aged 15 years, and of father unknown.
>
> *14 May 1879:* Death of DOUGUENA, Amélie.
>
> *22 May 1879:* Death of DOUGUENA.

The deaths of 24 New Hebridean women, or 8.6 percent of the 279 known to have given birth in the colony, were registered soon after the birth of a child to them. However, the statistic may be distorted because of the need to record infant deaths, giving the names of their mothers in the process, and the deaths of the infants might be related to the deaths of the mothers.

Conditions at the workplace were very hard for workers of both sexes. But for a woman there were additional hazards, and the very act of recruiting was risky. The promise of greater independence must have been alluring to inspire the courage for this dangerous course.

Chapter 9

The Children

The legal indenture of unaccompanied children was a phenomenon peculiar to the New Caledonian segment of the labor trade. Young children formed a substantial proportion of imported labor for the first thirty years of recruiting. Child labor was not unusual in nineteenth-century Europe, and in France itself, very young children were a normal part of the workforce as late as 1879.[1] Nevertheless, children who worked while living at home were vastly better off than children taken away from their families to work in a foreign country.

In Queensland after 1884, the legal minimum age for imported workers was sixteen, while in Fiji recruiters were permitted to take younger workers, at the rate of two for every adult, until 1891. In both colonies, however, regulations were flouted, and boys of twelve to fourteen were commonly found on plantations.[2] The Reverend R H Codrington asserted that boys as young as ten to eleven years were taken to Fiji before British annexation in 1874,[3] although missionaries were apparently satisfied that the British administration soon put a stop to this practice.[4] The Queensland inspectors, Drs Wray and Thomson, refused to pass 29 out of 108 recruits on a labor ship because they believed them "little over fourteen (14) years of age."[5] Of course, the age recorded was always an estimate. The crude method of examining prospective workers for the presence of armpit or pubic hair was commonly used by British government agents to determine minimum age, while inspection by a medical officer on arrival in the colonies was a further check.[6] But for New Caledonia, puberty was not a requirement. For the first seventeen years of the trade, the law allowed the recruiting of children, unaccompanied, from the age of six years; thereafter the legal minimum age was still only ten (figure 3).

Writing of recruitment for Fiji and Queensland, Peter Corris referred to some "very young recruits" who were taken in spite of the regulations, but by this he meant boys of about twelve to fourteen.[7] In

Figure 3 *Livret* of Lolole, recruited at about age eight in 1877. Being under ten, he would have received half the rations listed. His details, translated: Livret no. 2360 [his registration number]; Of Lolole; Born at Aoba [Ambae]; Caste[!] New Hebridean; Height 1 meter 160 mm [or 116 cm = 3 feet 9.75 inches]; Eyes Black; Nose Normal; Mouth Small; Hair Fuzzy, Red [or reddish-brown; would be limed]; Eyebrows Black; Chin Normal; Beard ——; Color [of skin] Copper; Distinguishing Marks: Tattoos on the chest. Scar on the back. The toe of the left foot is deformed. The third toe of the right foot is missing. Collection of Anne-Marie D'Anglebermes, Noumea.

the New Caledonian context, such recruits would not have been considered very young. The first labor code of 1874 laid down no minimum age, although a clause stating that children under ten need only receive half rations recognized that young children were routinely recruited.[8] The minimum legal age of six years was mentioned in proposals to reform the law following the *Aurora* investigation: "The minimum age of immigrants, currently fixed at six years, should be raised by two years."[9] The director of the Interior Department put the suggestion to the Privy Council in April 1881. He believed that the effective minimum should be eight years, but he set it at ten years in the government agents' instructions, reasoning that in order to make sure that the recruiter did not take recruits younger than eight it was better to raise the official limit to ten! The measure was accepted by the council.[10]

Discussions about reforms were cut short by the first suspension of the trade, but the new minimum age probably appeared in the government agents' instructions at the resumption of labor recruiting in 1884, because there was argument in the *Ferdinand de Lesseps* inquiry about whether a child the ship had recruited had reached the age of ten.[11] No revision appeared in the regulations, however, until the decree of 1893, wherein a provision forbade the recruiting of children of less than 110 centimeters in height (later reckoned at about nine years of age) unless they were accompanied by either mother or father; by 1904 the minimum for an unaccompanied child was still only ten years or a height of 114 centimeters.[12]

According to the 1874 regulations and all those that followed, the recruiting of a minor was not valid "without the express consent of those who have authority over him, given in the presence of two witnesses, or without an authorization of a justice of the peace or magistrate performing the functions of a justice of the peace, if it concerns natives of Oceania."[13] Such dignitaries were nonexistent in the places of recruitment at the time, and for decades afterward. The intervention of a justice of the peace could only have taken place after the recruit's arrival in the colony, and a refusal to authorize recruitment would have involved sending the child back on the next available ship, a course of action fraught with as much uncertainty for the children as indenturing them. No evidence of such intervention has been found, and in effect whether or not the consent of the child's guardians had been given depended on the word of the government agent, who often was not a witness to the recruitment. Except for a provision that the government agent was held to have "judicial police" powers, eliminating the putative need for judicial intervention in New Caledonia, the clause about the consent of guardians remained virtually unchanged in the 1893 decree.

Photo 13 New Hebridean workers (said to be from "Sandwich Island" [Efaté]) on the property of Kerveguen, a sugar planter at Dumbea, about 1869. Note the young age of some of them. Photograph by E Robin. Collection of S Kakou, Brignoles, France.

Although there was a provision that young children could make up no more than a fifth of each convoy,[14] a much higher proportion was regularly recruited. To Governor Courbet, "one of the saddest aspects of this kind of operation" was the large number of child workers imported. He cited randomly the cases of two recent convoys: that of the *Havannah*, reaching Noumea in October 1881 with 100 recruits, of whom 37 were under sixteen; and that of the *Annette*, arriving in January 1882 with 70 recruits, of whom 27 were under sixteen.[15] Of a list of 107 recruited on the *Marie* in 1884, 44 (41 percent) were children of nine to fifteen years. Among the *Annette* cohort of 1885, a third were fifteen or less, and a half of these were children of eleven and twelve years.[16] Miklouho-Maclay noticed the young age of recruits on ships "especially from New Caledonia."[17]

An even higher proportion of young children seems to have been recruited before 1880. Early in 1875, when addressing the question of giving religious instruction to New Hebridean "immigrants," Bishop Vitte pointed out that they were "nearly all young."[18] Ludovic Marchand remarked that the convoy of 52 recruited on the 1879 voyage of the *Venus* were "almost all children."[19] Albert Picquié claimed that the *Aoba,* sailing regularly from 1875 to 1880, recruited only children.[20] The death statistics of the 1870s indicate a large number of the very young: of those who died and whose ages were registered, 25.5 percent were aged between six and fifteen, the highest proportion of any decade. For 1874–75, a period of frenetic recruitment, the proportion of deaths of very young children is especially high. For example, of the many New Hebridean workers who died on the sugar plantations of the Dumbea district in 1874–75, the estimated ages of 83.0 percent are registered, and of these, 45.5 percent were children under sixteen, most between seven and twelve years.[21] Those who had been *recruited* as young children, and who died in the colony at or over the age of sixteen, would considerably inflate this figure.

The same sampling of those who died before reaching the age of sixteen produces a declining figure for the following decades. Of those whose age at death was estimated, the equivalent proportion of child deaths registered in the 1880s is 14.4 percent, for the 1890s 5.8 percent, and for the 1900s 4.6 percent. Over the whole period, of 3,668 New Hebrideans and Solomon Islanders whose ages at death were given (out of a total of 4,795 such workers whose deaths were registered in New Caledonia) 470 or 13 percent were under sixteen when they died, and 180 of these were twelve or under.[22] Again, this is the absolute minimum of the proportion *recruited* at a young age.

Why were so many children imported when the ideal worker on a short-term contract was obviously someone in the prime of life? Part of the answer lay in the labor regulations, for they included an extraordinary provision that made possible a long extension of indenture for child workers. Under Article 16 of the 1874 code, the term of engagement was not to be less than two years or longer than five, except for that of a minor, which "could be for a longer time, but would cease to be operative at the time when the indentured laborer attains his majority."[23] A loophole like that—allowing an indenture of up to twelve years—was bound to be exploited. As Marchand wrote to Schoelcher, "the settlers are attracted by the idea that they will be able to keep [children] until their majority, perhaps for eight or ten years."[24] Of course, as they grew older they became more valuable. They could even be traded off at a profit. The liberal newspaper *Le Progrès* cited the case of "Mme Ad... who had the misfortune to lose successively two little kanakas she had bought for three years. She went around crying poor-mouth and to console her, they gave her another for nine years and, when she left for France, she resold the kanaka, after enjoying his services for three years, for three hundred francs, the old passage money, plus an agreement to pay him all wages due, so that for three years she had had a kanaka absolutely free."[25]

The demand for domestic workers was an additional reason for the special interest in child workers. Although children as young as nine were employed sorting nickel at the mine face,[26] and on sugar plantations,[27] young children were most commonly employed as house servants, particularly as nursemaids. Several contemporaries commented on their prowess in this capacity. Marchand wrote to Schoelcher early in 1880, "The little blacks, such as those who came almost exclusively for a certain time, are employed as house servants, and often act as nursemaids, a job which they perform admirably; they are very fond of children and take better care of them than do most maids in France."[28] Julian Thomas shared this opinion: "I should think that some of these 'labour boys' make about the best and most careful attendants on children in the world."[29] A former public servant in the colony recalled the value of his nine-year-old New Hebridean servant:

> Yamoutha acted as a nursemaid to amuse our baby. He was very gentle and appeared intelligent. The child, grateful, never left her friend Yamoutha. They say that the New Caledonians refuse to serve foreigners. I have no difficulty believing it. Yamoutha, also, gave us to understand that he did not come of his own free will. We caught him in the evening wiping away a few furtive tears.[30]

Lee and Howard Walker, both in business in Noumea (including labor trading), also had "the little blacks" in their households as a matter of course, for domestic service and as sentinels, sleeping across the doorways at night.[31] Lee told his mother that he had two boys about ten years old and Howard had three, "and no one else to keep the house in order and you would be surprised to see how well they do it."[32] Young domestic workers were also in demand in the Australian colonies, and they were supplied via New Caledonia (see chapter 5). As I shall elaborate in chapter 14, the Marist Mission had a different employment in mind for child recruits, hoping to train them as harbingers of the Gospel in the New Hebrides.

Another reason given for the higher proportion of younger recruits in New Caledonia was that children were "easier to entice" with showy goods and false promises.[33] As well, because the preference for those in greatest demand—young men—was for Queensland first and Fiji second, New Caledonian ships had, to some extent, to fill up with young children. The raising of the recruitable age may partly account for the recruiting of fewer very young workers as time passed, but the reduction of competition after 1884, when British traders were unable to trade firearms, was perhaps a more important reason, because it increased the ability of French recruiters to sign on workers in the prime of life. Although very young workers were still being recruited, they were a smaller proportion, so effective were rifles in recruiting adult males. On the voyage of the *Annette* in 1885, the recruiter rejected the offer of a twelve-year-old at Pentecost, having already six recruits of that age aboard, believing that with Snider rifles he could now attract sufficient older recruits, and that if not, he always had the option of taking more children. In the event, out of a total of 58 recruits, the ship brought 9 of about twelve years or younger, and another 10 reckoned to be under sixteen, but they were also able to recruit 17 prize recruits—men with experience in Fiji and Queensland.[34]

It can hardly be argued that young children were parties to a free contract, understanding that they were to work for three or more years (or in their case until their majority) in a foreign land. Picquié put the matter bluntly: "Here the principal term of the contract is invalid. With these young Hebrideans there is no free will; and there is only one alternative; either they have been kidnapped, or their parents have sold them."[35]

Ships' journals spoke of parents or relatives offering children as recruits in exchange for a variety of goods, including axes, tobacco, and "sabres," but never firearms, which were reserved as payment for adult males.[36] The government agent of the *Lady Saint Aubyn* claimed that he took on a six-year-old boy "as an act of charity," because he was offered by his uncle who was unwilling to look after him following the death of his mother and father.[37] The Reverend F Bowie, medical missionary at Tangoa, Espiritu Santo, remarked (in relation to the interisland labor trade) that the people generally did not "sell" boys of six or seven years, "especially if they are their own children," implying that they might in some cases be prepared to allow or constrain older children, or other people's children, to recruit.[38] One of the kidnap victims who appeared in the *Aurora* inquiry complained that the recruiter had not parleyed with him before taking all the occupants of his canoe: "If he had talked with me, I had two young *canaques* with me, I would have given him one of them."[39] A man from Malakula already on board the *Aurora* was allowed to land after he offered his nephew of twelve or thirteen in his place and gave four pigs to the recruiter, because those on shore refused to give up the beach payment for him (a gun).[40]

With more scope under their regulations to enlist them, New Caledonian recruiters were always ready to take children. In the early years, when they were less able to obtain adult workers than were Queensland recruiters, they were prepared to kidnap young children. Later, they offered inducements to their elders to let them go. There was always a market for them, mainly as domestic servants and child minders, but also for jobs in the fields and mineral sorting at the mines.

Part Three

At the Workplace

Chapter 10
Work in New Caledonia

In April 1866, Brother Aimé Mallet happened to see a parade of New Hebrideans passing the presbytery. They were an early shipload of recruits to be offered for indenture to employers in New Caledonia, under the Henry contract of 1865. Mallet recognized the Hebrideans by their dress, for he had been part of a short-lived Catholic mission at Aneityum in 1848, so he went down to see what transpired. The recruits were marched up from the wharf and ranged in front of the *mairie* (city hall). When Mallet arrived there, Krieger, a naval officer, had drawn them up into two ranks "of which the first consisted entirely of young people about 10 to 15 years." Proceedings were summary. Krieger was supposed to ask them if they understood the purpose of their being there before employers signed them on forthwith. As traders themselves said, even had the language been understood, in these early days the conditions of the contract could not have been. But Mallet observed that not even the words were comprehended, let alone the implications. Krieger was assisted only by the government English interpreter (presumably the recruits spoke Bislama if they could communicate with Europeans at all). The interpreter "tried to speak to them in English, to ask them if they were willing to engage for work. The natives not understanding a word, officer Krieger said 'whether they understand or not doesn't matter much. It's only a formality and that's what they have come for'; it would have been more correct to say that that's what they were brought for, for how could they have made these savages understand that if they came aboard the ship they would be taken to a country and constrained to labor there for one or several years?"[1]

Observing Mallet trying to speak to one of the Tannese recruits, Krieger asked him if he could translate the proceedings into the "native" language, and Mallet had to explain that although he had a few words of Aneityumese, the language of neighboring Tanna was different and he was unable to help. Dispensing with this problem, Krieger allowed the employers to make their choice. "The group from Tanna, consisting of about 12 men, was chosen by M. Hoff, employee of M. Joubert, then a lot of about the same number of Efatese was reserved by M. Higginson, broker, then a lot by the Martin brothers, then another by M. B . . . , but I withdrew before the end of the placements. I noticed that they went into the *mairie* to register the contracts in writing before the clerk of court."[2]

This early manner of questioning and distributing the recruits evolved into a standard procedure and was written into law. Under the 1874 code, an Immigration Office was established in Noumea, to be part of the Colonial Secretary's Department. (It later became part of the Department of the Interior, then was linked with the Native Affairs Department, and in 1912 became a separate department.) An immigration comissioner was appointed to head the office: he was responsible for boarding the ship on its arrival to verify that recruits had come of their own accord, and for arranging for a medical officer to check that they were fit for the labor expected of them. In the first fifteen years of the trade, these measures were sometimes overlooked in the case of ships docking at the east coast ports of Pouébo, Houailou, Canala, and Thio, where recruits were distributed to employers before the ship went on to Noumea. After the scandals of 1880–1881, it became obligatory for recruiting vessels to call first at Noumea, and the formalities were observed. During the years from 1887 to 1890, when the introduction of so-called free labor was permitted during a labor-trade ban, ships unloaded at the east coast ports again, as well as at Noumea, without any inspection.

Employers who wished to engage labor could register in advance with the Immigration Office; large companies might have directly ordered a number of workers before the departure of the ship,[3] but others would rely on a labor broker and respond to their advertisements in the newspapers (figure 4).

Brother Mallet believed that the procedure he witnessed smacked "more or less of the negro slave trade" and recalled the remark of an official who said "if one wants to have any success in colonization one really must acquiesce in a few small injustices."[4] Mallet was not the last observer disquieted by the affinity to a slave market. By the 1880s the system—no longer directly controlled by the colonial administration—certainly looked much the same. In 1882 Léon Moncelon, who had taken part in it, described it: "Everyone here knows what the engagement procedure is like: the employer chooses from the bunch of men and women those who suit him, marks them on the back with a letter in chalk, then goes down to the office or place of registration. The owner of the black-birding ship[5] gets paid for the cost of the pas-

---

NEW HEBRIDEAN WORKERS

As the *Venus* is due to arrive soon with a new convoy, employers are requested to register their names with the undersigned

Joubert & Carter

Figure 4 Advertisement in *Le Néo Calédonien,* 8 April 1880.

sage; the employer pays him a sum of . . . per recruit (generally from 150 to 300 francs) and the receipt reads; 'for passage from the New Hebrides to Noumea'." This was an agreed fiction; "the so-called passage money is in reality considered the price of the black," which varied with the demand and estimated quality, like any other commodity. Although an employer of New Hebrideans himself, he could not accept that this procedure remotely resembled a contract between free agents, as it was supposed to be in law.[6]

Even before the administration stopped directly managing the labor trade, merchant firms—like Lomont, Hagen, Higginson, Rataboul & Puech—had begun to act as brokers, taking laborers wholesale and disposing of them retail, a practice that also existed in Queensland until stopped in 1876. Julian Thomas visited the warehouse of Rataboul & Puech in Noumea in 1883, where he watched his friend Brock "disposing of a cargo of 'niggers,' selling them at so much a head for a 3 years' term of service." Thomas was far from being an opponent of the labor trade, believing that the "niggers" brought to work for Europeans were "doing more good in the world than if engaged in killing and eating each other on their native islands."[7] Nevertheless he was uncomfortable at the marketing of human beings. They had been landed at the docks and "marched in gangs to the verandah of the owner's store, and there left for the inspection of intending purchasers until the sale commenced (photo 14). I say 'purchasers' and 'sale' advisedly, for the transaction was as openly and avowedly a sale as anything to be seen in the old days 'down South'"[8] (photo 15). He saw an Australian acquaintance enter and ask for a houseboy. "'That lot up there ain't sold,' said the good-natured factotum; 'there's one little fellow can speak English.' Then my friend examined the 'little fellow' as a veterinary surgeon would a horse. He

Photo 14 New Hebridean recruits in Noumea. Max Shekleton collection, Noumea.

Photo 15 Workers at Hagen's store, Noumea, 1885. Mitchell Library, State Library of New South Wales.

looked at his legs, and paid special attention to the glands of his throat. Some bargaining took place, and in the end 100 francs (£4) was given for the boy of fourteen, who thenceforward became the slave for three years of his purchaser. All engagements of island labor were of this nature, the prices given varying according to the value of the 'stock'."[9] According to Thomas, the "niggers" had little cause for complaint, but he nevertheless believed that "the first transaction certainly savors of slavery" although engaged in by the most "highly respectable citizens" of New Caledonia.[10]

A French opponent of the trade had written to a Paris periodical the year before in terms very little different from those of Thomas.

> [A]fter landing the natives are displayed in a shed. There the connoisseurs and the dealers go to make their choice. There they discuss the value of the human cattle; and the latter varies from 200, 250 to 300 francs, per head, according to its quality, a certain item is of a lesser price, another higher; they discuss the prices, as needs be they make lots of three or four heads; in a word, nothing resembles a cattle market more than such an exhibition. As the natives are successively auctioned or sold by private contract, they are taken to the office of the Director of the Interior where an official explains for form's sake to each immigrant that he must work for a white man for three or four yams, that is to say for three or four years.[11]

After the agreement was concluded between broker and client, it was formally recorded at the Immigration Office, where the new employer paid 10 francs for a *bulletin d'immatriculation* (registration of the worker with a number), and 5 francs for the employee's *livret* (passbook), in which the details of the laborer's history were to be recorded—wages paid, days absent, offenses, sickness. The *livret*, also a requirement in France from 1803 to 1890, remained in the hands of the employer. Recruits not selected in the first round remained at the depot until they were engaged.

Moncelon believed that the state thus legitimized an involuntary system. In his view, the state's responsibility ended when the recruit was landed and registered as fit for work: by registering the employer's choice without consulting the wishes of the recruit, the administration authorized a breach of contract that could never have taken place in France. His odd conclusion was not that there should be more regulation, but less: the state should opt out of the system altogether, allowing genuine contracting between the Oceanian and the employer. As the two parties were far from equal in resources, power, and comprehension of the engagement, such a proposition could only have resulted in worse conditions for the *engagé*, as it did when in 1887–1889 there was no regulation protecting introduced labor.

Term of Service

Apart from the apparent health and strength of the recruit, another variable for the "buyer" was the length of the contract. In New Caledonia the term of indenture was not the standard three years of Queensland and Fiji. At the beginning of organized labor recruiting the recruits "signed" for one year only, before having the option of repatriation. By 1867, a two-year contract had become the norm.[12] After 1870, the duration of the contract was from two to five years,[13] but according to the inspection report of 1874, the period was still "generally from two to three years" in 1873.[14] The *arrêté* of 1874 laid down that the contract could not be for less than two years nor more than five, with the notorious exception of children who could be kept until their majority (presumably twenty-one) without a renewal of contract.[15]

The two- to five-year limits were retained in the instructions issued to government agents in 1881, but it is clear that the lower limit, in practice, was three years by this time. Among the existing samples of cohorts of recruits in the 1880s, no one was enlisted for less than three years: out of a list of 107 on the 1884 voyage of the *Marie*, 9 recruits were engaged for three years, 53 were engaged for four years, and 45 for five years; the voyage of the *Annette* the next year signed on 58 workers, of whom 34 were engaged for four years, 15 for three, and 9 for five years. In the 1890s there was some pressure on Oceanians to recruit for five years, like the Asian laborers who were beginning to enter the colony,[16] but many island workers seem to have successfully insisted on the right to maintain the option of a three-year term,[17] no doubt because of the competition of Queensland and Fiji where the three-year term was standard. By 1893, when the metropolitan decree replaced the 1874 *arrêté*, the minimum period was officially raised to three years and the maximum left at five.[18] In the early years of the twentieth century, opposition to the longer term came from a different source—the planters in the New Hebrides, who opposed the export of labor altogether—and in 1907 they obtained an upper limit of three years through the action of their French resident commissioner.[19]

Shorter contracts became the rule as the number of New Hebridean recruits dwindled and competition for them increased. In 1901 Ballande successfully experimented with six-month contracts in order to attract recruits,[20] and by 1920 a one- to six-month contract was recognized in a regulation taxing the employment of New Hebrideans.[21] It would seem that, like their compatriots working for local planters,[22] recruits became more conscious of their bargaining power as competition heightened for their services.

Occupations

The formalities of the contract completed, the recruits followed their employer to the place of work, perhaps in Noumea, perhaps in "the bush." Imported Oceanians were employed in a far wider range of occupations in New Caledonia than in the British colonies, especially in Queensland after 1884, when laws were passed restricting Melanesian laborers to the sugar industry. In New Caledonia they were used for any kind of unskilled labor in all parts of the colony over the whole period, but the distribution varied, of course, with the extraordinary vicissitudes of the colonial economy and with the labor requirements of the administration itself. Only in the 1890s, when Asian labor began to be imported on a comparable scale, can one discern a kind of specialization by so-called "race," in which one ethnic group was considered best fitted for a certain function.

As has been noted, when Governor Guillain's administration had to cope with the influx of convicts, the urgent need of the government itself was an important reason for arranging the systematic importation of foreign Melanesians. Thus it happened, uniquely in New Caledonia, that the administration was an important employer of these people. In the 1860s it used them as convict guards on Ile Nou, as boat crews, and in the government workshop. Later they were also employed in the telegraph service.

Guillain's arrangement with Henry to underwrite convoys of New Hebrideans was also intended to make New Caledonia a flourishing plantation colony that could be self-sufficient, rather than simply exist as a penitentiary for exiled convicts. With the hope of establishing sugar and coffee, among other agricultural ventures, Guillain had recently attracted a number of settlers from Réunion who were in desperate need of labor, despite bringing with them a number of their Indian coolies. The earliest convoys, therefore, tended to go either to public works in Noumea, or to plantations in the interior (photo 16). An idea of the employment and location of the first official imports of New Hebrideans can be gained from two reports giving a breakdown of the distribution of workers. At the beginning of 1867, a cohort of 37 all went to private farmers: 11 went to four different mixed farms and cattle stations at Paita, 3 to a mixed farm at Naniouni, not far from Paita, 2 to a farm at Yaté, 4 to a sugar planter on the Dumbea River, 6 to a coffee planter at Nakéty and 5 to another at Canala, and 6 to a coastal trader near Canala.[23] Later the same year, no less than

Photo 16 New Hebrideans building a house on the property of G Martin on
Ile Ducos (in the Bay of Saint Vincent), 1865. Martin is the one on horseback.
Drawing by A de Neuville after a photograph by E de Greslan. From Jules
Garnier, "Voyage à la Nouvelle Calédonie," *Le Tour du Monde* 18 (1868): 25.

50 out of a cohort of 64 were employed by the administration itself:
25 went to a government workshop, 20 to Ile Nou as guards for convicts, and 5 to the Port Authority as boat crew; the remaining 14 were
divided among private settlers.[24] By 1869, 49 New Hebrideans were
employed on the Joubert sugar estate at Koé, on the Dumbea River,[25]
including a barge crew to transport produce down the river. In the
late sixties and early seventies the number employed on the coffee
plantations of Canala rose sharply, the workers being transported
directly to that port by the recruiting vessels.[26] The old collecting
trades of sandalwooding and bêche-de-mer fishing also employed
New Hebrideans, and they still continued to form a high proportion
of the crews of private trading ships as well as administration vessels.

Perhaps not part of the governor's development plan, but a role
that persisted for the imported workers, was their engagement very
early as house servants, in Noumea as well as in the country. As domestics in houses, hotels, and bars, as store laborers and humpers of
loads from the wharves, and as administration employees, nearly half
of the New Hebrideans worked in Noumea even in the first decade of
the labor trade, despite the stated intention of importing them to develop agriculture.

Photo 17 Working at the gold mine "Manghine," better known as Fern Hill, about 1873. Max Shekleton collection, Noumea.

After 1872, the administration, on a reduced budget, was under renewed pressure to house and service the influx of exiled *communards* (the rebels deported after the fall of the Paris Commune of 1871). The extra business they brought to the shopkeepers and bartenders of Noumea was exceeded only by that of the French troops brought in to quell the rebellion in 1878. Both public and private employers required extra labor to cope with these events.

From 1873 to 1884, there was a marked change in the pattern of the employment of the Oceanians as a result of the mining boom as well as a greatly increased demand for their services. As the British colonial secretary pointed out in April 1874, the mine owners "had already channelled such an inexpensive labor force on to their mines."[27] As competition for labor grew and passage money soared, smaller employers were increasingly hard-pressed to maintain or renew their supply of labor. Some considered that they had paid enough through the inflated passage money, and simply did not pay wages thereafter (see chapter 12).

The granting of the first mining concessions accounts for the considerable upsurge in the intake of New Hebrideans from 1873. They worked on the first gold-mining operation in the northeast, the Fern Hill (or Manghine) mine (photo 17). When in 1873 the copper mine opened in the Diahot region near Ouégoa in the northeast, they were sent to work it. They then went to the first nickel mines at

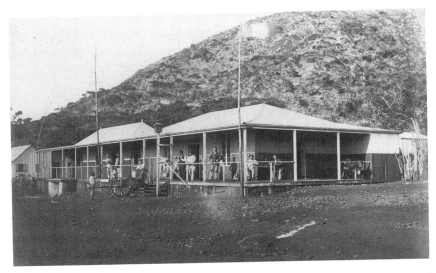

Photo 18 At Hagen's store, Thio, 1885. Mitchell Library, State Library of New South Wales.

Thio, Canala, and Houailou on the east coast, to Mont Dore in the south, and to the Chesterfield Islands to the northwest and Walpole Island southeast of the mainland to dig phosphate. Later they went to Kouaoua in the Canala district and finally to the mines of the northwest. Gangs of laborers did the heavy work of clearing the site and excavating, and built the road or tramway to transport the mineral to the coast. Once the mine was in operation, New Hebridean labor was at first used to dig the ore, but as an alarming number of them died from chest complaints, the administration suspended their employment in underground galleries in 1884.[28] Although this measure appears to have quickly become a dead letter, for they were certainly employed in the mines thereafter, the tendency was to use them only at the surface when other labor became available. There they sorted the ore and put it into sacks—work often done by young boys—and loaded them onto wagons that others either pushed or pulled along a tramway to the wharf, a distance, in the case of La Balade copper mine at Diahot, of six miles[29] (photos 19, 20). Travelers passing through the country often observed, as a colorful feature, gangs of New Hebridean workers at the mines, recognizing them by their distinctive clothing, or lack of it.[30] A nickel mine at Thio was christened *La Mine des Sans-Culottes* (the Bare-Bottom Mine) after its New Hebridean workers (photo 21).

Photo 19 Work at a nickel mine at Thio. Photograph by Hughan, 1870s or early 1880s. Mitchell Library, State Library of New South Wales.

    While the employment of New Hebrideans in mining attracted a good deal of attention because of publicity about their high death rate and because, since they worked in gangs, mine labor was more visible, probably only a little more than a quarter of them worked in the mines. At the end of 1882, at the peak of their employment in mining, it was estimated that 621 out of 2,366 working in the colony, or 26 percent, were employed at the mines, as against 774 or 33 percent at "stations in the bush" and 971, or 41 percent, in Noumea.[31]

    The figure for those at "stations in the bush" included cattle hands and domestics as well as agricultural laborers. Although the numbers employed in sugar, cotton, and tobacco growing had declined during this period—most such plantations were bankrupt by the end of the seventies—coffee plantations burgeoned and employed many New Hebrideans in field work and processing (photo 22). An entire boat-load of them was commissioned in 1879 by Laurie, a coffee planter at Canala, and his brother-in-law Evain also employed numbers of them. On the pineapple plantations established farther up the east coast, New Hebrideans were used both to plant and tend the crowns

Photo 20 Work at a nickel mine at Thio, 1870s or early 1880s. Photograph by Hughan. Mitchell Library, State Library of New South Wales.

Photo 21 New Hebrideans working at the *Sans-Culottes* nickel mine at Thio, 1870s. Photograph by Hughan. Mitchell Library, State Library of New South Wales.

Photo 22 Coffee drying at Laurie's plantation, Paravoué, near Canala, May 1874. Photograph by Hughan. Mitchell Library, State Library of New South Wales.

(photos 23, 24). Cattle stations on the west coast continued to employ them as stockmen—a popular job—and of course as house servants and rouseabouts. Visitors staying in hotels and boardinghouses on the west coast would find "labor boys" poling the barges that took passengers and their luggage to and from ships, carrying their luggage to their rooms, and waiting at their dinner tables.[32]

Coastal shipping, both state and private, employed a mixture of Loyalty Islanders and New Hebrideans as firemen, sailors, and boat crews, also popular jobs for which they had a high reputation. In 1879, the administration decided to replace its Loyalty Islands boat crews with New Hebrideans, and placed an order for thirty of them by the next recruiting ship.[33] Thomas remarked that on his voyage around the coast in 1883, a Santo man acted as steward, while half of the crew were New Hebrideans and the rest Loyalty Islanders. He pointed out that they "did all the steering and appeared to know their work as well as any white men."[34] In a petition against the suppression of the labor trade in 1882, the so-called Committee of Caledonian Interests claimed that navigation would suffer drastically from the ban, because there was no possibility of employing penitentiary labor for security reasons, and passage by sea was the chief means of transport to and from the country centers: "The coastal ships, whose role is indis-

Photo 23 Planting pineapples, Nakéty, east coast of New Caledonia. Photograph by Hughan. Mitchell Library, State Library of New South Wales.

Photo 24 Working on a pineapple plantation, Nakéty. Photograph by Hughan. Mitchell Library, State Library of New South Wales.

pensable by reason of our topographical situation and the deficiency of roads, can function only with New Hebrideans; . . . even the steamships and certain government ships use only blacks."[35]

In Noumea, New Hebrideans were seen everywhere, humping loads at the wharves or in the warehouses, moving goods in shops, laboring in hotels and bars, and also in the government service as orderlies, messengers, and convict guards. They were in every household of private settlers or government employees as domestic servants and child minders. Still by far the largest category of labor in the early eighties—not excluding convicts—"Hebrideans" were ubiquitous. Courbet reported in July 1882 that "here [in Noumea] as in the interior, the servants and laborers are, for the greater part, Hebrideans; coastal navigation recruits its sailors among them; plantations employ a great number, the mines employ the rest."[36]

A commission formed in 1883 for the purpose of discussing the merits of reintroducing the labor trade argued that New Hebrideans were irreplaceable in the coffee industry, where they were suited to the work and the only labor that the small settler could afford to pay. "[I]t is above all for the coffee planter that one can say that this immigration is a question of life and death, and coffee is one of the great resources of the country, one of the products on which the greatest hopes are founded. The picking goes on for a large part of the year; this is fairly light but unremitting work and the New Hebrideans are perfect for it. If they should disappear, and it is with all conscience that the Commission states this, the coffee planters are ruined and we have to give up the cultivation of this crop."[37] The commission added that the small concessionaire could afford a New Hebridean "content to live off the land," and receiving low wages at a fixed rate, so he could develop his land much faster. Both the free settler and the *libéré* concessionaire had need of them, for neither could afford any other form of labor.[38]

By the 1880s the occupational distribution was remarkably wide. Of 107 recruits brought by the *Marie* on 7 August 1884, 41 went to domestic service, 43 became laborers, 21 went to the mines, and 2 were employed as coastal sailors. The "laborer" category included both rural and industrial work (for example, 12 were engaged by Draghicewitz, who had a brickworks at Mont Dore and was a general trader in Noumea, and 21 by Gratien Brun, who had cattle stations on the west coast). Of the 21 who went to the mines, 16 were boys aged between eleven and fifteen employed by Puech to sort the nickel ore. The 41 employed in domestic service included all 7 women on the list, as well as 17 boys aged fourteen or under.[39]

The depression in the mining industry, which led to the closure of most of the mines early in 1885, varied the pattern of employment

Photo 25 Workers at the cobalt diggings, Bay of Lebris, north of Houailou. Max Shekleton collection, Noumea.

once again for a few years. Surviving mine workers were either repatriated or diverted to other occupations. Three of the *Marie* recruits, listed as employed by Puech sorting nickel at the mine-face, died before the end of their first term on a coffee plantation at Canala.[40] They were no doubt part of a contingent transferred from the mines when they closed down. But during the mining revival of the late eighties—the period of the second official ban—unregulated "free" New Hebridean labor was going, above all, to the mines. In the years 1888 to 1891, at least 157 imported Oceanians died at the mines, implying by way of a rough calculation that a total of about 628 were so employed at the time, a number curiously similar to that employed at what is considered the peak mining period in 1882.[41] Société Le Nickel specifically referred to 59 of its deceased workers as "free laborers," the only employer to use the category in the death notices, and a habit it dropped after an 1890 regulation enjoined employers to regularize the position of their migrant workers. The Méré mine near Houailou and new mines in the north near Pam appear to have opened and closed in this period. Judging from the death registrations at these places—the only measure available—they employed mostly Oceanian labor.[42] As New Hebridean workers were still being taken to the Chesterfield Island phosphate diggings,[43] and to other small mining enterprises including cobalt diggings (photo 25), the proportion engaged in mining returned to that of former days, despite comments to the contrary from contemporaries, perhaps because imported laborers were officially nonpersons during this period of the ban. Possibly the continuing periods of depression in nickel mining, becoming acute from 1892 to 1895 and again from 1903 to 1906[44]—when workers were once again diverted and fewer new ones imported—added to that impression.

The beginning of substantial imports of Javanese and Indochinese workers in the second half of the nineties tended to overshadow all reference to New Hebridean workers, although a continuous stream of them still arrived, and in the census of 1901 they still far outnumbered the combined total of Asian workers in the colony (1,008 to 638). As Asian workers began to replace Oceanians in the large mining enterprises and in plantation work, the categorization of occupation by race begins to appear in general comments on imported labor: Indochinese were the miners, Javanese the coffee workers, Loyalty Islanders the smartest sailors, and New Hebrideans ideal for domestic service. Popular generalizations, however, were not always in accord with the facts. In the same month, *La Calédonie* reported both that the New Hebrideans were used principally on coffee plantations, and that "We now only use [New Hebrideans] as domestic servants."[45] Certainly these two occupations probably accounted for most of the workers at this time, but imported Oceanians continued to be employed in a variety of occupations, then and later.

In the twentieth century, New Hebrideans were once again employed at the mines. In the years 1906 to 1910, when it became easier and cheaper to import Oceanian workers than in the previous decade, partly because of the new regulations of 1904, and partly because competition from Queensland had ceased, there was coincidentally a surge in mining activity, and New Hebrideans were employed in it, especially in the newer mines of the northwest. The Ballande mine at Kativiti in the Koné district, for example, employed a number of imported Oceanians in this period.[46] In 1912, mining employed more than a fifth of New Hebridean indentured workers,[47] and as late as 1927 work at the mines was still being given as the reason for the return of workers to the New Hebrides "in broken health."[48] Oceanians also participated in the mining industry as foundry laborers when foundries were established at Thio and Doniambo (Noumea), in 1908 and 1910 respectively. In 1931 the foundries united to become the one works at Doniambo.[49]

The proportion of indentured New Hebrideans in urban employment—always large—continued to rise gradually, and was augmented by the "free residents," who, having completed eight years of service and committed no crimes, were permitted to stay in the colony and were free to indulge their preference for working in town, a preference remarked as early as 1881.[50] Domestic service employed many, but the category of "commerce and navigation" was probably the largest employer of Oceanians in the first two decades of the twentieth century. In 1901–1902, the mercantile firm of Maison Ballande took in what was a large number for a single employer—193 Oceanians— presumably for laboring at their docks and stores, and for boat or barge rowing, all of them it seems, working in Noumea.[51] In 1912, 588 New Hebridean workers were officially under contract, and 125 were free residents. Of the indentured workers, 40 percent worked in "commerce and navigation," as against 23 percent in agriculture, more than 20 percent in mining, and under 17 percent in domestic service.[52] Of the 125 "free residents," one can safely assume that none were at the hated mines, and probably very few on the farm: they tended to drift to the towns, especially Noumea, and there take domestic or laboring jobs, with a preference for the latter for the comradeship it offered, particularly in off-duty hours. *Le Néo-Calédonien* commented on the haste with which time-expired workers left their first master to go to Noumea, preferably to work in a situation that gave them more social freedom.[53] That a continually higher proportion lived in the town is borne out by the distribution of death registrations in the *état civil*. While the small numbers of New Hebrideans imported after 1915 were said to be mainly employed in domestic service,[54] in 1921 the British consul in Noumea still listed "rough work in the stores in Noumea as well as in the interior" as a typical occupation for New Hebridean "boys."[55]

"The Fourth Question"

When Governor Feillet in 1899 proposed expanding the intake of Javanese labor, he said that there was not just one labor question, but three: the problem of agricultural labor, labor for public works, and mining labor. *La Calédonie*, virtually the mouthpiece of the governor, for once ventured a small point of difference with Feillet: "There should be, perhaps, a fourth question, which without being as acute as the others, has nevertheless its own importance, and that is [finding] domestic staff. The question of cook and nursemaid is a serious problem which torments numerous small households and solving it is not always easy."[56] The felt need for domestic labor—which Oceanians had been fulfilling for more than thirty years—had clearly not abated. Domestic service, in hotels and restaurants as well as in private homes, had been the most constant if not the largest employer of foreign Oceanians. Mines closed down and farms and businesses went bankrupt, but the demand for servants never wavered, in town or country, and this market profited rather than suffered from economic crises as workers were diverted from other occupations. Yet the use of scarce cheap labor for this purpose involved the settlers in uncomfortable contradictions.

The "labor question" dominated all other subjects in the columns of New Caledonian newspapers from the beginning to the end of the period under study, and pressure was applied to every administration to organize a supply of cheap labor, depicted as the sole requirement for a rapid development of the rich resources of the country. From the beginning of colonization, however, labor had been used in ways very difficult to justify as essential to economic development. When administration officials and troops were assigned convict labor as personal servants, and those with wives allowed to employ them as houseworkers and child minders, private employers were clear about the economic absurdity being perpetrated. Settlers who had no access to this source of labor called it a scandal and an outrage. In a developing country, convict labor should at least have been directed at creating infrastructure, such as road and bridge building, if private employers could not themselves employ them to clear their concessions or till their fields. The so-called *garçons de famille*—convicts in domestic service—were a favorite subject of derision and obloquy directed at the administration by private settlers.[57]

Despite these protests, and even laws against employing convicts as orderlies, the practice continued as long as the penal administration itself. But as soon as the import of Oceanians began and for as long as it lasted, the complaining settlers used them for the very same purpose. Public comment, however, became muted. When labor immigration was in jeopardy, settlers relied on the more persuasive economic argument: agriculture, mining, and commerce would be ruined if their cheap exotic labor were withdrawn. Only occasionally did the indisputable demand for domestics find its way into public comment, and then it sat rather uneasily with the clearer demands of the economy. *La Calédonie* involved itself in contradictions on the question of the importance of domestic labor in relation to industry and agriculture. Complaining of the current high cost of recruiting Oceanian labor, it argued that Loyalty Islanders proved unstable and defective "since the natives of these islands are unwilling, with very rare exceptions, to involve themselves in domestic labor."[58] It was clear that in rural areas there was no clear distinction between field and domestic duties; workers could be called on to do either, depending on the "will of the employer,"[59] and one presumes that the coffee-picking, for example, saw all hands in the fields. When Javanese workers were imported, the ability to employ them in this dual capacity was written into the contract with the Dutch East Indies government, but this, of course, was a superfluity in relation to the Oceanians, who had not even the appearance of a protecting state guaranteeing the conditions of their contract.

Personal service has always been the most elusive form of labor to classify, let alone to publicize or extol. The difficulty arose from the belief—as strongly held by emerging New Caledonian capitalists as by modern analysts—that if a factor cannot be analyzed in terms of economic function it is not fundamental. The efforts of some feminist writers to "economicize" some of the duties of the unpaid housewife, for example, seem to be motivated by the desire to appreciate their value. Such tasks as washing and ironing clothes and tidying the house, although appearing to simply add to the comfort of the family, are described as the "maintenance of the worker" as a unit of production. While some functions, like child care, may be seen in this light, whether workers are more efficient if they live in a tidy house and arrive at work in ironed clothes is decidedly difficult to demonstrate. Nor can freedom from the drudgery of household chores be shown to increase productivity: modern women workers who are not thus freed have not been shown to be less efficient at work. The cost is to their quality of life, not their productivity.

The desire for personal service as a "quality of life" factor is a side-stepped issue—and with good reason, for it is itself a complex of ingredients not all of which are present concurrently and all of which are difficult to encompass—yet it remains a strong motive in determining human priorities. In a colonial society there are many privations, and as the French are notably unwilling to migrate it was particularly difficult to attract settlers to French colonies. One of the positive factors for prospective settlers was (and still is) the opportunity of raising their standard of living, which by no means meant only an improvement in economic terms. How does one classify, for example, the gratification of deference from an inferior? It appears that some settlers in New Caledonia were prepared to trade a better economic condition in their home country for a higher social status in the colonies,[60] and Genovese has argued convincingly that the ownership of slaves in the American South brought a status that was highly sought, even when unprofitable.[61] But personal service not only conferred power and self-regard, it also brought material benefits that rarely earn a mention—more leisure, the ability to avoid the more laborious or boring tasks, and small comforts like a cool drink on a hot day upon command, a meal prepared according to one's own taste and timetable, clean pressed clothes always on hand. The pursuit of an improved lifestyle is often, but not necessarily, related to the quest for status and power. Both were highly motivating factors in the demand for domestic servants, but both can only with strain be related to economic production.

Even when laborers were employed in profit-making enterprises, it did not follow that the hiring of a laborer was productive. It might mean only that entrepreneurs spared themselves certain laborious jobs. As a contemporary French writer said, French citizens believed they were making a considerable sacrifice to leave their homeland, and had no intention of traveling twenty thousand kilometers to do the menial work they had to do at home, but instead expected to develop an estate on which someone else did the drudgery.[62] If married, a settler would have persuaded his wife to come or to join him, not as a housewife doing the meanest chores, but as mistress of a household. When, like many coffee and sugar planters in New Caledonia, settlers had come from societies such as Réunion, where a servile underclass had recently emerged from slavery, this propensity was even greater.

There was also a fifth question, discussed in chapter 14, influencing the demand for imported Oceanian labor: the New Hebrideans were important to their employers for security reasons, for they formed a buffer class between the settlers and those they feared—the convicts, the *libérés,* and the local Kanaks.

Chapter 11

Living and Working in New Caledonia: By Law or Custom?

When the recruits arrived at their workplace, an entirely new life began. They had to conform to a totally foreign régime, work set hours at strange tasks, adapt to a different climate, eat different food, obey orders from an employer who spoke a foreign tongue, and more often than not work and live with Islanders from other places whose languages were equally incomprehensible, and whose powers and intentions of sorcery were unknown. Above all, they had to reconcile themselves to having no recourse to kin support. In themselves these changes must have been traumatic.

The workers were to a large extent dependent on their masters for their living and working conditions. Regulations relating to hours of work, minimum rations of food and clothing, lodging, and discipline were laid down in the 1874 labor code, but there was a loophole clause in most sections allowing for variations to be written into the contract, supposedly agreed to by employers and employees. In 1893 a metropolitan decree superseded this code, and here minimum requirements were stated with no mention of alternative arrangements. But inspection was inadequate in both sets of regulations. Under the 1874 *arrêté* the commissioner of immigration was supposed to make four inspections a year of sites where indentured workers were employed: in fact, such visits were rare. In the 1893 decree, the head of the service was supposed to visit once a year, while the *syndics*—the officers responsible to him—were to do the rounds four times a year. The *syndics* in the interior were normally the district gendarmes who had many other responsibilities: although overburdened, some tried valiantly to do the job, but their reports sometimes went unheeded. The *Inspection mobile* from France, which reported on all aspects of the colonial administration, and on whose word promotions and replacements depended, was the most effective critic of abuses in the system, but it made only intermittent visits and on-the-spot surprise visits were not practicable. No local officer had the exclusive function of inspecting labor conditions.

Hours of Work

Daily hours of labor were prescribed in New Caledonia, unlike Queensland.[1] Hours were set at ten in summer and nine in winter: the workday was twelve and eleven hours long, respectively, but included two hours for meal and rest breaks. Sundays were normally free, but, as laid down in the 1874 code and repeated in the 1893 decree, there remained the obligation "not considered as work" of employees to attend to jobs necessary for the proper maintenance of the establishment—the care of animals, and service maintaining "*la vie habituelle*" on Sundays and holidays—bad news for house servants and farm laborers.[2] On the *livret* it was noted that an employee who was an agricultural laborer must work until 9 o'clock on Sunday morning, and a house servant must be on call all the time, as can be seen in Lolole's *livret* of 1877 (figure 3).

Neither the long hours of work nor the extra time filched from personal servants and from farm hands can be considered unusual by European standards for most of this period.[3] What rendered the situation ambiguous was the clause "except for special agreements which can be inserted into the contract of engagement," a contract over which workers could have no control.[4] As in most matters, the length of the New Hebridean's working day depended on the grace and good sense of the employer and the exigencies of the work: at harvest time, for example, sugar and coffee workers worked as long as was necessary to get the crop in. Joubert claimed that his New Hebridean employees worked "well and willingly" fourteen hours a day.[5] The worker would not have known the hour, so it is perhaps not surprising that although there were complaints of being worked "too hard," there was no appeal to the clock.

Wages

No minimum wage was set by the 1874 labor regulations. As before, wages were to be arranged by agreement and noted in the contract, but twelve francs a month became the standard wage for a man, and nine for a woman or child, with maintenance to be found by the employer. Wages were deducted for days absent from work (presumably through sickness or bad weather), but in the case of illegal absence two days' pay could be deducted for each day's absence. All days absent due to arrest and imprisonment had to be replaced at the end of the term.[6] In the 1893 decree, a minimum wage was set, without reference to agreements in the contract. The minimum wages of women and children were left at the customary sum of 9 francs a month, but men's wages were raised to a minimum of 15 francs.[7] Days off sick, as well as for any other reason, were now to be added to the term of engagement.[8]

Food

Employers were obliged to feed their workers, but early regulations were vague about minimum rations. The day after the first official shipload of indentured laborers arrived in Noumea (9 August 1865) a model contract was issued that set a weekly ration of 6.3 kilograms of rice and 450 grams of salt pork (to be delivered in one serving).[9] The recruits who arrived on the warship *Bonite* in 1867 were to receive a daily ration of 550 grams of biscuit, 200 grams of dried vegetables, 8 grams of olive oil, and 24 grams of salt, with no requirement of animal food.[10] In evidence to the NSW Royal Commission of 1869, Didier-Numa Joubert was unaware of any ration scale: he testified that employers were only expected to provide cornmeal and molasses for their workers. Any meat, fish, or poultry was procured by the workers themselves through arrangement with the indigenous people. He had heard of a list of rations prescribed by the government for Indian workers, but not of one for the "South Sea Islander."[11]

In the 1874 *arrêté*, the minimum daily ration was fixed as follows:

1. Biscuit, 500 gm; Ground corn, 600 gm; Rice, 400 gm. *OR* Rice alone, 800 gm *OR* Rice, 400 gms; taros, manioc, sweet potatoes, 1,500 gms.
2. Salt fish, 100 gms; fresh fish, 250 gms *OR* Salt meat, 125 gms; fresh meat 200 gms *OR* Dried vegetables, 120 gms.
3. Salt, 20 gms.

Child workers under ten years need receive only half these quantities.[12] The ration was not generous. It was appreciably less than that of Indochinese and Javanese workers who came later, and, in the same period, much less than was thought necessary to keep a convict at work.[13] Once again, the regulation did not apply when different provisions had been laid down in the contract.[14] Even if the law about rations had been closely supervised—and nothing suggests that it was—the employer could avoid prosecution through this loophole. However, Julian Thomas, who was capable of criticizing employers—especially French ones—when he believed them at fault, considered that in general "the labourers were fed well, irrespective of any ration scale. It would not be to the benefit of the employers to starve them. All throughout New Caledonia the labour boys were in good condition."[15] Unfortunately, in this as in other matters, a number of employers were incapable of enlightened self-interest. What the worker got to eat depended on what the employer chose to provide: far-sighted or affluent employers no doubt fed their workers well, while poor, stupid, or greedy employers fed them poorly.

New Hebrideans were the cheapest laborers to feed, and in 1882 this formed part of the argument of an employers' group for continuing to import them: it was absolutely essential, they said, that the colony have "cheap labor able to be fed exclusively on the products of the property."[16] These, it seems, were sometimes nothing but corn: on a recruiting voyage in the New Hebrides in 1875, a government agent collected many complaints about insufficient food. "They often told me: 'At Noumea men do not get enough to eat or only get corn; here we only give that to pigs.'"[17] An observer who wrote a litany of complaints to a French journal about their conditions also asserted that some New Hebridean workers were only given "an ear of corn to roast."[18] Domestic servants, who got the leftovers from the table, had a more nutritious and varied diet than many other workers;[19] they were also in a position to purloin food from the kitchen.

Meat was more readily available to employees on cattle stations. Governor Courbet reported in 1882 that such workers, employed in small numbers at each station, were the best fed of the New Hebrideans: there, in addition to a copious ration of rice, they regularly got salted meat, but their employers would also often kill a beast to provide fresh meat. Meat was, as in Queensland where it was cheap and readily accessible, sought after by Oceanians, although this preference held health hazards for them because they were used to a mainly vegetarian diet.[20] The large mining company, Société Le Nickel, perhaps concerned at the alarming death rate of its New Hebridean employees, made an effort to improve their diet by buying land to cultivate "native" crops,[21] and wise supercargoes on recruiting ships bought food where they recruited migrant workers and gave them yams, sweet potatoes, and taro on the voyage, for which those already aboard "quickly abandoned rice and salt beef."[22]

Incidental detail from a variety of sources, however, indicates that, as in many other areas where indentured labor was employed,[23] white rice was the staple food, sometimes the only food. In 1873, in an account of the comparative costs of employing his various kinds of labor, Numa-Auguste Joubert cited the cheapness of their rations as a cost advantage in favor of the New Hebrideans: he said he only had to give them 800 grams of rice per day, whereas he also had to give fish or ox-head to his Kanaks from Paita, Hienghène, and Maré, and curry to his Indians, although four years earlier his father had told Captain Palmer that he gave his Oceanians pork or fish twice a week.[24] The *déporté* Achille Ballière asked how these workers could be expected to produce a good day's work on nothing but boiled rice "that they have to cook themselves as well as they can, which means without salt or pepper, . . . yet they are lucky if they get rice. Often, very often, they have nothing but boiled corn."[25] One of the reasons Islanders gave to recruiters for their preference for Queensland was the monotonous diet of rice in "Noumea."[26] Rice was the staple of Ballande's workers in 1900, a newspaper describing it as "repulsively filthy" and probably contributing to the outbreak of plague among his workers.[27] Rice was a convenience food for employers. It expanded to many times its size when cooked, was easily transportable when raw, and was filling and cheap. That a diet of white rice caused beriberi was not known until the end of the nineteenth century.

Complaints of inadequate rations for New Hebridean workers were common, especially in the bush. The reports of the immigration commissioner indicated to Courbet that where workers were employed in large numbers, such as on coffee plantations, underfeeding of workers was more likely to occur. In one case a planter opted out of the business altogether: Courbet quoted the journal of a government agent who reported that Oceanians from four different islands in the New Hebrides—that is to say, without possibility of collusion—complained that "one of our principal coffee planters" had only given the workers tobacco and told them to find their own food, presumably by trading with local Melanesians; no one had been given the responsibility to see that they got enough to eat.[28] The coffee planter in question was probably one of those whom Courbet caused to be prosecuted as a result of the local inspections he ordered in 1880.[29]

At the end of 1881, during the trial of M de Gimel for cruelty to four of his female workers whom he had punished for stealing manioc, the women complained that they had taken it because they were not given enough to eat.[30] Their complaint was supported by Mrs Atkinson, a neighbor, and by de Gimel's *libéré* overseer, who said he was sometimes out of provisions for his *canaques* for as long as a fortnight at a time and was often forced to send them out to find their own food.[31] In the course of the same hearing, the immigration commissioner, Desruisseaux, described a visit of inspection to de Gimel's property that he made at mealtime. He confirmed that the laborers had manioc, sweet potatoes, and corn to eat, but complained that there was no meat. He then made the surprising statement that he had questioned de Gimel on this matter and had been assured by him that his rations met the legal requirements.[32] De Gimel was right—the provision of meat was not obligatory in the 1874 ration scale—but one might well feel less than confident in an official charged with protecting the rights of workers who depended on the word of an employer for this information.

The decree of 1893 set down a slightly more generous daily ration, making it closer to the ration of the Asian workers (although still less), and omitted reference to alternative arrangements in individual contracts:

Bread, 682 gms, or alternatively husked rice, 800 gms.
Beef, 250 gms, or salt pork or tinned meat, 200 gms.
Salt, 20 gms.
Sugar, 8 gms.
Tea, 3 gms.

The ration could be replaced, by government regulation for a specified time or in specified quantities, by fresh vegetables, root vegetables, and locally grown food.[33] The schedule duly appears in a specimen *livret* of a Solomon Islands worker in 1897.[34] For failing to supply these rations, an employer was liable to a fine of from 16 to 100 francs, not a daunting prospect.

Allusions to the malnourishment of workers did not cease as a result of the new schedule. Two Solomon Islanders before the court in 1894 for deserting their employer complained of maltreatment, including being given "practically nothing to eat." They got four months' jail for stealing food and escaping from imprisonment,[35] but their complaint was not investigated. As late as 1904, Councillor Blandeau referred to an employer who gave his workers insufficient food for four or five years and then refused to pay them.[36] None of the complaints was either contradicted or pursued; none of the employers was brought to justice.

Lodging and Clothing

As in Queensland,[37] the standard of housing was left to the discretion of the employer. The 1874 *arrêté* stipulated only that employers were obliged to provide "by sex and family" suitable and salubrious lodgings for their indentured workers.[38] The many descriptions of different kinds of "kanaka" housing that emerged in Queensland, however, are lacking in the record for New Caledonia; but scraps of information indicate that a similar variety of styles prevailed, that is, huts constructed by the recruits themselves, or wooden barrack-style buildings with bunks, built for them by their masters. At the beginning of 1882, when a sum of money was made available to construct a new depot for immigrant workers, their lodgings were said to be of *torchis*, that is, of mud laced with straw and gravel or (more likely in New Caledonia) of mud used to plaster interlacing twigs, like the "wattle-and-daub" of the early Australian colonists. These dwellings had been devastated by cyclones and repeatedly patched up, but were now pronounced absolutely unusable and to be replaced.[39] In the inventory of the property of Numa-Auguste Joubert to be auctioned in 1877, appear "sixteen houses for lodging *canaques*" that were thatched huts, presumably built by their inhabitants.[40] Julian Thomas described the lodgings of "labor boys" as "out-houses,"[41] probably referring to huts in the yard for domestic servants known in colonial New Guinea as "boy-houses." Where the place of death of New Hebridean workers was not given as a hospital or infirmary, it was usually reported as either "at the employer's place *(chez son engagiste)*" or "in a hut," including those deaths actually on the site of the mine. Where large numbers were employed, wooden buildings of substantial proportions might be used as communal labor quarters, and many deaths of workers for the large mining firm of La Balade occurred "in the house belonging to the company."[42]

The merchant André Ballande, with good intentions of making his workers feel "at home,"[43] had an intermediate solution: he had a large group of huts built on his property at the Bay of Moselle, apparently designed by an architect,[44] and divided according to ethnic community in order to reduce fighting among them.[45] It was probably inevitable that such quarters quickly developed into an insalubrious ghetto: they were the site of the first outbreak of bubonic plague in Noumea at the end of 1899. The anti-Ballande, anticlerical *La Calédonie* took full advantage, asking its readers, if they dared, to go and see the miserable, filthy slums the rich man's *canaques* were forced to inhabit, if they wondered how such a disease could occur in Noumea.[46] But poor hygienic conditions seem to have been the rule for the dwellings of immigrant workers, not only those employed by Ballande. As a category they were the most susceptible to plague, and Governor Feillet's circular to employers explained this partly by reference to the "dirty conditions in which they generally live."[47]

It seems clear that in general not much effort was devoted to the problem of housing servants, and in the subtropical to tropical climate of the colony employers no doubt felt that adequate accommodation could be quite simple, as it was in the workers' home islands; yet the cold in the mornings and nights of the winter season of June, July, and August was something outside the experience of most migrant workers, particularly those from the northern New Hebrides and the Solomon Islands, and certainly would have been severely felt by them. On mining sites in the mountains, the cold was more intense, and when it did not cause health problems would at the very least have been distressing. The rainy months would have been a miserable time for workers in flimsy lodgings.

In the matter of the supply of clothing, the 1874 *arrêté* again deferred to agreed arrangements in the contract, but in default of these, demanded as a minimum the provision of two cotton shirts, two pairs of cotton trousers, and two head kerchiefs per year per man, and two cotton shirts, two dresses or skirts, and four handkerchiefs per year per woman.[48] In the decree of 1893, a similar minimum ration of clothing was to be issued on board the recruiting ship, but the requirement of employers to clothe workers in the colony is not mentioned; however, to the clause about "salubrious lodgings" is added the obligation of the employer to provide a woolen blanket to each employee,[49] and a sample *livret* a few years after the decree spells out slightly more generous issues of clothing than in the 1874 regulations: "1 woollen blanket, 1 woollen shirt, 2 cotton shirts, 2 pairs of trousers [material unspecified], and two hats per man per year, and 1 woollen blanket, 2 shirts, 2 dresses or 2 blouses and 2 skirts [material unspecified], per woman per year."[50]

Lacking on-site inspection reports, one is dependent on stray observations for information about the actual clothing distributed to workers, as distinct from the garments prescribed by regulation. From a preamble to an *arrêté* of 1872, however, it is clear that until that date migrant workers habitually went about "in a state of nudity" (photos 1, 21). This *arrêté,* prescribing minimum clothing, was designed not for the comfort of the workers but to protect the white citizens from a sight that was to them "offensive to decency and public morality." It decreed: "Immigrants from Oceanian islands and archipelagoes may only be landed if they are clothed, the women in a dress, and the men in trousers or in a loin-cloth which covers them from the middle to the knees. It is forbidden to natives, of whatever provenance, to go about town, in the peninsula, on public roads and in the centers of colonization, without being decently clad."[51] The only possible source of clothing was the recruiter or the employer, but the penalty for infringement fell solely on unclad workers. Perhaps the regulation was intended to cover cases where workers discarded their clothing when it became uncomfortable in the heat of the day.

> All natives found insufficiently dressed in a public place will be immediately arrested and taken to the depot of the civil prison, where they will be clothed at the cost of . . . the local administration, which will be reimbursed through days of labor.
>
> Offenders will, in addition, be punished with from one to five days in prison and from one to five francs fine, which will be

doubled in the case of recidivism, without prejudice to more serious penalties which may be imposed by the public ministry according to the circumstances of the offence.[52]

Incidental observations about the dress actually worn tend to fall
into two classes: at one end, patronizing descriptions of indentured
servants on parade in their best finery, for which they might have paid
themselves, or which had been given by an employer; at the other, a
number of complaints about the inadequacy of the clothing supplied
in protecting them from the elements.

Julian Thomas could not resist the opportunity to amuse his readers by describing Hebridean workers disporting themselves in the
Place des Cocotiers on a Sunday afternoon "in gorgeous attire."[53] Several other residents and visitors made similar observations, including
Léon Gauharou, director of the Interior Department, who told a session of the *Council General* in 1895 that evidence of the excellent treatment of indentured workers in the colony appeared every Sunday in
the Place des Cocotiers where "our domestic servants dressed as gentlemen, lounge around with a cigar in the mouth, while *popinées* in silk
dresses and very bright rig-outs, look like ladies of noble birth."[54]
Workers in the interior were less likely to be noticed if they wore
scanty clothing; workers at the *Sans-Culottes* mine wore little more
than a G-string (photo 21). The coffee workers in photos 7 and 22
seem to be in minimum regulation dress—Mother Hubbards for the
women and lap-laps for the men.

Complaints of inadequate clothing in cold weather appeared
early. Governor Pallu de la Barrière remarked that the "creoles of
Bourbon [Réunion] who are numerous in this country" did not take
the trouble to cover their workers, although it could get very cold at
night, and "the New Hebrideans contract chest complaints which
decimate these poor people, always shivering as soon as the sun goes
down."[55] Inadequate covering was not always the fault of employers:
in 1870, an administration employee was convicted of pocketing funds
allocated for supplying New Hebrideans with blankets.[56] In 1882 another critic claimed that in most places in the bush New Hebrideans
"abandoned to the cupidity and brutality of their masters or people
working for them" were sent in the morning to bring in cattle "although naked . . . in the middle of high grass covered with icy dew
which drenches them up to the shoulders."[57] In a report of 1884,
Henri Courmeaux, a strong proponent of the indenture of New Hebridean labor, recommended that "the inadequacy of their clothing"
be remedied, since the colony was colder than their native land: he
believed that an improvement in this respect, as well as assuring them
a "good and healthy diet," would reduce the high rate of chest com-

plaints and dysentery among them.[58] As late as 1904, a councillor remarked that an employer had failed to clothe his workers properly throughout their five-year term.[59] He did not ask for an investigation by the authorities, nor was any charge for this offense brought before the court.

Discipline

The whole point of having an indentured workforce is that it is subject to tight control. Any discussion of the control of indentured workers must distinguish between official and unofficial methods. Penal sanctions were attached to a number of offenses outlined in the regulations, as they were under the indenture system everywhere. These provisions were liberally used by employers, as court records and newspaper notices show. Punishment by fines and imprisonment was also allowed officially but in 1907 considered illegal by visiting inspectors. More direct coercion, however, was used as well.

Under the 1874 *arrêté*, the immigration commissioner or his deputies, the *syndics*, were empowered to decree the immediate dispatch of workers to the prison workshop (*atelier de discipline*) or to the Orphelinat depot for a period of from eight to sixty days for "habitual insubordination."[60] All such days were to be added to the worker's term of engagement.[61] At the *atelier* the regimen was severe: the inmate had to work without pay for an hour longer than the normal working day, was on reduced rations, and while working was forbidden to speak or smoke. These disciplinary provisions were virtually unchanged in the 1893 decree that replaced earlier labor regulations.

In practice, offenses not in the regulations were added to the list of punishable acts (they were later condemned as illegal by the *Inspection mobile*). The arrest and imprisonment of workers for "illegal absence" or "escape" from the place of employment, "disorder," "ill-will" (*mauvaise volonté*), or single acts of "insubordination" at the workplace were reported daily in the newspapers; that the arrest was made at the request of the employer was also mentioned without comment: "The native Sandidi sent to the lock-up on the application of his employer for refusal to work and disorder in town due to drunkenness"; "Cacon, native, arrested on the complaint of his employer."[62] One employer, at least, refused on principle to avail himself of this control, finding it contrary to natural justice to be, as he said, "both plaintiff and judge."[63]

It was small wonder one of the reasons New Hebrideans gave to a government agent for not signing on for New Caledonia was "too much 'carabousse'" (calaboose or prison) there.[64] But "carabousse" was not the employers' favorite method of punishment, for it deprived them of their workers' services, sometimes at an inconvenient time. The problem was more severely felt by employers in the interior where there was no *atelier de discipline* and workers would have to be sent to Noumea. A system grew up—condoned by the Immigration Office but pronounced illegal by the visiting inspectors of 1907—of imprisoning workers in the lockup of the local gendarmerie. Other punishments that suited the requirements of rural employers received official sanction—again, illegally: fines were freely imposed on workers by the immigration commissioner on the evidence of employers, who often got their authorization by telegraph;[65] sometimes the fines were simply imposed by employers themselves. The effect of the fining system is treated at greater length in the next chapter: suffice it to say here that it was an attractive option to employers.

Toward the end of 1898, an ingenious system of Sunday imprisonment was devised to overcome the inconvenience to employers of losing working time. All through 1899 lists appeared in the newspapers on Fridays of *engagés*—now including local Melanesians and Asians as well as New Hebrideans and Solomon Islanders—who were to lose their precious Sunday break through "administrative punishment." Many names appeared for a succession of Sundays. Employers were asked to return "native employees under sentence" to the police station on Saturday evenings; Sunday imprisonment, the notice pointed out, was being implemented "to enable employers to avail themselves of their employees for longer hours."[66] It was part of the system of arbitrary imprisonment to be highlighted by the mobile inspection of 1907 as completely illegal. This measure seems to have been abandoned at the end of 1899, perhaps because of the outbreak of bubonic plague at that time, when unnecessary congregation or movement of "natives"—the prime plague victims—was considered risky.

Despite the severity of the *atelier de discipline* régime, many settlers argued that harsher punishments were necessary because, they said, workers regarded a term at the *atelier* as a holiday. The suggestion that labor at the *atelier* be made harder and more tedious was apparently taken up, for *Le Néo-Calédonien* reported with satisfaction that the inmates were now breaking stones for road-making; it hoped that "refractory servants, and all the New Hebrideans who disturb the peace on Sundays with their shouting and street-fights" would be sent to join them.[67] When criticism by the 1907 mobile inspection forced the administration to abandon all punishment outside the *atelier* system, it was still considered far too attractive to be a deterrent, and in 1909 the *Conseil général* decreed that henceforth indentured workers doing a spell at the *atelier* would be locked up during the whole of their term, except for three half-hour periods during the day, when smoking or any other form of distraction would be forbidden. The maximum publicity was to be given to this regulation so that *engagés* henceforth would know that there would be a "very severe penalty for their follies."[68]

The inconvenience of the legal sanction for many employers led to more summary sanctions becoming the rule. That Oceanian indentured laborers were routinely kicked, cuffed, and pushed about was never seriously disputed in the history of the labor trade. The fact is casually treated in the literature. In his 1882 report, Governor Courbet himself took minor physical violence for granted, concerning himself only with real cruelty: "The natives employed in Noumea by business houses and individuals, constantly under the eyes of authority, are almost all treated appropriately; at least it has never come to our knowledge that the manual corrections so lavishly meted out to them have ever deteriorated into acts of cruelty." The remark about "manual corrections" earned the penciled comment "this is already over the top!" from someone at the ministry in Paris not inured to colonial ways.[69] As in Queensland, Hawai'i, Fiji, and probably any other place where unfree labor was used, physical violence by employers or their overseers was habitually used to secure the obedience of workers.[70] As Courbet said, serious assault was probably uncommon in Noumea; if the presence of officialdom and the gendarmerie was not sufficiently inhibiting, public opinion might well be.

In rural areas, however, the settlers were a law unto themselves. Good employers looked after their workers; others treated them harshly, even cruelly, without having to fear much trouble from the law. Governor Pallu singled out the "créole" immigrants from Réunion as those with "the detestable habit of beating their colored workers," a habit they had brought with them from the former slave colony,[71] but they were by no means the only ones to use violence. In photo 22 it may be observed that the overseer of the coffee workers has a stick in his hand. The New Hebrideans on de Gimel's property at Saint Vincent on the west coast complained to Immigration Commissioner Desruisseaux that the overseer beat them with a whip; Desruisseaux claimed that he had laid a charge against de Gimel but it had been followed by an "*ordonnance de non-lieu*," a ruling that there was no case to answer. Perhaps Desruisseaux was in no position to press the matter, for de Gimel later pointed out that the commissioner himself used a whip on laborers.[72]

There was no provision in the labor regulations prohibiting corporal punishment. Charges of assault against workers could be brought before the courts in the normal way, but very few were, and those initiated by the administration were in Noumea. One man, Julien Déméné was prosecuted several times. In 1878, he was charged with aggravated assault on Tulera, his New Hebridean *engagé*: he was found guilty and fined 16 francs and costs.[73] Not surprisingly, Tulera later appeared on a list of deserters. The following year, Déméné was charged with having assaulted his employee Loubloubsara in 1875, causing his death, an event that had apparently gone unnoticed for four years: this time he was acquitted.[74] In 1881, he was prosecuted for having caused the death of four New Hebridean workers "through imprudence, inattention, negligence or non-observance of the regulations" and of beating and "using force and other assaults" on these four men and several other New Hebridean employees. He was acquitted on the first charge and given one month's prison for the second.[75] One might reasonably have expected, given his record, that an order debarring him from employing unfree labor would be made, but there was none, nor were any others guilty of abuse so debarred, although a proposal that they should be was made from time to time.[76] The extremely light penalties were in themselves no deterrent.

In the bush it appears that brutal behavior occurred with few or no ill consequences for the perpetrator. A propos of a demand from the Immigration Office that his New Hebridean employee Romboutoula be paid, Canala coffee planter Evain casually replied that the department's records were defective, as the man had died three years before as a result of blows from an iron bar given him by a *libéré* overseer.[77] There is no record of a prosecution in this case. Also in Canala, some years later, a *libéré* storekeeper, on the property of coffee planter Laurie, was alleged to have hit Manlié over the head with an iron bar.[78] A deserting Solomon Islander, Babai, claimed to have been beaten by his master, Champion, a settler in Bouloupari: Babai was punished, but his charge was not investigated.[79] When Tamakoira allegedly refused to load mineral at a mining site in Thio, he had a fight with his overseer, Benjamin Booth, who killed him with a knife: Booth was sentenced to two years in prison for "negligent homicide."[80]

Of course, Oceanians were not the only indentured laborers to suffer violence. Casual references to blows, kicks and supervision with *nerf de boeuf* (a cosh or blackjack) ready in hand appear just as frequently in reference to Asian employees.[81] In 1925 a law was passed in Indochina forbidding the corporal punishment of "natives," and New Caledonian employers found to their surprise that this extended to Indochinese workers abroad. An overseer was prosecuted shortly afterward for beating his "Tonkinese" worker with a *nerf de boeuf,* but he was let off with a suspended sentence, presumably because he did not know the rules had changed.[82]

The Customs of the Country

While the trial of de Gimel, mentioned earlier, was probably, as Courbet believed, atypical in the degree of callousness shown by the young settler, it is worthy of attention for the light it shed on what was considered customary practice in the interior. De Gimel's property was at

Saint Vincent, but the case was heard in Noumea and was amply reported in several issues of *Le Progrès,* whose *déporté* editor was defending the *libéré* overseer. The trial was attended by the British vice-consul, whose account formed the basis of the consul's report to the foreign minister to give him "some idea of the state of things now prevailing here, with respect to the treatment of imported laborers by their employers."[83]

De Gimel was accused of cruelty to four of his New Hebridean female workers. The fact that he was prosecuted at all was a matter of chance. The charge arose not from the complaint of his workers but from incidental information given by a former *libéré* overseer in the course of a case against de Gimel for cattle stealing. Nor would the word of a *libéré* by itself have carried much weight: the crucial corroborating testimony came from Mrs James Atkinson, wife of a young English settler. De Gimel was charged, under Article 311 of the penal code, with having committed violence against the four women.[84] Undisputed facts in the case were that, in an attempt to make them confess to stealing manioc, de Gimel had had them hanged by the neck, with the tips of their toes barely touching the ground. From time to time the rope was yanked so that they choked and believed they would die. Afterward they were put in the stocks.

Mrs Atkinson, who was a guest of the de Gimels during the absence of her husband, testified that during a meal the conversation turned to cruelties to colored workers and the way they were treated. De Gimel mentioned that he had four *popinées* to punish that very evening, and invited her to attend. After dinner, she went out and saw the four women in front of the verandah, "dirty and in rags, trembling and weeping." De Gimel asked them why they had stolen manioc; they did not reply. They were then led to the cellar, where two were tied with a collar and a rope to the ceiling; two others were hanged from trees outside. According to her, they were hanged for about twenty minutes; they were gasping for breath as the rope was tightened, and very distressed; they were screaming as much as they were able while half-suffocated. One was told, "You know you'll be killed if you don't answer [that is, confess]," and she replied, "It's all the same to me." [*Ça m'est égal* in the French report; her Bislama words were not recorded.] During the simulated hanging, said Mrs Atkinson, de Gimel continually hit the women hard in the face. Afterward he said, "Look how black my hand is from having hit those dirty niggers." Asked whether she had interceded with M de Gimel and his wife, Mrs Atkinson said she was told that she was stupid, that she was not familiar with "the customs of the bush," and that once he [de Gimel] had put a *canaque* on a bed of red ants after beating him for having picked the pocket of another *canaque.*

De Gimel replied that her account was "perfectly correct, but idi-

otic and exaggerated. Apart from that she has an excellent memory."
He said the whole thing was just a joke. His aim was just to intimidate
the women to make them confess. They did not suffer at all. Their
feet never left the ground for an instant. He confirmed that the next
day they were put in irons. He vigorously denied the story of the red
ants, saying that this had occurred during the time of his predecessor,
Schiele. He might have slapped the women two or three times while
they were tied up; he couldn't remember. The following illuminating
exchange then occurred between the judge [president of the court]
and the accused:

Judge:	And you think that without such treatment it would be impossible to be obeyed by New Hebridean *engagés?*
De Gimel:	It would be impossible.
Judge:	Then don't take any, don't use *canaques.*
De Gimel:	Mrs Atkinson has exaggerated. She is very young, very naive, she's just come from England. Many English claim to love the niggers and they do the same as us, if not worse.
Judge:	We are in the presence of facts which as admitted by you are regrettable.
De Gimel:	I have admitted putting natives in irons, but all my neighbors, all the settlers do the same. The Immigration Commissioner himself keeps a whip behind the door and he uses it on the *canaques* we send him. So you would have to prosecute everybody. One has to consider the customs of the country.

As Courbet said, referring to this incident, "certain property-owners
have almost come to look upon [such treatment] as lawful."[85]
    More revealing still of the customary mentality, perhaps, was the
levity with which the trial was conducted and reported. The fact that
the victims were women seemed to add to the hilarity. The first witness was described in the newspaper report as "a big girl very well put
together by Jove," and when she denied having relations with the
overseer it was comically portrayed as "with the virtuous indignation
and modesty of an outraged native virgin." When another woman
came up to the bench to show the rope with which she had been
hanged, it was "amid the laughter of the court."[86] The British vice-
consul reported that much grossness was omitted from the newspaper account, and that the judge had to reprimand both de Gimel
and his wife for "joking, laughing, grimacing, and making loud comments on the evidence."[87] But the judge himself, it seems, could not
refrain from lighthearted comments, such as "Come now, it's disgusting. Making *popinées* go down to the cellar at eight o'clock in the

evening," and "one certainly can't have much to do in the bush to go in for such exercises after dinner."[88] The tone of the whole proceedings gave the strong impression that de Gimel's behavior, while somewhat bizarre, was not considered a serious matter. The principle of physical assault, arbitrary punishment, and the use of irons elicited no censure from the court; the accused had simply gone a little too far. On the grounds that the defendant "had only meant to intimidate" his workers, he was let off with a derisory fine of 10 francs—the same amount (although almost a month's wages to them) often exacted from New Hebrideans for being drunk and disorderly. The *libéré* informant, who had executed de Gimel's orders, was fined 15 francs. When the prosecution of this case was set in train, the director of the Interior Department boasted that in cases of malnourishment and cruelty "the immediate intervention of the Administration has borne witness to its vigilance,"[89] but the penalty mocked such intervention, which was in any case rare.

After the trial, other "customs of the country" had to be attended to. De Gimel alleged that Mrs Atkinson had contravened the rules of hospitality by informing against him while she was his guest: James Atkinson took pains to point out that he had not laid the charge against his neighbor, for it was unthinkable for a gentleman to report what his wife had seen while a guest under his roof. Social conventions, it appears, took precedence over the question of cruelty to New Hebridean laborers. The explanation did not save Atkinson from being "called out" by de Gimel. Dueling was of course illegal, but "custom" prevailed. With pistols at twenty-five paces, the duel took place at the Magenta racecourse on the evening of 6 January 1882. Both missed, but honor was satisfied.[90]

The British vice-consul considered the whole trial a travesty of justice: he pointed out that the doctor testified that there were no signs of violence on the women's bodies, but that he did not say, because he was not asked, that his inspection was made weeks after the incident. The *prosecuting* counsel asked for a light sentence! The court adjourned for five minutes "to consider its judgment," and although (timed by the clock in the courtroom) the vice-consul saw the judge walking on the verandah for three of those five minutes, His Honor reappeared with a judgment that occupied ten minutes in the reading, suggesting that it had been written some time beforehand. Consul Layard concluded his report, "After reading this case I am sure Your Lordship will not wonder that I have strongly urged against our India fellow-subjects being brought as coolies to this country. God forbid such should ever be allowed. I have marked this dispatch 'Confidential' as I have no wish to be requested to stand target for M. de Gimel at 25 paces!"[91]

Transfer of Workers

From time to time, through the overcommitment of employers, their bankruptcy, death, or departure from the country (the last very frequent in New Caledonia) indentured laborers were often consigned to a new master before the expiry of their contract. The intention of selling the remaining part of the indenture was advertised thus in the newspapers:

> *For transfer: the contract of a New Hebridean couple.*
> *Apply to Messrs. Barrau and company.*[92]

or

> *For transfer: contract of a young New Hebridean canaque valid to the 6th of*
> *September 1897. Offers received up to the 14th instant by M. Victor Giraud,*
> *official receiver in the Courché bankruptcy.*[93]

Opponents of the labor trade drew the parallel with slavery. Victor Schoelcher claimed that the *engagé* was traded like property: "When property is sold, the *engagé* working on it is lumped with the domestic animals of the farm; like them, whether he likes it or not, he passes into the hands of the purchaser. Considered a tool with two arms, he is handed over to the buyer along with the other tools of wood and iron, in a word with all the things belonging to the property."[94] Certainly, bills of sale referred to indentured workers under the same head as other property. The auction of the bankrupt Joubert's property in 1877 included in its advertisement, after the outbuildings, the heading *"Engagés,"* stating that "thirteen *canaques* . . . the said *engagés* having a term more or less long to do," were part of the sale. Another notice from Noumea appearing in an Australian journal reported that X of New Caledonia had "sold all the working bullocks and engagements of native labor."[95]

The law provided that transfers were to take place in the presence of the *syndic* and were only to occur with the mutual consent of the interested parties,[96] but as in Hawai'i and Queensland,[97] many transfers took place informally. The British resident commissioner for the New Hebrides believed that such traffic took place even between island groups: "[E]very year many natives, male and female, recruited nominally for service in this Group, are, soon after engagement, transferred, or to use the term commonly employed, 'sold', with or without their consent, and, I believe without reference to the French Residency, to people in New Caledonia."[98] His view is supported by advertisements in the newspapers by the Société Française des Nouvelles Hébrides, such as the following:

Transfer of New Hebridean workers.
For transfer, the contract for three years of several canaques and
popinées. Apply to the Société Française des Nouvelles-Hébrides at
Noumea.

As discussed in chapter 6, it also explains the many entries on the passenger list of steamers coming from the New Hebrides in the twentieth century, such as "one boy for M. Bourdois, 1 popinée for Mme. Choyen."[99]

In 1907, Inspector Revel found that indentured laborers often passed from one employer to another without any official intervention. No prosecutions had taken place, so nobody in Noumea took any notice of the regulations, not bothering either to declare that a worker had left their service or that another had entered it. Revel remarked that the illegality was so well tolerated in Noumea that the *procureur-général* himself (head of the Justice Department) was guilty of it.[100]

Moreover, Noumea also became an entrepôt for supplying Melanesian servants to the Australian colonies. As it was illegal to indenture island laborers in New South Wales and Victoria, and only legal for work in the sugar industry in Queensland after 1884, servants for Australia were ordered through Noumea. Ludovic Marchand had heard of this practice from a government agent on a Queensland ship, but he had himself observed it when he sailed to Sydney on the *City of Melbourne.* "There were several young blacks from the New Hebrides on this ship who were being sent from Noumea to Sydney. Two out of three of these remarkably handsome and well-proportioned persons were addressed (like parcels) to the General Manager of the Australian Navigation Company, and one to the purser of a ship of that company. These gentlemen, like so many others, not being able to procure New Hebridean servants for themselves in Australia, have them taken to Noumea which thus serves as an entrepôt for blackbirding in the provinces of New South Wales and Victoria."[101]

The British labor trader William Wawn learned of the practice from a French recruiter: "Many of these boys [recruited by French ships], it is said, are persuaded to go to Sydney from Noumea and take service there, for which their late masters receive a money equivalent as high as £10 per head."[102] A church document in 1883 analyzing immigration statistics mentioned that, out of 5,148 workers recruited between 1874 and September 1882, 100 had "left for Sydney," without having been paid.[103] The transfer of New Hebridean workers from Noumea to Australia does not seem to have troubled New Caledonian authorities any more than the transfer to Noumea of those recruited for service within the New Hebrides. In a report of 1888 on the history

Photo 26 Aboard the recruiting ship *Effie Meikle* (1880s). Mitchell Library, State Library of New South Wales.

of 56 Utupuans who were recruited by the *Effie Meikle* in June 1881, the director of the Interior Department named 4 who had "gone to Australia," whereupon, it seemed, his responsibility for them ceased.[104] New Hebrideans traded to Australia were not necessarily all children, but probably all became domestic servants, otherwise they would have had problems with organized white labor, opposed to the intake of non-European workers.

Custom and Law Enforcement

Laws governing conditions of work for indentured laborers were, by the standards of the time, reasonably protective. Some of the French regulations were earlier and better than those laid down in British colonies, such as the limitation on the hours of work. The problem lay in their enforcement.

The duty of policing labor regulations on the ground fell to the *syndic* or district officer, usually the local gendarme, who had a vast number of other responsibilities. Special labor inspectors were never appointed, although this measure had been suggested as early as 1877 by Inspector Cuinier, on a mission from France to inspect all aspects of the colony. Cuinier found that the administration failed to provide adequate supervision and protection to its New Hebridean labor: "Not all the employers fulfil their obligations and there result from this some occurrences likely to compromise this source of labor. A supervisory committee composed of settlers has just been appointed. I fear that it will be still less attentive than the administration in supervising the fulfilment of contracts. One would find, it would seem, more safeguards in the creation of a position of a salaried Inspector."[105] Fifty-two years later, in 1929, Inspector Gayet was still recommending that an independent inspector of labor be appointed as a minimum measure of reform, having observed that a tour of inspection ordered by the local department in 1927 had been resisted by some Caledonian employers "who do not understand that the supervision of the administration over labor . . . is not simply vexatious, but constitutes a safeguard indispensable to the recruitment and maintenance of indentured labor."[106]

Despite its many shortcomings, Queensland's system of appointing inspectors of Pacific Islanders probably produced better results. After 1868 there was a salaried inspector responsible to the Immigration Department in every district in Queensland in which Pacific Islanders were employed. Although at least one early inspector was assiduous in reporting abuses, the system as a whole was fairly ineffective until 1880, when an act was passed defining their role as defender of the workers' interests.[107] However, the fact that the workers had someone to turn to in the locality, and the mere threat of on-the-spot intervention, probably reduced the incidence of gross abuse. Further Queensland legislation in 1885 strengthened the force of inspectors' complaints to the authorities.[108] The district inspector was supposed to supervise the half-yearly payments of the laborers' wages, to hear complaints, which he was bound to investigate, inspect the workplace, give advice to workers, or perform practical functions like banking savings on their behalf. Although some were complaisant and unwilling to antagonize employers, others gained the confidence of the Islanders, who did not hesitate to go to them if they thought they had been wronged. Inspectors were never sufficiently numerous, nor could even the most conscientious of them prevent transgressions of the law; they could, however, ensure that the regulations were taken seriously. In New Caledonia, two visiting inspectors pointed out that the nonenforcement of labor regulations in the colony was one reason why prospective recruits chose other destinations,[109] and officials in the islands relayed complaints of returns against former employers, warning of damage to the colony's reputation,[110] but colonial custom was slow to change.

Chapter 12
"Perpetual Theft"

> [N]ative workers in the colony are cheated as much as possible
> out of their wages, and the Immigration Office has always given
> this perpetual theft all needful cooperation. It is unconscious
> complicity—but how culpable!
>
> CHIEF INSPECTOR FILLON, 1907

The hardships borne by indentured laborers were, in theory, compensated by wages that could be converted into coveted goods to be taken home. In the first few years, no complaints were recorded about the rewards given for their labor. But after the state opted out of its managerial role at the end of the 1860s, there was a grave problem in the just payment of wages.

Under the provisions of the 1874 labor code, the laborer received scant protection in this matter. There was no fixed minimum wage: wages were to be arranged by agreement between employer and employee (Article 35) but to be noted on the contract. The code was based on the notion of a free contract between employer and employee, although it was patently absurd to consider the parties on an equal footing for negotiation, nor could the workers verify any oral agreement by reading the contract.

Wages were to be paid in cash every three months before a *syndic.* In the case of nonpayment of "all or part" of wages due at the expiry of the contract, the employer would be given a month to pay, after which the immigration commissioner "could, after obtaining the authority of the Colonial Secretary, take him to court for the recovery of the money on behalf of the employee" (Article 28). Infractions were to be heard in a magistrate's court *(tribunal de simple police),* and the penalty for nonpayment was a fine of 10 to 15 francs, with the possible addition, according to circumstances, of imprisonment for three to five days (Articles 61 and 62).

Even on paper, the sanctions provided virtually no deterrence to employers who chose to cheat their workers. In the event of prosecution, the penalty was derisory: the fine was roughly equivalent to a month's wages, and rather less than the fine normally applying to a European caught drunk in public. The month's grace to pay at the end of the contract was already serious for the laborer: if discharged workers were not on board the repatriating vessel on the appointed day, they lost their right of repatriation. They were, in any case, obliged to work for their employer or some other employer up to the moment of their departure, or else be sent back to the depot to labor on public works without pay (Article 73). The prospect of delays occasioned by legal procedures to recover the money, should they occur, was even more daunting. Considerable pressure was therefore exerted on employees whose masters owed them money either to reengage in the hope of recouping it or to return home empty-handed. Both options were frequently taken.

No change occurred in the regulations concerning wage payment until the decree of 1893, which for the first time set a minimum wage: 15 francs for men and 9 francs for women and children (Article 55). But it did not change the procedures for redress against employers who failed to pay. The fine for those convicted was raised to between 50 and 100 francs, but all mention of imprisonment was dropped.[1] In practice, the prosecution of an employer for failure to pay was unlikely, although some cases did occur.

Weak though the labor legislation was, settlers found it unnecessary and vexatious. A form of "custom law" replaced it. Before the 1893 legislation, the customary rate of payment for a first engagement was commonly about 12 francs for a man and 9 francs for a woman or child, although 15 francs was sometimes paid for a man and as little as 6 for children. A higher rate was considered the due of a reengaged worker. The wage was often paid by advances in kind or by payment in kind at the expiry of the contract, two practices expressly forbidden by both the 1874 and 1893 codes. Advances in kind were extremely advantageous to employers, who generally also supplied the goods, marked them up to pay themselves a handsome profit, and had the opportunity of keeping the worker continually in their debt. Cash payments were often irregular, if they occurred at all, and the requirement to pay every three months before an official was flouted as a matter of course.

Evidence that laborers were regularly defrauded of their wages is abundant. As early as 1870 a writer claimed that in that year alone, the administration received complaints of failure to pay wages against some of the local big-men—settlers Blanchot, Bouscarel, Sleath, Peyraud, Jean-Baptiste Dezarnaulds, and Joubert. Of these only Sleath was obliged to pay. As for the others, "more or less protected by the Church or the administration, they continue to consider [the workers] like their own cattle; they don't pay them and they keep them forever." The writer justly asked, "How many other blacks not knowing how or not being able to complain have the same problem?"[2] Independent confirmation for the case of Joubert comes from his 1877 bankruptcy papers, which reveal that he had not paid his New Hebridean and Indian workers.[3]

In September 1879, Marchand wrote to Schoelcher that some employers of indentured laborers managed to avoid paying their workers at all, merely giving them a few worthless articles and bad guns at the end of their term.[4] Five years later, government agent Dangeville unwittingly confirmed Marchand's claim in extraordinary detail. As he was about to repatriate nine men at Tomman Island, south of Malakula, he heard them murmuring among themselves, and inquired the reason. They replied that they had worked for Laurie of Canala for five to five-and-a-half years but now were returning with only bad guns and shoddy goods. On examining their guns and their boxes, he could only agree with them. The guns, he said, were not worthy of the name, they were "children's toys" and in bad condition; the chests were made of old planks, and although small, were far too large for what they contained—rubbishy goods (which he listed and costed item by item) worth 100 to 150 francs at the most—a sixth of what they were supposed to have earned.[5] To avoid reprisals from their friends on the beach, Dangeville exchanged the worthless guns for two muskets from the ship, keeping the originals to send with his complaint to the administration.

Dangeville also reported that men he repatriated to Gaua in the Banks Group complained of being underpaid and kept beyond their time by their employers, the missionaries at St Louis, east of Noumea. Because the returns were well treated on board, he said, the *Marie* had no trouble from their relatives on the beach; but they summed up their feelings pretty well: "Noumea no good. Noumea no pay," they explained, refusing to send fresh recruits to the ship.[6] Since 1879 New Hebrideans had been telling French naval commanders in the islands that the reputation of "Noumea" as a bad payer made them prefer Queensland and even Fiji.[7] There were other reasons for the unpopularity of "Noumea" as a destination but "small fellow pay"[8] was a recurrent theme.

Labor trading was a competitive affair and by 1880, at last, there was some awareness that the failure of some New Caledonian employers to pay their workers made Queensland and Fiji more attractive. At the *Aurora* Commission Inquiry in 1880, the commissioners asked whether the preference for Queensland was related to the fact that laborers were better rewarded there, and learned from a settler, Douglas Carter, that he was employing a New Hebridean called Bili who had not yet been paid by his first employer, Penaud, for whom he had worked for three years. Bili had intended going home at the end of his first term, but could not "for lack of money." As return passage money was supposed to have been paid in advance to the Immigration Office, he may have meant by this that Bili was ashamed or afraid to go home empty-handed, although it is quite possible that Bili's first employer also neglected to pay his installments of repatriation money to the department. Carter added that he knew other laborers in the same situation as Bili.[9] Both Dangeville and Carter appeared to assume that these cases were, though unfortunate, not common. Dangeville said that the rest of his returns were satisfied with their rewards, and he believed that the ex-employees of substantial industrialists and the administration itself paid their workers regularly, on the evidence of well-filled boxes and contented returns. This may have been true, for large employers had the resources and the incentive to be more farsighted in this matter; but it is also the case that cheated employees were less likely to be among those repatriated—and, of course, a high proportion of the many who died (at this time more than 60 per thousand per annum in years free of epidemics) were probably never paid.

The evidence of failure to pay is too general to exempt whole classes of employers. Between July 1874, when the registries of the Immigration Office seem to have begun, until September 1882, the time that the first suspension of the labor trade took effect, official records show that 5,148 Oceanians were introduced.[10] According to a document held at the archives of the archdiocese in Noumea, the records of 3,632 of these, or 70.55 percent, bore no mention of any payment. Of those, 1,046 had died and 810 had been repatriated unpaid: the rest, presumably, reengaged in the hope of making up their losses.[11] Those repatriated might, however, have been paid according to "custom," in goods of the employer's choice, at the expiry of their contract, without any payment having been inscribed on their *livret*.

The law about payment in cash every three months was treated with contempt. In 1875 Governor Pritzbuer had issued a warning that article 43 of the 1874 code, forbidding payment in kind to workers in lieu of cash wages, was to be strictly observed.[12] Subsequent warnings of almost identical wording appeared again and again in the *Moniteur* to 1891, suggesting that employers continued to disregard them. Indirect evidence of this, however, is rendered superfluous by the brazen assertion of the *Néo-Calédonien* that the law was, and should remain, a dead letter. When in 1881, under the stronger administration of Governor Courbet, a more serious attempt was mounted to supervise proper payments to indentured laborers, the newspaper protested vigorously. It published a letter from an employer described as "very experienced," arguing that the original *arrêté* had been the brainchild of Governor de la Richerie, who had a passion for vexatious regulations, but it had never been applied. He pointed out that the three governors who succeeded him—Alleyron, Pritzbuer, and Olry—had all allowed Article 43 to "sleep in the dust." Yet now when business was in a critical situation,[13] it appeared that employers were to be forced to pay cash to their workers every three months instead of paying them in goods at the expiry of their contract "as has been the practice up to this time."[14] So entrenched was this custom that one settler, at least, mistook it for law: in a letter to his mother, Vernon Lee Walker, an employer as well as a labor trader, explained to her that "The buyer [*sic*] has to give them wages at the rate of from 9 to 15 francs per month, but does not pay them until their engagement is finished."[15]

This customary method of payment would have enabled "buyers" to entirely escape payment of wages to workers who died before the end of their contract, and in the 1870s and 1880s that constituted more than a quarter of them. Perhaps employers considered this just, because they would not have got full value for the passage money they had paid to the broker if the worker died prematurely. From another perspective, it cannot have promoted concern for the health of workers as they neared the end of their term.

In 1885 the immigration commissioner announced that employers who had not settled accounts with their indentured workers of all origins, or who owed money to the Immigration Fund (advances of repatriation payments, hospital dues, deferred wages, and so on) would no longer be able to engage such labor.[16] Even this obvious measure, which did not go as far as *withdrawing* labor from recalcitrant employers, let alone punishing them, proved unenforceable. The so-called free immigrants who came during the second banning of the labor trade had not even paper guarantees to protect them. The reforms in the 1893 decree related mainly to recruiting procedures, since kidnapping scandals had caused some unfavorable press in Europe: in the matter of payment of wages, little changed. The problem remained acute beyond the end of the century.

Fines

In his report of 1892, Commandant Gadaud not only complained about the failure of employers to fulfil their engagements, but also alluded to the practice of fining workers for infractions, keeping them in constant debt.[17] The administration had freely adopted the practice of fining workers on the complaint of their employers for "illegal absence" or "refusal to work," as well as for petty offenses such as drunkenness, or being found in the town after 8 PM. The practice proved to be illegal, but the imposition of fines suited the administration, always short of money, and was favored by most employers, who did not thereby stand to lose the services of employees at an inconvenient time and reaped the benefit that laborers might be forced to work an extra period in order to repay the debt incurred by the fine. In one revealing case, however, an employer called Maestracci actually requested that the fine and costs incurred by his worker Bozérou be foregone by the administration. He said that Bozérou had been punished by the courts in December 1883 for "drunkenness and rebellion," receiving one month's jail and a fine of 200 francs, which with costs amounted to 327 francs: he had done the prison sentence but had not been able to pay this sum, which was equal to fifty percent more than the total of his wages for the two years he had worked for his master. The reason for Maestracci's petition—which was granted—was that Bozérou had saved the life of a settler, Charles Simon, a few days before.[18] More than a year had passed since the infliction of the penalty, without protest from Maestracci, so it is fair to assume that workers not having done such noble deeds simply had to suffer this loss. The justice system was hard on Oceanians, whose court costs included an extra ten or fifteen francs (at least a month's wages) for the services of an interpreter.[19]

Fining in the courts was bad enough, but some employers inflicted fines themselves, putting employees in their debt. The Paris paper *l'Eclair* quoted an example that it claimed came from a report of a *syndic* sent to the bush in January 1898 to examine stories of wages overdue for three or four years: according to an extract sent to the *Comité de la Défense des Indigènes,* reproduced in the paper (and reprinted in the local paper *La Calédonie* with much negative comment), the *syndic* was received with great hostility, especially in Canala and Hienghène, where the settlers claimed that the governor supported their right not to pay in the prescribed manner. One even denied the administration's right to interfere in any matter concerning "his" *engagés,* "whom, he said, he considered less than his dogs." Weathering the storm, the *syndic* established that a large number of employers had assumed the right to impose fines on their workers and never paid them wages. According to *l'Eclair,* the report was filed and never acted on,[20] a familiar fate for the reports of *syndics* that were adverse to the settlers. Indeed Governor Feillet appeared to be quoting from the very same report when he mentioned in a letter to the minister for colonies in the following year that a settler was threatening to make trouble for him at the ministry in France and also in "certain organs of the Press." Feillet wanted to put the minister in the picture first, in case the settler, Pesnel of Nakéty, made good his threats. Pesnel had paid his workers by advances in kind, which was not regular but "a constant practice in the colony, and the administration, who cannot prevent it, in fact leaves . . . the employers and employees to arrange this to their own satisfaction." Such a remark supported the claim of the settler quoted in *l'Eclair* that the governor had no objection to this method of payment. But Feillet could not condone Pesnel's imposition of fines "on various pretexts: laziness at work, loss or deterioration of tools, etc." Moreover, he owed the deferred pay of his workers—a sum of 90 francs—to the department's funds. Pesnel had reacted badly to remonstrances, had shown an "incorrect" attitude, and had unjustly attacked the officer concerned.[21]

Matters had not improved by 1904, when some members of the *Conseil général* expressed disquiet at the continued abuse of the rights of indentured laborers. Blandeau quoted the case of an employer who, having worked his laborers for four or five years on insufficient rations and given them next to no clothing, not only evaded his responsibility to pay them at the end of their term, but also contrived to have them still in his debt. He questioned the ability of the administration to deal with the maltreatment of indentured laborers. He was supported by James-Bernard Dezarnaulds (the son of Jean-Baptiste Dezarnaulds), who said that when wages were owed to workers, more often than not the department was content to put the matter in the hands of its lawyers, where it rested for years. He requested a list of arrears in wages, a demand he was forced to repeat two years later. Léon Vincent expressed regret that employers who had not paid their workers were still able to hire new workers from the Immigration Office (so much for the decision of 1885 not to allow recalcitrant employers to engage more labor!) and Sylvestre Leconte insisted that the Immigration Office refuse absolutely to allot labor to employers who owed money to either the department or their workers. Dezarnaulds asked the administration to enforce the 1893 decree strictly.[22] Apart from a humanitarian concern, the heightened interest in reform was probably linked to the increasing difficulty in recruiting workers.

This debate also made clear that not only had employers been able to cheat their workers, but they had also managed to defraud the administration by not paying the advances of passage money and other due payments, a theme I shall take up later. The colonial secretary replied weakly that he had sent a circular to all employers requesting payment of dues that had resulted in the return of 20,000 francs: he admitted that 86,000 was still outstanding,[23] a figure the *Inspection mobile* in 1907 found to be grossly understated.

In a *Conseil général* debate of 1906, Councillor Laroque, director of the firm Ballande et Fils, voiced concern at the amount of money anticipated by the Immigration Office as receipts of fines on indentured laborers for the year 1907: the amount came to 26,000 francs, constituting nearly 23 percent of the department's entire revenue. As the fines were inflicted arbitrarily by the *syndics* and not by the courts, he argued that it was immoral that the money should go into the de-

partment's funds, quaintly suggesting that it be earmarked for charitable works instead. His colleagues demolished his proposal, the
acting immigration commissioner, Engler, declaring that the fines
were not as heavy as they appeared, considering that they were now
spread among Asians as well as New Hebrideans and indentured
Kanaks. In reply to a question about arrears in wages, raised again by
Dezarnaulds, the secretary-general finally disclosed that the sum of
4,699.79 francs was owing to indentured laborers of diverse backgrounds,[24] which was an average of about two days' wages for every
laborer in the colony.[25] This sum also was grossly underestimated.

Although it was common talk in Noumea that some employers
cheated their indentured workers out of their wages, among other
abuses, it was still usually said in the same breath that the bad boss was
the exception rather than the rule. In 1907, the report of the *Inspection mobile* shattered that myth. Inspectors Revel and Fillon found that
evasion of payment was widespread, and that this was hardly surprising when nonpaying employers were never prosecuted by the
Immigration Office, nor had their workers withdrawn from them, nor
were prevented from engaging new ones: "Rare indeed are the employers who come to pay their workers before the *syndic* every three
months. . . . It is not just a few months of arrears that have been tolerated, but years; whole engagements have been allowed to run out
without any wages being paid; the poor wretches who have lost, or will
lose, the fruit of their labor in this way are innumerable."[26] Inspector
Revel quoted the case of a New Hebridean woman who had completed two contracts without having been paid anything, as well as
an Indochinese and a Javanese couple who were owed years of wages
without hope of redress, emphasizing that these were by no means
exceptional cases: "And these cases could be multiplied at random
from the registers."[27] He believed that the total owed to indentured
workers of all backgrounds would undoubtedly exceed 100,000 francs
for employees in Noumea alone—a far cry from the 4,000-odd admitted by the secretary-general in the council debates of the previous year.

Revel ordered that a list of arrears in wages be drawn up and every
effort made to recover the money owed to those "unfortunate people
who have worked so hard and waited too long for it."[28] Fillon commented that total reparation was not possible: some workers had
died, some had been repatriated, some had deserted. It was unlikely
that accounts were in sufficiently good order to determine the exact
state of affairs: "Numerous *engagés* will remain victims of their masters' duplicity and the blind negligence of Immigration."[29]

In his reply, Engler asserted that it was impossible under current
regulations to enforce the prompt payment of wages. He explained

that his department sent a series of three warning notices to the defaulter, after which the matter was put in the hands of the administration's lawyer.[30] Revel's comment on this echoes that of the councillor James-Bernard Dezarnaulds in 1904: "It has never got any further than sending the matter to the lawyer: the courts have never had to decide the issue."[31] As for withdrawing workers from defaulting employers, Engler protested that he had no legal power to do it; only the courts could implement such a measure. No need whatever to do it ex officio in order to do it promptly, replied Revel. Immigration had only to notify a justice of the peace, who could cancel the contract as a matter of urgency and at the cost of the employer. Inspector Fillon added with some asperity, "And no justice of the peace has ever been notified."[32]

In the matter of fining indentured workers, the *Inspection mobile* condemned the system operating in the colony as unjust and illegal. Workers were arrested on the complaint of employers for labor offenses, and were arbitrarily fined or imprisoned as if they had committed offenses under the *indigénat,* or Native Regulations, which did not apply to them. The only legal penalty—applicable only by the immigration commissioner or *syndics,* and not by the administrative police—was a term in an *atelier* or at the Orphelinat depot, where they were to work without pay for the administration.[33]

The inequity and severity of punishment was alarming, concluded the inspectors. They cited the case of the New Hebridean woman Yakoali, who had been fined 10 francs on 3 January 1906, another 10 francs on 18 January, given fifteen days at the *atelier* on 19 February, and another thirty days on 30 May. The Immigration Office did not take the trouble to find out why she had violated her contract, but a rapid inspection of her *livret* would have shown them that she had simply never been paid. As a consequence of this severity, the woman was forced to work for a settler who had then disappeared from Noumea, also without paying her for her work. "When one compares this severity with the laxity vis à vis the employers," noted Revel, "the conclusion is distressing."[34] Yakoali was never to benefit from the interest in her case, for she died in Noumea a few months later, at the age of about thirty.[35]

The administration itself, according to the inspectors, joined in the business of cheating the indentured laborers. Laborers detained at the depot not only had to work for nothing, but were also (illegally) charged for their keep, a debt that was extracted from their wages when they began to earn money after their discharge. This was bad enough in the case of those detained for breach of contract, who paid twice for their offense, but since some inmates were also there because they were awaiting engagement or for a ship to repatriate them, and had committed no offense, the injustice was outrageous. In this way, said the very thorough Inspector Revel, the commune of Noumea had used 6,508 days of free labor in 1903, 8,626 in 1904, and 7,359 in 1905, since when it had continued to have four to twelve men at its daily disposal without spending a sou. The government gardens at Anse Vata also benefited from free labor from the depot to the tune of one or two men per day.[36] Fillon commented: "Disorder, arbitrary decisions, whimsy—it's all there! And that's not all yet!"[37]

The recruits' greatest grievance against the labor market of New Caledonia was thoroughly documented by the report of the *Inspection mobile*. The defrauding of employees was not only widespread, it was virtually sanctioned by the administration. The inspectors concluded that the Immigration Office had proved its impotence to ensure respect for the regulations, and that it had neglected its role of protection, using the police powers put at its disposal only against those whom by law they were supposed to defend.[38]

In theory, the report of this *Inspection mobile* turned the Immigration Office upside down, as one local councillor put it.[39] Engler was fired and given an official reprimand. His assistant Gayon was also reprimanded. Fillon remarked of him: "Born in New Caledonia, [he] has constantly given proof in the course of his duties of inexcusable weakness and partiality."[40] The Immigration Office was to be separated from the Native Affairs Department in future, and for the moment abolished, immigration being made directly responsible to the governor.[41] A commission was set in train to make effective the regulations that already existed. Governor Liotard promptly enacted the appropriate *arrêtés*. A list of wages due to those currently working was drawn up by the office: the total came to 96,803.5 francs.[42] In addition, an enormous list of unclaimed estates (*successions et biens vacants*) dating back to 1890, appeared in the *Journal Officiel* in June 1907, representing 519 indentured laborers (of all origins, now including local Melanesians) who had died, deserted, or been repatriated, and who had money owing to them.[43] The many for whom there were no proper records, as Revel had predicted, did not make either list. As if echoing Revel, Councillor Reverchon pointed out that the books of the Immigration Office were in such a mess that nobody knew how much employers owed their workers, so officials were obliged to get their information from interested parties, while Councillor Devambez spoke of the "complete anarchy" that was still permitted by the current regulations.[44] In any case, as the inspectors realized, the list was just a gesture: few expected that workers in the colony or their heirs in the New Hebrides would respond to a notice in a French newspaper in New Caledonia and lay claim to the estate.

Despite these measures, there was no revolutionary change in the modus operandi of the Immigration Office. Governor Liotard himself was gone by 1908, and so was the liberal government in France that had sent the *Inspection mobile*. At the end of 1907, Leconte pointed out during a meeting of the *Conseil général* that arrears of pay were due to workers at the Kataviti mine near Koné, and that the administration could easily make employers pay them but had not done so because the system of recovery was defective—a charge made before the inspection and apparently still valid. By way of reply, the secretary-general pointed out that the commission was in process of revising the regulations.[45] In mid-1908 Councillor Devambez asked what had happened to this commission, which was supposed to have reported in the previous session but from which they had heard nothing.[46] In the same year indigenous chiefs and parents were still complaining that they had never been paid for the work of their children sent to pick coffee on settlers' plantations.[47] In 1911, in almost exactly the same words used by Inspector Fillon, Councillor Martin observed "Rare indeed are the employers who observe the rule" relating to the quarterly payments of wages.[48]

It was sometimes true that it was a hardship in the bush to go on a long journey in order to make these payments before a *syndic*, but the townspeople and those at large mining centers, the majority of employers, did not have this excuse. In 1911 the secretary-general claimed that debts owing to the Immigration Office for repatriation were at least diminishing, that the system of payment was now "generally respected," and that M Solari, the head of the office, looked after it personally.[49] However, Solari had been one of the employers singled out by the Fillon inspection as an official (then principal clerk to the secretary-general) setting a bad example by not conforming to labor regulations,[50] so one does not know how much confidence to put in his personal efforts, or in the fact that he was promoted to head of the Immigration Office only four years after being censured.

In 1929 the *Inspection mobile* still made a number of complaints about arrears in payment, both to workers and to the (now separate) Immigration Department, as well as other abuses, pointing out that promises of reform in response to the special inspections of 1925 (of Indochinese labor) and 1928 (of Javanese labor) had not been followed up by appropriate action.[51] There is some evidence that after this the regulations were better observed in the matter of wage payments if not in other respects. Reform in this respect offered some guarantees to the increasing number of Asian and indigenous workers who were indentured up to the Second World War, but for the large majority of New Hebridean workers, improvements came too late. As Inspector Fillon feared, many had worked for nothing.

In cheating their workers, employers clearly acted against their own long-term interests. Cheap labor was the most valuable commodity in the Pacific: all subscribed loudly to that view. It was possible to recruit New Hebrideans to work abroad for an agreed reward. New Caledonia was a popular labor destination in the 1860s, when the trade was better supervised, and it was the nearest of all to the major source of supply. With a more generous attitude, New Caledonian employers could have made a killing. After recruiting for Queensland and Fiji was stopped, in the early years of the twentieth century, New Caledonia had only the competition of the internal market of the New Hebrides itself, soon to acquire an even worse reputation in the matter of labor abuses. Yet the administration had to resort to the more expensive procedure of importing laborers from the French colony of Indochina and the Dutch colony of the East Indies (whom they began cheating in the same fashion). Why did the settlers poison the goose that laid the golden egg?

To Governor Liotard, responding to the criticisms of the inspectors in 1907, the matter was easily explained: the employers' mentality was the product of a convict colony. In response to the charge that the Immigration Office had cooperated in the theft of laborers' wages, he said, "Unfortunately this is strictly correct. The settlers have always been heard and the indentured laborers have always been silenced. The Immigration section should never have been entrusted to an official born in New Caledonia. There has developed among the inhabitants of this country a special mentality through contact with the *bagne*. I have observed this strange mentality in some people esteemed honorable in New Caledonia."[52] But of course the mentality in New Caledonia was no different from that in colonies elsewhere, where the privileges of white settlers appeared to them to be part of the natural order. New Caledonian employers were by nature no greedier, no more shortsighted, and no less humane than their counterparts in Fiji or Queensland, but they were less constrained to observe regulations imposed in their own long-term interest.

Again, it was a case of nonenforcement of the law rather than the law itself. Regulations about payment were earlier and better in New Caledonia. Payment of workers only at the end of their term had also been common in Queensland in the first seventeen years of the labor trade; no regulation ordering the periodic payment of wages existed there until six years after one had been enacted in New Caledonia. And when in 1880 a Queensland regulation was passed, it decreed that wages were to be paid every six months, rather than every three months, in the presence of the district labor inspectors.[53] Thereafter, although many abuses came to light in the British colonies, the failure to pay due wages did not seem to have been a problem, whereas in New Caledonia abuses surrounding the payment of all workers were not resolved by the administration until well into the twentieth century.

Some difficulties were peculiar to New Caledonia. A phenomenon of the colony, even more than in most colonies, was the transient nature of many of its inhabitants. Many, including officials, soldiers, and penitentiary personnel—all employers of "New Hebridean" labor— spent only a few years in the colony. This problem was perhaps envisaged by the framers of the regulation requiring payment every quarter: in theory anyone who left the country could be no more than three months in arrears. In practice, residents could defer payment until the expiry of the contract, then, like the employer of Yakoali, quietly slip from the scene. As the gendarme commandant Rentz noted in his circular to *syndics* in 1907, "If you do not see to the application of this regulation [about quarterly payments] it can happen that indentured laborers can remain unpaid for a long time and that their employers disappear without leaving an address."[54]

The records show clearly that many settlers were simply unable to pay. Some went bankrupt as a result of problems endemic to plantation agriculture in the Pacific—wild fluctuations of prices for tropical commodities, droughts, fires, floods, hurricanes, and plagues of locusts, and, more fundamentally, the uncompetitiveness of their small-scale production combined with the great distance from the markets it served. Some were so poor themselves that they could never have afforded, on any rational plan, to employ labor in the first place. Yet they were allowed to do so; nor was their failure to pay any bar to their hiring fresh labor.

Settlers in the bush argued that the regulations about payment were over-rigid and unenforceable. Employees themselves demanded advances in kind, they said, when they ran short of things like tobacco and clothing. It might be a two- or three-day journey to find the *syndic* before whom they were supposed to settle accounts, and they and their workers would lose this time. As well, few settlers in the bush had any cash. Many simply had an account with a big merchant firm like Ballande, and were themselves only paid in kind when the ship came around with their supplies. These arguments appear to have convinced many officials, including Governor Feillet.[55] But gendarmes on the spot, acting as *syndics,* tended to take a more cynical view. In 1903 Commandant Rentz reported that the settlers of Sarramea requested permission to settle their wages before their Municipal Commission, on the grounds that to go before the *syndic* at La Foa would involve losing a day's work from their employees. This, he said, could appear plausible to the uninformed, but in his view it was their "bad faith" that gave rise to an excuse "without the least validity," for the *syndic* had in fact visited *them,* and had even arranged to come on a

Sunday so that work would not be interrupted. Settler Baguil had objected that he was obliged to pay in kind to furnish his workers with certain commodities they needed, since La Foa was far away and they could not go there themselves without losing a day's work. But, said the *syndic,* "The truth is that the said Baguil finds it easier to supply the goods himself. The profit he makes on them doubtless pays him his workers' wages in part, if not in whole. I must explain that settlers who reside at stations as far and farther away than Sarramea come regularly to La Foa to pay their workers . . . in cash."[56] They usually came on Sundays, and workers took advantage of the visit to shop at the stores in La Foa; often workers came in on other Sundays just to shop.[57] As for the seemingly reasonable request to pay before the Municipal Commission, it was hardly disinterested, for the president of that body was one of the most recalcitrant of the employers and had met the gendarme with a torrent of abuse when asked to pay overdue wages.[58] The argument about the lack of cash in the bush had some foundation, although settlers could have paid their wages as they paid other debts—by a note on Ballande, or the company they dealt with, that would have been honored in the stores.

None of these excuses, however, could plausibly be made in Noumea, which held the largest concentration of indentured laborers. Yet nonpayment of wages was very prevalent in Noumea, where, as Inspector Fillon pointed out, "supervision and immediate action could be particularly effective."[59] Fillon suspected that it was worse in the bush, extracting at random from the registers several bad cases from Hienghène, Koumac, La Foa, and Pouembout, but in 1929 the *Inspection mobile* found this abuse to be worse in the capital.[60]

Understaffing of the Immigration Office was a local factor underlined by the inspection missions and evident since the introduction of indentured labor to the colony. For much of its history, the office was just a subsection of the Department of the Interior or the Native Affairs Department, although it had always had its own budget. The staff had always been inadequate for its nominal functions, which included registering the names and details of the laborers, issuing passbooks, collecting dues for hospital and other services, receiving installments for repatriation payments and deferred wages, liaison with the *syndics* in the bush, overseeing disciplinary measures, prosecuting infractions of the labor laws, undertaking tours of inspection, and a variety of other chores. In 1907, the complaint of the *Inspection mobile* was that additional jobs were taken on by staff, apparently only for the sake of the extra pay. Assistant-Head Gayon acted as *syndic* for Noumea, cashier-bookkeeper, and deputy to the head of the Department of Native Affairs.[61] Until it was pointed out by the inspectors, wrote Revel, it did not occur to the acting head of the Immigration

Office that the accumulation of several jobs was likely to prevent their being performed properly: "The *syndic* [Gayon], who should have been the first to point out that he could not carry out the obligations with which he was entrusted, did not protest against the accumulation of extra allowances from which he profited."[62] As for the acting head himself, he was also head of the Topographical Service and allowed the Immigration Office to be run by Gayon.[63] Fillon commented that on his own admission, Engler had not had the time to look after immigration, although he never failed to collect the 125 francs per month extra pay for acting as head.[64]

In 1929, at a time when there were about eleven thousand indentured laborers of various origins in the colony, the full-time staff of the Immigration Department in Noumea consisted of an elderly head of department, an assistant, and a bookkeeper, plus an auxiliary clerk and seven typists who had other duties, and two interpreters from the ranks of the Asian laborers.[65] Those performing the office of *syndics* for the town were the auxiliary clerk and a young woman typist, both of whom lacked the training, the status, and the authority to enforce the settlement of payments or investigate complaints.[66] Both admitted to the inspector that they allowed debts or advances not registered on the *livret* to be deducted from wages when supervising the settlement of payments, despite an *arrêté* of 21 June 1902 specifically requiring this essential evidence.[67] While the general lack of funding of the colonial administration can be seen as a symptom of the neglect with which the metropolitan government treated its Pacific colonies, the conclusion is still inescapable that in Noumea itself the function of supervising the labor laws had a low priority.

Some *syndics* in the bush—generally gendarmes—defended the rights of laborers against high odds: they were overwhelmed with work, isolated, subject to pressure by local settlers, and not confident that they would be backed by the department in Noumea. One gendarme reported the following incident when he was *syndic* at La Foa: When he requested that a certain Lachaud pay his colored labor, Lachaud arrived, furious, brandishing a letter from the head of immigration authorizing him not only to pay his workers without the intermediacy of a *syndic* but also to punish them on his own authority.[68] *Syndics* frequently encountered abuse and threats. Gendarme Lafourcade was asked "What's the point of bothering about half-savage people" when he asked a settler to pay his workers (in this case Javanese) the considerable sums he owed them;[69] the same settler had boasted to a gendarme that "everything he solicits [from the authorities] even if it is against the regulations, is granted him."[70] Commander Rentz heard settler Thomas of Pouembout protesting vehemently to a gendarme who had requested that he settle accounts with his workers in the proper manner, "I'll do what I like, and we will see who gets the better of it."[71] The reports of *syndics* did not necessarily get as far as the department. For example, the report on the recalcitrance of the settlers of Sarramea went no farther than the platoon commander of the gendarmerie, who marked it "To be filed." Verifying that this report had never reached the Immigration Office, Inspector Fillon commented, "Platoon Commander Maudet could have, in the same manner, blocked other *procès-verbaux* and reports for the Immigration Office that were sent to him by gendarmes of the interior acting as *syndics*."[72]

Fundamentally, the problem was that the colonial administration after 1870 was too weak and too easily manipulated to enforce the most basic of the regulations. It was the role of the government in other colonies—and arguably the role of the state in all capitalist societies—to oblige employers to restrict their immediate benefits for the sake of their ultimate advantage. It has to be assumed that few employers impose this discipline on themselves in their own long-term interest. But officials in Noumea were generally themselves employers of indentured labor and in any case unwilling to alienate their fellow whites by appearing to penalize them in the cause of the blacks. Governors, high officials, and gendarmes coming from France were transitory. Local people who had fallen into disfavor had only, as a gendarme chief remarked, to "bring the force of inertia to bear"[73] against a bad report, wait for a reforming official to depart, and in the meantime make his life intolerable and his promotion precarious.

On the beaches in the islands, recruiting practices could be policed by fear of local retribution, but at the place of work in a foreign land, imported laborers had no such bargaining power. The role of the state was crucial. Without pay, workers had nothing to show for their labor and their subjection; they were ashamed to return home with empty hands.

Chapter 13
Sickness and Death

No one disputed the fact that the rate of sickness and death among indentured laborers, especially mine workers, was extremely high. The habit of listing the names of dead foreign workers among those in the "Trusteeship of unclaimed estates" (*Curatelle aux successions et biens vacants*), regularly published in the *Moniteur,* publicized the extraordinary number of imported Oceanians—and later Asians—who died, often within a short time of arrival. The appearance of list after list of the strange-sounding names (figure 5) made it impossible to deny that these workers, with few exceptions recruited under the age of twenty-five, fell sick and died at many times the rate of Europeans of any age. These dismal catalogues made an impact in France as well as in the colony. Yet the register was a very limited indication of the number of actual deaths, insofar as it recorded only the names of those known to the authorities to have possessions or money, or to have money owing to them.

It is impossible to determine the death rate of the *engagés* in New Caledonia as fully as it has been computed for Queensland and Fiji,[1] given the absence of corresponding statistics. To make an estimate, one has to rely on the registration of deaths in the *état civil* (register of births, deaths, and marriages). Fortunately the birthplace of the deceased was always attempted on the registration form; for these workers at least "Nouvelles-Hébrides" was given, and often also the name of the island of origin. The numbers for each year, from all districts, were added together and divided by the average number of migrant laborers present over the year. Obtaining that average number presented difficulties. First, one is dependent on the survival of informed estimates, or calculations therefrom using the known number of arrivals and departures for the next or previous years; second, the numbers of workers shifted in the course of a year, as some left and new ones arrived. Like Ralph Shlomowitz,[2] I have resolved the

(Deux-Sèvres), cultivateur, marié à Pélagie Nivet, et décédé à l'hôpital de l'île Nou, le 13 juillet 1882 (sans autre ronseignement).

KINTZ, condamné libéré, matricule 2975, noyé près de Canala dans la nuit du 7 au 8 juillet 1882 (sans autre renseignement).

LEROY (Alexandre), condamné libéré, matricule marchand à Pouébo, décédé le 29 juillet 1882, à Amos, par suite de submersion de son canot (sans autre renseignement).

MAMOUYASSI, Néo-Hébridais, matricule 4417, engagé Higginson, à Thio, y décédé le 2 octobre 1881 (sans autre renseignement).

TOGOROMOLÉ, Néo-Hébridais, matricule 4572, engagé Higginson, à Thio, y décédé le 25 octobre 1881 (sans autre renseignement).

LINGA, Néo-Hébridais, matricule 4683 engagé Higginson, à Thio, y décédé le 11 novembre 1881 (sans autre renseignement).

OUIDOUA, Néo-Hébridais, matricule 4409, engagé Higginson, à Thio, y décédé le 10 novembre 1881 (sans autre renseignement).

PALÉMOUGO, Néo-Hébridais, matricule 4743, engagé Higginson, à Thio, y décédé le 11 novembre 1881 (sans autre renseignement).

PÉTROMOLÉ, Néo-Hébridais, matricule 4757, engagé Higginson, à Thio, y décédé le 12 novembre 1881 (sans autre renseignement).

OUMBA, Néo-Hébridais, matricule 4613, engagé Higginson, à Thio, y décédé le 18 novembre 1881 (sans autre renseignement).

MÁTHANI, Néo-Hébridais, matricule 4295, engagé Higginson, à Thio, y décédé le 26 novembre 1881 (sans autre renseignement).

OUMASSANA, Néo-Hébridais, matricule 4428, engagé Higginson, à Thio, y décédé le 15 décembre 1881 (sans autre renseignement).

BELLÉ, Néo-Hébridais, matricule 4734, engagé Higginson, à Thio, y décédé le 21 décembre 1881 (sans autre renseignement).

TRAVÉA, Néo-Hébridais, matricule 4669, engagé Higginson, à Thio, y décédé le 28 novembre 1881 (sans autre renseignement).

LONGANNE, Néo-Hébridais, matricule 2984, engagé Evain, à Canala, y décédé le 4 décembre 1881 (sans autre renseignement).

YAMAC, Néo-Hébridais, matricule 1146, engagé Girard, à Houaïlou, y décédé le 25 décembre 1881 (sans autre renseignement).

TAMA, Néo-Hébridais, matricule 3803, au Service du port, à Pam, y décédé le 28 décembre 1881 (sans autre renseignement).

AMBOLECK, Néo-Hébridais, matricule 3601, engagé Laurie, à Canala, y décédé le 30 octobre 1881 (sans autre renseignement).

VAKOUA, Néo-Hébridais, matricule 4804, engagé Noblot, à Canala, y décédé le 15 décembre 1881 (sans autre renseignement).

TUÉ, Néo-Hébridais, matricule 4114, au Service de l'Administration pénitentiaire, décédé le 10 novembre 1881 (sans autre renseignement).

ORO, Néo-Hébridais, matricule 4732, engagé Castex, à Nouméa, y décédé le 18 novembre 1881 (sans autre renseignement).

RAMEL, Néo-Hébridais, matricule 1710, engagé de Casteljau, décédé le 21 octobre 1881 (sans autre renseignement).

VÉRITIA, femme Néo-Hébridaise, matricule 4717, sans engagement, décédée le 10 novembre 1881 (sans autre renseignement).

PIELLE, Néo-Hébridais, matricule 3697, au Service du Port, à Nouméa, y décédé le 2 novembre 1881 (sans autre renseignement).

OUASSE, Néo-Hébridais, matricule 4494, engagé de Gérolimo Draghicewitz, décédé lors du naufrage de l'Henriette, à Thio, le 2 novembre 1881 (sans autre renseignement).

TÉLIS, Néo-Hébridais, matricule 3300, engagé de Gérolimo Draghicewitz, décédé lors du naufrage de l'Henriette, à Thio, le 2 novembre 1881 (sans autre renseignement).

MÉTIOR, Néo-Hébridais, matricule 3301, engagé de Gérolimo Draghicewitz, décédé lors du naufrage de l'Henriette, à Thio, le 2 novembre 1881 (sans autre renseignement).

MÁLUO, Néo-Hébridais, matricule 3314, engagé J. Daly, à Nouméa, y décédé le 4 mars 1879 (sans autre renseignement).

MAN, dit Jack, Néo-Hébridais, matricule 2496, engagé Deschamps, à Nouméa, y décédé le 5 janvier 1882 (sans autre renseignement).

JUDITH, femme Néo-Hébridaise, matricule 4536, engagée Desmazures, à Nouméa, y décédée le 9 janvier 1882 (sans autre renseignement).

TAOUA, Néo-Hébridais, matricule 4721, engagé Castex, à Nouméa, y décédé le 14 janvier 1882 (sans autre renseignement).

LISBURNE, femme Néo-Hébridaise, matricule 4399, engagée Tranchant, à Nouméa, y décédée le 4 février 1882 (sans autre renseignement).

AVALAIS, Néo-Hébridais, matricule 3098, engagé Simon et Tauveron, à Nouméa, y décédé le 6 février 1882 (sans autre renseignement).

NAIGUÉGUÉ, Néo-Hébridais, matricule 4203, engagé Morgan, à Nouméa, y décédé le 13 février 1882 (sans autre renseignement).

MAKENBOY, Néo-Hébridais, matricule 2340, engagé Le-

baigue, à Nouméa, y décédé le 13 février 1882 (sans autre renseignement).

TITIHO, Néo-Hébridais, matricule 3283, engagé Joubert et Carter, à Nouméa, y décédé le 19 février 1882 (sans autre renseignement).

CHÁLBALEY, Néo Hébridais, matricule 2572, engagé Ah-Ben, à Nouméa, y décédé le 20 février 1882 (sans autre renseignement).

BONTO, Néo-Hébridais, matricule 4620, engagé Tournier, à Nouméa, y décédé le 28 février 1882 (sans autre renseignement).

TANTIOMARIE, Néo-Hébridais, matricule 4551, engagé Fruitet, à Nouméa, y décédé le 8 mars 1882 (sans autre renseignement).

PALETO, Néo-Hébridais, matricule 4132, engagé au Service local, à Nouméa, y décédé le 22 juillet 1882 (sans autre renseignement).

LOBO, Néo-Hébridais, matricule 4576, engagé de la Société le Nickel, à Nouméa, y décédé le 20 janvier 1882 (sans autre renseignement).

VAGUÉA, Néo-Hébridais, matricule 4681, engagé de la Société le Nickel, à Nouméa, y décédé le 29 janvier 1882 (sans autre renseignement).

MOLO, Néo-Hébridais, matricule 4603, engagé de la Société le Nickel, à Nouméa, y décédé le 31 janvier 1882 (sans autre renseignement).

TOUÉSSE, Néo-Hébridais, matricule 4701, engagé de la Société le Nickel, à Nouméa, y décédé le 8 février 1882 (sans autre renseignement).

MANGOU, Néo-Hébridais, matricule 4085, engagé de la Société le Nickel, à Nouméa, y décédé le 1er mars 1882 (sans autre renseignement).

OUARI, Néo-Hébridais, matricule 4083, engagé de la Société le Nickel, à Nouméa, y décédé le 6 mars 1882 (sans autre renseignement).

MALONGUÉ, Néo-Hébridais, matricule 4639, engagé de la Société le Nickel, à Nouméa, y décédé le 6 mars 1882 (sans autre renseignement).

OUSAORÖH, Néo-Hébridais, matricule 4420, engagé de la Société le Nickel, à Nouméa, y décédé le 12 mars 1882 (sans autre renseignement).

KARAKELÉ, Néo-Hébridais, matricule 2757, engagé de la Société le Nickel, à Nouméa, y décédé le 12 mars 1882 (sans autre renseignement).

WILLAPÁU, Néo-Hébridais, matricule 4267, engagé de la Société le Nickel, à Nouméa, y décédé le 26 janvier 1882 (sans autre renseignement).

LIA, Néo-Hébridais, matricule 4639, engagé de la Dumbéa, y décédé le 2 février 1882 (sans autre renseignement).

OTARI, femme Néo-Hébridaise, matricule 2050, engagée Russeil, à la Dumbéa, y décédée le 31 mars 1882 (sans autre renseignement).

SANDEREIZIA, Néo-Hébridais, matricule 3405, engagé Robson, à Nouméa, y décédé le 20 avril 1882 (sans autre renseignement).

Les personnes qui auraient des droits auxdites successions, sont invitées à les faire connaître et à en justifier au curateur de l'arrondissement judiciaire de Nouméa, soussigné.

Les créanciers sont également invités à produire leurs titres au curateur et les engagistes sont priés, conformément aux articles 43 et 44 de l'arrêté du 8 août 1882, de se libérer entre les mains du curateur des salaires dûs à leurs anciens engagés dans le mois à partir du présent avis.

Nouméa, le 28 août 1882.

Le Curateur,
WADDY.

PONTS ET CHAUSSÉES

Le Service des Ponts et Chaussées recevra jusqu'au lundi 11 septembre, à 4 heures du soir, des offres pour la fourniture de 250 pieux de 7 à 8 mètres de longueur et de 25 centimètres de diamètre moyen, en bois de niaouli, bois de fer, houp, chêne-gomme ou autre essence de bois dur, livrables au chantier du pont de la Dumbéa dans le délai d'un mois.

Les conditions générales des marchés en date du 10 janvier 1870 sont applicables au présent concours.

ENREGISTREMENT ET DOMAINES

VENTE AUX ENCHÈRES PUBLIQUES

Le samedi, 16 septembre 1882, à huit heures et demie du matin, sur la place du Marché et, ensuite, à la Direction du port de Nouméa, il sera procédé, par le Receveur des Domaines, assisté de qui de droit, à la vente publique, aux enchères :

1° Des chevaux ci-après désignés, d'origine australienne, provenant de l'escadron de gendarmerie de la Nouvelle-Calédonie, à savoir :

ABONDANT, bai brun, âgé de quinze ans, taille 1 mètre 56 ;
AZAIS, alezan clair, âgé de quinze ans, taille 1 mètre 56 ;
AGÉSILAS, rouan charbonné, âgé de sept ans et demi, taille 1 mètre 58.

2° De la canonnière la Bayonnette, telle qu'elle se composera au jour de la vente, à savoir : coque, mâture, cuisine, etc.

Figure 5 Part of a *"Curatelle aux successions et biens vacants." Moniteur*, 6 September 1882.

second problem by using a figure representing the number present midway through the year by halving the sum of the population at the beginning and end of the year, when a mid-year figure is not fortuitously given. The result of these calculations appears in appendix table 3.

Even the *état civil* is deficient in recording the deaths of migrant laborers. Deaths aboard recruiting and repatriating vessels, signaled in ships' journals, are not recorded in it. On rare occasions it is possible to infer an outbreak of disease on a recruiting ship: for example, in April 1882, a few entries in the *état civil* mentioned that the deceased New Hebrideans were recruits of the *Havannah* who had just arrived. Since the date of the ship's arrival in port is known, one can calculate that no fewer than 6 of its 101 recruits died within a few days of arriving at Noumea, 3 of them children aged nine to twelve. Moreover, a penciled comment in the margin reads, "See the register of burial permits for other *canaques* of the same provenance who were not registered."[3] It seems probable that others died *during* the *Havannah*'s voyage, but there is no way of confirming this. Even New Hebridean deaths in the colony were not always registered: for example, some who were killed in accidents or murdered, and are mentioned by name in court cases or newspapers, are simply not in the records. And in the list of unclaimed estates for 1907, drawn up after the *Inspection mobile*'s complaints, are the names of dozens of "New Hebrideans" who had disappeared "without trace" from immigration files.[4] A few of these names turn up in the death notices of the *état civil*, but others must have died anonymously in the territory, for they could not have been repatriated without reentering official records, unless they became one of the many "Toms," "Dicks," "Harrys," "Djimys," "Sams," or "Louis" that appear there. One has also to take into account that many recruits came as so-called free labor between 1887 and 1890, during the second ban on the labor trade, and were nonpersons so far as official records were concerned. Those enlisted in 1887 had time to die or be repatriated before retrospective enrollment was demanded. It is known by chance that of 20 recruited at San Cristobal in 1887 and sent to the mines, only 11 returned.[5] However, suspiciously few of the names on private contracts in this period appear in the death registries, at a time when conditions were harsh. For example, 49 workers were privately contracted in 1889 to work for Charles Laurie, who normally had high death rates on his coffee plantation, yet not a single one of those names appears in the death registry within the period of their three-year contracts.[6]

The adverse publicity arising from publishing the names of New Hebridean dead in the list of unclaimed estates may even have led to a deliberate reduction of registrations in the *état civil*, at least in the bush where such events were easier to conceal. A letter from the officer of the *état civil* in Poya to the *procureur* in 1882 apologizes for the inclusion of New Hebrideans on his register, explaining that he had drawn up the list before "instructions from Noumea ordered me not to make mention on the registers of the district of the occurrence of deaths among the New Hebrideans."[7] No more New Hebridean names appeared in the death registries of Poya-Népoui until 1884.

Clearly, death rates computed from the *état civil* represent minimum figures. This can be dramatically illustrated by checking one instance of a list of known deaths against those registered in the *état civil,* making liberal allowance for variations in name in the French spelling. In 1912, the British district agent on Tanna obtained the names, from various village headmen, of local people who had gone to New Caledonia "in recent times" (estimated by him as three years, but by me as a much longer period, probably between the late 1890s and 1912).[8] After collecting information from twenty-six villages, he reported on 352 Tannese who had gone to work in New Caledonia in that period, including 58 who were still there, some of these having recruited in the same year as the report. Of the 352, 202 were known to have died in the colony,[9] but only 20 of these deaths are registered in the *état civil.*[10] This may not be a typical sample, as the period included no less than three outbreaks of bubonic plague when niceties like the registration of deaths of foreign colored labor might well have been overlooked, but it confirms the need for caution in using the registered deaths. The problem is not peculiar to New Caledonia. In Queensland it was not compulsory to provide a death certificate for indentured Oceanians until 1880: as Owen Parnaby pointed out, 2,200 of the 60,000-odd Islanders who came to Queensland were never accounted for.[11]

Although the use of the register of unclaimed estates to calculate death rates produced even more minimal figures, observers found them shocking enough. Governor Courbet used the register to calculate the mortality of New Hebrideans over six quarters, or eighteen months. It gave, he said, an average of about 30 deaths per quarter, over the period 1879 to 1882—about 5 percent of the workers per year, or 50 per thousand. "That is an enormous figure," he said, "given the absence of a contagious disease or any accidental cause."[12] This calculation is evidently based on his own figure of 2,456 New Hebrideans present in April 1881, and 120 (30 per quarter) deaths listed in the "Unclaimed estates" for the year. However, the *état civil* registered 156 New Hebridean deaths for 1881, 63.6 per thousand, a much higher figure than the one that alarmed Courbet, but still to be considered a minimum. It accords fairly well with the figure given by Henri Courmeaux, reporting to the Ministry of the Navy and Colonies, for the period 1874 to 1882, if one assumes that the term of engagement for all was four years. Courmeaux says that of 5,148 New Hebrideans introduced over those years (one presumes he dated them from April 1874, when registrations under the labor code began), 1,221 of them died, or 24 percent of the total introduced[13]— 6 percent per year, or 60 per thousand. Over this period, however, there would have been a high proportion of three-year engagements, raising the annual rate to something approaching 80 per thousand. But his death figures are too low: the *état civil* registered 1,527 deaths from April 1874 to the end of 1882, more than 29.6 percent of recruits indentured since the 1874 labor code, making the annual rate something between 74 per thousand per year (dividing by a four-year term) and 98.9 per thousand (dividing by a three-year term). One has to allow for the fact that the 1874–1882 period included the epidemic year of 1875, when the death rate rose to more than 151 per thousand, so the average annual rate was unusually high. But in other, non-epidemic years, Courbet's figure of 50 deaths per thousand was often exceeded, especially in years following a heavy intake of recruits, for, as Shlomowitz discovered for Queensland and Fiji,[14] foreign workers were at most risk of death in their first year of service (see figure 6), possibly due to their lack of immunity when exposed to a new disease environment. The average age at death for New Hebrideans in the period 1874–1882 was something between 17.8 and 19.9 years (appendix: table 4). As late as 1912 the death rate was more than 37 per thousand, and the average age at death was under thirty.

A vivid picture of the high mortality rate can be obtained by analyzing a whole convoy, selected randomly by the accidental survival of records. One such convoy was that of the 107 New Hebrideans arriving on the recruiting ship *Marie* in August 1884, whose names were listed in the *Moniteur* along with other details, including the term of their engagement.[15] It is a good sample, because the years of their initial contract were not epidemic years and the recruits came from several different islands, all of them sources of recruiting for over a decade. The *état civil* shows that of the 107, 55 died in New Caledonia: the other 52 are assumed to have been repatriated, although some of them may simply have not made the registry of deaths. Of the 55 whose deaths were registered in the colony, 29 died within the (by then) average four years of service, or 68 per thousand per year: 11 died within the first year, 8 in the second year, 5 in the third year, 5 in the fourth year. Another 12 died within ten years of being in New Caledonia. Only 6 of the remaining 14 who are known to have stayed in the colony passed the age of thirty.

Another sample is less representative, because the workers came from Utupua in the Santa Cruz group in 1881, a new area for recruit-

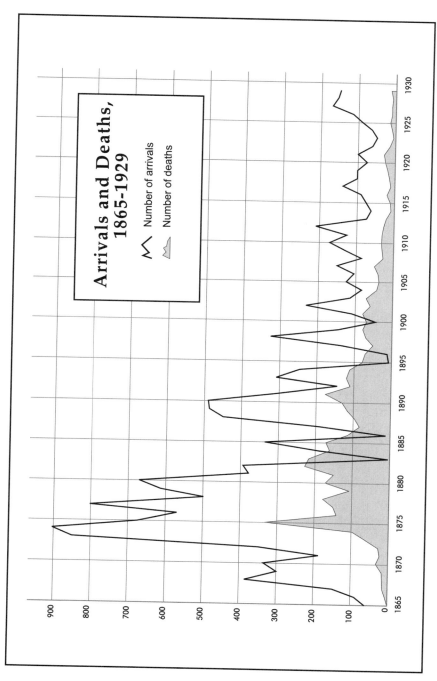

Figure 6

ing at the time, where there was probably less immunity to unfamiliar diseases. The list of Utupuan recruits exists because of an inquiry from the Royal Navy in 1888, acting on a report from the Melanesian Mission that 100 people had been recruited from Utupua to New Caledonia "some three or four years back," but only 5 had been returned. The director of the Interior Department replied that only 56 had been recruited, *seven* years ago, on the *Effie Meikle,* giving a list of their names with short observations about what had happened to them: 23 of them, he noted, had died.[16] By following the names as well as some registration numbers, the recruits can be traced in the *état civil.* To begin with, there appear to have been at least 59 recruits from Utupua aboard the *Effie Meikle.* Of the 55 who worked in the colony (4, according to the director's report, "had left for Australia"), at least 35 died in New Caledonia, 28 of them during their first four years in the colony: of these, 20 had died by the end of the first year of service, 6 in the second year, and 2 in their third or fourth year. (The Utupua people might have been mistaken in the number of recruits and the year of their leaving, but they were perfectly accurate in saying that only 5 had been returned by 1888: while the official report listed 6 who had been repatriated by then, the death of one of those named had been registered in 1882.) For this cohort, the death rate for the average term of four years was therefore 127 per thousand per year— an extremely high figure. Even using the figures cited by the director of the Interior Department (omitting 1 of the 23 who died later), it would have been 106 per thousand per year.

To those who died in the colony should be added those who died during or soon after repatriation.[17] Governor Courbet complained about the practice of repatriating workers in a wretched state of health instead of leaving them in hospital at the expense of the employer.[18] While a doctor was employed to ensure that no cases of contagious diseases went aboard a repatriating ship, the governor found that on the *Annette* "six *canaques* belonging to Mr Morgan had been put aboard after the doctor's visit." He concluded that the law should be modified to ensure that Hebrideans suffering from noncontagious diseases whose death was imminent should be kept at the hospital at the expense of their employers.[19] But such a regulation *had* been introduced seven years before—many years before it saw light in Queensland[20]—requiring that returns should have a certificate of good health before being embarked, and that those found to be sick should remain at the charge of their employer until they were fit.[21] The *Annette* case was simply another instance of the law being ignored.

The captain of the *Effie Meikle* complained about the state of health of the repatriates aboard his ship returning to the New Hebrides in 1881: "Out of eight, only two were healthy, a third was paralyzed, and the other five, in a state of complete enfeeblement, were continually bed-ridden."[22] Things had not greatly changed by 1904, it seems, for a member of the *Conseil général* in that year asked that the Immigration Office be given the power to cancel contracts and take *engagés* away from inhumane employers: among those, he specified employers who "discharge their indentured workers in a deplorable state of health, drained by fatigue, suffering from tuberculosis."[23] Frank Paton, a missionary on Tanna at the receiving end of a repatriation voyage told a confirming story: "Early on Monday morning the French steamer stopped off our landing and sent a boat ashore. . . . As the boat neared the shore we saw a recruit on board with his box. He looked wet and miserable enough in the boat, but when he was set on shore he presented one of the ghastliest sights I have ever seen, racked with a fearful cough, and so weak that he could not walk out of the water, but stood helplessly gazing about him." Half-carrying him to the mission house, Paton and his wife revived him with hot tea and fed him every two hours until he became stronger. Paton added: "Netian's story is only too common in these far lands. He left Tanna four years ago for Noumea, and was worked there till all his strength had gone, and was then shipped back to die in his native land. . . . Out of six recruits landed from Noumea within the last few years, only one has lived, and he was a boy."[24] This was no isolated case, for in his report on Tanna in 1912, the British district agent reported that of 93 Tannese who had been repatriated "in recent years," only 52 returned well and strong: of the 41 others, 1 died on the voyage home, 37 were returned dying or gravely ill and died within a year of repatriation, 1 returned a cripple, 1 a leper, and 1 a permanent invalid.[25] The effect on prospective recruits of the return of their clansmen in these conditions was obvious. As the commander of the French warship *Dives* said of another repatriating ship, "[I]t is clear that the sight of this cargo of the dying is hardly likely to induce natives to replace them on board."[26]

Frank Paton collected the cases of death and morbidity of the *engagés* from one district during the later period of Tannese participation in the labor trade: "Between 1898 and 1908 fifty-five natives recruited from one small district of Tanna for New Caledonia. Of these 39 died in New Caledonia, four returned and died shortly after arrival, four returned lepers or hopeless cripples, and eight returned well."[27] This represents a death rate of 71 per thousand in the colony; adding the four who died soon after repatriation, it rises to 78. The high death and morbidity rate of recruits from Tanna is particularly significant because it was an island whose people, having been in continous contact with Europeans from the 1840s, might have been expected to be more resistant than others to foreign diseases.

When Paton made these calculations, recruiting for Queensland had long since ceased, and his conclusion that "this is typical of the effects of French recruiting"[28] should not be read to imply that the effects of British recruiting were any better. Deaths, chronic disease, and crippling injuries were also common among Queensland returns.[29]

Causes of Death

The cause of death was, unfortunately, not one of the required details on the death registry, although it was sometimes given in rural areas. When it was, "chest complaints," tuberculosis, and dysentery were the most common causes. Several contemporary writers attempted to explain the high rate of mortality and morbidity, most of them associating it with the mining industry. Julian Thomas believed that along with dysentery, consumption carried off most of the "labour boys."[30] Edmond Cotteau, on a scientific mission in the interior, noted that about a quarter of those who worked in the mines died of consumption.[31] Even the *Néo-Calédonien* spoke of the "frightful mortality" among mine workers from "galloping consumption and dysentery."[32] An anonymous document among the records of the archbishopric in Noumea divided up the reported deaths of 1882 according to occupation: on the basis of these figures, while the overall death rate for that year stood at slightly more than 83 per thousand (an underestimation due to the writer's use of official figures), deaths at mine sites were at the rate of 121 per thousand, as against 40 per thousand on stations in the bush, and 88 per thousand in Noumea.[33] It would seem, therefore, that occupation—particularly mining—is implicated as a cause of death, for 1882 was neither a year following a peak in intake nor an epidemic year. The relatively low figure for workers in rural areas in 1882 may relate to the greater dispersal of rural workers, as disease spread more rapidly among aggregations of workers living cheek by jowl in Noumea, as well as at the mines.

Information from the individual convoys of the *Marie* in 1884 and the *Effie Meikle* in 1881 appears to reinforce the conclusion that mine work was an important factor in the death rate. The recruits in the Utupua sample arrived at the height of the mining boom—June 1881: at least 15 of the 26 who died in the first two years of service were employed at the mines.[34] That their death rate exceeded even the average for mine workers in 1882 can probably be attributed to the combination of their mine work with their extra vulnerability to local diseases. On the other hand, when the recruits in the *Marie* sample arrived (August 1884), mining was in a state of depression and had virtually ceased a few months later: some of these recruits had even been transferred to other work before January 1885, as was noted in chapter 10. Although the death rate in the *Marie* sample was very high, it was much lower than the rate for those employed in mining. As noted earlier, the death rate among Tannese workers from the late 1890s to the end of the first decade of the twentieth century was very high considering their long contact with Europeans; it may relate to their being employed in the revival of mining in that period, as well as to their exposure to episodes of bubonic plague.

It could be argued that part of the reason that contemporaries blamed mining for the high death rate was, once again, the dramatic impact of the lists of dead workers and their employers in the published register of unclaimed estates: the names of those working for the mining firm of Société Le Nickel formed at least half of the list, but allowance must be made for the fact that the company kept better records than small employers, routinely listing those who died with money owing to them. However, in the New Hebrides the clansmen of the dead also gave the high mortality in the mines as a reason for refusing to offer recruits for New Caledonia, and they were not affected by vagaries in the lists of deaths. In his report to the minister, Commander Bigant of the French warship *Sâone* explained that the increasing unpopularity of New Caledonia as a labor destination was the high mortality at the mines,[35] a grievance also picked up in the New Hebrides group by British Commodore James G Goodenough.[36] Since the general rate of death was high, not only in New Caledonia but in Queensland (with an average death rate of 54.44 per year among its Oceanian workers over the period of its labor trade),[37] their singling-out of mine work for comment is significant.

Explaining why workers became ill and died from working in the mines is not a simple matter, for several reports confirm that the Société Le Nickel at least was more careful about rations and clothing for its workers, and not overworking them, than were other employers. Puzzled for the same reason, the *Néo-Calédonien* decided, unsatisfactorily, that mine work simply was "unsuitable for these unfortunate people."[38] The newspaper was reduced to using the hoary old neo-Darwinian explanation that mere contact with the white race was fatal to "inferior races": "European civilization is obviously detrimental to them, but must one for that reason give up all ideas of colonization?"[39]

One may perhaps conclude that mine work was much harder than that to which New Hebrideans were accustomed, that the damp and dust of the mines affected their lungs, that they were unused to the cooler conditions of the mountains, and that their close confinement in the barracks at mine sites facilitated the spread of disease. In the early 1880s, two physicians independently wrote about the endemic nature of consumption and dysentery in the New Hebrides itself, one based in Tanna in the south and the other visiting Tanna, Erromango, Efaté, Malakula, Ambrym, and Santo during a three-year period at the French naval station in the Pacific.[40] If they were right, the conditions of mining in New Caledonia might simply have produced the perfect climate for the exacerbation of these diseases. The naval medical officer, Dr Monin, used almost the same words about the New Hebrideans in their own country as observers did about indentured New Hebrideans in New Caledonia: "The principal causes of death are consumption and dysentery," adding, in this case, "anemia following bouts of [malarial] fever,"[41] which was not a problem in the French colony.

As I have shown, the death rate in *non*-mining occupations was still high. An early observer, writing before the mining era, complained that the New Hebridean workers were weak and sick half the time from malnutrition, because their masters fed them nothing but boiled rice.[42] Governor Courbet offered a possible explanation of the general high mortality rate, and the ministry in France added its own diagnosis. Courbet asked: "Is it due to the facility with which the Hebrideans contract chest complaints, or to their propensity to drunkenness?"[43] To which, after his comments on the young age of many recruits and the failure of some employers to feed them properly, the marginal comment at the ministry ran: "This mortality is due to the young age of the immigrants who are overburdened with work and are not fed. It is not astonishing that they are afflicted with chest complaints. It is barbaric!"[44] Neither comment is very useful, except when they were both right: when the excessive consumers of alcohol were very young, the combination was probably fatal. The *Néo-Calédonien* reported one case of a death due directly to alcohol poisoning: "Last Sunday a New Hebridean in the service of M Goudin died suddenly on the road, while carrying two buckets of water. The autopsy, made at the request of the employer, revealed that this death was solely the result of a case of alcoholism."[45] This must have been Matana, who was only about twelve years old, the only employee of Goudin to die within days of the report.[46] Another case was brought before the justice of the peace at Canala of a boy called Kamaara, a New Hebridean employed on a coffee plantation, who was found lying on the side of the road two kilometers from Canala, asleep, under the influence of drink given him by his older comrades.[47] He died the next year, 1885, at the estimated age of thirteen: from his registration number it can be inferred that he was recruited (from Santo) in 1879, at the age of seven. As for the ministerial comment about the general effects of harsh conditions on young recruits, it is true that about a third of those who died in 1882 were under sixteen, but they do not appear to have died at a faster rate than older recruits, because a third is probably less than the proportion of the total recruited under sixteen at that time.[48]

Alcohol abuse was, of course, not helpful in maintaining health, especially when the liquor consumed was inferior, to say the least. Among Protestant missionaries like Dr Nicholson on Tanna, who complained that one of his flock had returned from Noumea "a chronic alcoholic,"[49] it was a popular diagnosis of ill health. The newspaper *La Calédonie* for once agreed with a missionary synod in the New Hebrides that blamed the New Caledonian labor trade for causing depopulation in the group "because we teach our employees the use of spirituous liquors."[50] The abuse of alcohol also indirectly caused deaths and injuries among New Hebrideans through brawling.[51]

Deaths in accidents at sea or at the workplace were another factor, because most of the hard and dangerous work was done by indentured laborers. Among deaths in the line of duty must be numbered the 19 who died at the hands of Kanaks during the 1878 rebellion, of whom, incidentally, the names of only 10 appear in the *état civil*.[52] For female recruits, childbirth was an additional hazard, as mentioned earlier. However, one would need to know something about the rate of death in childbirth in their home islands before deciding that it was more unsafe in the colony. From a medical missionary's account of childbirth in Tanna, for example, one might conclude that parturition was at least as dangerous there as in their new surroundings.[53] On the other hand, Melanesian proscriptions about the spacing of children could not be enforced in New Caledonia, increasing the risks of childbirth there.

Epidemic diseases, of course, caused peaks in the death rate, and they were not uncommon in Noumea. The newspapers believed it was because of poor sanitation.[54] As late as 1921 the *Bulletin du Commerce* asked why it was that Noumea had so many epidemics, although "the air" was healthy (perhaps referring to the lack of malaria). It answered that the town was full of pools of filthy stagnant water, from the products of household sinks and slop pails which eventually spilt out on to the public roads and footpaths.[55] Writing only a few months later, the British consul complained that there was "no attempt at modern sanitation" in Noumea, for lack of public funds.[56] Bubonic plague occurred in 1899–1900, 1905–1906, 1912, and 1920–1921. In 1903, *La France Australe* complained that typhoid was endemic in the town.[57] The "native" quarters, however, were more insanitary than the rest of the town, and since they also lived in aggregations and close together, indentured laborers were the first and greatest casualties of contagious diseases. New Caledonia suffered the influenza pandemic in 1919–1920, with a recurrence in mid-1921, and although this outbreak was worldwide and not attributable to local conditions, the crowded living quarters of the *engagés* would have facilitated its spread.

The highest peak in the death rate of imported Oceanians occurred in 1875, when a devastating measles epidemic struck in a year following the year of the highest intake of workers. Of 336 recruits who died in that year, 265 died in the first six months, when the epidemic was raging. Many died soon after arriving, to the annoyance of employers who had paid passage money and government charges for them. Numa Joubert, a sugar planter on the Dumbea River, hoped to be relieved at least of the fees paid to the administration for such workers. He requested that the 1,125 francs he owed the Immigration Office for *livrets* and registration charges be waived for 75 New Hebridean workers who died as a result of the measles epidemic between January and April 1875, pointing out the losses he had sustained because they "had not done any work from the time of their engagement to the day of their death."[58] The director of the Interior Department recommended that he be given a remission of 375 francs, but the Privy Council sympathized with the "well-founded" request of Joubert, "who was unable to use his immigrants because of the measles epidemic which decimated them soon after their landing"; they gave him a full rebate.[59]

The administration took some preventive measures against the spread of diseases. In 1881, apparently in response to a clamor in the newspaper,[60] it was decreed that all immigrant workers should be vaccinated against smallpox.[61] In the same year the administration ruled that "immigrants of all colors" should be screened for leprosy.[62] The first cases of leprosy to be officially notified in New Caledonia were those of four New Hebrideans in 1883.[63] Two years later, a labor ship's journal recorded that a recruit from Santo thought to be "leprous" was rejected and returned on the orders of the doctor.[64] Toward the end of the century, concern about the spread of leprosy became a panic. In November 1898 a health check of all *engagés* was ordered with a view to discovering cases of leprosy. At the Immmigration Office, the whole of December was spent in the medical examination of 1,200 *engagés,* of whom 2 were found to be afflicted with leprosy.[65]

The leprosy scare was dwarfed by the outbreak of plague at the end of the following year. As previously mentioned, it began in the compound housing Ballande's New Hebridean laborers and was soon rife in the quarters of other indentured laborers. The health department was led to make some interesting admissions about the poor conditions of the laborers. Noting that so far cases had occurred "only among natives," a communiqué from the administration announced prophylactic measures of isolation and disinfection. All dirty and unhealthy places were to be cleaned up, "notably the places where natives and *engagés* live." Europeans had nothing to fear, they announced, from a disease that "like most plagues, only raged where there was filth, overcrowding and poverty."[66] The next day Governor Feillet himself issued a circular echoing the same sentiments. Since the disease had so far only struck "natives" in Noumea, explicable by the "filth in which they habitually live, and the wretched physiological condition in which they all more or less are," the city would be divided into two sectors, each with its own doctor. No "native or Asian" could pass from one to the other, or anywhere else in the colony, without a *passeport sanitaire*—a health passport—given by the doctor of the relevant sector. Employers were to take particular care that their *engagés* did not go out after 8 PM.[67] A special part of the cemetery was set apart to receive Oceanians or Asians suspected of having died of the disease, and they were to be buried two meters deep between layers of quicklime.[68]

"We have only one wish," said *La Calédonie*, "and that is that the European population of our town be preserved from this terrible scourge. Everything leads us to hope so."[69] The two sectors of the town were divided by "Cape Horn" (the hill on which the cathedral is built). The first sector comprised the Orphelinat (the buildings then serving as a depot and hospital for "natives"), the Quartier Latin, the Vallée du Génie, the Faubourg Blanchot, and the Vallée des Colons—presumably the danger spots—and the second the city proper and the two Vallées du Tir (map 2). A fresh outbreak of plague late in 1905 also began in laborers' barracks. When the third outbreak began in the same way in 1912, the local authorities even had convicts erect three corrugated iron fences around the high risk areas, hoping to keep the disease away from Europeans (photo 27). The fences were meant to contain rats and mice, as well as humans, so they were to be driven into the ground for at least ten centimeters. Gates were built to allow the passage of approved humans, who were disinfected by medical assistants before crossing. The seaward half of the town was cut off from the Rue Austerlitz, bounded by the Rue de la République and the Bay of Moselle (map 3). Another fence enclosed the Vallée du Tir, and another from the coast of Montagne Coupée to Montravel.[70] The fences were built with remarkable alacrity. The townspeople acquiesced, while bemoaning the "state of siege" and their lack of free movement in the divided city. Business was severely interrupted. Ballande stores had a box built into the fence in the Rue

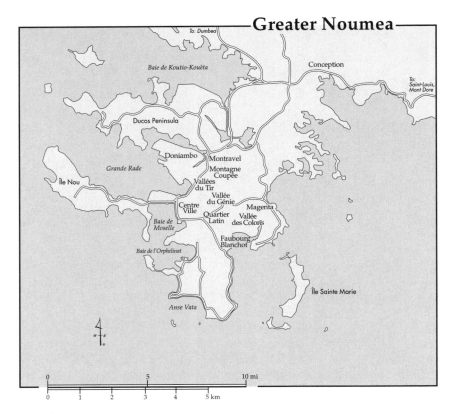

Map 2

Photo 27 Convicts in Noumea building one of the fences to quarantine plague-infected areas, 1912. Max Shekleton collection, Noumea.

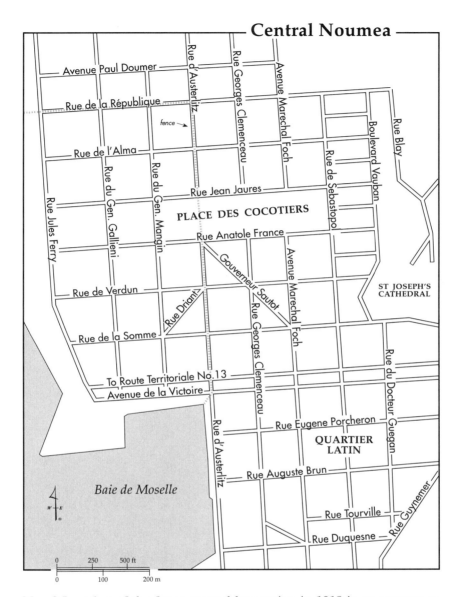

Map 3 Location of the fence erected by convicts in 1912 in an attempt to confine the plague to the seward area of Noumea.

Alma where customers could place their orders: they promised to deliver by automobile.[71] Other drastic measures were taken. All Ballande dock workers were sent to the islet of Sainte-Marie for a period of quarantine.[72] Employers were required to see that their workers stayed home overnight, and any *engagés* found sleeping elsewhere but in their quarters were to be punished. No late passes were to be given for any reason whatever. However, plague did not spare the whites of the town, and it subsequently ravaged the rural centers and the reservations of the indigenous communities. The death toll from the 1905–1906 episode was less than that of the outbreak of 1899– 1900, although the number infected was greater, and the number of white casualties diminished in 1912, so perhaps the precautions were effective.

Care of the Sick and Burial of the Dead

After the 1874 labor regulations, the administration had certain responsibilities concerning the health of imported workers. It was required to employ a medical officer to examine recruits when they arrived and before they were repatriated. It also enacted measures against the spread of contagious diseases among workers in the colony, for of course these threatened the white community as well as the black. Apart from such measures, employers were responsible for the health care of their workers for the duration of their term. They were to see that their *engagés* received appropriate medicine or medical care when sick, and they had to pay for the cost of hospital care when necessary. There existed an excellent hospital at Noumea, the Military Hospital, which also received private patients. "Immigrants of all colors" (Oceanian and Asian indentured laborers) could be treated in separate rooms of this hospital at a cheaper rate, which in 1881 was 3.75 francs a day. From 1880, however, the Orphelinat depot established its own infirmary (comparable to Queensland's "Native Hospital") at even cheaper rates (in 1883 the rate was 1.50 francs per day) (photo 28). In the 1880s, the Société Le Nickel had its own hospital at Thio,[73] and arranged for regular medical check-ups of its workers (photo 29).

Many employers became inured to the sickness and death of their workers: deaths sometimes occurred at the rate of several a month to the one employer, and more often during epidemics. It was, presumably, to dodge the cost of hospitalization and burial that workers were often repatriated in a state of morbidity.[74] From 1881, nearly all foreign Oceanian workers who were hospitalized went to the infirmary of the Orphelinat. According to Julian Thomas, writing in 1887, "Once there they generally die. The medical men here have enough to do

Photo 28 The "native hospital," or infirmary, at the Orphelinat, 1885. Mitchell Library, State Library of New South Wales.

Photo 29 The doctor's visit to New Hebridean workers at a nickel mine at Thio. Photograph by Hughan. Mitchell Library, State Library of New South Wales.

amongst white people." He believed that employers were lacking in humanity toward sick "labour boys," who, by and large, were left to nurse each other, or "packed off to the Orphelinat, and there is generally an end of him. You see the poor fellows crawling along on the road, for their employers have not the humanity to send them in vehicles." Although convinced of the superiority of the white race, he admitted a case of an Islander putting an employer to shame: "A poor old man from his own island, bent double with pain, was crawling past Mr Johnston's house to the Orphelinat. Toki, as Aeneas did Anchises, and Cassius Caesar, took up the sick man on his back, and with tottering limbs bore him for a mile to the so-called hospital."[75] As in Queensland,[76] the plight of the sick indentured laborer was pitiable. According to observers in Queensland as well as New Caledonia, attitudes to sick workers hardened in the final months of their indenture: they argued that in the first years of indenture the care of workers was a protection of the employer's investment in the "purchase price," but, since many only paid their workers at the end of their term, the closer the workers came to the end of their time the more they represented a debt to be paid out.[77]

As late as 1909 a member of the *Conseil général,* M Blandeau, drew attention to the fact that employers were dodging their reponsibility of caring for sick *engagés* because of the costs of transport and hospitalization. By that year the cost of the infirmary had risen to 2 francs a day, to which was added a fee of 6 francs for driving the sick from Noumea to the Orphelinat and back. He pointed out that in the bush matters were worse, for the cost of the fare to Noumea had to be added. He cited cases of unnecessary deaths that had resulted from lack of treatment. Other councillors agreed with Blandeau, including the head of the Immigration Office. He proposed that employers subscribe to an insurance scheme for workers, and that was accepted by the *Conseil général.*[78] Whether or not it was ever implemented is unclear.

A doctor made a daily visit to the infirmary of the Orphelinat, but the inspectors in 1907 found it in a run-down and unhygienic condition, and the warden, unable to get repairs done, forced to improvise. "From the material point of view the Depot is abandoned by the administration." There was virtually no staff. The lower death toll of the 1906–1907 plague episode was in their opinion due to the remarkable work of Madame Lechanteur, the sole nurse and "valiant wife" of the warden of the Orphelinat: she had selflessly nursed the sick throughout the epidemic and indeed managed the whole establishment because her husband was no longer capable of doing so.[79] Finding that the warden had been given a medal for his work during the epidemic while his wife received only an honorable mention, they asked that she also be awarded a medal of honor: "The Inspection has at last found an *irreproachable* party in the Immigration Office, and the least known to the section Head and the *syndic* who have never been there!"[80]

The cost of the burial of workers was borne by importers of labor and employers, from the time of the first labor code in 1874 to 1893. But the decree of 1893 allowed burial costs to be deducted from any sum left behind by the deceased worker—a "macabre" clause, according to Inspector Gayet in 1929.[81] Death was so common an occurrence among recently arrived laborers that burial was sometimes a summary matter, especially during times of epidemic. In 1875 a report was received at the British Foreign Office (because some of the people involved were English nationals) describing the indifference of importers of labor to the plight of their human cargo; it had something to say about the attitude to the death and burial of some of them.

> In one instance my informant saw a consignment of between forty and fifty who on landing were confined in a wooden shed the sides of which open in the day were battened at night. Eight died on the first night, and at one time my informant saw four of the dead lying amongst the living. He reported the fact between 9 and 10 pm to the Consignee's Clerk, and the Clerk said it was nothing unusual and they would have to lie there till morning. The Clerk and his employees were English. In the back yard my friend saw three bodies sewn up in blankets, thrown on the mud, exposed to the rain and waiting for interment at a prescribed hour on the following day.[82]

With slight variation, the story fits the convoy of 40 New Hebrideans consigned to William Caporn & Company, brought by the *Reine Hortense*, a small schooner of only fifteen tonnes, on 3 March 1875. The *état civil* registered the deaths of 4 recruits at the Caporn premises on 15 March and 4 more the following day. Since the deaths of 51 recruits were registered in the colony soon after their arrival in that month and 80 the next—the peak months in the measles epidemic—Caporn's establishment was probably not exceptional. Indeed, in the following month a notice appeared in the *Moniteur* reminding the public of the health regulations in respect of interments, as it had come to the attention of the town government that "several New Hebrideans or natives had been buried without being encased in a coffin."[83]

In the bush, deaths of laborers were often registered days or weeks after the event, and in a few instances after the legal limit of three months, when the certification of death became a matter for the courts. The employer in the country presumably waited until several deaths occurred before he or his agent made the trip to inform the *état civil* officer.[84] In these cases, one has to assume that the body was buried long before the death was recorded, so there could have been little chance that an independent assessment of the cause of death could be made. It probably also meant, as is stated in a few cases, that the bodies were buried on the property.

The high sickness and death rates were probably the outcome of a variety of factors. Shlomowitz's study suggests that an important cause was the mere transfer of workers to a new disease environment to which they had no immunity. His hypothesis is based partly on the observation that the highest incidence of death among recruits occurred within the first year of service, and this was equally true in New Caledonia. Significant variations in the death rate can, however, also be correlated with occupation, as I have shown. This is most clearly evident in the case of mine workers from Tanna, who, although not as vulnerable as the Utupuans of more recent contact, had a high death rate despite the fact that Tanna had experienced contact with Europeans for more than fifty years. As well, high death rates in the first year could also be the result of harsh and unaccustomed working and living conditions or poor nutrition, for one might expect the weaker to go to the wall rapidly, while the stronger (not only those who were reengaged) hardened up. Proper attention to the sick was also a relevant factor. It is difficult to avoid the conclusion of several contemporary observers that the difference between indentured labor and slavery was, in respect of physical care, to the advantage of slavery, for slave owners had a long-term interest in looking after their property.[85]

Chapter 14
"Hebrideans" in Colonial Society

The imported laborers occupied a lowly rank in New Caledonian society in the nineteenth and early twentieth centuries, but they were only one of a number of underclasses. There were also the convicts, the *libérés,* the Asian workers, and the indigenous Kanaks. The free whites saw the New Hebrideans as the least sinister of all their inferiors, and generally inoffensive and trustworthy.[1] They were often contrasted with the "insolent" and "thieving" Loyalty Islanders and later with the "violent" and "thieving" Indochinese. The most frequent complaint about them was their disposition to drunkenness and, consequent upon it, their rowdy brawling in the streets.

The court records bear out the settlers' impression that the Hebrideans were not a threat. Like all underprivileged classes in most times and places, they were overrepresented before the various courts, but the charges were generally trivial offenses such as drunkenness, being late in the town, making a row, or fighting with each other. There were two cases of rape, a few of assault, and one of the murder of a spouse through jealousy. Theft was rare among them, and when it occurred, it was usually the pilfering of food or a bottle of wine or spirits from the master's store. In court they usually admitted their guilt in disarming fashion. Worthy attempts were made to level the playing field in the justice system: a lawyer was sometimes found to represent defendants, however lowly, and in the case of foreigners and local Melanesians, there was an effort to have an interpreter. Inevitably, however, low rank, language problems, and cultural misapprehensions weighted the process against them from arrest to sentence. Sentences for minor misdemeanors approximated those of white settlers charged with the same offenses, but the fines of 10 to 16 francs weighed much more heavily on indentured laborers earning only 9 to 15 francs a month. Costs tended to be higher for them than for other accused, as they had to pay for interpretation into Bislama or a local language. For blows resulting in injury or death to fellow workers or Kanaks, sentences were not usually as severe as those involving white victims, just as free Europeans responsible for death or injury to "natives" rarely felt the full weight of the law.

However, a few gruesome violent episodes for which New Hebrideans were arraigned did occur. In August 1867, four were charged with the murder of Louis Pascal, their employer, and his wife and two children, on a sugar plantation on the Dumbea River. Three of the workers were found camped near Noumea: they confessed to the crime and blamed the fourth, Soupésalé, as the instigator. Soupésalé, discovered already working for another settler in Yaté, claimed that he had been ill-treated by Pascal. Unfortunately, his version of events did not appear in the only extant account of the trial, in the *Moniteur*. The four men had arrived in New Caledonia a fortnight before and could only have been on the Dumbea property for a few days.[2] One is left wondering whether such ill-feeling could have built up between master and man so quickly, or whether Soupésalé's revenge may also have had something to do with the manner of his recruitment. When the men were found guilty by the criminal court, the sentence was death by guillotine. A public execution was arranged, calculated to inspire terror in all immigrant workers, and causing some curiosity because the "instrument of death" erected on the Ducos Peninsula had recently arrived from France. Twenty other New Hebridean laborers were brought from the Dumbea district to witness the drama. On 25 September 1867, before their fellow workers, "the natives from round about," plus "a large number of settlers," the four New Hebrideans had the dubious distinction of being the first people guillotined in New Caledonia.[3]

Toward the end of the following year, another four New Hebrideans were accused of killing their employer, the master of a fishing vessel, Augustin Déméné, his first mate, Franck Lazario, and a Kanak woman and her baby while the vessel was off islands near the north coast of New Caledonia. No account of their defense is extant, but the court admitted extenuating circumstances. Two of the accused were sentenced to life with hard labor, one—too young to be sent to jail—to twenty years in a "house of correction," and another convicted of robbery only and sentenced to a year's jail.[4] Ten years later, two Malakulans were sentenced to death for the murder of a local Kanak.[5]

Not until 1913 was there another case of a family attacked by its "Hebridean" servant, in fact a Solomon Islander with a touching history. Miskana came to New Caledonia at the estimated age of twelve, about 1891, and went to work for the Paladini family in Paita. He passed for an excellent worker, and was well known to all the settlers in the region. In 1904, he had a son by a Torres Island woman, Ladge.

She died two and a half years later, and the child died six months after her.[6] After that, Miskana showed signs of derangement, and was frequently heard to say, "I see my wife and child in the sun; I must go and join them." One day when he was working on the property, Paladini criticized him for being slow on the job: furious, Miskana turned on him with the tomahawk in his hand, cutting him to pieces. When Paladini's wife came to the rescue, she was chopped up as well, along with the baby in her arms and the three-year-old child at her side. Taking a gun from the house, Miskana then fled into the bush. A search was mounted, his description and a picture of him appeared in *La France Australe* (photo 30) and a reward of 500 francs was offered for his capture dead or alive. For months there appeared in the newspapers pieces about the "Unfindable Miskana"; some said he had committed suicide, some that he had taken refuge with a tribe of the interior. There was a supposed sighting on the islet Sainte Marie; a Lifuan who had worked with him in Paita said that he had seen him near Yaté, where he was living with a *popinée*, after having robbed a *libéré*. Police followed all the trails, to no avail. Eight months after his disappearance, Miskana's skeleton was discovered only seven kilometers from Paita, identified beyond doubt by the objects he carried.[7]

These isolated violent episodes do not seem to have affected the general trust placed in Hebridean servants. Citizens counted on them for protection against the other people they had to live among, especially nomadic escaped convicts or *libérés* and the virtually unknown but greatly feared Kanaks. In Noumea the chief anxiety was theft. In innumerable court cases the person who surprised or apprehended a thief in the store or private house was a "Hebridean" who had clearly been assigned the job of night watchman. The English settler Lee Walker described how his young New Hebridean servants guarded his person and property: "In the yard I have two good watchdogs loose all night, also two or three boys [New Hebrideans] to sleep outside. In the house I see to everything being 'made-fast' myself and have the two little boys (youngsters about ten years of age . . .) each one sleeping across the doors."[8] The mention of New Hebridean servants sleeping in the kitchen or in the shop for security reasons is a common detail in accounts of thefts or assaults in court cases.[9]

The security provided by the "faithful" New Hebridean had been an important part of the settlers' argument against the suppression of the labor trade in 1882: "Our children, our families, all our intimate secrets cannot be handed over to convicts. The public servants themselves have to resort to New Hebrideans. The settler who leaves home every day for his business affairs can leave his family in all confidence under the protection of his *engagés*."[10] In the bush, New Hebridean servants were even more important for personal security. Who was

Photo 30 Miskana (sometimes spelled Misskana), the Solomon Islands worker wanted for the murder of the Paladini family. This picture appeared in *La France Australe,* 6 November 1913, together with the offer of a reward of 500 francs for finding him dead or alive.

their best protection, the settlers asked in a petition to the president of the Republic, against the growing numbers of escaped convicts and *libérés* roaming the country? Their answer—their New Hebridean workers: "It is a truism recognized by everybody here that the New Hebrideans are the terror of malefactors of all sorts: they constitute for us a sort of natural gendarmerie."[11] When the labor trade was suspended in 1885, a member of the *Conseil général* believed that the insecurity of white settlers in the bush was increased by the departure of the New Hebrideans "which leaves the inhabitants at the mercy of escaped convicts and *libérés*."[12]

In his report of 1884, Henri Courmeaux added this security function to his list of the advantages in the reintroduction of New Hebrideans: "The New Hebrideans never make common cause with the escapees, as some *libérés* do, on the contrary they are in this respect vigilant guardians, victims like ourselves and at our side during the insurrection of 1878; on the contrary they provide complete security to the settlers; and it is thanks to them that it is possible to use other categories of workers in the bush, because they [the New Hebrideans] serve as a counterbalance to them and a safeguard to the colonists."[13] The efforts of the New Hebrideans in assisting the northern expedition against the Kanaks at Pouébo in 1868 also received the praise of the commandant.[14] When the indigenous people rebelled, New Hebridean workers had no option but to join ranks with those on whom they depended.

Reliance on the buffer function was apparently not misplaced. The *Sydney Morning Herald* correspondent reported that employers counted on the cooperation of the Hebrideans when disputes arose at mining sites: "At the least altercation between the *libérés* and the overseers, 8 or 10 appear, without being ordered to, and woe betide the thief or aggressor. He is tied up and taken to the gendarmerie. The fidelity and honesty of these blacks is a most extraordinary thing."[15]

Stories of New Hebrideans capturing escaped convicts and thieves were common in the newspapers, and peppered the reports of court cases.[16] In 1892, Tom, a New Hebridean worker, was acquitted of murder after he shot a marauder on his master's property at Tonghoué.[17] Pita was posted by his master to watch his vegetable garden, as there had been a series of thefts from it, and a hungry escaped convict was suspected. Pita caught and killed the thief *in flagrante delicto,* but he turned out to be a poor settler down on his luck. Evidence was given that Pita had a good record and that he had already captured several *évadés.* He was acquitted.[18]

Being a "natural gendarme," however, was dangerous work. Encounters with thieves breaking and entering, and the capture of escaped convicts sometimes led to the injury or death of the faithful

servant. Thus one Palacol was murdered by an escapee as he escorted
him to a police post.[19] Fifteen New Hebrideans were killed on
Bérard's property at Mont Dore during the revolt of the 1850s[20] and
nineteen New Hebridean domestics and laborers were among those
killed on the west coast in the rebellion of 1878.[21] Even the domestic
watchdog role had its dangers, not only from intruders but also from
the master, as Lee Walker related to his mother.

> Last night, or rather this morning about two o'clock I heard some-
> one trying to open one of the doors. I got up quietly and sneaked
> along on my hands and knees until I arrived at the opposite door,
> when through the glass I saw a head. I took aim at it (for my motto
> is—"Shoot first, and sing out afterwards") and had my hand on the
> triggar [sic] to shoot, when I noticed that the head was wooley
> [sic], so that I knew that it must be a canaque so I sang out and got
> for an answer "It's me master." It was one of the little boys, who was
> trying to open one of the doors without waking me, but couldn't.
> Poor little beggar I do not think he quite understood how near he
> was [to] being shot. He is my favourite boy, not more than ten
> years old, and has only come from the New Hebrides about a
> month ago. He is such a pretty little fellow and is just beginning to
> talk English. I did not sleep a wink afterwards thinking how near I
> had been to killing the poor little devil.[22]

New Hebridean servants had no choice but to be faithful to the
masters on whom they depended. While the settlers had their problems with their *engagés,* these were greatly outweighed, it seems, by
the advantage of this loyalty. When the Malakulans were convicted of
murder in 1878, a local newspaper commented that it would be good
policy for the state to show clemency on this occasion, this being the
year of the rebellion in which New Hebrideans had bravely fought beside their masters: "Thanks to the alarm given by them [at Ouarail]
many settlers, and notably those of the Ouameni valley, escaped a certain death. Several [New Hebrideans] fell under the assaults of the
murderers."[23] The stocks of the victim's race—he was a Kanak—were,
of course, correspondingly low during this crisis.

Free Time

In Noumea, after a hard day's work and a meal, there was little spare
time left before the cannon sounded at 8 PM, signaling that workers
were no longer free to leave their quarters without the written permission of their master. Many domestic servants were probably unable to get out at all, being on call all the time, but those working the
boats or laboring in the stores or on the wharves managed to get to-

gether for some social life on Sundays and in the evenings after work. Some did not make it back by curfew time, and arrests for being "late in town" were nearly as common as those for drunkenness. In the bush there was little opportunity during the week for meeting anyone apart from fellow farm laborers. Sunday, however, was liberty day, although not all of it for workers tending animals.

How did the New Hebrideans spend their precious free time? Unfortunately, the chief source for reports of the workers' diversions are complaints in the newspapers. Editorials and letters regularly deplored the drunk and disorderly conduct of Hebrideans, and denounced the inadequacy of police action against it. Such behavior concerned the citizenry of Noumea only because it affected them directly: they had not only to witness this "disgusting" spectacle in the streets as they passed, but also they were liable to be hit in a cross fire of stones or other missiles.

Although they came from a biased source, the frequent reports of these activities were not inventions. The dozens of arrests for drunkenness, fighting, and noisy behavior reported on Monday mornings support the impression that for many indentured laborers the chief object in view for Sunday was to procure and consume enough liquor to obliviate the misery of the rest of the week, as it had been for British factory workers in the days of the gin palaces. Drunken brawls and gang fighting caused many casualties among the workers. The gang fights were not confined to New Hebrideans and Solomon Islanders; indentured Kanaks—until the twentieth century mostly Loyalty Islanders—were warmly involved. Gang solidarity varied according to the ethnic group present. Battle lines were sometimes drawn between two of the larger groups present—for example, between Malakulans and Tannese.[24] Sometimes the New Hebrideans joined forces to fight the Loyalty Islanders, who, on occasion, split into two camps—for example, the Lifu against the Maré men—with the New Hebrideans taking the side of one or the other.[25] Knives and knuckle-dusters were sometimes used,[26] but generally it was a battle of stone throwing.

More words appeared in print on this aspect of the New Hebrideans' lives in the colony than on any other. Numerous appeals for more severe punishments for the offenders, more police, and more arrests, appeared continuously in the newspapers from 1880 to 1912. On Monday mornings, particularly, there would almost always be an editorial or a piece called "Our Natives," "The Canaques Again," or "Battle of the Canaques," describing the Sunday street brawling, enumerating the arrested or deploring the number who got away, and invariably calling for more drastic repression. From a thousand accounts over a thirty-year period, here are a couple of samples. From *Le Néo-Calédonien:*

The Santo boys get excited and propose battle with the Malakulans. Each of the parties is supported, one by the Ambryms, the other by the Ambaens, or *vice versa*. Blows and shouting. Sunday is the great day. If you go to the suburbs you find the fight organized in more systematic fashion. This is what is happening every day . . . . [The administration] knowingly allows this splendid periodic daily disorder, to go on in the middle of the town.[27]

From *Le Progrès,* the paper edited by a deported Communard:

The New Hebrideans continue to present to us every Sunday the disgusting spectacle of their wild orgies. Last Sunday it was a band of forty, at least, who, in broad daylight, attacked those passing by with a volley of stones, along with the usual yelling. Similar events occurred the same day in different parts of the town. It is truly scandalous, and it is not worth having a police force if one cannot cross certain streets on Sunday without running the risk of being knocked senseless. Fortunately, the gendarmerie showed up at the Vallée de l'Infanterie around five or six o'clock. Six *canaques* were arrested and locked up. The others fled like a flock of sparrows. The inhabitants of Noumea demand an exemplary punishment for those caught.[28]

As late as 1912, there were complaints about a band of about a hundred New Hebrideans brawling in front of the Hotel National on the corner of Solferino and Inkerman Streets.[29]

Despite the unanimous condemnation of these scandals by the white community, divisions appeared when remedies other than fierce repression were suggested. Everyone was clear that the consumption of liquor was at the base of the fights, but the question of banning the sale of liquor to "natives" drew an ambivalent response, for, to quote a report to the house of Ballande in 1899: "Many settlers now draw the better part of their income from the sale of liquor, notably to the natives."[30]

While one lobby argued for the ban, another argued that it would only promote bootlegging, and the sale of poisonous laced liquor to "natives." The fluctuation of local regulations reflected this ambivalence. An *arrêté* of 1887 forbade all Oceanians from entry to bars, then two years later, all sales of alcohol to Melanesians were banned.[31] There followed a clamor in the press that the abuse of alcohol had not decreased. It was true that during the period of prohibition—as elsewhere—illicit liquor was freely available: the only change was that the price went up and the quality down.

Libérés figured largely among those prosecuted for dispensing liquor to "natives"; it was said that many made a living out of it, but they were by no means the only offenders. *L'Avenir* also reported that very young vendors were going around with a liter or two of rum strapped to their waist, selling it by the glass.[32] In 1897, *La Calédonie* argued for the repeal of the law on the grounds that drunkenness was worse than ever, and that illegal liquor was usually a "veritable poison": at least if blacks were allowed to drink in the bars they would get good liquor and the bar owners, who had to pay license fees, would get the profits.[33] The administration shifted first one way and then the other. The ban was lifted once more in 1899 but reimposed by metropolitan decree in 1901, coming into force in the colony in the following year.[34] Once again it was lifted, but reimposed in 1903.[35] Yet another interest, however, had to be placated, this time in France, for the local regulation became unjustifiable to the ministry on the grounds that it would be injurious to the French wine industry, then [1915] in a state of crisis.[36] Later in the year the rule was modified to except "healthy beverages," notably wine, with "less than 12 degrees of alcohol."[37] Oceanians, either local or immigrant, were also refused entry to bars, once again, and were not supposed to be given drink when clearly already drunk. This law, however, was generally admitted to be ineffective: in any case, a newspaper observed, there were droves of *canaques* always to be seen hanging around outside the bars after liquor.[38] A total ban was finally put on the sale of alcohol to, or the procurement of alcohol for, all "natives" in 1918.[39] The law was openly flouted. In 1929, Inspector Gayet found that bar owners sought out *liberés* as intermediaries, and small shops made a living above all out of the clandestine sale of small quantities to Melanesians, a practice protected by a "culpable tolerance." While in the previous year 407 "natives" had been punished for drunkenness, only 1 bar owner had been prosecuted, and none had lost their license.[40]

From the point of view of colonists, the drunk and disorderly behavior of New Hebridean laborers presented an inconvenience, but one they hoped to cure by repression despite forty years of vain attempts. On the other hand alcohol was for many of them a source of profit, and even those who did not profit directly from the sale of liquor gained indirectly from the fact that workers, having spent their earnings on grog and being too ashamed to go home empty-handed, remained to reengage or to work as "free residents" for the rest of their lives.

Although drunken brawling was condemned ad nauseam, few settlers felt constrained to provide any alternative recreation for their Oceanian workers, again perhaps reflecting the ambiguity of interests on this subject. For town-based workers, parading in the Place des Cocotiers had its limitations as a Sunday entertainment, but there is only one reference to an effort by an employer to organize alternative amusements: André Ballande issued a directive that his indentured workers be given the means of going fishing after mass, with a "little feast, free of alcohol, to enliven the outing."[41] He also ordered that his barracks be subdivided according to ethnic group, to try to reduce violence.[42] It is not known whether his local managers put the suggestions into effect, but if so, it did little to diminish the drunken brawling among his workers, who were frequently among those arrested for this offense, and who became known for their adeptness at evading police by disappearing over the wharves.

Plenty of evidence indicates that procuring and consuming liquor with a view to a few hours' camaraderie and excitement was an important preoccupation of the Oceanian laborers. But accounts of other activities in their precious moments of freedom are very meager, and the vociferous complaints of settlers should not be allowed to dominate the record. It is very likely that many occupied themselves more peacefully in their leisure time.

According to *La Calédonie,* New Hebrideans amused themselves every day by playing with "little spears" in the streets of the capital, presumably in mock battle. Characteristically, the newspaper mentioned it only in order to condemn it. The authorities should ban the practice, it argued: What if a citizen passing by should be hurt by a misthrown spear?[43] Describing how the workers readily joined in the principal diversion of Noumean inhabitants on Sunday afternoons, that is, listening to the music of the excellent convict band in the Place des Cocotiers, Julian Thomas marveled that they were allowed to mingle there on equal terms with the whites, as they certainly would not have been in a British colony: "Liberty, Brotherhood and Equality are certainly shown in Coconut-square where you see native labor boys and girls from the New Hebrides occupying the seats, lying on the grass and walking around under the trees as much at home as if they were the full equals of the white race with whom they mix."[44]

Like other observers, he felt constrained to regale his readers with descriptions of their dress and behavior.

> The women on this day come out in gorgeous attire, and I feel a reflected glory in that "Topsy," who brings me my tea of a morning, is decidedly the best dressed, which shows the kindness of her mistress, Mrs. Strokarck. The females follow the fashion of the French ladies, and they affect only slightly to notice the native boys of their acquaintance whom they meet. Some of the males smoke pipes and cigars, and appear to be thoroughly enjoying themselves. The manner in which they walk round behind parties of French officers, and unconsciously imitate the gait and gestures of those they follow, is very amusing.[45]

Photo 31 Widam, from Gaua in the Banks Islands. From J Durand, "Bois d'Ebène," *La Revue des Revues,* 1900. In Durand's article Widam is described as "a *canaque* of the native police," but he was working as an orderly in the penitentiary administration at this time (1899–1900), when he would have been about thirty-nine years old. Before that he was a servant in Noumea. Sixteen years later he appeared as a witness, describing himself as a "business employee." Bibliothèque Bernheim, Noumea.

Another British visitor in 1887 describing the "principal diversion" of Noumea, the convict concert in the park, noted that "French naval and military uniforms and Kanakas from the various Pacific Islands, in marvellous states of dress and undress predominate."[46] Presumably the Hebrideans socialized with other workers there, as well as enjoying the music and parading in their best clothes. Thomas also described them "walking in the evening, hand in hand," and congregating around bonfires in the square, reveling in "imitations of the war-cries and dances of their native homes."[47] He observed too that they were included in the festivities of 14 July 1883, at which they were seen entertaining others by their own entertainment: "the 'helots' of the convict colony of France were allowed their saturnalia. In the afternoon . . . the 'labour boys,' were allowed to compete in climbing a greasy pole. The trophies were gaudy scarfs, shirts, and other articles of clothing. The fun caused was immense. Three or four natives would be on the pole together, when, perhaps, the top one would slip, and down they would all come."[48]

In the bush, Marc Le Goupils, who farmed a property near Bouloupari for several years, also recalled that parading about in Sunday best was a source of pleasure to his Hebridean workers. "European elegance," he said, held no secrets for his Hebridean servant Nani:

> The first advances on her wages we let her have were spent on her toilet. On Sunday afternoons after lunch, the road which runs across our paddock looked like the grand boulevards. All the New Hebridean women parading: eleven men and four women, the latter all in frills and furbelows! Nani was dressed in a pink frock . . . . During her stay in Noumea, Nani would have observed in detail the smartest *popinées* in the capital during the Sunday concerts given by the convict band in Coconut Square. From the play of the parasol as well as from her dress she drew all the effects that the most provocative demi-mondaine could draw. It was a revelation.[49]

Dancing at night was a common recreation of workers on Le Goupils's property. In competition with his Kanak workers who performed the *pilou pilou*, his sixteen "Hebridean" hands asked if they could put on their own "*pilou.*" As most of them came from different islands in the New Hebrides—one had been kidnapped from Pentecost Island at the age of about five, too young to have learnt the dances of his native land—and two of them were not from the New Hebrides at all but from the Solomons, there was some problem

Photo 32 Two women workers in Noumea, 1915. Max Shekleton collection, Noumea.

Photo 33 New Hebrideans in Noumea contributing their dances to the fifti-
eth anniversary celebrations of the French colonization of New Caledonia,
24 September 1903. Max Shekleton collection, Noumea.

about *which* "native" dance to perform. In the end, all accepted a man
from Ambae as choreographer and rehearsed his "hebridean *pilou*"
every night, finally performing in paint and feathers for their employer and his wife on Easter day.[50]

From indirect references in the newspapers, it is clear that Hebridean workers in Noumea went to the races, to shows, and later to
the cinema. A Hebridean charged with stealing money from his employer explained that he needed to have a suit made to go to the
races.[51] The producers of a traveling variety show complained in a
letter to the newspaper that police had prevented "natives" from at-
tending the performance, by enforcing the eight o'clock curfew,
whereas they had been freely allowed to go to Wirth's circus, which
had played in Noumea just a few weeks before. Although they undoubtedly bought only the third-class tickets at 1 franc, they must
have made up a significant part of the audience, for the producers
complained that they suffered severe financial loss from the restric-
tion. Supporting them, *La France Australe* explained that it was an
act of spite by the police, who had been criticized by the organizers
for neglecting the duty they had been paid for—preventing *canaques*
entering without paying by crawling under the tent—as a result of
being inside the tent themselves instead of outside![52] In 1919, "natives" and *engagés* of all kinds were allowed to be in the town after

curfew on nights when there were cinemas and concerts, except on Sundays, provided they were given permission by their employers and were home half an hour after the end of the show.[53]

In their limited free time, New Hebrideans were mainly left to their own devices. While not restricted by the racial barriers of some other colonies, they mixed with the rest of Caledonian society without becoming part of it. They found camaraderie among fellow workers regardless of community of origin, even if only to drink and fight together. They visited each other after hours,[54] as one would expect. It is not unlikely that they visited and were received by indigenous tribes as well, for they traded for food with them and sometimes deserters took shelter there. Like the Europeans, they also sought access to their women. There are several accounts of this causing trouble, but as enduring relationships also formed between Hebridean men and indigenous women, and between indigenous men and Hebridean women, some must have reached an understanding with local communities.

Shopping around for goods to take home was another popular occupation in free time.[55] *La Calédonie* noted approvingly that they spent at least two hundred thousand francs a year in the country.[56] While some dissipated what money they earned in buying grog, others saved it and took great care in choosing the items for their box.[57] In the bush, "labor boys" no doubt went hunting, fishing, and exploring the countryside as they did in Fiji and Queensland, but accounts of such activities are so far lacking for New Caledonia. It is likely that many spent their Sundays just talking or simply sleeping.

New Hebrideans and the Church

There seems to have been no real counterpart in New Caledonia to the missionary activities of the Queensland Kanaka Mission, which played an important role in the lives of Oceanians on the sugar plantations of Queensland. Although the presence of numerous rootless men and women in the colony offered an excellent opportunity for the church to proselytize—for many would doubtless have welcomed the charitable concern, social life, and moral solace that it could have provided—the clergy, it seems, were already overwhelmed by the task of maintaining a hold on the various segments of the New Caledonian population. In 1874, Bishop Vitte described to his superiors six different categories of people within the colony, all requiring special care: the convicts under sentence (who became all the more difficult to manage when they graduated to being *libérés*); the *déportés*, with their abominable Voltairian opinions; the free whites, among whom greed and scandalous behavior prevailed; the native Caledonians, with their superstitions and debauches; the half-castes, who combined the vices of both races from which they descended; and the foreign workers, who were in turn different from each other, at that time including Indians and a few Africans, as well as Oceanians. The mission had insufficient resources to cope with these six different ministries: it was impossible to spare priests to serve the needs of the introduced workers. The Indians were probably lost to "Buddha" (!) and considered that they had fulfilled their religious obligations by abstaining from beef. The "blacks," on the other hand, were probably convertible, but because they worked under a tight regimen it was difficult to assemble them in one place at one time, and the problem of their different languages seemed insurmountable.[58]

Bishop Vitte also keenly felt the Catholic "abandonment" of the New Hebrides archipelago for more than twenty years following the first attempt at evangelization in 1848; the Protestants, by contrast, had been very active there, and "at stake are more than a hundred thousand souls that the demon of heresy threatens to ensnare."[59] But the bishop was unable to spare any priests for a new venture in the group. He hit upon the notion of availing himself of the New Hebrideans at hand in New Caledonia: "As a large number of New Hebrideans, even very young, are brought to New Caledonia by merchants, I will try to procure a few children, in order to make Christians of them and pioneers of the Gospel. I have already entered into negotiations with a businessman of Noumea to this end."[60] Seven months later, he mentioned in a letter that he had succeeded. "We have bought [*sic*] nine natives from these islands, still young, and who, I hope, will be able to learn enough French and religion to become one day the introducers of missionaries among their unfortunate compatriots."[61] One might have thought it more pressing for the clergy to learn the languages of the children, if they were to go to the New Hebrides to evangelize, than for the children to learn French.

In his next report, Vitte elaborated the project: "Not being able to go to the Hebrides, Eminence, I have procured at great expense nine natives of these islands, from ten to fifteen years, and I have placed them in our school at St. Louis to be brought up with the little Caledonians. My goal is to make missionaries of them in their respective countries." He explained that he did not aim to produce, as the Protestants did, teachers to be sent ahead—whose only function was to spell out the Bible, praise their ministers, shout against Rome, and not get involved in too many scandals—but simply catechists under the guidance of the priest: "Will I succeed with the Hebrideans? It is doubtful. Three out of nine are already dead; three appear to be going the same way, and the others are scarcely robust. Is it the effect of an epidemic, which this year [1875], here and in Fiji, has carried them off by thousands? Is it bad luck in the choice, or the product of a scrofulous temperament weakened by the climate of their country? I don't know."[62]

As for the rest of the foreign workers, he added, they were going down the same track as the pagan Kanaks, given over to their own impurities and debaucheries as well as adding to them the drunkenness of the whites, except that the foreign workers did it with more ease because no priest could look after them, either through not knowing their language or for other reasons. Apart from a "rather nice chapel" built for "these poor blacks," and some organization of meetings to attract them to it, the church had made no more progress in relation to them.[63]

The experiment in creating catechists out of child recruits apparently continued, for Father Goubin related that the mission acquired three New Hebridean children in 1877. He did not feel constrained to explain his casual remark that "barely three months ago we bought some little New Hebrideans, two boys and a girl," to the distress of the modern editor of his letters who searched for such an explanation: "Apart from the fact that slavery had been abolished in 1848—and we are in 1877—one would have a poor view of a Catholic Mission acquiring children." But the mention of the "purchase" was purely incidental to a story of a miracle. The little girl, whose face was eaten away by a skin disease, was said to have been cured by the application of some water from Lourdes.[64]

Two other New Hebrideans were employed by the mission in 1879, but whether as laborers or prospective missionaries is not known. When they were repatriated in 1884, they complained to the captain of the ship that they had been kept for five years instead of three, and given only 6.25 francs a month for their work all that time, although wages were usually raised for time-expired workers. The captain, who checked their boxes and found them meagerly furnished, sympathized with them and forwarded their complaint.[65] It is just possible that there had been a gigantic misunderstanding between the mission and the recruits, the fathers believing that they were educating them for higher service and the young men that they were working for a stingy master. The mission evidently made efforts to baptize laborers they came across who were in danger of death, for a missionary later made efforts to track down in Malakula a returned laborer who had been baptized for this reason at St. Louis, but, although the man had kept his Christian name of Mathias, he had lost interest in Christianity.[66]

I have found no further mention of a mission to the imported New Hebrideans, and it would appear that after the failure of the catechist project, the church found this responsibility beyond its capability. It was later necessary, after all, for André Ballande to pay for a special chaplain to the Indochinese workers in order to have their spiritual needs attended to.[67] A previous Protestant tutelage was not the obstacle that stood in the way of instructing the New Hebrideans, for up to the mid-1880s only a few of the islands in the group had been touched by Christian teaching of any sort, and not many ten years after that. The catechists and auxiliaries who eventually went with the renewed attempt of the Marists, in 1887, to evangelize the New Hebrides, were converted New Caledonian Kanaks.[68] It was rather as assimilated residents, than as contracted laborers, that New Hebrideans in New Caledonia later came into contact with the church, requesting legitimation of their new status through baptism or marriage.[69]

Unlike the British, the French government did not have the pressure of a vigorous missionary lobby continually raising the specter of slavery and demanding the suppression of recruiting in the Pacific. While individual priests in New Caledonia expressed disquiet about aspects of the Oceanian labor trade, as well as about the exploitation of Asian and local Melanesian labor,[70] the hierarchy seemed to accept the system at face value. In 1874, when kidnapping was at its height, Bishop Vitte naively believed that the New Hebrideans wished to be colonized by France because "the natives of these islands come in droves to seek food, work and safety in New Caledonia."[71] He worried about the souls of introduced workers who remained uninstructed in the faith and who died in numbers without being baptized, but he did not express concern about their being taken from their homes. It was an accident of history that in France the human rights movement descended from French revolutionary thought, which was also hostile to the church. An alliance such as the British one between evangelical Christians and Benthamite liberals was much more difficult in the French context.

Chapter 15
Life after Indenture

At the end of their term, workers had the option of reengaging or returning home. After eight years of continuous indenture, they were eligible to apply for free residence provided they had not been convicted of any crimes or had not incurred any disciplinary penalty during their last two years of employment, a rule that seems to have been fairly strictly adhered to, unlike others. Very few of those convicted in the courts appear in the death registers, apart from those who died during their term of imprisonment.

The Returns

No official figure for the number who were repatriated is extant, but it was probably a little less than half of those indentured. Figures for the repatriated are drawn from shipping notices and not as reliable as those for arrivals: the shipping notice of arrivals was an advertisement to potential customers, but there was no incentive to be precise about the numbers repatriated. Nevertheless, most of the time shippers did report the number of returns on board, along with their other passengers and their cargo, but some merely stated that they had "a number of natives to repatriate." Allowing 30 (less than the average) for each ship declaring that it had an indeterminate number to repatriate, the total comes to over 7,700, or just under half the number of arrivals. This is consistent with Courbet's analysis in 1882 that about a quarter of each contingent reengaged (some of whom would die in the colony and some would finally be repatriated),[1] together with my own that more than a quarter died during their first term, averaged at four years (see appendix table 3). The figures given in a church document relating to the eight years between 1874 and 1882—apparently based on administration statistics for that period—show a somewhat lower rate of return—only 45 percent repatriated of those whose first term had been completed.[2] As these years contain the enormously high death rate for 1875, the year of the measles epidemic, the return rate could have been lower than average.[3] From the list of 107 names of the *Marie*'s cohort of recruits in 1884, 55 appear in the registry of those who died in New Caledonia over the next fifty years, leaving 52, or slightly less than half, presumed repatriated. It appears that the newspaper *La Calédonie* was fairly accurate in its impression that "barely a half of those [New Hebrideans] who recruit will return to their native land."[4]

Indentured laborers were guaranteed repatriation unless they applied for and were admitted to free residence. Under the regulations, the employer was responsible for the expense of returning workers to their homeland at the expiry of their contracts, and was required to pay regular installments of the return passage money to the Immigration Office during the period of indenture. If the worker either died during the term or was admitted to residence, this money was not returnable to the employer.[5] However, as I have shown, it proved difficult for the administration to collect these fees.

The return passage from Noumea was made in conditions inferior to those on repatriating ships from Queensland, to the detriment of fresh recruiting where returns were landed. An official report attributed this to the low rate paid to ships for repatriating Oceanian workers—25 francs (£1 or US$4.75) a head—compared with five times that amount paid to Queensland vessels (£5).[6] Perhaps in response to this criticism, the fee was raised to 50 francs in 1885, but an aggrieved government agent pointed out that this was a poor reward to ships for the expensive delays caused by the requirement of finding the precise home of the return; he contrasted it with the then rate of 175 francs (£7) paid to ships repatriating from Fiji.[7] The New Caledonian rate nevertheless remained the same under the revised labor code of 1893,[8] and was still the same in 1912.[9]

As in Queensland,[10] abuses in repatriation practices quickly came to light. Some workers were kept beyond their term, resulting in a poor reception for repatriating ships hoping for more recruits.[11] Moreover, time-expired workers who had to wait for a ship to repatriate them were not only forced to work either for a private employer or for the administration during their wait, but were sometimes charged for their board and lodging as well, until the 1907 *Inspection mobile* put an end to the practice.

Being landed at the wrong beach was an ever-present risk. It could result, at best, in returns being stripped of their hard-won box of goods, or at worst, in their death, for most islands were divided into mutually hostile districts. However, finding the right place often proved difficult. Government agents commonly found that they had

been given insufficient information to fulfill their obligation to return laborers safely to their homeland, even if they conscientiously
tried to do so. Earlier officers had been too lax about stating the exact place of origin: some had been careless, while others had not realized the necessity for precision. The returns were themselves often
unsure of the place where they had recruited, especially if they had
been away for a long time, or came from the bush and therefore
found it difficult to recognize the passage on the coast where they
had been recruited, or had been recruited when very young.[12] Others
found that their community had moved as a result of events during
their absence.[13] The more negligent government agents, of course,
yielded to the impatience of the captain to land the returns some-
where or other so that the ship did not incur expensive delays.[14] As
late as 1898, when a government agent reported several complaints
by returns or their friends that another French ship had landed returns far from their homes, it brought him a "*blâme*" from Governor
Feillet for having "accepted as true and without checking them
[how could he?], statements from natives known for their lies."[15] The
problem of assuring the return of the New Hebrideans to their own
"place" was still in evidence in 1907,[16] and although the administration believed that the appointment of a French resident officer under
the terms of the New Hebrides Condominium would allow more
supervision of repatriation, it is difficult to understand exactly how
the new arrangement would have helped. It seems highly unlikely
that the resident's staff supervised landings at the passage, and later
complaints would have been too late for the victims, and in any case
hard to distinguish from local feuding.

An abuse brought to the attention of Governor Courbet was that
some captains kept repatriates until the end of the recruiting journey,
so that they could employ them to help work the ship.[17] The newspaper *Le Néo-Calédonien,* a stout defender of the labor trade, also had
information that returns were not always landed at all but were sometimes brought back to Noumea as new recruits by the very ship paid
to repatriate them. Even when the return consented, under pressure
from the shipowner, to be reengaged, the reporter believed that the
administration should oppose the practice, otherwise the bleeding
hearts would have some reason to shout about slavery![18] An instance
of this kind of abuse was reported by Miklouho-Maclay: the skipper of
an American schooner on which he was a passenger told him that he
had been offered a few returns from a Noumea ship for a small sum.[19]
Finally, the practice of putting moribund workers, near the end of
their term, aboard repatriating ships in order to avoid the cost of
hospitalization continued beyond the end of the nineteenth century,
despite regulations aimed at preventing it.

How did the returns fare when they arrived back in their home community? There is so far little evidence that those from New Caledonia raised their status at home through using their knowledge of the colonial language to act as interpreters for passing ships, as those from Queensland are said to have done. Occasionally government agents spoke of meeting returns in their home islands who worked as intermediaries for the recruiters, which would have brought them transitory reward and importance, but nothing beyond that. Commandant Bigant, looking for French-speaking contacts to smooth the way of his half of the Joint Naval Commission in the New Hebrides, reported that most of the returns he had met were indistinguishable from the other local people and could not even understand French, having only been addressed in Bislama while in New Caledonia: "Apart from one man living in Ambrym who had kept his French habits, speaking and writing our language very well, the others have returned to savage ways, no longer wearing clothes and very difficult to recognize."[20] The knowledge of Bislama, however, helped them in communication with Europeans in general and also provided a lingua franca with people from other communities in the islands.

How workers repatriated from New Caledonia were regarded in local terms, rather than as harbingers of European manners and politics, and whether their term abroad helped or hindered them in achieving status, can only be inferred from reports of how returns from other colonies behaved. British missionaries in the New Hebrides complained that they had acquired an addiction to alcohol and that they brought back leprosy,[21] but there is very little other information specific to those from the French colony. Inevitably, most of those who had been living in a foreign society for quite long periods must have experienced changes in outlook. Among the returns from other colonies some were said to be more than content to settle back into their allotted role in their own community, while many now seemed impatient with the assumptions and authority prevailing in their old villages. Some used their new knowledge or sometimes their new weapons to claim superiority, were more assertive, and aspired to leadership of new movements, as Corris so graphically described.[22] There is no reason to doubt that returns from New Caledonia would have shared these various patterns of behavior.

But in one respect the repatriates from New Caledonia differed from those of other colonies: very few had been touched by Christianity, for reasons discussed earlier, unlike Solomon Islanders and New Hebrideans from Queensland, many of whom were converted by the Queensland Kanaka Mission, or the Gilbertese who worked in Tahiti and brought Catholicism back to the Gilberts. They would not therefore have had a religious motive for forming their own little en-claves on the coast as some returns from Queensland did,[23] but it would be useful to know whether some from New Caledonia set up their own communities for a different reason, perhaps out of an in-ability to readapt to the life of their old villages.

There are accounts, too, of returns who, profiting by their expe-rience of plantation agriculture, began to clear land and produce cash crops,[24] including a story of a return from New Caledonia—a Solomon Islander who during the period of his indenture had lived with Martine, an indigenous woman. When he was repatriated, he bought land with the money he had earned and began a coffee plan-tation, using the skills he had learnt abroad. Martine followed him to his homeland, and some years later a visitor to the Solomons re-ported that the pair were living in harmony and doing very well.[25] No doubt many of the New Hebrideans reported successfully cash-cropping on their own account in 1927[26] had also profited from their experience on foreign plantations, some of them in New Caledonia.

The return of female recruits was problematic, as I have described, because many of them left without the consent of their community. On the other hand, the case seems to have been different if a woman returned with her lover to *his* homeland. Several cases are known of cheerful acceptance of this situation by the community to which the man returned. The Kanak woman Martine apparently had no prob-lem when she returned with a Solomon Islander to his "place." Nor did the Pentecost woman who returned to Tanna with her Tannese lover: a missionary (J Campbell Rae) testified that they "live happily together" and, being childless, adopted a Tannese boy.[27] Two Mala-kula women asked to be repatriated to Efaté with the men with whom they had lived for seven years in Queensland, and who had paid their return passages: the local missionary (Macdonald) agreed that this was the best solution.[28] A government agent aboard a New Caledon-ian recruiting ship reported that an Ambrym woman signed on at Malakula: she had returned there from Queensland with her Mala-kula lover, but now wanted to go home. So she recruited alone for Noumea on condition that she would be repatriated to Ambrym when her term was finished![29] Under the regulations, children born to New Hebrideans during their stay in New Caledonia were guaranteed repatriation with them when they left, but there is no information about how this provision worked in practice.

Many of the people of these regions had responded of their own accord to an apparent opportunity to increase their wealth and status, as most other peoples in the world have done, but one knows little about whether such expectations were ever fulfilled. Precise research by a local historian or anthropologist could no doubt throw light on whether or how returns used their hard-won experience in the French colony, or how they adjusted to their return. Useful references to the role of ex-indentured laborers are found in the works of some anthropologists, but a great deal remains to be discovered about how the workers' experience abroad translated to the daily life of their reintegration. Were they, because of their experience, more, or less, attracted to the Christian missions that were springing up when they returned? Did they find it more difficult to accept the rule of their elders? Were the concerns of village life now less appealing? Anthropologists living for long terms in communities once involved in the labor trade might well be able to provide some answers.

Those Who Stayed

Much less is known about the life of laborers who elected to stay in New Caledonia than about those who stayed in Queensland or Fiji. The "free resident" New Hebrideans were able at least to bargain for higher wages and to choose their job and place of residence. Not surprisingly, most chose to stay in Noumea rather than in the bush, and nearly all the deaths of older Hebrideans occurred there. The most common employment given with their deaths is "laborer" or "servant."

Despite harsh conditions, the women seem to have survived better than the men, some establishing families and achieving a degree of independence. Up to 1930, 17 female recruits had reached the age of sixty or more, compared with only 20 men, despite the very large preponderance of males. Scraps of evidence show that the lives of these women in the colony had by no means been easy. One of them, a Santo woman, revealed in court that she had a child by her *libéré* overseer and that she had been beaten by the plantation owner after she had complained to the immigration officer about not being paid. At the time of her court appearance she was aged about thirty-seven, and was being detained in Noumea by order of the magistrate, for an unspecified offense.[30] Surviving all these problems, she died in Yaté, in the southeast of the Grande Terre, still in service, aged sixty.[31] Another woman, who had come to New Caledonia from Pentecost around the year 1890 aged about twenty, began work in Noumea as a domestic servant. At the end of 1896, she gave birth to a son, "father unknown," who lived for fourteen months. In 1900 she had a daughter, the father this time an Ambrymese servant. In time, the daughter also became a domestic in Noumea, where she had a stillborn child, "father unknown," in 1922. She then went into the laundry business with her mother. She had at least two other children, who married in

Noumea. She died in 1928, at age twenty-eight, but her mother was still going strong at the time, her age given as sixty.[32]

There is some evidence of assimilation into local society. The register of births records liaisons of New Hebridean women with Kanak, Asian, and white men, and of New Hebridean men with Kanak women as well as with New Hebridean women from different communities. Some of these relationships appear to have been stable, as more than one child was born to them and recognized by the father. Some contracted legal marriages with their partners. Many of the children of New Hebridean women, particularly, but not exclusively, those born of liaisons with white men, married settlers, and their descendants would be indistinguishable from other inhabitants of the territory today.[33] In 1947, Governor Parisot made a general mention of some of the ethnic New Hebrideans living in the colony.

> There exists in the colony a certain number of natives born in the New Hebrides group, most of them old, or descendants of Hebridean natives. One mostly encounters them in Noumea, living among Europeans. Those born in New Caledonia have generally gone to European schools. They are therefore socially closer to Europeans than the natives of New Caledonia and its Dependencies who normally live in the tribes and spend their whole lives attached to that social unit.[34]

A few scraps of information about individuals have come to light. One little Hebridean was adopted about 1872 by Hortense Vendegou, known as Queen Hortense, high chief of Kunié (the Isle of Pines). Although he did not inherit the title, he retained the name Vendegou, married, and has living descendants on the island.[35] Other descendants of Hebrideans are said to live as a *"tribu"* on the east coast. Among the sources are signs that time-expired or "free resident" New Hebrideans were assimilated to either European or indigenous ways of life. Records in the archbishopric's archives refer to some seeking baptism in the Catholic Church, one of whom lived with the indigenous people of Ndé, near Paita, "recognized as one of their own," who wished to marry a local woman, herself a convert.[36] There is a reference in the correspondence of the Gendarmerie during the Second World War to a New Hebridean called Willy, then a free resident, who lived with an indigenous woman from the tribe of Grondu, near Ponérihouen: Willy was working for the American troops camped near the airport at Tontouta and was observed acting as interpreter for regular meetings between American soldiers and "the native leaders of Ponérihouen," which attracted the alarm and investigation of the local gendarme commandant, worried that they were being incited to rebellion.[37] A free resident Tannese who had worked for Maison Barrau for more than twenty years, and in the colony at least three years before that, was in 1955 asked by his family to return to Tanna; he refused in no uncertain manner.[38]

The hazards of recruitment, work in a foreign land under poor conditions, and repatriation were such that one must wonder that any succeeded in completing the cycle. But it seems that about a half of them did, and that hundreds also remained after indenture to live out their lives in the colony.

Chapter 16
"Nothing More Convenient"

The myth that New Caledonia was a sleeping beauty, needing only a supply of cheap labor as the kiss of life, was retold so often that it passed almost without question among colonizers and settlers. The shortage of labor and the need for the administration to do something about it was a perpetual subject of discussion in the newspapers. Official reports to France usually agreed that the place would take off if only one could find enough cheap labor. The small size of the territory, the poverty of most of its soil, and above all its distance from its markets, rarely intruded on the story. There were exceptions. The continual comparisons made between the development of Australia and New Caledonia drew the exasperated comment from Rear-Admiral du Petit-Thouars that "the only point of similarity existing between the two countries is that both of them are situated in the southern hemisphere."[1] He believed that the number of New Hebridean workers in the colony a few months before he wrote his report—2,023 on 1 January 1879—roughly corresponded to the demand. He recommended that the government should revert to the original conception of the colony as a place to send convicts as well as a depot for supplying and repairing ships in the South Pacific.[2]

The proponents of development proved too strong, however, especially as mining spread to every part of the country. Except in the years of depression—1885–1887, 1895–1897, 1900–1902, 1930—the calls for cheap labor were as strident as ever. The neighboring islands remained the preferred source. Convict labor was not as available to settlers as it had been in the Australian colonies; *libérés* were said to be unreliable and anyway far too expensive for most settlers; the local Melanesian population, even when they came under control, were considered too independent and a security risk, apart from the fact that they were only employable for short periods and were almost twice as costly as the New Hebrideans. As Governor Courbet said, after he first suspended the labor trade in 1882:

> One must not disguise the fact that Hebridean immigration is universally missed. . . . Nothing more convenient, in fact, than the Hebridean. Despite his savage nature and by reason of simply being far from his country and separated from his kin, he is docile and inoffensive: he submits passively to the will of the master, whatever form it takes, he is little aware of his rights and rarely claims them. And when someone trains him they have him for three or five years. . . . The employer cares little about how he was recruited, that is the business of the recruiting agency and the administration.[3]

To these virtues of "Hebrideans" in the eyes of the settlers, was added their role as a buffer against rebellious Kanaks, escaped convicts, and fractious *libérés*. As well, unlike Asian workers, they spent their wages in the colony. Expressing gratification that, after two years of depression the labor trade with the islands was to be resumed, *La Calédonie* said it all:

> The New Hebridean immigrants give us good service as workers, in Noumea as well as in the bush. More disciplined and submissive than the Loyalty Islanders, less to be feared than the Tonkinese and the Annamites, they are highly sought after by employers.
>
> This recruitment is to be encouraged from yet another point of view; it gives rise to business benefiting the commerce of the country; not only through the purchases [by shipowners] of the trade goods with which recruiting is conducted, but because the New Hebrideans generally spend in Noumea the greater part, if not the whole, of their wages.[4]

"Disguised Slavery"?

The reasons for the demand for "Hebridean" labor are clear, but accounting for island societies supplying that demand is more difficult, unless one accepts the popular belief that all so-called recruits were kidnapped. However, recent historians, while acknowledging that kidnapping took place, have produced good evidence that island societies cooperated in recruiting labor for Queensland and Fiji. This study confirms similar evidence for the trade to New Caledonia, but suggests that the extent and interpretation of island participation should be modified.

First, it seems that Adrian Graves is right in pointing out that modern scholars have underestimated the extent of coercion, treating it as a short-lived phenomenon of the early stages of recruiting.[5] The New Caledonian experience certainly tends to undermine their claim that it became "unnecessary and impossible"[6] to kidnap Islanders after they became experienced in the business of recruiting. The proposal that they could hardly be abducted "from the same beaches, on the same islands, . . . for forty years or more"[7] neglects the fact that familiarity with European ships diminished prudence. When Islanders confidently crowded around the boats or went on board to trade or chat, a new opportunity was provided for unscrupulous recruiters to abduct them. The 1890s was not too late for kidnapping, according to Moore's oral evidence from a Queenslander (Len McGann) whose father worked on the recruiting ship *Sybil*.[8] Indirect kidnapping through chiefs and big-men, especially in the Solomons, also occurred quite late in the trade, and was difficult to detect and impossible to prevent by any regulation. Kidnapping declined but remained possible for the duration of the labor trade.

Island societies certainly cooperated with cruising labor vessels to obtain the trade goods they brought. The ships traded for vegetables and for water all around the groups, and often employed local people as interpreters, messengers, and extra hands, giving valued items in exchange. They were a source of commerce for all Melanesian communities, not only those that sold labor. This trade continued the process, begun by traders collecting sandalwood, of distributing European cloth, iron and steel tools, tobacco, and muskets throughout the islands of the New Hebrides and the Solomons.

Commerce in labor, however, was of a different order. After all, people were traded, not goods. It involved taking young people from their villages to a life of hardship and, for the first thirty years of the trade, a one-in-four chance of death at the average age of seventeen to twenty-four. It was a worse prospect than enlisting for the First World War. In his summary of the historiography of the labor trade in general, Doug Munro rightly concluded that the "basic question of motivation to enlist is perhaps still one of the least understood aspects of the labour trade."[9] In the places where trade goods like steel axes, knives, and cloth were not yet common they were most welcome, and labor was readily exchanged for them, but there was a limit to the absorption of these goods, as I have shown for the sandalwood trade.[10] It is difficult to conceive that, after a stock of them had been supplied, they would continue to be acceptable in exchange for young men who might never return.

The only insatiable demand in the labor trade, attested by all, was the demand for modern firearms. The most powerful incentive to recruiting was the offer of a good breech-loading rifle: no longer the slow-loading and unreliable musket of sandalwooding days, the Snider rifle was an effective weapon. The acquisition of a number of them was capable of making local warfare more deadly.[11] Sometimes it changed the balance of power among communities, equalizing the position of coastal peoples relative to inland peoples, and sometimes it encouraged aggressive warfare.

The present study reinforces the conclusion of other writers that the acquisition of effective firearms was a powerful motivating force, but it also suggests that it should be elevated to the main factor driving cooperation with recruiting. When the British colonies banned the supply of firearms in 1884, recruits and their sponsors turned to French and German ships instead. While most historians recognized this change of preferences, they looked on it as only a temporary blip.[12] However, the advantage, to French traders at least, was not temporary. It may have appeared that the British trade made a quick return to favor late in 1885 and throughout 1886, but in fact during that period the New Caledonian trade was effectively suspended. When it resumed under another guise in 1887, the complaints of British traders about unfair competition recurred.[13] In important pools of labor like Tanna and Malaita, where alternative sources of firearms were few, Noumea recruiters did a roaring trade: in the 1890s no other item was acceptable there. More remarkable still, ships from Noumea were able to recruit women from Tanna, something that had been a rarity before.

The steep decline in the numbers recruited for Fiji after 1884—falling from 1,266 in 1884 to 295 the next year, and going no higher than 368 thereafter[14]—surely related to the ban on firearms. And in both Queensland and Fiji, under-age youths, some of poor physique, formed a higher proportion of those recruited in the 1890s than in the two previous decades,[15] also signaling that British traders had less negotiating power than before, whereas the opposite in age trends occurred in New Caledonia. It is arguable that a striking improvement in working conditions and the increased value of beach payments offered in alternative goods (even gold)[16] were compensatory measures that Queensland and Fiji had to take to remain competitive after the firearms ban. In direct contrast, New Caledonia was able to obtain the most desirable recruits in the 1890s—including those who had already served in the British colonies—by giving Snider rifles as beach payment for them, without even having redressed their endemic problem of the nonpayment of wages.

While concurring that breech-loading rifles were the things most valued by the Islanders, most writers have not given this factor full weight in their general analyses. Peter Corris referred to the offer of rifles as "the most powerful inducement the recruiters could hold out" to potential recruits or their sponsors, and pointed out that "[t]o lack a store of guns could mean the failure of a voyage."[17] He related that in 1878 a group of Melanesians confronted the premier of Queensland to tell him that no more recruits would be forthcoming if he were to ban firearms as beach payments or as purchases from their wages.[18] He also stressed the "importance of firearms to the islanders" indicated by the risks they took to smuggle them home when they were banned.[19] But when summarizing the stimuli to recruiting he referred only to the "great desirability of European goods" without giving special status to the "most powerful inducement" of modern weapons.[20] Graves also rated the desire for firearms as the strongest incentive, but subordinated it, and weakened it, by connecting it to the Islanders' need to fight to secure land to maintain subsistence, part of his general picture of the destruction of Melanesian subsistence agriculture by European traders and missionaries.[21] But, as already noted, there was in fact a disjunction, not a correlation, between local rates of recruiting and European inroads into the subsistence economy.

The reasons for the desirability of powerful weaponry probably do not need to go beyond the competition for prestige and power between groups, already present in the culture of most Melanesian communities, but whatever the reasons, no one questions the efficacy of this factor in promoting the labor trade. International cooperation in the ban of firearms, sought by the British but in effect refused by the French, German, and United States governments,[22] might very well have killed off the labor trade altogether, as both traders and recruits predicted. It would at least have forced a significant improvement in working and recruiting conditions everywhere in order for indenture to have survived.

Differentiating Participation

The participation of a society should not be confused with the free choice of individuals within it. Did the "majority," as one historian said, make "a definite decision to leave their islands" to spend three or more years abroad?[23] Was this choice, as he said, made by the recruits themselves? Except in the case of runaways, it does not seem likely. In most island societies of the period, men young enough to be interesting to recruiters rarely made such important decisions for themselves as leaving the community to work in a foreign land. As was later observed, such matters were determined by their elders in long consultations. For example, when the people were forced to work on plantations to pay taxes to the colonial government, the number of young men to go away to work, and which of them should make up the quota, was decided by their seniors. It does not follow that the young people, used to direction, were necessarily forced or were even unwilling to go, although that was no doubt true in some cases. But it is different from their "making a definite decision to leave."

Most scholars have appeared unwilling to distinguish the motives of the recruits from those of their sponsors, and often merge the two. Deryck Scarr concluded that the success of the labor trade as a business "required the substantial consent of all concerned,"[24] but he distinguished different interests among the concerned Islanders only in the negative case, when people of authority tried to *prevent* young men from leaving.[25] Corris, while aware of "pressures from within their own societies" driving people to leave, saw these mainly in terms of the "unsatisfied needs and aspirations" of the recruits themselves. For the general "rounded portrait" of the trade he was content to quote Scarr's "substantial consent of all concerned."[26] He spoke of a period of European coercion after which "systematic recruiting was well understood and willingly entered into by the islanders," as if "the islanders" were one and indivisible in their attitudes.[27] Roger Keesing likewise wrote of "the islanders" using the trade for their own ends but failed to note that there were a variety of interests among "the islanders."[28] Kerry Howe left the impression that the members of a Melanesian society were of one mind when he wrote of the trade as a "cooperative venture" and "on the whole a voluntary exodus."[29] Clive Moore specifically extended this cooperation to the recruits themselves: presenting an alternative interpretation to the view that the trade was purely a matter of kidnapping, he stated, "[W]e know that the majority came willingly."[30] But do we?

The New Caledonian episode throws this distinction into relief through one of its specific elements—the legal recruitment of children from the age of six (later ten). The question of voluntary enlistment by the recruits themselves arises most starkly here. In the case of young children, the notion of a free contract is impossible to accept. One must ask, with *Le Progrès*, what sort of guarantee surrounded such an engagement. "When a little *canaque* is brought [here] by a recruiter, who is going to be convinced that he engaged himself freely and knowingly for five years, nine years or even until his majority?"[31] Corris allowed that there were cases where a "generous recruiting present excited the cupidity of adults so that they urged the recruiting of boys so young that they had a very imperfect grasp of what they were undertaking,"[32] but he believed this occurred only very late in the trade "when competition for recruits was at its height."[33] However, if it was sometimes possible to excite cupidity in adults to cause them to exert pressure on boys, why not throughout the period? And why not on young men?

It is hard to argue against the view of Corris's eighteen informants who signed on for British colonies in the early years of the twentieth century, but it is not a strong counter to the views of Europeans who were writing about their immediate experience throughout the period. All of them seventy to eighty years old, Corris's informants were survivors and had been recruited when, as he himself said, in British colonies "the regulation of recruiting was at its most strict, when conditions on the plantations were at their best, and when the rewards for labor migration were at their highest."[34] Selective memory may also have played a part. It would have suited Europeans engaged in the labor trade to take the view that "[t]he attractiveness of the travel and rewards the labor recruiters offered, and the circumstances of young men in the island communities, account sufficiently for the decision of the majority of those who entered the recruiting boats."[35] But many recruiters and government agents (though not all)[36] thought otherwise. Their opinion that it was often someone else's decision seems therefore worthy of more respect.

The "attractiveness of travel" undoubtedly carried weight with individuals, but if it was so important, how does one account for the difficulty of obtaining recruits when there were ways of acquiring wealth at home? In places where copra and bêche-de-mer trading stations were established, where Islanders could obtain valued goods through selling local produce, recruiters from New Caledonia found it virtually impossible to obtain recruits. Exactly the same observation has been made by historians of British labor trading.[37] Judith Bennett pointed out that to get similar wages for three years' work abroad, Islanders able to sell commodities to traders at home had to work only six to twelve months.[38] This was quickly recognized, and where and when valued European goods could be obtained in alternative ways, there was very soon a fall-off in recruiting.[39] So the attraction of foreign parts for individuals seems to have been exaggerated as a motive for recruiting.

The notion that the beach payment was an inducement to a sponsor to use his influence over prospective recruits has been denied by scholars who said that it merely reproduced customary patterns of Melanesian behavior: it was not, in fact, strictly a *payment* but a recognition of the need for compensation for the absence of a relative, following the "Melanesian principle of reciprocity."[40] It was not tantamount to *buying* a recruit, as some reformers argued, despite the fact that the Pidgin term for it was "buying boy." Furthermore, they said, unless an agreed present were given, kinsfolk were likely to complain to the next warship that the recruit had been "stolen," that is, not paid for.[41] Both these things are true, but neither affects the case that the gift was an inducement for people to offer as recruits those over whom they had control. This, indeed, was what it was designed to do. The goods advanced by Europeans were planned to be as tempting as possible, not just something to smooth the path of negotiations. The offer of Snider rifles was, and was meant to be, an overwhelming enticement: in other contexts Corris referred to them as "persuasive presents"[42] and "the most powerful inducement."[43] Nor was the "gift" given to induce future obligation on the part of the receiver, as in the Melanesian gift exchange system. It was an on-the-spot bargain, as in normal trading *between* groups: no gift, no recruit, the payment being strictly in proportion to the perceived value of the recruit.

W G Ivens may have unwittingly fostered the notion that the beach payment was part of traditional gift-giving by saying that it was "thoroughly in accord with native ideas," and done by the missionaries themselves. But he was clear that the Melanesian concept involved was that of trading, not gift-giving within the community. He said that it was "known *in the native tongue everywhere* as buying,"[44] as his dictionary shows.[45] He believed the practice harmless only when the beach payment consisted of goods of small value. R H Codrington also pointed out that on Vanua Lava, where he knew the local languages, the words buying and selling were not only the Pidgin terms used in labor trade exchanges, but also the words used in the local tongues, the same they used for buying and selling pigs.[46]

Some recruits undoubtedly dreamed of seeing the world and of acquiring wealth (especially a rifle), and perhaps even a wife, through this their only chance of leaving home. In communities as closed as Melanesian villages, labor vessels also provided an escape hatch for dissidents, law-breakers, and refugees of various kinds. In general, however, consent to sign on was not necessarily an indication of free and informed choice. Consent could occur from corporate decision, from credence in false promises, from the effects of natural disasters, and from misfortune in war. Even when and where the trade was relatively well regulated, there was no way of eliminating those pressures.

Reputation as a Factor in Choice

Active participation was shown in deliberate choices about whether to let young men go at all, and if so, to what destination. Preferences for one colony over others—and changes in these preferences—were clear over the whole period. Recruiters came to realize that these choices were based on much better information and far more astuteness than most Europeans commonly attributed to Pacific Islanders. This has been observed by historians of the British labor trade,[47] and it is emphatically shown in the New Caledonian sector, which, being for long periods out of favor with recruits, was forced to consider the subject.

The good name of a destination was a factor in choice as well as the material gains to be obtained from it. New Caledonia enjoyed the advantage of being closer to the source than any of the other markets, but it was unable to capitalize on this by taking a longer-term view of its responsibilities to recruits. Its reputation was good until government control weakened at the end of the 1860s; then it became the least attractive destination for migrant workers until the mid-1880s. The process was cumulative, for being held in low esteem only increased pressure on recruiters to obtain recruits by force or fraud, thereby adding to the poor reputation of "Noumea" ships. The playing field was leveled only when the British authorities banned the trade in firearms in 1884, but too often this advantage was offset by fresh acts of injustice, causing another decline in reputation.

Slavery at the Workplace?

Even where individual consent—sometimes eagerness—to sign on is quite evident, the debate about coercion, as Miklouho-Maclay pointed out, is not over. Those who saw indenture as "disguised slavery" were referring not only to kidnapping but also to the next stage in the system, the working life in the colony. The introduced laborers were not slaves, because they had legal rights, their children were born free, and, assuming they lived to the end of their term, they could choose to be repatriated. However, I do not, like Moore, seriously object to the statement in a Queensland textbook that the indentured laborers were "given a status little better than slaves."[48] Once in the colony, recruits could not choose their job or their master, and their bargaining power, at least in the case of first indentures, was virtually nil. They could not express themselves freely in the language of the master and were subject to an unknown system of law and wholly foreign conditions of life. Laws protecting them were often a dead letter. In practice if not in theory, they could be transferred or "sold," to use the usual expression of the times, to another master without their consent. In New Caledonia, many were never paid. Bereft of the support of kinsfolk, they were dependent on a foreign employer with power to punish and humiliate. If it was temporary slavery for those who survived the period of their indenture and the perils of repatriation, for the quarter of them who did not—either in Queensland[49] or New Caledonia—it was also a sentence of death at an early age. Notwithstanding the presence of labor inspectors and stricter enforcement of the law in the British colonies, no instances of harsh conditions and ill-treatment in New Caledonia are without their counterparts in Fiji and Queensland,[50] because the system itself was a fertile soil for abuses. In the end, the fate of indentured workers rested with the intelligence and good conscience of their masters, not the best guarantee in the world. The wonder is that many employers fulfilled their responsibilities conscientiously.

Under the best circumstances, indenture was never a free contract between equal parties. Unlike boys indentured to a master craftsman in seventeenth and eighteenth century Europe, with whom they have been compared,[51] indentured Oceanians had no social contact with their employer, and rarely acquired a skill, as apprentices did, that led to opportunity and status when they became free. On the employers' side, they could not see such workers as potential fellow citizens of equal status, as a master might have seen apprentices. They had therefore no incentive but to get as much work as they could from them in the three or more years of the bond.

As Du Petit-Thouars pointed out,[52] the people-export business was by far the most important industry in the New Hebrides and the Solomon Islands in the last quarter of the nineteenth century, dwarfing copra and maize production. Having exhausted the sandalwood trade, entrepreneurs scoured the islands for brawn and muscle. Although it provided a temporary solution to the labor problem in New Caledonia, as elsewhere, the labor trade had few apparent positive consequences for the donor communities as a whole. The same can be said for the indenture of Asian and local laborers that followed. It may have served enterprising individuals within those societies, but growth in individual wealth or status mainly followed preexisting power, the apportionment of the wealth gained depending on the position of the individual in the donor societies, as it did in the host societies. In southern Melanesia, labor trading increased the use of steel tools, which cut the amount of time needed to clear land and cultivate crops, but against this must be offset the destruction caused by warfare encouraged by the acquisition of effective firepower.

The foreign Oceanians were the staple of the colony's labor force in the nineteenth century, and were valued ancillary workers in the twentieth century. Their work laid the foundations of the mining industry and of coffee and livestock culture; it made the country more attractive and safer for European settlers, who refused to tolerate substitute labor and twice campaigned successfully for the restoration of the trade in Oceanians. But the price of awakening the sleeping beauty was paid by the donor communities: hardship for those left at home, and for those abroad a bleak life and a grave toll in sickness and death.

Appendix: Tables

Table 1
Estimated numbers of arrivals and departures of recruits,
1865–1929

Year	Arrivals	Departures	Year	Arrivals	Departures
1865	61		1889	482	77
1866	92	38	1890	488	59
1867	151	112	1891	306	33
1868	485	76	1892	144	101
1869	299	120	1893	308	176
1870	336	376	1894	243	254
1871	187	176	1895	9	132
1872	349	128	1896	15	80
1873	847	176	1897	138	132
1874	902	184	1898	326	143
1875	674	582	1899	144	53
1876	566	209	1900	44	15
1877	805	417	1901	110	15
1878	495	197	1902	234	102
1879	613	314	1903	117	53
1880	671	330	1904	83	55
1881	379	124	1905	126	74
1882	393	56	1906	106	74
1883	4	6	1907	156	92
1884	189	172	1908	86	128
1885	338	285	1909	130	88
1886	13	83	1910	174	69
1887	183	184	1911	125	36
1888	456	88	1912	211	62

(continued)

Table 1 (*continued*)

Year	Arrivals	Departures	Year	Arrivals	Departures
1913	76	51	1922	61	50
1914	63	51	1923	51	46
1915	77	47	1924	64	32
1916	91	43	1925	90	32
1917	140	38	1926	116	57
1918	101	63	1927	170	31
1919	101	68	1928	155	86
1920	77	71	1929	151	31
1921	100	39			
			TOTAL	15,478	*7,372

Sources: Figures are mainly from shipping reports, as described in the Note on Sources. Various supplementary sources include reports from the Department of the Interior and the *Inspection mobile,* Privy Council proceedings and quarterly figures in *Le Moniteur* and the governor's correspondence.

Notes: In the years up to and including 1880, when some ships were offloading and repatriating on the east coast, without being reported in Noumea newspapers, official figures, when available, were sometimes preferable, although probably an underestimation. For the reasons given in the Note on Sources, shipping reports for departures were less reliable than those for arrivals, and where available, official figures were preferred.

*Eleven ships' reports did not state the number being repatriated, but indicated only that they had "a number of natives to repatriate," or some such phrase. Allowing a conservative average of 30 per ship, this would add 330 to the total number of repatriates, bringing it to 7,702.

Table 2
Registered deaths of foreign Oceanians, by year, 1866–1929

Year	Number	Year	Number	Year	Number
1866	7	1888	97	1910	33
1867	14	1889	116	1911	32
1868	15	1890	128	1912	27
1869	16	1891	177	1913	21
1870	33	1892	109	1914	10
1871	23	1893	120	1915	12
1872	25	1894	112	1916	20
1873	64	1895	79	1917	11
1874	97	1896	72	1918	14
1875	336	1897	53	1919	19
1876	141	1898	70	1920	25
1877	150	1899	78	1921	30
1878	178	1900	49	1922	16
1879	107	1901	79	1923	8
1880	172	1902	60	1924	11
1881	156	1903	70	1925	16
1882	227	1904	42	1926	11
1883	218	1905	38	1927	10
1884	161	1906	41	1928	8
1885	174	1907	52	1929	12
1886	116	1908	28		
1887	84	1909	31		

Source: New Caledonia registry of births, marriages, and deaths *(état civil)*.

Table 3

Estimate of foreign Oceanian populations and death rates from official figures

	(1)		(2)	(3)	(4)	(5)
	Population given		Estimated mid-year population	Deaths	Deaths per thousand	Notes
Year	Number	Date				
1870	720	15 June	720	33	45.8	
1871	—		—	23	—	
1872	—		—	25	—	
1873	1193	1 May	1358	64	47.1	
1874	1665	27 April	1772	97	54.7	
1875	2343	1 Jan	2221	336	151.2	
1876	—	—	2187	141	64.5	
1877	1650	1 Jan	1780	150	84.3	
1878	1909	1 Jan	1966	178	90.5	
1879	2023	1 Jan	2104	107	50.9	
1880	2185	1 Jan	2270	172	75.8	
1881	2354	1 Jan	2452	156	63.6	
	2456	1 April				
1882	2819	1 July	2819	227	80.5	
1883	2706	1 Jan	2349	218	92.8	
1884	2446	15 July	2440	161	66.0	A figure of 1900 for 1 January was given to the *Conseil général*, but it is not credible, given the previous figures and the ar-

Year	(col 1)	date	(col 2)	(col 3)	(col 4)
1885	—	—	—	174	—
1886	—	—	—	116	—
1887	1769	1 June	1771	84	47.4
1888	1881	1 Jan	1982	97	48.9

rivals, departures, and deaths after them. It may perhaps refer to current engagements, omitting the reindentured and free residents, or perhaps refers only to New Hebrideans in Noumea and adjacent districts, as sometimes happened. I have therefore used the figure quoted by Courmeau in his report to the ministry in France (1884).

This was the first year of a suspension of the labor trade, and therefore there were virtually no arrivals, while departures and deaths diminished the previous population.

Official figures for 1888–1889 failed to count the "free laborers" (nonindentured) introduced from mid-1887 to the end of 1889. These are newly drafted recruits, not time-expired residents: my mid-year estimates add them, and subtract deaths and repatriates, for those years.

Note: The population figures in column 1 are from official records of various sorts: letters, reports, censuses, the proceedings of the *Conseil général*, and occasionally in *Annuaires* (yearbooks). They are unsatisfactory, not only because they are given at various times of the year and are not there for every year, but also because different figures sometimes appear in different sources for the same year, and one has to infer which was more likely to be reliable. I have estimated mid-year population figures (column 2) from arrivals, departures, and deaths before or after the given date, or, where two figures are available in sequence, the sum of the two divided by two. The population figures given for 1897–1911, and again for 1919–1921, are of indentured laborers only (denoted by asterisks). Therefore, since the total population was greater than the figure given, and death registrations do not discriminate between indentured and unindentured, the death rate (column 4) cannot be calculated for those years, but official figures for the number of indentured laborers are still given as a matter of interest. The figures in column 3 are from the registry of deaths

(continued)

Table 3 (continued)

Year	Population given Number	Date	Estimated mid-year population	Deaths	Deaths per thousand	Notes
1889	2082	1 Jan	2227	116	52.1	
1890	2371	1 Jan	2347	128	54.5	
1891	2672	1 Jan	2720	177	65.0	
1892	2768	1 Jan	2735	109	39.9	
1893	2688	Aug	2745	120	43.7	Of the population given, 1250 were New Hebridean "free residents" (PVCG 1893, August session).
1894	2788	1 Jan	2727	112	41.1	
1895	—	—	—	79	—	Although no estimates have been found for population present in 1895 and 1896, there were very few arrivals in these two years because of an economic recession, and deaths and repatriates would have diminished the existing population, so the figure would have been lower than that for 1894.
1896	—	—	—	72	—	
1897	*1511	1 Jan	—	53	—	*See introductory note.
1898	*1405	1 Jan	—	70	—	
1899	*1365	1 Jan	—	78	—	
1900	*1310	1 Jan	—	49	—	
	*1282	1 Oct	—			
1901	*1223	1 Oct	—	79	—	
	*1338	3 Nov	—			
1902	*1025	1 Oct	—	60	—	

1903	—		—	70	—	
1904	—		—	42	—	
1905	*778		—	38	—	
1906		15 April	—	41	—	
1907			—	52	—	
1908			—	28	—	
1909			—	31	—	
1910			—	33	—	
1911	*728	5 March	—	32	—	The population given includes 6 Wallisians.
1912	713	30 Nov	721	27	37.4	
1913	—		—	21	—	
1914	—		—	10	—	
1915	563	15 Dec	616	12	19.5	Of the population given, 522 were indentured (including 57 Wallisians) and 41 were now free residents.
1916	666	31 July	666	20	30.0	The population given includes 518 indentured (of whom 50 were Wallisians) and 148 free residents.
1917	631	1 July	631	11	17.4	Of the population given 492 were indentured (including 33 Wallisians) and 139 free residents.
1918	—		—	14	—	
1919	*620	(no date)	—	19	—	Of the indentured population given, 57 were Wallisians.
1920	—		—	25	—	
1921	*414	1 July	—	30	—	Of the indentured population given, 27 were Wallisians.
1922	—		—	16	—	
1923	—		—	8	—	
1924	—		—	11	—	

(continued)

Table 3 (continued)

	(1)		(2)	(3)	(4)	(5)
	Population given		Estimated mid-year population	Deaths	Deaths per thousand	Notes
Year	Number	Date				
1925	—		—	16	—	
1926	—		—	11	—	
1927	—		—	10	—	
1928	—		—	8	—	
1929	465	29 June	465	12	25.8	The population given includes 403 New Hebrideans (all re-indentured), 9 Wallisians (indentured), plus 18 free residents (16 New Hebrideans and 2 Wallisians), plus 35 in a "*situation irrégulière*" (26 New Hebrideans and 9 Wallisians).

Table 4

Mean age at death 1866–1929

Year	Mean age at death (years)	Year	Mean age at death (years)	Year	Mean age at death (years)	Year	Mean age at death (years)
1866	21.5	1882	19.9	1898	28.8	1914	36.3
1867	22.9	1883	21.6	1899	27.0	1915	34.5
1868	20.9	1884	22.3	1900	29.9	1916	31.5
1869	21.4	1885	22.3	1901	28.2	1917	44.2
1870	23.2	1886	23.2	1902	27.9	1918	27.2
1871	22.1	1887	23.5	1903	24.1	1919	36.4
1872	20.4	1888	22.8[c]	1904	27.3	1920	35.5
1873	22.6	1889	21.3[d]	1905	28.7	1921	34.4
1874	17.8	1890	21.0	1906	27.2	1922	21.0[g]
1875	19.0[a]	1891	22.4	1907	29.1[e]	1923	
1876	19.2	1892	23.3	1908	27.9	1924	
1877	18.1	1893	23.4	1909	30.8	1925	
1878	18.3	1894	24.0	1910	34.6[f]	1926	39.7
1879	18.4	1895	24.4	1911	28.1	1927	
1880	19.9	1896	26.9	1912	29.8	1928	
1881	19.2[b]	1897	27.0	1913	33.1	1929	43.1[h]

Notes: In the état civil an estimate of the age at death was given in 75 to 99 percent of cases for most years. Years where the provision of age estimates falls below this rate are noted. In years in which there are too few ages given to make an average worth taking, the mean age column is left blank. Second-generation New Hebrideans and Solomon Islanders are excluded from the calculations of mean age. The mean age tends to rise in later years, mainly because there were then a significant number of time-expired or free-resident foreign Oceanians.

a Fewer than half the death registrations in this year carried an estimate of age. The mean age of these is probably higher than it would have been had more ages been given. It was the year of the measles epidemic, and many died soon after arrival and were hastily buried, six of them without even a name. Because many of the measles victims were young children, the true mean age is probably lower.

b Only 50 percent of ages given this year.

c Only 66 percent of ages given this year.

d Only 58 percent of ages given this year.

e Only 67 percent of ages given this year.

f Only 55 percent of ages given this year.

g It is not clear why the mean age at death plummeted this year. It may be that the flu epidemic of 1921 carried off ailing older people who might otherwise have died the next year.

h Out of 12 deaths, 9 ages at death were given. They range from 14 to 66 years.

Notes

Chapter 1: The Pacific Island Labor Trade and New Caledonia

1. Ward 1948; Morrell 1960; Parnaby 1964 (Parnaby's views are somewhat revised in Parnaby 1972).
2. Graves 1984, 112.
3. McArthur and Yaxley 1967, 20.
4. Calculations made from figures (subtracting Solomon Islanders) in the following sources: Parnaby 1964, 203–204; Price and Baker 1976, 114–116 (Queensland); Siegel 1985, 37 (Fiji); Courbet 1882*b* (New Caledonia); Firth and Munro 1990 (Sāmoa); Bennett 1976 (Hawai'i). Parnaby (1972, 142) gives a total of 15,000 laborers in Fiji and Queensland about this time, but says that about half were Solomon Islanders, so his proportion of New Hebrideans is only 7 percent of the 100,000 estimated New Hebrides population; but Solomon Islanders were no more than 14 percent of recruits in Queensland in this year, and about 40 percent in Fiji, so he underestimates the New Hebridean population abroad by almost half.
5. Bridge 1883.
6. Steel 1880, 221.
7. Quoted in Ivens 1918, 226.
8. Especially Scarr 1967; Corris 1973; Saunders 1982; Moore 1985; Moore, Leckie, and Munro 1990; Graves 1993; Mercer and Moore 1978.
9. Munro 1993, 90.
10. Munro 1993, 90.
11. Quoted in Steel 1880, 414.
12. Campbell 1873, 207, 204.
13. Miklouho-Maclay 1882.
14. Moore 1981, 78.
15. Saunders 1982; Corris 1972; 1973, 68–98; Moore 1985, 123–273; Graves 1993, 74–110.
16. Corris 1973, 111–125; Moore 1985.
17. Mercer and Moore 1976, 1978; Mercer 1995.
18. Meleiseā 1976.
19. Moore 1981, 81–85.
20. Panoff 1979, 172.

21. The most important of these studies are Ward 1948; Morrell 1960; Parnaby 1964; Scarr 1967; Corris 1973; Saunders 1982; Moore 1985; Graves 1993.

22. Bennett 1976.

23. Firth 1976; Munro and Firth 1987; Firth and Munro 1990.

24. Firth 1973.

25. Gascher 1974, chapter 8. Most of the information regarding the New Hebrideans in New Caledonia in Winslow 1990 was added by one of the editors from an early unpublished paper of mine, without specific acknowledgment of my authorship.

Chapter 2: The Colony Established

1. It was not less logical than bestowing the name of the Hebrides on the steamy, verdant tropical islands he had just left. J C Beaglehole suggested that since he knew of New Britain and New Ireland to the north, and had himself named New South Wales, he decided to round out the United Kingdom in the South Pacific with Scotland and the Hebrides islands; there was already a Nova Scotia, so he used the Latin name of Caledonia for Scotland (Beaglehole 1969, 2:562, n 1).

2. Beaglehole 1969, 2:531, n 5.

3. Shineberg 1967.

4. Merle 1995, 35.

5. Merle 1995, 115.

6. Douglas 1972, 417–418.

7. Douglas 1980, 32–33.

8. *Moniteur,* 7 October 1866.

9. Douglas 1972, 418.

10. Douglas 1972, 421–422.

11. Douglas 1972, 419.

12. Douglas 1972, 420.

13. Douglas 1972, 418.

14. Douglas 1972, 417–424; 1980, 46–49.

15. NSW Royal Commission 1869, 2.

16. Shineberg 1967, 190–198.

17. Douglas 1980, 32.

18. Shineberg 1967, 193.

19. *Moniteur,* 6 August 1865.

20. Shineberg 1967, 139–141 and passim.

21. Guillain 1865; MNC 1865.

22. *Moniteur,* 6 August 1865; 25 November 1865.

23. *Moniteur,* 6 July 1865, 10 August 1865.

24. *Moniteur,* 30 September 1866.

25. Rapport Statistique 1870.

26. *Inspection mobile* 1874 [for 1873]; Shipping reports 1874 [1874].

27. Durand 1870–1871, 10; *Australasian,* 7 October 1871.

28. Hoff 1873.

29. *Inspection mobile* 1874.

30. Courbet 1882*a*.

31. Suckling 1873.
32. *Décret* 1852, Articles 16 and 17.
33. *Moniteur,* 23 June 1867, 18 August 1867.
34. *Arrêté* 1874, Article 16.
35. NSW Royal Commission 1869, 9.
36. NSW Royal Commission 1869, 72–73, 74.
37. NSW Royal Commission 1869, 46.
38. NSW Royal Commission 1869, 74.
39. *Décret* 1852, Article 8.
40. Douglas 1972, 423–424.
41. Gascher 1974, 223.
42. *Inspection mobile* 1874.

Chapter 3: Entrepreneurial Recruiting in the 1870s

1. Head of Native Affairs Bureau to Colonial Secretary, 22 August 1870; copy in *M & D* 4:194–197.
2. 3 September 1870, *M & D* 4:198–199.
3. Aitkin 1871, 30 July.
4. Aitkin 1871, 5 August.
5. Brooke 1871, 14 August.
6. Ramsay 1871.
7. Markham 1872*b*.
8. Subenclosure 1 in Markham 1872*a*.
9. Gaultier de la Richerie 1872.
10. Notes on the French Labor Trade, 1876.
11. *Arrêté* 1875*a*.
12. *Moniteur,* 28 April 1875.
13. *Moniteur,* 22 September 1875.
14. Pritzbuer 1876.
15. Rouzaud 1875.
16. Du Petit-Thouars 1879.
17. See also Courmeaux 1884.
18. D'Arbel 1882.
19. Gadaud 1892. See chapter 8.
20. Courbet 1882*a*.
21. Bigant 1890*a*.
22. *Néo-Calédonien,* 8 August 1882.
23. Picquié 1880.
24. Giles 1968, 80.
25. From the shipping columns of *Le Moniteur.* See Note on Sources.
26. Interior Report 1881.
27. Marchand 1879.
28. Marchand 1879.
29. Marchand 1879.
30. *Arrêté* 1878.
31. Marchand 1880.
32. Courbet 1882*a*.

Chapter 4: The Kidnapping Inquiries and the Suspension of the Labor Trade, 1880–1882

1. Courbet 1880*a;* J C Wilson 1880; Gaggin 1880; Wecker 1880; Macdonald 1880.

2. *Aurora* Commission 1880*a*, 3.

3. *Aurora* Commission 1880*a*, 7–10.

4. Unless otherwise noted, the following account of the inquiry comes from *Aurora* Commission 1880*a*. Only direct quotations are noted separately.

5. This may be an error of transcription. The "bourbonnais" was black, a man known as "Black Tom," later described in court as a native of Martinique. Alternatively, use of the term may relate to a Melanesian habit of referring to foreign blacks, especially those who had identified with European culture, as "whites."

6. *Aurora* Commission 1880*a*, 83–84.

7. Appointed under the reform discussed in chapter 3, of appointing government clerks as agents, instead of the shipowner's nominee.

8. *Aurora* Commission 1880*a*, 84–88.

9. *Aurora* Commission 1880*b*.

10. *Aurora* Commission 1880*a*, 108.

11. *Aurora* Commission 1880*a*, 100.

12. *Aurora* Commission 1880*b*.

13. *Aurora* Commission 1880*b*.

14. Report of court proceedings, *Progrès*, 17 September 1882.

15. *Aurora* Commission 1880*b*.

16. *Aurora* Commission 1880*b*.

17. Courbet 1882*c*.

18. *Néo-Calédonien*, 23 October 1885.

19. *Aurora* Commission 1880*b; PVCP* 1881.

20. GA Instructions [1881].

21. *Venus* Inquiry 1880.

22. Cordeil 1882.

23. Report of court proceedings, *Progrès*, 17 September 1882.

24. The following account is from the resumé of court proceedings in Cordeil 1882.

25. Lafarge 1882.

26. Cordeil 1882.

27. Lafarge 1882.

28. Courbet 1882*c*.

29. Courbet 1882*a*.

30. *PVCP* 1881.

31. *PVCP* 1881. See also Courbet 1880*b*, 1882*a*.

32. Corris 1973, 29.

33. *Aurora* Commission 1880*a*, 90.

34. *Aurora* Commission 1880*a*, 132–133.

35. *Aurora* Commission 1880*a*, 186–189.

36. Scarr 1967, 150.

37. Moore 1981, 80.

38. Moore 1981, 80.

39. Moore 1981, 85–89.
40. Corris 1977.
41. Moore 1979, 12–13.
42. *BONC* 1882, 272–273.
43. Courbet 1882*c.*
44. *Néo-Calédonien,* 4 and 18 July 1882.
45. Courbet 1882*c.*
46. Courbet 1882*c.*
47. *Tribunal Correctionel* 1886; *état civil* 1887, Noumea, Deaths.
48. *Etat civil* Noumea 1886, Deaths.
49. Courbet 1882*a.*
50. Jauréguiberry 1882.

Chapter 5: Settlers Triumphant

1. Courbet 1882*a.*
2. Courbet 1882*f;* Immigration Commission 1883; *Moniteur,* 14 January 1884.
3. *Moniteur,* 18 January 1884; 16 February 1884.
4. Parnaby 1964, 172–179; Scarr 1967, 189–190, 196; Scarr 1970, 228.
5. Rannie 1912, 107.
6. Scarr 1967, 196; *Telegraph,* 1892.
7. Legrand 1886.
8. Courbet 1882*b,* 1882*d.*
9. Lacascade 1885; Le Boucher 1885*a.*
10. Petit 1885.
11. *PVCP* 1884, 4 September.
12. *Arrêté,* 1884.
13. Le Boucher 1884*a.*
14. *FLP* 1884.
15. Le Boucher 1884*a.*
16. Gauharou 1884.
17. Le Boucher 1884*b.*
18. *France Australe,* 30 October and 23 November 1889.
19. *Moniteur,* 23 March 1885.
20. Le Boucher 1885*b;* MNC 1885; *PVCG,* 17 August 1885.
21. Layard 1887.
22. *Indépendant,* 31 August 1886.
23. Layard 1887.
24. Thomas 1887*b;* Shipping reports 1887.
25. Shipping reports 1887.
26. Thomas 1887*b.*
27. Shipping reports 1887–1889.
28. Héricault 1889; Chanvalon 1889.
29. Interior Report 1889.
30. *Journal Officiel,* 22 June 1907.
31. *M & D,* 10:40; *Journal Officiel,* 24 August 1889; *PVCG* 1889, September session.
32. Bigant 1889.

33. Bigant 1889.
34. Interior Report 1889.
35. Interior Report 1893.
36. *Journal Officiel,* 8 March 1890.
37. *Calédonie,* 23 February 1892.
38. *Calédonie,* 13 October 1892.
39. *Calédonie,* 13 October 1892.
40. Wawn 1888–1900, 29 October 1888.
41. Price and Baker 1976; Siegel 1985.
42. *Calédonie,* 10 August 1893.
43. Gray 1892.
44. *Telegraph* 1893.
45. Revel 1907*b.*
46. Bigant 1890*a.*
47. Bigant 1890*a.*
48. Bigant 1890*a.*
49. Bigant 1890*b.*
50. Pardon 1890.
51. Bigant 1890*b.*
52. Grossin 1890.
53. *Calédonie,* 10 January 1893.
54. Bigant 1890*d.*
55. *Moniteur,* 24 June 1885; *Indépendant,* 20 June 1885; Cour Criminelle 1885.
56. *Indépendant,* 6 August 1887; Doze 1887; Bigant 1890*b;* O'Reilly 1957, 27; WPHC IC 1893, 69/93.
57. *Calédonie,* 2 September 1893.
58. O'Reilly 1957, 27.
59. Doze 1887.
60. Doze 1887.

Chapter 6: The New Century

1. 1901 census in *Journal Officiel,* 5 April 1902; *Annuaire* 1902.
2. Shipping reports in *France Australe,* 1911.
3. Brunet 1908, 68–69.
4. Politis 1908, 11.
5. *Arrêté* 1904.
6. *France Australe,* 3 November 1906.
7. Revel 1907*b,* 10.
8. King 1919.
9. King 1919.
10. Shipping reports in *France Australe,* 1925.
11. Pinard 1906; Liotard 1906.
12. *PVCG* 1902, November session.
13. WPHC IC 1906–1912.
14. Anglo-French Conference 1914.
15. King 1919.

16. *France Australe,* 15 November 1906.

17. *Arrêté* 1920.

18. Scarr 1967, 233.

19. *France Australe,* 23 April 1894; *Calédonie,* 9 December 1897; Nicholson 1909; Macmillan 1908; Nicholson 1910; Paton 1913.

20. Annual Report 1912.

21. *France Australe,* 29 October 1912.

22. Nicholson 1912*b.*

23. GBFO 1911, FO 371, 1175/22289.

24. *France Australe,* 25 September 1912; Census of 1921, in *Journal Officiel,* 15 October 1921; Gayet 1929*b,* 2.

25. Gayet 1929*b,* 21.

26. *Annuaire* 1946.

27. Gayet 1929*b,* 21.

Chapter 7: Men and Motives

1. Scarr 1967, 139–145; Corris 1973, 2–5.

2. Courbet 1882*a.*

3. Rubinstein 1981, 140–141.

4. Funabiki 1981, 173.

5. Rubinstein 1981, 137–138.

6. Corris 1973, 114; For a graphic example, see Gilding 1982, 76–79.

7. Ivens 1930, 42–43.

8. Shineberg 1967, 155.

9. Clain 1885, entries for 19 and 20 January.

10. Hagen 1893, 379.

11. Petit 1885.

12. Wawn 1888–1900, 29 October 1888.

13. *Moniteur,* 8 February 1871.

14. Dangeville 1884–1885; Clain 1885.

15. Clain 1885, entry for 21 January.

16. Ayscough 1900; see also Forrest 1899; *Southern Cross Log,* 15 February 1900, 23.

17. *Southern Cross Log,* 15 February 1900, 22.

18. Clain 1885, entry for 27 January.

19. Clain 1885, entry for 29 January.

20. Dangeville 1884–1885, entry for 30 October 1884.

21. Hagen 1893, 367.

22. Clain 1885, entry for 29 January.

23. Dangeville 1884–1885, entry for 11 September 1884.

24. D'Arbel 1882.

25. Dubois 1890.

26. Dangeville 1884–1885, entries for 19 and 24 September, and 21 October 1884.

27. Olry 1882.

28. *Calédonie,* 15 June 1893 (*Lady Saint Aubyn* report). See also Chauliac 1893; *Aurora* Commission 1880*a,* 240, 241.

29. Corris 1973, 56.
30. Nicholson 1912*b.*
31. Bigant 1889.
32. Moore 1981, 85 n 48; see also Ivens 1918, 227.
33. Corris 1973, 57–58.
34. D'Arbel 1882.
35. Rouzaud 1875.
36. Corris 1973, 60; Scarr 1967, 143.
37. See, for example, evidence of recruiter Tom at the trial of Madézo, in Layard 1882*b;* evidence of Champion at *Venus* trial, 1882.
38. "Tout est dit": Courbet 1882*a.*
39. *Aurora* Commission 1880*a,* 145.
40. Bigant 1889.
41. Scarr 1967, 143–144; Corris 1973, 54.
42. Exceptions being Graves 1984, 128–132; Munro 1993, 94.
43. Corris 1973, 60–61; 55.
44. Wawn 1888–1900, entry for 4 September 1889.
45. Ivens 1930, 264–265; 200–201.
46. Rannie 1912, 36.
47. Rannie 1912, 185–186.
48. Corris 1973, 62.
49. Corris 1973, 61.
50. Graves 1993, 220; 1984, 115.
51. Courbet 1882*a;* Hagen 1893, 363, 382.
52. Munro 1993, 94.
53. Moore 1985, 47.
54. Dangeville 1884–1885, 21 December 1884.
55. *Calédonie,* 15 June 1893.
56. Adams 1987, 7.
57. Lamadon 1893; Le Mescam 1893.
58. *Calédonie,* 10 August 1893.
59. Corris 1973, 55.
60. Lainé 1898, General Observations.
61. Clain 1885, entry for 29 January.
62. Rouzaud 1875.
63. Pallu de la Barrière 1882*a.*
64. D'Arbel 1882.
65. *Aurora* Commission 1880*a,* 48–49.
66. *Aurora* Commission 1880*a,* 66; 228–229; Scarr 1967, 143–144.
67. *Aurora* Commission 1880*a,* 145.
68. D'Arbel 1882.
69. For a modern reference to the prestige associated with travel, see Bolton 1993, 271.
70. Courbet 1882*a.*
71. Hagen 1893, 363, 382.
72. Corris 1973, 61; see also 59.
73. Hagen 1893, 374.
74. Nicholson 1912*a.*

75. Bishop G A Selwyn, cited in Corris 1973, 45.
76. Annand 1890.
77. Rae 1919.
78. Dangeville 1884–1885, entry for 9 October 1884.
79. Rouzaud 1875.
80. Rouzaud 1875.
81. D'Arbel 1882.
82. Hagen 1893, 384. Hagen gives an earlier date, but, as explained in the list of references, his account amalgamates four voyages. As it happened, the incident that followed is documented in other records, and relates to his voyage of December 1890 to March 1891.
83. Case 46 in RNAS 38.

Chapter 8: The Women

1. Indian women in Fiji, however, formed a greater proportion of migrant labor—just under 29 percent of the total workforce—as by law, for every 100 men there had to be 40 women imported (Gillion 1962, 56).
2. Corris 1973, 46. The figures on which the proportion for Queensland and Fiji is calculated are not as satisfactory as others for the labor trade in these colonies. Those for New Caledonia have mainly to be inferred from a variety of sources.
3. *Moniteur,* 30 September1866; Shipping reports 1866–1881; Interior Reports 1878, 1880; Courbet 1880*a*.
4. Shipping reports 1880–1899.
5. That is, 495 out of 4798, or 10.3 percent; Computer file.
6. If the names of those still living, in the records, were added, the proportion of women would be more than 12 percent, so the lower figure can be considered conservative.
7. Saunders 1980; Jolly 1987; Lal 1985*a*, 1985*b*; Shameem 1987, 1990.
8. Figures calculated from Courbet 1882*a* and newspaper shipping columns for the first three months of 1881.
9. Rouzaud 1875.
10. GA Instructions [1881].
11. GA Instructions 1885.
12. Saunders 1980, 27; Jolly 1987, 129.
13. Corris 1973, 45.
14. King 1911.
15. King 1912.
16. Macmillan 1911 (he followed up cases in New Caledonia); Bowie and Bowie nd.
17. Rae 1919.
18. Jolly 1987, 124–126.
19. Dangeville 1884–1885, 83–86.
20. Dangeville 1884–1885, 85.
21. King 1911.
22. Macdonald 1875–1879, entry for 27 September 1876. Her husband was described as "an old man," and she had evidently eloped with a much younger one, given that he was of recruitable age.

23. Dangeville 1884–1885, 117.

24. *Indépendant,* 16 June 1885. The couple are not named in the newspaper, but have been identified as these two through the *état civil.*

25. Rae 1919. He witnessed many runaways and attempted runaways of women, mostly, in this period, for the internal trade of the New Hebrides.

26. Macdonald 1875–1879, entry for 1 March 1879 (his emphasis). Macdonald did, however, pursue the matter, but found that it was too difficult to decide who was telling the truth about the woman's status.

27. Paton 1896, 6. The incident took place on 14 August 1896.

28. See, for example, Jouenne 1890.

29. This occurred in 1910; *Q J* 71 (January 1911): 7.

30. Dangeville 1885.

31. Le Maréchal 1884.

32. Petit 1885.

33. GA Instructions 1885.

34. Clain 1885, entry for 16 January.

35. Coates 1887.

36. Annand 1890.

37. Legendre 1891.

38. Legendre 1891.

39. *Etat civil* Noumea 1891. Dr Legendre claimed that Beriri was found to be suffering from venereal disease when she came aboard the *Marie* (1891). In this case she may have been taken straight to the native hospital in Noumea, where she died.

40. Probably on the *Né-Oublie; Calédonie,* 23 February 1892.

41. Bigant 1890*a,* 1890*b;* Davis 1890.

42. *Q J* 75 (January 1912).

43. Mahaffy 1913*a,* 1913*b.*

44. Repiquet 1911.

45. The war of correspondence is in GBCO, 225/107; the outcome, in WPHC IC 243/1913, 444/1913, and 1337/1913.

46. GBCO, 225/107.

47. Cariou 1931, 23–24.

48. NHJC 1911.

49. Jacomb 1912.

50. Jacomb 1911.

51. Quoted by Mahaffy 1912*a.*

52. Mahaffy 1912*d.*

53. Rannie 1912, 82.

54. Quoted in Scarr 1967, 158–159n.

55. GA Instructions 1885.

56. Lacascade 1885.

57. King 1911.

58. Repiquet 1912.

59. See Allen 1981*b,* 3.

60. Fiji figures from Siegel 1985, 40. In Fiji the proportion of 19.1 percent for Ambae women was exceeded by that for women from Kiribati, where the normal method of recruiting was by couples or families. For New Cale-

donia, the figure is from a sample of females whose death is registered and whose provenance is known. Sampled as a proportion of all known Ambae female recruits (alive or dead) to the total of known female recruits (alive or dead) whose provenance is known it is a little higher, at 21.76 percent.

61. Calculations from computer file. Ambae sent slightly more than its fair share in relation to its proportion of the total population of the group. Ambae probably had a population of about 4,000–5,000 in the last quarter of the nineteenth century. Even if the lower estimate of 70,000 for the New Hebrides as a whole is taken, the Ambae proportion is only around 7 percent of that of the group; Gilding 1982, 72; McArthur and Yaxley 1967, 18.

62. *Moniteur,* 20 August 1884. The list was of those engaged at the Immigration Office. Presumably the other 28 recruits were either ordered in advance by employers, or not yet engaged by the time of the newspaper report.

63. See, for example, Dangeville 1884–1885, 89 (3 November 1884) and 97 (7 November 1884).

64. Saunders 1980, 34.

65. Petit 1885.

66. Clain 1885, entry for 3 March.

67. *Néo-Calédonien,* 23 September 1881.

68. D'Arbel 1882.

69. Siegel 1985, 40.

70. Fletcher 1923, 175.

71. Rodman 1981.

72. See also Bolton 1993.

73. Allen 1981*c*, 125. See also Allen 1981*a*.

74. Rannie 1912, 161.

75. Hagen 1893, 367–368.

76. Dangeville 1884–1885, 89.

77. Dangeville 1884–1885, 22–24.

78. Hawkins 1887–1888, entry for 19 March 1888.

79. Corris 1973, 49.

80. Petit 1885.

81. Wawn 1870–1874, 21; Courbet 1882*a*.

82. Inference from *état civil,* where the names and provenance of spouses were usually given in Births and Deaths in New Caledonia.

83. Saunders 1980, 26–27. She went on to add an explanation that is much more a reason of state—the opposition to a permanent colored immigration in Queensland—and another, implicitly, relating to the pressure of "Melanesian customs"; but neither of these explanations was distinguished from her first, about the concerns of "rural capitalists."

84. Saunders 1980, 26–27.

85. Du Petit-Thouars 1879.

86. Rae 1919.

87. Corris 1973, 53.

88. Melanesian Mission 1881.

89. In the *état civil* the death of a New Hebridean infant in New Caledonia was often the first mention of its existence; sometimes the fact that the birth was "never declared" was added to the death notice. There would be

many who survived, whose birth was not recorded, and some whose death was not noticed, particularly if they had been stillborn, or died within a few days of birth.

90. Fletcher 1923, 58–60.

91. Hoff 1879.

92. These appear regularly in the *état civil* from the earliest days of colonization, and the children were quite commonly recognized by the European father, much more commonly than the children of imported women laborers.

93. *Etat civil;* they often appear through the death of one or more infants, more likely to be reported than the birth.

94. *Progrès,* 15 May 1884; see also 5 April 1884.

95. *Progrès,* 16 August 1884.

96. Picquié 1880.

97. Thomas 1887*a*, 3 September.

98. Miklouho-Maclay 1882.

99. Saunders 1980, 39.

100. *Progrès,* 16 August 1884.

101. Moncelon 1882.

102. Stoler 1991, 58–59.

103. Le Goupils 1928, 128.

104. Schiele, the previous owner of the plantation.

105. Report of court case against M de Gimel; *Progrès,* 15 January 1882.

106. *Progrès,* 15 January 1882.

107. *Progrès,* 29 January 1882.

108. Melanesian Mission 1881.

109. Le Goupils 1928, 183–184; 202–205.

110. *France Australe,* 28 May 1894.

111. Marchand 1880.

112. Many instances of births in successive years appear in the registers. This would have been uncommon in most parts of Melanesia, where there were prohibitions against sexual intercourse during a mother's lactation period, and for periods of up to two years after parturition.

113. I have no direct evidence of this, but it is noted in connection with Oceanian women in Queensland (Saunders 1980, 37) and the deaths of indentured Indian women in Fiji (Shameem 1987).

Chapter 9: The Children

1. Noiriel 1990, 8.

2. Corris 1973, 47; Thomas 1886, 333–334.

3. Quoted by Steel 1880, 414.

4. Steel 1880, 416–417.

5. Quoted by Miklouho-Maclay 1882.

6. Miklouho-Maclay 1882, quoting Drs Wray and Thompson; Corris 1973, 47.

7. Corris 1973, 48.

8. *Arrêté* 1874, Article 37.

9. *Aurora* Commission 1880*c*.

10. *PVCP* 1881.

11. *Néo-Calédonien,* 12 September 1884.

12. *Décret* 1893; *Arrêté* 1904.

13. *Arrêté* 1874, Article 17.

14. GA Instructions [1881]. This restated one of Pritzbuer's reforms of 1875.

15. Courbet 1882*a*.

16. *Moniteur,* 20 August 1884.

17. Miklouho-Maclay 1882.

18. Vitte 1875*a*, 12.

19. Marchand 1880.

20. Picquié 1880.

21. *Etat civil* 1874–75, Noumea and Dumbea, Deaths. At least 123 New Hebridean workers died in that district in 1874–75, of whom the ages of 110 are estimated. Of those, 50 were children under sixteen, of whom 28 were under twelve.

22. Calculations from *état civil* 1865–1930. Whether the estimated age of death was given depended on the diligence of the informant or the *état civil* officer.

23. *Arrêté* 1874, Article 16.

24. Marchand 1880.

25. *Progrès,* 22 January 1882.

26. *Moniteur,* 20 August 1884.

27. *Etat civil* Dumbéa 1870–1876, recording the deaths of many young children at the sugar plantations, particularly in 1875.

28. Marchand 1880.

29. Thomas 1887*a*, 9 July.

30. Godey 1886, 121–122. Godey arrived in New Caledonia in 1875 and left in 1878.

31. Walker 1885.

32. Walker 1885.

33. Marchand 1880.

34. Clain 1885, from list of recruits at end of journal.

35. Picquié 1880.

36. See, for example, Clain 1885, entry for 30 January.

37. Hagen 1893, 354.

38. Bowie 1899.

39. *Aurora* Commission 1880*a*, 211.

40. *Aurora* Commission 1880*a*, 173. This is the account of the recruiter involved. Another by the other recruiter varies slightly in detail: *Aurora* Commission 1880*a*, 99.

Chapter 10: Work in New Caledonia

1. Mallet 1866. Dr Bronwen Douglas kindly brought this document to my attention.

2. Mallet 1866.

3. *Progrès,* 28 May 1882.

4. "words almost verbatim of one of our administrators" (Mallet 1866).

5. *Négrier,* the word used for a slave ship.
6. Moncelon 1882.
7. Thomas 1887*a,* 3 September.
8. Thomas 1886, 149.
9. Thomas 1886, 149.
10. Thomas 1887*a,* 3 September.
11. "A" 1882. An extract with a furious rejoinder was published in *Le Néo-Calédonien,* 31 October, but interestingly this part describing procedure was not part of the extract quoted for the purpose of rebuttal.
12. *Moniteur,* 6 January 1867; NSW Royal Commission 1869, 45.
13. Durand 1870–1871, 10; *Australasian,* 7 October 1871.
14. *Inspection mobile* 1874.
15. *Arrêté* 1874, Article 16.
16. *PVCG* 1898, session 25 November, 160.
17. *PVCG* 1895, November session, 162–163.
18. *Décret* 1893, Article 41.
19. *PVCG* 1907, 273.
20. Ballande 1902.
21. *Journal Officiel,* 23 October 1920.
22. Smith-Rewse 1924.
23. *Moniteur,* 20 January 1867. They had arrived by the *Challenge* a few days before. Names and locations are given in the report; occupations are drawn from other evidence.
24. *BONC* 1867–1868, 256.
25. NSW Royal Commission 1869, 3.
26. *Moniteur,* 9 July 1868; 14 February 1869.
27. Replies to a questionnaire addressed to the Colonial Secretariat, 27 April 1874, in RNAS 32.
28. Glasser 1904, 518.
29. Lemire 1884, 196; Anderson 1880, 200, 206; Thomas 1886, 100–101.
30. Thomas 1886, 100, 101; Anderson 1880, 200, 206; Lemire 1884, 196.
31. Marist Mission Report 1883.
32. Thomas 1886, 160, 54–55; *Histoire authentique,* 1909, 20.
33. *PVCA* 1879.
34. Thomas 1886, 163–164.
35. CCI 1882.
36. Courbet 1882*c.*
37. Immigration Commission 1883.
38. Immigration Commission 1883.
39. *Moniteur,* 20 August 1884.
40. *État civil* Canala 1886 and 1887, Deaths. They were: Caveyron, aged 12, employed August 1884 by Puech, sorting nickel; died June 1886 at Canala (employed by Laurie, coffee planter) aged 14; Leo, aged 20, employed August 1884 by Puech, sorting nickel; died November 1887 at Canala (employed by Laurie, coffee planter) aged 23; and Salabano, aged 12, employed August 1884 by Puech, sorting nickel; died September 1887 at Canala (employed by Laurie, coffee planter) aged 15.
41. To be conservative, I used the average death rate of one in four,

rather than the rate specific to mining. I say "at least 157" because where the occupation of the deceased was not quite clear, I did not include it.

42. *Etat civil* Thio, Houailou, and Pam 1888–1892, Deaths.

43. Shipping reports 1887–1889 (coastal).

44. Brou 1979, 36.

45. *Calédonie,* 2 August 1899; 21 August 1899.

46. *Etat civil* Koné 1906–1910, Deaths.

47. Annual Report 1912.

48. New Hebrides Inquiry 1927, 22.

49. Brou 1979, 39–40.

50. *Néo-Calédonien,* 29 April 1881; see also Courbet 1882*a.*

51. Between 1900 and 1909, 54 known Oceanian employees of Ballande died; all of them worked in Noumea. Over the same decade, of all the Oceanian workers whose deaths are registered, 310 out of 487 died in Noumea (Computer file).

52. Annual Report 1912.

53. *Néo-Calédonien,* 12 April 1881; Computer file.

54. King 1919.

55. Dunlop 1921.

56. *Calédonie,* 14 December 1899.

57. A typical editorial tirade against *garçons de famille* may be found in *Le Néo-Calédonien,* 1 March 1881.

58. *Calédonie,* 23 February 1892.

59. *Calédonie,* 14 December 1899.

60. Merle 1991, 242–244.

61. Genovese 1966, 28–36.

62. Jeanneney 1894, 142.

Chapter 11: Living and Working in New Caledonia

1. Saunders 1982, 73–74; Parnaby 1972, 140–141.

2. *Arrêté* 1874, Article 41.

3. In France in 1900 the working day of industries with a mixed work-force of men, women, and children was limited to eleven hours, in 1902 to ten and a half hours, and in 1904 to ten hours for all workers, but employers frequently evaded the law in various ways. The six-day working week was enacted in 1906, with generous exemptions for various categories of workers (Stone 1985, 125–135).

4. *Arrêté* 1874, Article 41.

5. NSW Royal Commission 1869, 3.

6. *Arrêté* 1874, Articles 39 and 42.

7. *Décret* 1893, Article 55.

8. *Décret* 1893, Article 65.

9. *BONC* 1865, 172.

10. *BONC* 1867, Décision no. 98.

11. NSW Royal Commission 1869, 50.

12. *Arrêté* 1874, Article 37.

13. Muljono-Larue 1996, 48–50.

14. *Arrêté* 1874, Article 37.

15. Thomas 1886, 150.
16. *Néo-Calédonien,* 4 July 1882.
17. Rouzaud 1875.
18. "A" 1882.
19. *Néo-Calédonien,* 11 August 1882.
20. Saunders 1982, 83.
21. *PVCG,* 6 May 1892.
22. Rouzaud 1875.
23. Notably, on plantations in the New Hebrides itself, where the habits of settlers could be expected to be most similar (British Resident Commissioner 1920).
24. *Moniteur,* 15 January 1873; NSW Royal Commission 1869, 3.
25. Ballière 1875, 224.
26. Scarr 1967, 140.
27. *Calédonie,* 6 January 1900.
28. Courbet 1882*a.*
29. Courbet 1881.
30. *Progrès,* 5 and 8 January 1882.
31. *Progrès,* 29 January 1882; 5 February 1882.
32. *Progrès,* 29 January 1882.
33. *Décret* 1893, Article 61.
34. WPHC IC 1897, 221/97.
35. *Calédonie,* 2 February 1894.
36. *PVCG,* 22 November 1904.
37. Saunders 1982, 77 and following.
38. *Arrêté* 1874, Article 36.
39. *Moniteur,* 4 January 1882.
40. *Moniteur,* 15 January 1877.
41. Thomas 1887*a,* 9 July.
42. *Etat civil* Ouégoa, Deaths.
43. Ballande 1899*b.*
44. *Calédonie,* 10 January 1900.
45. Ballande 1899*b.*
46. *Calédonie,* 6 January 1900.
47. *Calédonie,* 23 December 1899.
48. *Arrêté* 1874, Article 38.
49. *Décret* 1893, Article 62.
50. WPHC IC 1897, 221/97 (sample *livret* of a Solomon Island worker in New Caledonia).
51. *Moniteur,* 21 August 1872.
52. *Moniteur,* 21 August 1872.
53. Thomas 1887*a,* 9 August.
54. *PVCG* 1895, November session.
55. Pallu de la Barrière 1882*b.*
56. Thompson 1982, 104.
57. "A" 1882.
58. Courmeaux 1884.
59. *PVCG,* 22 November 1904.

60. *Arrêté* 1874, Article 52.

61. *Arrêté* 1874, Article 42.

62. *Calédonie,* 7 February 1895; 13 March 1894.

63. Le Goupils 1928, 97.

64. Rouzaud 1875.

65. Revel 1907*b*, 16–17; Revel 1907*a*, 2, 3 (comment of Denis).

66. *Calédonie,* 4 April 1899.

67. *Néo-Calédonien,* 25 April 1882.

68. *PVCG* 1909, November session.

69. Courbet 1882*a*.

70. Saunders 1982, 76; Saunders 1988, passim; Beechert 1985, 74; Corris 1973, 83. Minor arbitrary violence was taken for granted in Papua New Guinea up to World War Two.

71. D'Arbel 1882 (marginal notes by Pallu de la Barrière).

72. *Progrès,* 12 February 1882.

73. *Tribunal Correctionel,* 13 June 1878.

74. Cour Criminelle, 28 June 1879.

75. *Tribunal Correctionel,* 24 March 1881.

76. For example, the proposal of Leconte in *PVCG* 1904, November session.

77. *Indépendant,* 6 February 1886; *état civil* Canala 1883, Deaths.

78. *France Australe,* 9 October 1889.

79. *Calédonie,* 26 January 1894.

80. *Néo-Calédonien,* 10 April 1883.

81. See, for example, Le Goupils 1910, 124–127.

82. *France Australe,* 7 August 1925.

83. Layard 1882*a*.

84. The following account of the trial, unless otherwise noted, comes from reports in successive issues of *Le Progrès* (8, 15, 22, and 29 January 1882).

85. Courbet 1882*a*.

86. *Progrès,* 8 January 1882.

87. Layard 1882*a*.

88. *Progrès,* 12 February 1882; 22 January1882.

89. Interior Reports 1881.

90. *Néo-Calédonien,* 10 January 1882.

91. Layard 1882*a*.

92. *Calédonie,* 27 October 1904.

93. *France Australe,* 7 March 1895.

94. Quoted by *France Australe,* 20 October 1890.

95. *Town and Country,* 9 August 1879, 258.

96. Revel 1907*b*, 12.

97. Beechert 1985, 69; Moore 1981, 83–84.

98. King 1919.

99. *France Australe,* 17 January 1921.

100. Revel 1907*b*, 12.

101. Marchand 1880.

102. Wawn 1893, 404.

103. Marist Mission Report [1883].

104. Gauharou 1888.
105. Cuinier 1877.
106. Gayet 1929*a*, 61–62.
107. Graves 1993, 142–150.
108. Parnaby 1964, 151.
109. Cuinier 1877; Gayet 1929*a*, 61–62.
110. Rouzaud 1875; D'Arbel 1882.

Chapter 12: "Perpetual Theft"

An early version of this chapter appeared as Shineberg 1991.
1. *Décret* 1893, Article 59.
2. Durand 1870–1871, 10.
3. Camouilly 1877–1878.
4. Marchand 1879.
5. Dangeville 1884–1885, 46, 48, 50.
6. Dangeville 1884–1885, 122.
7. Du Petit-Thouars 1879, 102; Gadaud 1892; d'Arbel 1882.
8. Day 1881, entry for 1 July. Here the complaint included Fiji, where the pay was half the monetary rate given in New Caledonia and Queensland, while in New Caledonia the problem was nonpayment and poor purchasing power.
9. *Aurora* Commission 1880*a*, 146–147.
10. Courmeaux 1884.
11. Marist Mission report [1883].
12. *Moniteur,* 18 August 1882.
13. The terms *crisis* and *critical situation* were used so constantly of New Caledonian business that one has either to believe that this was its constant state, or conclude that such language was needed to obtain concessions from the administration.
14. *Néo-Calédonien,* 21 October 1881.
15. Walker 1885.
16. *Moniteur,* 18 March 1885.
17. Gadaud 1892.
18. *PVCP,* 1885*a*, 6 January.
19. *Tribunal Correctionel,* passim.
20. *Calédonie,* 15 February 1899, quoting *l'Eclair,* 5 January 1899.
21. Feillet 1899.
22. *PVCG,* 22 November 1904.
23. *PVCG,* 22 November 1904.
24. *PVCG,* 10 December 1906.
25. More in the case of Oceanians, less for other categories. The secretary-general's office estimated the total number of indentured laborers as 4,854 (*PVCG,* 30 November 1906).
26. Revel 1907*b*, 14.
27. Revel 1907*b*, 15.
28. Revel 1907*b*, 15.
29. Revel 1907*b*, 15 (Fillon's comment).

30. Revel 1907*b*, 14 (Engler's response).
31. Revel 1907*b*, 14 (Revel's comments on Engler's response).
32. Revel 1907*b*, 14 (Fillon's comment).
33. Revel 1907*b*, 16.
34. Revel 1907*b*, 17.
35. *Etat civil* Noumea 1907, Deaths.
36. Revel 1907*b*, 18.
37. Revel 1907*b*, 18 (Fillon's comment).
38. Revel 1907*b*, 20.
39. *PVCG,* 18 December 1907.
40. Fillon 1907, 21.
41. Fillon 1907, 1.
42. *Inspection mobile* 1907.
43. *Journal Officiel,* 22 June. There were 150 Indochinese, 19 Javanese, 128 New Hebrideans, and 223 local Melanesians, mostly Loyalty Islanders. The number does not tell very much, for it relates only to those for whom there were proper records: it does not even tell anything about the ethnic proportions of the laborers, as the records of some were kept better than others.
44. *PVCG,* 12–18 December 1907.
45. *PVCG,* 19 December 1907.
46. *PVCG,* 1908, April-June session.
47. *PVCG,* 1908, April-June session. Councillor Laroque implied that the administration itself was pocketing the money due the children.
48. *PVCG,* 1911, Budget session, November.
49. *PVCG,* 1911, November session.
50. Revel 1907*b*, 17.
51. Gayet 1929*a*, 57.
52. Revel 1907*b*, 17 (Liotard's comment).
53. Parnaby 1964, 141–143.
54. Rentz 1907.
55. Feillet 1899.
56. Rentz 1903.
57. Rentz 1903.
58. Rentz 1903 (report of Lafourcade).
59. Fillon 1907, 11.
60. Gayet 1929*a*, 59.
61. Revel 1907*b*, 1.
62. Revel 1907*b*, 11.
63. Fillon 1907, 21.
64. Revel 1907*b*, 18 (comment of Fillon).
65. Gayet 1929*a*, 15–17.
66. Gayet 1929*a*, 59–60.
67. Gayet 1929*a*, 59.
68. Revel 1907*a*, 2 (comment of Denis).
69. Rentz 1903 (report of Lafourcade).
70. Rentz 1903 (report of Lafourcade).

71. Rentz 1903.
72. Revel 1907*a*, 2 (comment of Fillon).
73. Revel 1907*a*, 2 (comment of commander Rentz.)

Chapter 13: Sickness and Death

1. Shlomowitz 1987, 47–51.
2. Shlomowitz 1987, 40.
3. *Etat civil* Noumea 1881, Deaths.
4. *Journal Officiel,* 22 June 1907.
5. Hagen 1893, 384; RNAS 38, case 46; Hagen says that only eleven out of *fifty* survived, but his story, based on that of the angry returns, may be exaggerated, so the Royal Navy account is preferred.
6. Héricault 1889; Computer file.
7. G Annec to *procureur,* 16 January 1882 (in *état civil* 1882, Poya, Deaths).
8. Most of these deaths *found* in the *état civil* did indeed occur in the early twentieth century, but there are some from as early as 1896, and it seems likely that those questioned gave the names of those who had departed within recent memory rather than within the last three years, which the district agent (wrongly) assumed to be the unvarying duration of a labor term in New Caledonia, and as I show later, indigenous people having to rely on their memories were somewhat vague in estimating time. It is unlikely to have gone much further back than 1896, however, as the beginning of renewed large recruitment from Tanna was about 1893 and the news of deaths would have taken time to percolate.
9. Mahaffy 1912*a;* Wilkes 1912.
10. *Etat civil* all districts, 1890–1912, Deaths. The names on the list were matched against the registered deaths by sound, allowing liberally for a different French spelling.
11. Parnaby 1964, 147.
12. Courbet 1882*a.* Using his figures, it is 4.89 percent, so he has rounded off the figure.
13. Courmeaux 1884.
14. Shlomowitz 1987, 47–49.
15. *Moniteur,* 20 August 1884.
16. RNAS 38, case 26.
17. The same should be said of Queensland statistics: it was reckoned that an additional 2,000 died in the islands as a result of diseases they had contracted in Queensland (Graves 1993, 75).
18. Courbet 1882*a.*
19. Courbet 1882*a.*
20. Parnaby 1964, 148 nn 118 and 119.
21. *Arrêté* 1875*b.*
22. Ollivaud 1881.
23. *PVCG* 1904, 22 November.
24. Paton 1897.
25. Wilkes 1912; Mahaffy 1912*b.*
26. Quoted by Courbet 1882*a.*

27. Paton 1913.
28. Paton 1913.
29. Corris 1973, 115–116.
30. Thomas 1887*a*, 9 July.
31. Cotteau 1888, 237.
32. *Néo-Calédonien,* 25 January 1884.
33. Marist Mission Report [1883].
34. *Etat civil* 1881–1882, Deaths.
35. Bigant 1890*a*.
36. Quoted in Scarr 1967, 177.
37. Shlomowitz 1987, 50.
38. *Néo-Calédonien,* 25 January 1884.
39. *Néo-Calédonien,* 22 August 1884.
40. Macmillan 1883, 100; Monin 1883, 59. Macmillan's article was kindly brought to my attention by Dr Barry Smith of the Australian National University.
41. Monin 1883, 59.
42. Ballière 1875, 199.
43. Courbet 1882*a*.
44. Courbet 1882*a*.
45. *Néo-Calédonien,* 9 November 1883.
46. *Etat civil* Noumea 1883, Deaths.
47. *Tribunal de Simple Police,* 28 July 1884; he had been fined 10 francs a few months before this, along with several comrades, for causing a fire in the bush through carelessness (*Tribunal de Simple Police,* 4 February 1884).
48. Of the total of 228 deaths for 1882, the age at death is estimated and given for 163. Of these, 54 are estimated as aged less than sixteen, or 33 percent. In that year Courbet estimated the proportion of those recruited under the age of sixteen as 40 percent (*Etat civil,* all districts, 1882, Deaths; Courbet 1882*a*).
49. Nicholson 1912*b*.
50. *Calédonie,* 18 October 1904.
51. Of 294 court cases involving New Hebrideans recorded in my files, 83 were for assault, usually on other New Hebrideans, while drunk. Of such cases, 7 caused the death of fellow workers, 1 caused a man to lose an eye, and 1 sent to jail for the offense died shortly afterward.
52. *Histoire authentique* 1909, 54–55, 114–117.
53. Macmillan 1883.
54. *Calédonie,* 12 December 1899; *France Australe,* 28 October 1903.
55. *Bulletin du Commerce,* 22 July 1921.
56. Dunlop 1922.
57. *France Australe,* 28 October 1903.
58. *PVCP* 1875.
59. *PVCP* 1875.
60. *Néo-Calédonien,* 8 July 1881.
61. *Moniteur,* 20 July 1881.
62. *Moniteur,* 27 July 1881.
63. Servent 1995, 13.

64. Clain 1885, entry for 3 February.

65. *Moniteur,* 19 November 1898 (regulation); *Calédonie,* 3 January 1899 (screening).

66. *Calédonie,* 22 December 1899.

67. *Calédonie,* 23 December 1899.

68. *Calédonie,* 23 December 1899; *Journal Officiel,* 30 December 1899.

69. *Calédonie,* 22 December 1899.

70. *France Australe,* 11 November 1912.

71. *France Australe,* 13 November 1912.

72. *France Australe,* 23 October 1912.

73. *Etat civil* Thio, Deaths. In the 1880s the place of death given was sometimes "Hospital of the SLN, Thio."

74. Courbet 1882*a.*

75. Thomas 1887*a,* 9 July.

76. Graves 1993, 94–99.

77. "A" 1882; Laurent 1904, 80; Inspector Sheridan, quoted by Parnaby 1964, 142; Graves 1993, 101.

78. *PVCG* 22 December 1909.

79. Revel 1907*c.*

80. Revel 1907*c* (comments of Fillon, his emphasis.)

81. Gayet 1929*b,* 19.

82. Notes on the French labor trade 1876.

83. *Moniteur,* 14 April 1875.

84. Late reports of deaths are all in rural areas: *Etat civil* Paita, St Vincent, Canala, and Hienghène.

85. Ballière 1875, 200; Miklouho-Maclay 1882, n 1; Laurent 1904, 80.

Chapter 14: "Hebrideans" in Colonial Society

1. Courbet 1882*d;* Immigration Commission 1883.

2. *Moniteur,* 29 September 1867.

3. *Moniteur,* 29 September 1867.

4. Cour Criminelle 1869.

5. Cour Criminelle 1878.

6. *Etat civil* Paita 1906 and 1907, Deaths. The birth of the child (unregistered) is calculated from the death notice.

7. *France Australe,* 29 September 1913; 3, 4, 14, 16 and 18 October 1913; 6 and 14 November 1913; 10 March and 18 May 1914. Miskana's story acquired elaborations during his period of star status, including an account of his repatriation in 1901, when he was attacked and robbed while landing, and escaped by swimming back to the recruiting ship.

8. Walker 1885.

9. See, for example, *Néo-Calédonien,* 9 March 1883.

10. CCI 1882; see also *Progrès,* 16 July 1882.

11. Settlers' Petition 1882.

12. *PVCG* 1886, 75.

13. Courmeaux 1884.

14. *Moniteur,* 13 June 1869.

15. *Néo-Calédonien,* 7 November 1882.

16. For example, *Néo-Calédonien,* 29 October 1880; 30 June, 18 July 1882; *Colon,* 5 February 1890; *France Australe,* 24 February 1890; *Calédonie,* 28 March 1894.

17. *Calédonie,* 22 December 1892.

18. *France Australe,* 22 August and 31 October 1890; Cour Criminelle, 30 October 1890.

19. *Néo-Calédonien,* 19 and 28 December 1882.

20. Douglas 1980, 33.

21. *Histoire authentique* 1909, 54–55, 114–117.

22. Walker 1885.

23. *Nouvelle-Calédonie,* 4 July 1878.

24. *Neo-Calédonien,* 28 January 1884.

25. *Calédonie,* 22 March 1894; 30 August 1908.

26. *Progrès,* 22 January 1882.

27. *Néo-Calédonien,* 12 April 1881.

28. *Progrès,* 8 January 1882.

29. *France Australe,* 19 March 1912.

30. Ballande 1899*a*.

31. *Journal Officiel,* 23 February 1889.

32. *Avenir,* 17 February 1891.

33. *Calédonie,* 9 July 1897.

34. *Journal Officiel,* 1 November 1902.

35. *Calédonie,* 18 March 1903.

36. *PVCG* 1915, December session, 295.

37. *Calédonie,* 15 June 1903.

38. *PVCG* 1915, December session, 295–296.

39. *Arrêté* 1918.

40. Gayet 1929*b*, 16.

41. Ballande 1899*b*.

42. Ballande 1899*b*.

43. *Calédonie,* 22 January 1894.

44. Thomas 1887*a*, 9 July.

45. Thomas 1887*a*, 9 July.

46. Gallop 1887, 42.

47. Thomas 1886, 151.

48. Thomas 1886, 343–344.

49. Le Goupils 1928, 178–179.

50. Le Goupils 1928, 179–181.

51. *France Australe,* 29 March 1895.

52. *France Australe,* 30 September 1895.

53. *France Australe,* 23 September 1919.

54. Thomas 1887*a*, 9 July.

55. Rentz 1903.

56. *Calédonie,* 8 September 1897.

57. See, for example, the story of Garai in Le Goupils 1927, 130–131.

58. Vitte 1874.

59. Vitte 1877.
60. Vitte 1874.
61. Vitte 1875*a*.
62. Vitte 1875*b*.
63. Vitte 1875*b*.
64. Chaulet 1985, 26.
65. Dangeville 1884–1885, 12 December 1884.
66. Doucéré 1934, 71.
67. Shineberg and Kohler 1990, 16–18.
68. *APF* 1887, 290; Doucéré 1934, 62.
69. Passant 1913*a;* Noblet 1926.
70. Mallet 1866; Shineberg and Kohler 1990, 16–18; Marist Mission Report [1883].
71. Vitte 1874.

Chapter 15: Life after Indenture

1. Courbet 1882*a*.
2. Calculation from figures in Marist Mission Report [1883].
3. Subtracting the "excess" deaths for that year leaves 49 percent.
4. *Calédonie,* 13 October 1892.
5. *Arrêté* 1874; *Décret* 1893.
6. D'Arbel 1882.
7. Clain 1885, entry for 10 February.
8. *Décret* 1893, Article 93.
9. *PVCG* 1912, June session, 253.
10. Scarr 1967, 158–159.
11. Rouzaud 1875; Dangeville 1884–1885, 45, 121 (entries for 3 October and 12 December 1884).
12. Courbet 1882*a*.
13. Clain 1885, entry for 10 February.
14. Courbet 1882*a*.
15. Lainé 1898; *Journal Officiel,* 27 August 1898.
16. *PVCG* 1907, December session.
17. Courbet 1882*a*.
18. *Néo-Calédonien,* 11 March 1881.
19. Miklouho-Maclay 1882.
20. Bigant 1889.
21. *Calédonie,* 18 October 1904; *Q J* 1911, no 74; *Q J* 1913, no 81.
22. Corris 1973, 135–147.
23. Corris 1973, 136.
24. Corris 1973, 146.
25. Passant 1913*b*. Not even the name of the island is given.
26. New Hebrides Inquiry 1927.
27. Rae 1919.
28. Acland 1884.
29. Dangeville 1884–1885, 53–55.
30. *Progrès,* 15 February 1882.
31. *Etat civil* Yaté 1904, Deaths. Under the terms of my permission to con-

sult the *état civil* beyond the one-hundred-year limit, I am not permitted to give further details.

32. *Etat civil* Noumea 1928, Deaths. Under the terms of my permission to consult beyond the one-hundred-year limit, I am not permitted to give further details.

33. *Etat civil* all districts, passim. Under the terms of my permission to consult beyond the one- hundred-year limit, I may not give further details.

34. Parisot 1947. I am indebted to Dr Stephen Henningham for this reference.

35. Informants from Kunié, the Isle of Pines.

36. Passant 1913*a;* Noblet 1926; Noblet 1928.

37. Guigen 1942–1943. I am indebted to Dr Stephen Henningham for this reference.

38. Barrau Company 1955. Barrau's letter states that he had been recruited in New Caledonia, so he would have already served for at least three years before this.

Chapter 16: "Nothing More Convenient"

1. Du Petit-Thouars 1879.
2. Du Petit-Thouars 1879.
3. Courbet 1882*c.*
4. *Calédonie,* 20 July 1897.
5. Graves 1984, 113, 114.
6. Corris 1973, 29.
7. Moore 1985, 47.
8. Moore 1979, 12–13.
9. Munro 1993, 91.
10. Shineberg 1967, 151–152.
11. Ivens 1930, 43–44.
12. Corris 1973, 38; Howe 1984, 337.
13. Scarr 1967, 196; Telegraph 1892.
14. Siegel 1985, 46.
15. Scarr 1967, 149; Corris 1973, 44, 46–47.
16. Corris 1973, 43–44; Ivens 1918, 224.
17. Corris 1973, 37.
18. Corris 1973, 37.
19. Corris 1973, 112.
20. Corris 1973, 59.
21. Graves 1984, 135–137.
22. Scarr 1967, 189–190, 196.
23. Moore 1985, 47.
24. Scarr 1967, 139.
25. Scarr 1967, 143–144.
26. Corris 1973, 2, 4.
27. Corris 1972, 239.
28. Keesing 1974, 215.
29. Howe 1984, 330, 340. Howe bracketed this assessment with my emphasis on the cooperative elements in the sandalwood trade, but I made

clear several times in the book that the migration of labor—even in the sandalwood trade—entirely changed the nature of the power relationship (Shineberg 1967, 190, 198, 215–216).

30. Moore 1992, 67. See also Moore 1985, 47.

31. *Progrès,* 22 January 1882.

32. Corris 1973, 44; see also 59.

33. Corris 1973, 44.

34. Corris 1973, 43.

35. Corris 1973, 61.

36. Hagen 1893, 374.

37. Bennett 1987, 83; Munro 1995, 241.

38. Bennett 1987, 87.

39. Bennett 1987, 83; Munro 1995, 241.

40. Scarr 1967, 143; Corris 1973, 55. Scarr 1970, 242.

41. Scarr 1967, 143.

42. Corris 1968, 87.

43. Corris 1973, 37.

44. Ivens 1918, 224; emphasis mine.

45. Ivens 1929, 107, 254.

46. Quoted in Steel 1880, 414.

47. Scarr 1967, 140–142; Corris 1973, 40–43.

48. Moore 1981, 87.

49. Graves 1993, 75; Parnaby 1964, 201.

50. For examples, see Corris 1973, 83, 70–73; Saunders 1988, 192–207; Parnaby 1972, 140.

51. See, for example, Huetz de Lemps in de Deckker 1994, 340.

52. Du Petit-Thouars 1879.

References

Only items quoted have been listed here.

"A"
  1882 Letter signed "A," Noumea, 7 July 1882, in *La France Maritime et Coloniale,* 8 September. An extract from it, with comment, was published in *Le Néo-Calédonien,* 31 October 1882.
Acland, Commander W A Dyke
  1884 Commander Acland to Commodore Erskine, 23 June: Extracts from the Proceedings of HMS *Miranda,* copy 36. In WPHC IC, 186/84.
Adams, Ron
  1987 Homo Anthropologicus and Man-Tanna. *Journal of Pacific History* 21 (1): 3–14.
Aitkin, Reverend Joseph
  1871 Extracts from a diary kept by the late Reverend Joseph Aitkin of the Melanesian Mission, between 29 May and 24 September. Subenclosure B of enclosure 1 in Belmore 1871.
Allen, Michael
  1981a Introduction. In *Vanuatu: Politics, Economics and Ritual in Island Melanesia,* edited by Michael Allen, 1–8. Sydney: Academic Press.
  1981b Rethinking Old Problems: Matriliny, Secret Societies and Political Evolution. In *Vanuatu,* 9–34.
  1981c Innovation, Inversion and Revolution. In *Vanuatu,* 105–134.
Anderson, J W
  1880 *Notes of Travel in Fiji and New Caledonia, with Some Remarks on South Sea Islanders and Their Languages.* London: Ellisen.
Anglo-French Conference
  1914 Proceedings [of conference on the New Hebrides Convention]. Australian Archives, Canberra. 2218, vol 20 (3): 66.
Annand, Reverend Joseph
  1890 Letter to H[er] B[ritannic] M[ajesty's] Consul in Noumea. Tangoa, Santo, 19 December. In Correspondence from RNAS, Case 49. Copy in WPHC IC, 102/1892.

Annuaire
1871–1946 *Annuaire de la Nouvelle-Calédonie et Dépendances.* Noumea: Government Printery.
Annual Report
1912 Movement of Labor and Functioning of the Immigration Department. Section 8, Annual Report [New Caledonia]. Archives d'Outre-Mer, NC carton 271.
Anti-Slavery Papers
1909–1917 Manuscripts on British Empire, S22, G395. Rhodes House Library, Oxford.
AOM, Archives d'Outre-Mer
1853–1945 Archives d'Outre-Mer, Aix-en-Provence. A series on the New Hebrides (NH) and two series on New Caledonia (NC) were consulted (Série Géographique and Affaires Politiques; they are divided into numbered "cartons." The numbers do not overlap so the series is not specified in notes, which take the form "Archives d'Outre-Mer, NC carton —, or NH Carton —").
APF, Annales de la Propagation de la Foi
1887 *Annales de la Propagation de la Foi,* vol 59. Lyon: Société de la Propagation de la Foi.
APM, Archivio dei Padri Maristi
1846–1937 *Archivio dei Padri Maristi,* Oceania, Nova Caledonia, 3b, General Correspondence 1846–1937. Rome. Pacific Manuscripts Bureau microfilm 168.
Arrêté
1874 *Arrêté* of 26 March. In *Moniteur,* 1 April 1874; also in RNAS 32.
1875a *Arrêté* of 16 March. In *Moniteur,* 24 March 1875.
1875b *Arrêté* of 16 August. In *Moniteur,* 25 August 1875.
1878 *Arrêté* of 6 May. In *Moniteur,* 15 May 1878.
1884 *Arrêté* of 4 September. In *Moniteur,* 10 September 1884.
1904 *Arrêté* of 18 October. In *Journal Officiel,* 22 October 1904; also in BONC 1904, 738–742.
1918 *Arrêté* of 14 January 1918, promulgating *décret* of 6 November 1917. In *Journal Officiel,* 19 January 1918.
1920 *Arrêté* of 6 October. In *Journal Officiel,* 23 October 1920.
Aurora Commission
1880a Proceedings of the Commission of Inquiry charged with casting the greatest possible light on the acts of which the *Aurora* and *Lulu* have been accused. Archives d'Outre-Mer, NC carton 63.
1880b Report of the Commission to the Governor of New Caledonia, 6 December 1880. In *M & D,* vol 4.
1880c *Modifications à la règlementation sur l'immigration, proposées à la Commission d'enquête* [*Aurora* Commission], *dans le cours de ses interrogations.* Enclosure in *Aurora* Commission 1880b.
Australasian
1871–1873 *The Australasian.* Weekly newspaper. Melbourne.
L'Avenir
1888–1891 Weekly newspaper, then twice weekly, then thrice weekly. Noumea.

Ayscough, Lieutenant
  1900 Letter to Resident Commissioner of the Solomon Islands, 21 October 1900. In WPHC IC 156/01.
Ballande, André
  1899a Report to Ballande, 4 January. Archives de l'Archevêché de Noumea, 135.7.
  1899b Ballande to Bishop Fraysse, 19 May 1899. Archives de l'Archevêché de Noumea, 135.7.
  1902 Letter to the Minister for Colonies, 11 January 1902. Archives d'Outre-Mer, NH, A1 (2).
Ballière, Achille
  1875 *Un voyage de Circumnavigation: Histoire de la Déportation par un des Évadés de Nouméa*. London: Henry S King.
Bandler, Faith
  1977 *Wacvie*. Adelaide: Rigby.
Barrau Company
  1955 Letter from Maison Barrau (signature illegible), 6 April. Archives Territoriales de la Nouvelle Calédonie, 109 W 5*, in report of M Guiart.
Beaglehole, J C
  1966 *The Exploration of the Pacific*, 3rd edition. London: Adam and Charles Black. First published 1934.
  1969 *The Journals of Captain James Cook*. Cambridge: Cambridge University Press.
Beechert, Edward D
  1985 *Working in Hawaii: A Labor History*. Honolulu: University of Hawai'i Press.
Belmore, Earl of
  1871 Despatch 2 from Governor of New South Wales [Belmore] to Earl of Kimberley, 28 December 1871, with enclosures and subenclosures. In GBPP 1873.
  1872 Despatch 4 from Governor of New South Wales [Belmore] to Earl of Kimberley, 20 February 1872, with enclosures. In GBPP 1873.
Bennett, Judith A
  1976 Immigration, "Blackbirding," Labour Recruiting? The Hawaiian Experience 1877–1887. *Journal of Pacific History* 11 (1): 3–27.
  1987 *Wealth of the Solomons: A History of a Pacific Archipelago, 1800–1978*. Pacific Islands Monograph Series, 3. Honolulu: University of Hawai'i Press.
Bigant, Commander
  1889 Letter to the Governor of New Caledonia, 17 September. Archives de la Marine, Paris. Dossier H, BB4 1996.
  1890a Letter to the Governor of New Caledonia, 10 August. Archives de la Marine, Paris. BB4/1996.
  1890b Letter to Minister for the Navy and Colonies, 15 September. In *M & D*, vol 10.
  1890c Letter to Minister for the Navy and Colonies, 14 November. In *M & D*, vol 10.
  1890d Letter to Commander in Chief of the Naval Division of the Pacific, 13 December. Archives de la Marine, Paris. BB4 1996.

Blackwood, Peter
    1981 Rank, Exchange and Leadership in Four Vanuatu Societies. In *Vanuatu,* edited by Michael Allen, 35–84. Sydney: Academic Press.
BOEFO, Bulletin Officiel des Etablissements français de l'Océanie
    1864 *Bulletin Officiel des Etablissements français de l'Océanie,* Année 1864. Mitchell Library, Sydney.
Bolton, Lissant M
    1993 Dancing in Mats: Extending "*Kastom*" to Women in Vanuatu. PhD thesis, University of Manchester.
BONC, Bulletin Officiel de la Nouvelle-Calédonie
    1865–1904 *Bulletin Officiel de la Nouvelle-Calédonie.* Pacific Manuscripts Bureau Document microfilm 46–58.
Bowie, F G
    1899 Reverend F Bowie to Captain Farquhar, HMS *Wallaroo,* 5 August. WPHC IC 238/99.
Bowie, F G, and J T Bowie
    nd Report on the New Hebrides for the British and Foreign Anti-Slavery and Aborigines Protection Society. [1912]. In Anti-Slavery Papers.
Bridge, Captain Cyprian
    1883 Letter to Western Pacific High Commissioner, 9 August 1882. Enclosure 2, in Correspondence Respecting the Natives of Western Pacific and the Labour Traffic, GBPP 1883.
British Resident Commissioner
    1920 British Resident Commissioner to High Commissioner, 13 July. In GBCO 225/172.
Brooke, Reverend Charles
    1871 Extracts from the journal of the Reverend Charles Hyde Brooke, 12–14 August. Florida [Nggela]. Subenclosure D of enclosure 1 in Belmore 1871.
Brou, Bernard
    1979 Un siècle de crises et de booms: Les hauts et les bas de l'économie calédonienne. *Bulletin de la Société d'Etudes Historiques de la Nouvelle-Calédonie* 40:35–42.
Brunet, Auguste
    1908 *Le Régime International des Nouvelles-Hébrides.* Paris: A Rousseau.
Bulletin du Commerce
    1899–1927 *Bulletin du Commerce et des Tribuneaux de la Nouvelle-Calédonie.* Newspaper. Twice weekly. Noumea.
La Calédonie
    1892–1907 Newspaper. Appeared three times a week, then daily. Noumea.
Camouilly, Charles
    1877–1878 Distraint on the Property of Joubert. Notariat: Depot des Papiers Publics des Colonies. Archives d'Outre-Mer, NC.
Campbell, Frederick A
    1873 *A Year in the New Hebrides, Loyalty Islands and New Caledonia.* Geelong: Mercer.
Cariou, Marc
    1931 Historique de la Plantation Marc Cariou. Typescript. 199W, Archives Territoriales de la Nouvelle Calédonie, Noumea.

CCI, "Committee of Caledonian Interests"
    1882 Petition to the Governor from the "Committee of Caledonian In-
        terests," 29 June 1882. In *Néo-Calédonien,* 4 July.
Chanvalon, Maître
    1889 Contrats d'Engagement entre Lucien Bernheim et les Indigènes
        suivants . . . Actes Civils publics, Service de l'Enregistrement. Archives
        Territoriales de la Nouvelle Calédonie, Noumea. 27W 232.
Chaulet, Jean-Luc, editor
    1985 *Lifou Pacifique-sud: Une chronique de la Nouvelle-Calédonie de 1876 à
        1916 d'après la correspondence de Benjamin Goubin, Missionaire et Ardéchois.*
        Annonay, France: Colombier.
Chauliac, Captain
    1893 Letter of Chauliac, commander of the *Scorff,* to Minister for the
        Navy and Colonies, 21 April. Archives de la Marine, Paris. BB4
        1996.
Clain, P
    1885 Journal of Government Agent Clain, aboard the *Annette,* 8 January
        1885–10 March 1885. Archives d'Outre-Mer, NC carton 63.
Coates, Arthur
    1887 Sworn statement, 14 November, and extracts from his diary as
        government agent of the *Winifred.* In WPHC IC, 289/87.
Le Colon de la Nouvelle-Calédonie
    1889–1890 Daily newspaper. Noumea.
Computer file
    1865–1930 Author's computer file of more than 6000 individual workers,
        with names and attributes derived from a variety of sources, as de-
        scribed in Note on Sources.
Cordeil, Paul
    1882 Resumé of court proceedings by Paul Cordeil, head of the Depart-
        ment of Justice, 18 September. Enclosed in Courbet 1882*e.*
Corris, Peter
    1968 "Blackbirding" in New Guinea Waters, 1883–1884. *Journal of Pacific
        History* 3:85–105.
    1970 Pacific Island Labour Migrants in Queensland. *Journal of Pacific
        History* 5:43–64.
    1972 Review of *Cannibal Cargoes* by Hector Holthouse, and *The Blackbirders*
        by Edward Docker. *Journal of Pacific History* 7:239–240.
    1973 *Passage, Port and Plantation: A History of Solomon Islands Labour
        Migration 1870–1914.* Melbourne: Melbourne University Press.
    1977 Review of *Wacvie,* by Faith Bandler. *The Australian,* 20–21 August
        (weekend magazine).
Cotteau, E
    1888 *En Océanie: Voyage autour du Monde en 365 jours, 1884-1888.* Paris:
        Hachette.
Courbet, Contre-Amiral A
    1880*a* Letter to Minister for the Navy and Colonies, 3 September. In
        M & D, vol 4.
    1880*b* Letter to Admiral Cloué, Minister for the Navy and Colonies,
        24 December. In *M & D,* vol 4.

1881 Letter to Minister of the Navy and Colonies, 13 May. Archives d'Outre-Mer, NC carton 63.

1882*a* Report on New Hebridean Immigration. Enclosed in Courbet to Minister for Navy and Colonies, 17 February. Archives d'Outre-Mer. NC carton 63.

1882*b* Letter to Minister for Navy and Colonies, 6 July. Enclosed in Minister for Navy and Colonies to Minister for Foreign Affairs, 4 December. Archives d'Outre-Mer. NC carton 63.

1882*c* Letter to Minister for Navy and Colonies, 7 July. Archives de la Marine, Paris. BB4/1577.

1882*d* Letter to Minister for Navy and Colonies, 3 August. Enclosed in Minister for Navy and Colonies to Minister for Foreign Affairs, 4 December. Archives d'Outre-Mer, NC carton 63.

1882*e* Letter to the Minister for the Navy and Colonies, 19 September. Archives de la Marine, Paris. BB4 1577, vol 3.

1882*f* Extract of the report of Admiral Courbet on the overall situation of New Caledonia to the Minister of the Navy and Colonies, Paris, 6 December. Archives d'Outre-Mer, NC carton 282.

Cour Criminelle
1859–1896 Records of Judgments. Archives Territoriales de la Nouvelle Calédonie, Noumea.

Courmeaux, Henri
1884 Report of the mission to New Caledonia and the New Hebrides. Archives d'Outre-Mer, NC carton 180.

Cuinier, Inspector
1877 Extract of a report of inspection of New Caledonia by the colonial Inspector in Chief, M Cuinier, 18 April. Archives d'Outre-Mer, NC carton 173.

Dangeville, Government Agent
1884–1885 Journal of Government Agent Dangeville, aboard the *Marie*, 6 September 1884–1 January 1885. Archives d'Outre-Mer, NC carton 63.

1885 Report to the Director of the Interior, 8 January. Archives d'Outre-Mer, NC carton 63.

D'Arbel, Lieutenant
1882 Report on Recruitment in the New Hebrides, 20 November. Enclosed in letter to Governor Pallu, 8 December 1882. Archives d'Outre-Mer, NH carton 282.

Davidson, J W, and Deryck Scarr, editors
1970 *Pacific Islands Portraits*. Canberra: Australian National University Press.

Davis, Commander
1890 Letter to Commander Bigant, Efaté, 8 November. Enclosed in Rear Admiral Scott to J Thurston. WPHC IC 362/1890.

Day, J
1881 Journal of Government Agent Day, *Sea Breeze*, 8 April to 19 July. National Archives of Fiji. Microfilm in Records Room, Division of Pacific and Asian History, Australian National University.

Décret

1852 *Décret du Prince Président de la République du 13 février 1852, sur les immigrants dans les colonies françaises ainsi que sur les engagements et la police du travail.* Reproduced in RNAS 32; also in BOEFO, 51–63.

1893 *Décret rélatif à la réglementation de l'immigration océanienne en Nouvelle-Calédonie.* Reproduced in BONC, 11 July 1893, 386–464.

De Deckker, Paul, editor

1994 *Le Peuplement du Pacifique et de la Nouvelle-Calédonie au XIXe Siècle.* Paris: Harmattan.

Docker, Edward Wybergh

1970 *The Blackbirders: The Recruiting of South Sea Labour for Queensland.* Sydney: Angus & Robertson.

Doucéré, Monseigneur Victor

1934 *La Mission Catholique aux Nouvelles-Hébrides.* Lyon: Librairie Catholique Emmanuel Vitte.

Douglas, Bronwen

1972 Culture Contact in New Caledonia, 1774–1870. PhD thesis, Australian National University, Canberra.

1980 Conflict and Alliance in a Colonial Context: Case Studies in New Caledonia, 1853–1870. *Journal of Pacific History* 15 (1): 21–51.

Doze, Lieutenant

1887 Letter to the Commander of the Local Station in New Caledonia, 12 October. Archives de la Marine, Paris. BB4 1995.

Dubois, Government Agent

1890 Notes on the voyage of the *Ika-Vuka,* from Government Agent Dubois. *France Australe,* 13 and 15 December.

Dunlop, T D

1921 H[er] B[ritannic] M[ajesty's] Consul [Dunlop] in Noumea to Winston Churchill, 19 May. Australian Archives, CRS A981 New Caledonia, vol 1, 1921–1926.

1922 Report of the British Consul in Noumea to the British Ambassador in Paris, 30 January. Australian Archives, correspondence files, alphabetical series, 1901–1943, CRS A981, New Caledonia part 1.

Du Petit-Thouars, Contre-Amiral

1879 Report to Admiral Jauréguiberry, Minister of the Navy and Colonies, 22 April. In *M & D,* vol 4.

Durand, G

1870–1871 Extrait d'une correspondance sur la Nouvelle-Calédonie. Brussels: A van Naegen. Typescript in Mitchell Library, Sydney.

L'Éclair

1899 Paris newspaper. Issue for 5 January. Bibliothèque Nationale, microfilm D89.

Etat civil

1865–1930 Archives of the *état civil* for all districts of New Caledonia. Records less than one hundred years old were read, for statistical purposes only, by permission of the *procureur de la République* in Noumea.

Evans, Raymond, Kay Saunders, and Kathryn Cronin
   1988 *Race Relations in Colonial Queensland: Exclusion, Exploitation and Extermination.* St Lucia: Queensland University Press.
FCA, French Consul-General in Australia
   1899 French Consul-General in Australia to Minister for Foreign Affairs, 19 January. Enclosed in Minister for the Navy to Minister for Foreign Affairs, 17 March. Archives d'Outre-Mer, NH carton A1 (2).
Feillet, Paul
   1899 Governor Feillet to Minister for Colonies, 3 June. Archives d'Outre-Mer, NC carton 5.
Fillon, Inspector
   1907 Inspector Fillon to Minister for the Navy and Colonies, 16 April. Summary of reports and recommendations on Immigration and Native Affairs to *Inspection mobile.* Archives d'Outre-Mer, NC carton 209.
Firth, Stewart
   1973 German Recruitment and Employment of Labour in the Western Pacific before the First World War. DPhil thesis, Oxford University.
   1976 The Transformation of the German Labour Trade in New Guinea, 1899–1914. *Journal of Pacific History* 11 (1): 51–65.
Firth, Stewart, and Doug Munro
   1990 *German Regulation and Employment of Plantation Labour in Samoa, 1864–1914.* Working Papers in Economic History 37. Adelaide: Flinders University.
Fletcher, James
   1923 *Isles of Illusion: Letters from the South Seas,* edited by Bohun Lynch. London: Constable.
FLP, *Ferdinand de Lesseps* papers
   1884 Report of the inquiry into the *Ferdinand de Lesseps* incident, and related documents. Archives d'Outre-Mer, NC carton 64.
Forrest, A E C
   1899 Letter to Resident Commissioner Woodford, including an enclosure from Bishop Wilson, 28 August, recounting the case of the *France.* WPHC IC 241/99.
La France Australe
   1889–1930 Newspaper. Noumea. Twice weekly, then daily.
Funabiki, Takeo
   1981 On Pigs of the Mbotgote in Malekula. In *Vanuatu,* edited by Michael Allen, 173–188. Sydney: Academic Press.
GA Instructions
   [1881] General Instructions to Government Agents, from the Director of the Interior, nd. Apparently enclosed in Director of Interior to Governor, 27 April 1881. Archives d'Outre-Mer, NC carton 63.
   1885 Instructions to Government Agent P Clain from the Director of the Interior. In Clain 1885.
Gadaud, Commander
   1892 Letter to Minister for Navy and Colonies, warship *Saône,* Noumea, 22 October. Archives de la Marine, Paris. BB4 1996.

Gaggin, J. Government Agent
   1880 Extracts from his journal on board schooner *Stanley*, 23–26 May.
        Enclosure 2 in Courbet 1880*a*.
Gallop, Reg
   1887 Papers. Mitchell Library, Sydney. MSS 488.
Gascher, Pierre
   1974 *La Belle au Bois Dormant: Regards sur l'Administration Coloniale en
        Nouvelle-Calédonie de 1874 à 1894*. Noumea: La Société d'Etudes His-
        toriques de La Nouvelle-Calédonie.
Gauharou, Léon
   1884 Director of the Interior to M Russeil, government agent of the
        Ferdinand de Lesseps, 22 September. Archives d'Outre-Mer, NC car-
        ton 64.
   1888 Director of the Interior to Consul Layard, 28 October. (In reply to
        a British request for information on recruits who had not returned to
        Utupua.) In RNAS 38, case 26.
Gaultier de la Richerie, Eugène
   1872 Letter to Governor of New South Wales, nd; enclosure 2 in Belmore
        1872.
Gayet, Inspector
   1929*a* Report of Inspector Gayet *[Inspection mobile]* on the Immigration
        Department. Archives d'Outre-Mer, NC carton 746.
   1929*b* Report of Inspector Gayet *[Inspection mobile]* on the performance of
        M Harrelle, Commandant of the Gendarme squadron, Head of the
        Department of Native Affairs and Oceanian Labor. Archives d'Outre-
        Mer, NC carton 746.
GBCO, Great Britain Colonial Office
   1878–1930 Original correspondence; despatches to High Commissioner,
        Western Pacific. Public Record Office, London. 225. Microfilm in Na-
        tional Library of Australia, Canberra.
GBFO, Great Britain Foreign Office
   1853–1920 General Correspondence. FO 27 (France); FO 371 (Political);
        FO 58 (Pacific Islands). Public Record Office, London. Microfilm in
        National Library of Australia, Canberra.
GBPP, Great Britain Parliamentary Papers
   1872*a* Vol 39: Report of Proceedings [of HMS *Rosario*]. Various letters
        and reports of Lieutenant Markham to Commodore F H Stirling,
        RNAS, 1 November 1871 to 12 February 1872.
   1872*b* Vol 43: Further Correspondence respecting the Deportation of
        South Sea Islanders.
   1873 Vol 50: Communications respecting outrages committed upon na-
        tives of the South Sea Islands.
   1874 Vol 45: Correspondence respecting outrages committed upon na-
        tives of the South Sea Islands.
   1883 Vol 47: Correspondence respecting the Natives of the Western
        Pacific and the Labour Traffic.
   1892 Vol 56: Correspondence relating to Polynesian Labour in the
        Colony of Queensland.

 1893–1894 Vol 61: Further Correspondence relating to Polynesian Labour in the Colony of Queensland.

Genovese, Eugene D
 1966 *The Political Economy of Slavery: Studies in the Economy and Society of the Slave South.* London: MacGibbon & Kee.

Gilding, Michael
 1982 The Massacre of the *Mystery:* A Case Study in Contact Relations. *Journal of Pacific History* 17 (2): 66–85.

Giles, W E
 1968 *A Cruise in a Queensland Labour Vessel to the South Seas,* edited by Deryck Scarr. Pacific History Series, 1. Canberra: Australian National University Press.

Gillion, K L
 1962 *Fiji's Indian Migrants: A History to the End of Indenture in 1920.* Melbourne: Oxford University Press.

Glasser, Edouard
 1904 Rapport à M le Ministre des Colonies sur les richesses minérales de la Nouvelle-Calédonie. *Annales des Mines* (Paris). 10th series, vol 5:503–620, 623–693.

Godey, Charles
 1886 *Tablettes d'un ancien fonctionnaire de la Nouvelle-Calédonie.* Paris: Challamel.

Graves, Adrian
 1984 The Nature and Origins of Pacific Islands Labour Migration to Queensland, 1863–1906. In *International Labour Migration: Historical Perspectives,* edited by Shula Marks and Peter Richardson, 112–139. Hounslow, Middlesex: Maurice Temple Smith for Institute of Commonwealth Studies.
 1993 *Cane and Labour: The Political Economy of the Queensland Sugar Industry, 1862–1906.* Edinburgh: Edinburgh University Press.

Gray, Reverend W
 1892 Letter to Honourable Sir Samuel Griffith, Aniwa, 10 September. Enclosure 1 in Sir H W Norman to the Marquess of Ripon, 6 March 1893. In GBPP 1893–1894, no 2.

Grossin, Lieutenant
 1890 Letter to Bigant, Commandant of the *Saône,* enclosing the complaint of the sailors of the *Ika Vuka* (26 October 1890), and the report of his investigation. In Bigant 1890*d.*

Guigen, Adjutant
 1942–1943 Report of Adjutant Guigen on the activities of the tribes of Goa, Goyetta and Tchamba in 1942 and 1943. In Register of Correspondence of the Brigade of Ponérihouen, 1945. Archives Territoriales de la Nouvelle Calédonie, 107W 160.

Guillain, Rear-Admiral Charles
 1865 Extract of a letter of Governor Guillain to the Minister for the Navy and Colonies, 31 May. Archives d'Outre-Mer, NC carton 282.

Hagen, A
 1893 Voyage aux Nouvelles-Hébrides et aux Iles Salomon. *Tour du Monde*

(Paris) 65 (22–24): 337–384. Dr Hagen traveled as government agent in the *Mary Anderson* and three voyages of the *Lady Saint Aubyn* in 1890–1891. The account is an amalgam of all four voyages masquerading as one.

Hawkins, Joseph Edward
    1887–1888 Log of the *Nautilus*. Mitchell Library, Sydney. MS 2842.

Héricault, Léonce
    1889 Engagements Indigènes. Archives Territoriales de la Nouvelle Calédonie. Archives Notariales, 23W D5.

Hilliard, David
    1978 *God's Gentlemen: A History of the Melanesian Mission 1849–1942*. St Lucia: Queensland University Press.

Histoire authentique
    1909 *Histoire authentique de l'insurrection des indigènes de la Nouvelle-Calédonie en 1878: Réproduction des documents officiels*. Noumea: Viard. Manuscript copy in Mitchell Library, Sydney.

Hoff, C
    1873 Letter to the editor, *Le Moniteur*, 24 September.
    1879 Letter to the editor, *La Nouvelle-Calédonie*, 9 April.

Holthouse, Hector
    1969 *Cannibal Cargoes*. Adelaide: Rigby.

Howe, K R
    1984 *Where the Waves Fall: A New South Sea Islands History from First Settlement to Colonial Rule*. Sydney: George Allen & Unwin; Honolulu: University of Hawai'i Press.

Immigration Commission
    1883 Re-establishment of Immigration from the New Hebrides and Neighbouring Islands. Extract from the Report of the Commission named 4 April 1883 by Pallu de la Barrière, Governor of New Caledonia, to study different questions concerning free colonization. Archives d'Outre-Mer, NC Affaires Politiques, carton 282.

L'Indépendant
    1884–1890 *L'Indépendant de la Nouvelle-Calédonie*. Newspaper, Noumea. Thrice weekly.

Inspection mobile
    1874 Report of Inspector-in-Chief of *Inspection mobile*, November 1873– April 1874. Archives d'Outre-Mer, NC carton 178.
    1907 Sums due to Immigrants. 22 April. Archives d'Outre-Mer, NC carton 209.

Insurrection
    1882 *Insurrection des tribus canaques des circonscriptions de Bouloupari à Koné. Massacres des 25 et 26 juin et 11 septembre 1878. Listes nominatives des victimes*. Author unknown. Noumea: Imprimerie civile. (Copy in Mitchell Library.)

Interior Reports
    1878 Report of the Director of the Interior Department, 10 February. Archives d'Outre-Mer, NC carton 32.
    1880 *Situation présentant l'effectif des Néo-Hebridais, Africains et Asiatiques au*

31 Décembre 1879. 1 January 1880. Archives d'Outre-Mer, NC carton 282.

1881 Report of the Director of the Interior to the Privy Council, 27 April. In *PVCP* 1881.

1885 Report of the Director of the Interior to the Privy Council, 6 January. In *PVCP* 1885, no 11.

1889 Report of the Director of the Interior to the Privy Council, 12 December. In *PVCP* 1889.

1893 Report of the Director of the Interior to the *Conseil général.* In *PVCG* 1893, August session.

Ivens, W G

1918 *Dictionary and Grammar of the Language of Sa'a and Ulawa, Solomon Islands.* Washington, DC: Carnegie Institution.

1927 *Melanesians of the South-East Solomon Islands.* London: Kegan Paul, Trench, Trubner.

1929 *Dictionary and Grammar of the Language of Sa'a and Ulawa.* Second (revised) edition. London: Oxford University Press; Melbourne: Melbourne University Press.

1930 *The Island Builders of the Pacific.* London: Seeley, Service.

Jacomb, Edward

1911 Letter to French Resident Commissioner for the New Hebrides, Vila, 18 October. Copy in Anti-Slavery Papers 1909–1917.

1912 Letter to Minister for Colonies, Paris, 4 January 1912, enclosing a translation of Jacomb 1911, with additional information. In Anti-Slavery Papers 1909–1917.

Jauréguiberry, M le Vice-Amiral

1882 Letter, Minister of Navy and Colonies (Jauréguiberry) to Courbet, 5 May. Archives de la Marine, Paris. BB4 1577.

Jeanneney, A

1894 *La Nouvelle-Calédonie Agricole.* Paris: Challamel.

Jolly, Margaret

1987 The Forgotten Women: A History of Migrant Labour and Gender Relations in Vanuatu. *Oceania* 58: 119–139.

Jouenne, Dr

1890 Letter of Dr Jouenne, government agent of the *Marie,* to Commander Bigant, at sea, 4 November. Enclosed in Bigant 1890*c.*

Le Journal Officiel

1886–1930 *Le Journal Officiel de la Nouvelle-Calédonie.* Noumea. Weekly.

Keesing, Roger

1974 Review of *Passage, Port and Plantation* by Peter Corris. *Journal of Pacific History* 9: 215–217.

King, Merton

1911 British Resident Commissioner of the New Hebrides [King] to French Resident Commissioner,̈ 29 December. GBCO 225/107.

1912 British Resident Commissioner to French Resident Commissioner, 9 January. GBCO 225/107.

1919 British Resident Commissioner to High Commissioner for the Western Pacific, 24 February. WPHC IC 878/19.

Lacascade, T
1885 Director of the Interior (Lacascade) to Governor of New Caledonia, 14 January. Archives d'Outre-Mer, NC carton 282.

Lafarge, Maître
1882 Report of the President of the Superior Court, 14 September. Enclosed in Courbet 1882*e*.

Lainé, L
1898 Journal of L Lainé, Government Agent on the *Jeannette,* Captain Gaspard, from 10 January to 28 May 1898. Archives d'Outre Mer, NH E2, carton 34. Microfilm in Records Room, Division of Pacific and Asian History, Research School of Pacific and Asian Studies, Australian National University.

Lal, Brij V
1985*a* Kunti's Cry: Indentured Women in Fiji Plantations. *Indian Economic and Social History Review* 22:55–71.
1985*b* Veil of Dishonour: Sexual Jealousy and Suicide on Fiji Plantations. *Journal of Pacific History* 20 (3): 135–155.

Lamadon, M
1893 Letter of Director of the Interior (Lamadon) to British Consul, 22 March. Local Correspondence, in WPHC papers.

Laurent, Ensign H H
1904 La Colonisation aux Nouvelles-Hébrides. *Revue Maritime,* August, 73–92.

Layard, E L
1882*a* British Consul in Noumea (Layard) to Foreign Minister, 14 February. In GBFO 84/1614, XC/A16790.
1882*b* Layard to Commodore Erskine, 10 May, with enclosure of shorthand notes taken at the trial of Madézo on 6 May by the correspondent of the *Sydney Morning Herald* (Hughan). In RNAS 16.
1887 British Consul Layard to High Commissioner for Western Pacific, 25 October. In WPHC IC, 282/1887.

Le Boucher, A
1884*a* Confidential letter of Governor Le Boucher to Minister for Navy and Colonies, 4 September. Archives d'Outre-Mer, NC carton 64.
1884*b* Governor Le Boucher to Minister for Navy and Colonies, 27 November. Archives d'Outre-Mer, NC carton 64.
1885*a* Governor Le Boucher to Minister for Navy and Colonies, 21 January. Archives d'Outre-Mer, NC carton 282.
1885*b* Telegram to Minister for Navy and Colonies, 14 March. Archives d'Outre-Mer, NC carton 282.

Lecomte, Commander
1895 Report of the Commander of the *Scorff* to Minister for Navy and Colonies, 22 May. In *M & D,* vol 12.

Legendre, Dr
1891 Letter from government agent on board the *Marie* (Legendre) to Governor of New Caledonia, 31 December. Copy in WPHC IC 102/1892.

Le Goupils, Marc
  1910 *Comment on cesse d'être colon: Six années en Nouvelle-Calédonie.* Paris: B Grasset.
  1927 Sous les Niaoulis: Souvenirs d'un Planteur Calédonien (1898–1904). *Revue des Deux Mondes* 41:111–143.
  1928 *Dans la Brousse Calédonienne: Souvenirs d'un Ancien Planteur, 1898–1904.* Paris: Perrin.
Legrand, Lieutenant
  1886 Letter to governor of New Caledonia, written aboard the French cruiser *Dives,* 11 April. Archives d'Outre-Mer, NH carton A1 (2).
Le Maréchal [?]
  1884 Inquiry into the Operations of the Recruiting Ship *Marie* in the New Hebrides, 20–24 December. [Signed "Officer in Charge of the Inquiry, Le Maréchal."] Archives d'Outre-Mer, NC carton 63.
Le Mescam, L
  1893 Letter to the Reverend W Gray, missionary on Tanna, New Hebrides, 23 March. WPHC papers.
Lemire, Charles
  1884 *Voyage à Pied en Nouvelle-Calédonie.* Paris: Challamel.
Liotard, Governor
  1906 Governor Liotard to Commissaire Délégué aux Nouvelles-Hébrides, 16 October. Archives d'Outre-Mer, NH carton 5.
M & D, Mémoires et Documents
  1865–1918 *Mémoires et Documents, Océanie,* vols 4–21. Archives des Affaires Etrangères, Paris.
Macdonald, Reverend Daniel
  1875–1879 Diary. National Library of Australia, Canberra. MS1748.
  1880 Declaration on board the *Dayspring* off Epi, 2 July. Enclosure 4 in Courbet 1880*a.*
Macmillan, Reverend Thomas
  1883 On the Natural Obstetrics of the Aborigines of the New Hebrides. *Australasian Medical Gazette* 2 (February): 97–100.
  1908 Newsletter, Tanna, January. In *Quarterly Jottings* 60 (April).
  1911 Newsletter, Tanna: In *Quarterly Jottings* 73 (April).
Mahaffy, A W
  1912*a* Letter to High Commissioner, 19 September. WPHC IC 1917/1912.
  1912*b* Letter to High Commisioner, 17 October. WPHC IC 2010/1912.
  1912*c* Letter to High Commissioner, 4 November. WPHC IC 2259/1912.
  1912*d* Letter to High Commissioner, 11 November. WPHC IC 2260/1912.
  1913*a* Letter to High Commissioner, 30 January. Enclosed in New Hebrides Despatch, 31 January. WPHC IC 418/1913.
  1913*b* Letter to High Commissioner, 7 February. WPHC IC 434/1913.
Mallet, Brother Aimé
  1866 Letter to Révérend Père Forestier, 30 April. Archivio dei Padri Maristi, Rome. Pacific Manuscripts Bureau microfilm 168.
Marchand, Ludovic
  1879 Letter to Victor Schoelcher, 18 September. In Schoelcher Papers [1877–1885].

1880 Letter to Victor Schoelcher, 2 February. In Schoelcher Papers [1877–1885].

Marist Mission report

[1883] "Information on New Hebridean immigrants introduced into New Caledonia between 1874 and 1882." Undated anonymous report in Archives de l'Archevêché de Noumea, 111.1.

Markham, Lieutenant

1872*a* Letter from Lieutenant Markham, RN, late Acting Commander of HMS *Rosario*, to Earl of Belmore, 10 February, with enclosures. Enclosure 1 in Belmore 1872.

1872*b* Report of Proceedings of HMS *Rosario*, 12 February. In GBPP 1872*a*.

Marks, Shula, and Peter Richardson

1984 *International Labour Migration: Historical Perspectives.* Hounslow, Middlesex: Maurice Temple Smith for Institute of Commonwealth Studies.

Martin, Jules

1910 Acting French Resident Commissioner (Martin) to High Commissioner, 8 October. Archives d'Outre-Mer, NH carton 7.

McArthur, Norma, and John Yaxley

1967 *Condominium of the New Hebrides: A Report on the First Census of the Population 1967.* [Sydney]: Government Printer.

Melanesian Mission

1881 Report of the Melanesian Mission for 1881. *Sydney Morning Herald,* 8 May 1882. Reproduced from *Auckland Church Gazette,* nd.

Meleiseā, Mālama

1976 The Last Days of the Melanesian Labour Trade in Western Samoa. *Journal of Pacific History* 11 (2): 126–132.

Mercer, Patricia M

1995 *White Australia Defied.* Townsville: James Cook University.

Mercer, Patricia M, and Clive R Moore

1976 Melanesians in North Queensland: The Retention of Indigenous Religious and Magical Practices. *Journal of Pacific History* 11 (1): 66–88.

1978 Australia's Pacific Islanders. *Journal of Pacific History* 13 (2): 90–101.

Merle, Isabelle

1991 The Foundation of Voh 1892–1895: French Migrants on the West Coast of New Caledonia. *Journal of Pacific History* 26 (2): 234–244.

1995 *Expériences Coloniales: La Nouvelle-Calédonie 1853–1920.* Paris: Benin.

Miklouho-Maclay, Nikolai

1882 Letter to Commodore Wilson [nd]. Appendix to Wilson 1882.

MNC, Minister for Navy and Colonies

1865 Minister for Navy and Colonies to Governor of New Caledonia, 26 September. Archives d'Outre-Mer, NC carton 282.

1885 Telegram to Governor Le Boucher, 16 March. Archives d'Outre-Mer, NC carton 282.

Moncelon, Léon

1882 La vérité sur l'immigration (The truth about immigration). *Néo-Calédonien,* 8 August.

Monin, Dr
    1882 Contributions à la Géographie Médicale—Nouvelles-Hébrides, part 1. *Archives de médicine navale* 38:401–441.
    1883 Contributions à la Géographie Médicale—Nouvelles-Hébrides, part 2. *Archives de médicine navale* 39:58–67.
Le Moniteur
    1860–1886 *Le Moniteur de la Nouvelle-Calédonie.* Noumea. Official weekly. In mid-1886 renamed *Journal Officiel.*
Moore, Clive
    1979 *The Forgotten People.* Sydney: Australian Broadcasting Commission.
    1981 Kanakas, Kidnapping and Slavery: Myths from the Nineteenth-Century Labour Trade and Their Relevance to Australia's Immigrant Melanesians. *Kabar Seberang: Sulating Maphilindo* 8–9:78–92.
    1985 *Kanaka: A History of Melanesian Mackay.* Port Moresby: Institute of Papua New Guinea Studies and University of Papua New Guinea Press.
    1992 Revising the Revisionists: The Historiography of Immigrant Melanesians in Australia. *Pacific Studies* 15 (2): 61–86.
Moore, Clive, Jacqueline Leckie, and Doug Munro, editors
    1990 *Labour in the South Pacific.* Townsville, Qld: James Cook University.
Morrell, W P
    1960 *Britain in the Pacific Islands.* Oxford: Oxford University Press.
Muljono-Larue, Fidayanti
    1996 *L'Immigration Javanaise en Nouvelle-Calédonie de 1896 à 1850.* Points d'Histoire, 10. Noumea: Centre Territorial de Recherche et de Documentation Pédagogiques, Nouvelle-Calédonie.
Munro, Doug
    1993 The Pacific Islands Labour Trade: Approaches, Methodologies, Debates. *Slavery and Abolition* 14 (2): 87–108.
    1995 Revisionism and Its Enemies: Debating the Queensland Labour Trade. Review of *Cane and Labour* by Adrian Graves. *Journal of Pacific History* 30 (2): 240–249.
Munro, Doug, and Stewart Firth
    1987 From Company Rule to Consular Control: Gilbert Island Labourers on German Plantations in Samoa, 1867–96. *Journal of Imperial and Commonwealth History* 16:24–44.
Le Néo-Calédonien
    1880–1889 Newspaper, Noumea. First weekly, then twice weekly, then thrice weekly.
New Hebrides Inquiry
    1927 Report of the Commission of Inquiry into the Position of the British Settlers in the New Hebrides. Suva: Government Printer. Australian Archives, Canberra. 19 (New Hebrides), A981.
NHJC, New Hebrides Joint Court
    1911 Public Prosecutor of Joint Court of New Hebrides Condominium to Commandant of Police, British Division, Vila. In GBCO 225/107.
Nicholson, Reverend J Campbell
    1909 Newsletter [from] Lenakel, Tanna, September. *Quarterly Jottings* 67 (January 1910).

1910 Article in *Auckland Weekly News,* 1 December. Cutting enclosed in GBFO 371/1290.

1912*a* From Our First Mission Station. Lenakel, Tanna, July. Newsletter. *Quarterly Jottings* 79 (January 1913): 7.

1912*b* From Our First Mission Station. Lenakel, Tanna, 12 November. Newsletter. *Quarterly Jottings* 80 (April 1913): 12.

Noblet, Father Adrien

1926 Letter to Bishop Chanrion, Paita, 27 December. Archives de l'Archevêché de Noumea. 71.2.

1928 Letter to Bishop Chanrion, Paita, 4 June. Archives de l'Archevêché de Noumea. 71.2.

Noiriel, Gerard

1990 *Workers in French Society in the 19th and 20th Century.* New York: Berg.

Notes on the French labor trade

1876 Copy of an account [not bearing the name of the author] of the French labour trade in 1875, sent by Sir Robert Herbert, late premier of Queensland, then permanent undersecretary in the Colonial Office, to the Foreign Office, 14 July. GBFO 27/2294.

La Nouvelle-Calédonie

1878–1879 Weekly newspaper. Noumea.

NSW Royal Commission

1869 Royal Commission Appointed to Inquire into Certain Alleged Cases of Kidnapping of Natives of the Loyalty Islands, etc. Together with Minutes of Evidence and Appendix. Sydney. Proceedings in RNAS 21.

Ollivaud, Jules

1881 Extract of journal, on board the *Effie Meikle. Progrès,* 25 December.

Olry, Jean, Vice-Amiral

1882 Letter of Governor Olry to Minister for Navy and Colonies, 14 April 1880. Archives d'Outre-Mer, NC carton 282.

O'Reilly, Father Patrick

1957 *Hébridais: Répertoire bio-bibliographique des Nouvelles Hébrides.* Publications of the Société des Océanistes, 6. Paris: Musée de l'Homme.

Pallu de la Barrière, Léopold

1882*a* Instructions to M Marin d'Arbel, 23 October. In Des Granges Papers. Microfilm in Records Room, Division of Pacific and Asian History, Research School of Pacific and Asian Studies, Australian National University.

1882*b* Governor Pallu to Minister for Navy and Colonies, 8 December. Archives d'Outre-Mer, NC Affaires Politiques, carton 282.

Panoff, Michel

1979 Travailleurs, recruteurs et planteurs dans l'Archipel Bismarck de 1885 à 1914. *Journal de la Société des Océanistes* 35 (64): 159–173.

1991 The French Way in Plantation Systems. *Journal of Pacific History* 26 (2): 206–212.

Pardon, Noel

1890 Governor Noel Pardon to Under-Secretary of State for Colonies, Noumea, 20 May. Archives d'Outre-Mer, NC carton 63.

References

Parisot, Governor
  1947 Governor Parisot to Minister of France Overseas, 29 October. Archives Territoriales de la Nouvelle Calédonie, 44 W 592, no 848, SG 1.
Parnaby, Owen W
  1964 *Britain and the Labor Trade in the Southwest Pacific.* Durham, NC: Duke University Press.
  1972 The Labour Trade. In *Man in the Pacific Islands,* edited by R Gerard Ward, 124–142. Oxford: Clarendon Press.
Passant, Père Louis
  1913*a* Letter to Bishop Chanrion, Paita, 28 February. Archives de l'Archevêché de Noumea. 71.2.
  1913*b* Letter to Bishop Chanrion, Paita, 19 June. Archives de l'Archevêché de Noumea. 71.2.
Paton, Reverend F H L
  1896 Lenakel News, no 2, November. *Quarterly Jottings* 16 (April 1897).
  1897 Letter from Lenakel, Tanna, 28 January. *Quarterly Jottings* 17 (July).
  1913 Slavery under the British Flag: Representations Made by Unofficial Bodies & Individuals, 1924–1940. Australian Archives, Canberra. CRS/A981, New Hebrides, 72, III.
Petit, F G
  1885 Report on the operations of this recruiting ship *[Marie],* from 21 February to 18 August. Archives d'Outre-Mer, NC carton 64.
Picquié, Albert
  1880 Letter to Victor Schoelcher, 16 January. In Schoelcher Papers [1877–1885].
Pinard, Albert
  1906 Consul-General of France at Sydney (Pinard) to Governor of New Caledonia, 28 September. Enclosed in Liotard 1906.
Politis, N
  1908 *Le Condominium Franco-Anglais des Nouvelles-Hébrides.* Paris: A Pedone.
Price, Charles A, and Elizabeth Baker
  1976 Origin of Pacifc Island Labourers in Queensland, 1863–1904. *Journal of Pacific History* 11 (2): 106–121.
Pritzbuer, Contre-Amiral L de
  1876 Confidential letter to Minister for Navy and Colonies, 23 February. Enclosed in Minister of Navy to Minister for Foreign Affairs, 17 May. In *M & D,* vol 4.
Le Progrès
  1881–1885 *Le Progrès de la Nouvelle-Calédonie* (1881–1884), then *Le Progrès de Nouméa* (1884–1885). Newspaper appearing at first weekly, then thrice weekly, then twice weekly.
PVCA, Procès-verbaux du Conseil d'Administration
  1879 *Procès-verbaux du Conseil d'Administration.* Archives d'Outre-Mer, Paris. NC carton 109.
PVCG, Procès-verbaux du Conseil général
  1880–1930 *Procès-verbaux du Conseil général.* Archives Territoriales de la Nouvelle-Calédonie, Noumea.

PVCP, Procès-verbaux du Conseil privé
1875 Extract of *Procès-verbaux du Conseil privé,* 15 October. Archives d'Outre-Mer, NC carton 282.
1881 *Procès-verbaux du Conseil privé.* March-April session. Archives Territoriales de la Nouvelle-Calédonie, Noumea. 44W 21*.
1884 *Procès-verbaux du Conseil privé.* Archives d'Outre-Mer, NC carton 125.
1885a *Procès-verbaux du Conseil privé.* Volume 1. Archives d'Outre-Mer, NC carton 127.
1885b *Procès-verbaux du Conseil privé.* Volume 2. Archives d'Outre-Mer, NC carton 128.
1889 *Procès-verbaux du Conseil privé.* Archives d'Outre-Mer, NC carton 134.

Q J, Quarterly Jottings from the New Hebrides, South Sea Islands
1897–1919 "Periodical issued by the John G Paton Mission Fund [Presbyterian Mission] for the evangelization of the remaining cannibals on these islands." Edited by A K Langridge. Pacific Manuscripts Bureau microfilm documentary series, 34–37.

Rae, Reverend J Campbell
1919 Newsletter [from] Lenakel, Tanna, 20 March. *Quarterly Jottings* 106 (October).

Ramsay, Government Agent
1871 Extract from the journal of Ramsay, Government Agent of the *Isabella,* 12 August, quoted in Brisbane Immigration Officer [Gray] to NSW Colonial Secretary, 27 November. Enclosure 4 in Belmore 1871.

Rannie, Douglas
1912 *My Adventures among South Sea Cannibals: An Account of the Experiences of a Government Official among the Natives of Oceania.* London: Seely, Service.

Rapports statistiques
1866–1874 Enclosures in letters from governors of New Caledonia to Minister for Navy and Colonies. Archives d'Outre-Mer, NC carton 28.

Rentz, Lieutenant E
1903 Report of Lieutenant E Rentz [Inspection mobile], commandant of the gendarmerie of the district (Koné), no 162, 5 August, and enclosing the reports of gendarme sergeants Lumier, Denis, Jasseron, and Lafourcade. Enclosed in Revel 1907a.
1907 Note de Service, 21 March. Enclosed in Revel 1907a.

Repiquet, Jules
1911 Letter from French Resident Commissioner Repiquet to British Resident Commissioner King, 5 December. Copy in GBCO 225/107.
1912 French Resident Commissioner to the New Hebrides, to British Resident Commissioner King, 14 January. GBCO 225/107.

Revel, Inspector
1907a Report of Inspector Revel *[Inspection mobile]* on the performance of Sergeant-Major Denis (Gendarmerie), Immigration Syndic for the district of Koné, to July 1906, with comments by Denis, Commandant Rentz, Inspector Fillon, and Governor Liotard. Archives d'Outre-Mer, NC carton 209.

1907*b* Report of Inspector Revel *[Inspection mobile]* on the performance of M Engler, Acting Head of the Department of Immigration, with comments by Inspector Fillon, M Engler, and Governor Liotard. Archives d'Outre-Mer, NC carton 209.

1907*c* Report of Inspector Revel *[Inspection mobile]* on the performance of M Lechanteur, head warden and accountant of the Native Depot. Archives d'Outre-Mer, NC carton 209.

RNAS, Royal Navy Australian Station
1857–1900 Correspondence: 13–19, Pacific Islands; 20, High Commissioner; 21, Kidnapping; 32, New Caledonia; 33–35, New Hebrides; 38, New Guinea and Solomon Islands. Includes some printed materials, some manuscripts, and copies of letters from other departments. [National Archives, Wellington. Microfilm read at Australian National Library, Canberra.]

Rodman, Margaret
1981 A Boundary and a Bridge: Women's Pig-killing as a Border-Crossing between Spheres of Exchange in East Aoba. In *Vanuatu,* edited by Michael Allen, 85–104. Sydney: Academic Press.

Rouzaud, Government Agent
1875 Report on the Recruitment of New Hebrideans. Enclosed in Governor Pritzbuer to Minister for Navy and Colonies, 8 September. Archives d'Outre-Mer, NC carton 282.

Rubinstein, Robert L
1981 Knowledge and Political Process on Malo. In *Vanuatu,* edited by Michael Allen, 135–172. Sydney: Academic Press.

Saunders, Kay
1980 Melanesian Women in Queensland, 1863–1907: Some Methodological Problems Involving the Relationship betweeen Racism and Sexism. *Pacific Studies* 4 (1): 26–44.

1982 *Workers in Bondage: The Origins and Bases of Unfree Labour in Queensland, 1824–1916.* St Lucia: University of Queensland Press.

1988 The Black Scourge. Part 2 in *Race Relations in Colonial Queensland: Exclusion, Exploitation and Extermination,* by Raymond Evans, Kay Saunders, and Kathryn Cronin, 147–234. St Lucia: Queensland University Press.

Scarr, Deryck
1967 *Fragments of Empire: A History of the Western Pacific High Commission 1877–1914.* Canberra: Australian National University Press; Honolulu: University of Hawai'i Press (1968).

1970 Recruits and Recruiters. In *Pacific Islands Portraits,* edited by J W Davidson and Deryck Scarr, 225–251. Canberra: Australian National University Press.

Schoelcher, Victor
[1877–1885] Papiers de Victor Schoelcher relatif aux colonies françaises, volume 1. MS in Biblothèque Nationale, Paris.

Servent, Pascale
1995 Le lèpre: Essai pour le Licence d'Histoire, mention Géographie. Typescript in Archives Territoriales de la Nouvelle Calédonie, Noumea.

Settlers' Petition
  1882 Petition of the Settlers of New Caledonia to the President of the Re-
        public, nd. Reproduced in *Néo-Calédonien*, 4 July 1882.
Shameem, Shaista
  1987 Gender, Class and Race Dynamics: Indian Women in Sugar Pro-
        duction in Fiji. *Journal of Pacific Studies* 13:10–35.
  1990 Girmitiya Women in Fiji. In *Labour in the South Pacific*, edited by Clive
        Moore, Jacqueline Leckie, and Doug Munro, 148–154. Townsville:
        James Cook University.
Shineberg, Dorothy
  1967 *They Came for Sandalwood: A Study of the Sandalwood Trade in the South-
        West Pacific 1830–1865.* Carlton, Vic: Melbourne University Press.
  1972 Guns and Men in Melanesia. *Journal of Pacific History* 6 (1): 61–72.
  1991 Noumea No Good, Noumea No Pay: "New Hebridean" Labour
        in New Caledonia, 1865–1925. *Journal of Pacific History* 26 (2): 186–
        205.
  1994 La Main-d'oeuvre Néo-Hébridaise en Nouvelle-Calédonie, 1865–
        1929. In *Le Peuplement du Pacifique et de la Nouvelle-Calédonie au XIXe
        Siècle*, edited by Paul De Deckker, 192–207. Paris: Harmattan.
  1995 "The New Hebridean Is Everywhere": The Oceanian Indentured
        Labor Trade to New Caledonia, 1865–1930. *Pacific Studies* 18 (2): 1–22.
Shineberg, Dorothy, and Jean-Marie Kohler
  1990 Church and Commerce in New Caledonia: Ballande and the
        Bishops, 1885–1935. *Journal of Pacific History* 25:1–20.
Shipping reports
  1865-1930 Information drawn from the ship-movement columns of all
        the newspapers in New Caledonia over this period, as described in
        Note on Sources.
Shlomowitz, Ralph
  1987 Mortality and the Pacific Labour Trade. *Journal of Pacific History* 22
        (1): 34–55.
Siegel, Jeff
  1985 Origins of Pacific Islands Labourers in Fiji. *Journal of Pacific History*
        20 (1): 42–56.
Smith-Rewse, G B
  1924 British Resident Commissioner's Report on the New Hebrides for
        January to June 1924, 4 December. In WPHC IC 3149/24.
Southern Cross Log
  1898–1911 Periodical. Auckland and Sydney: Melanesian Mission. Micro-
        film in National Library of Australia, Canberra.
Steel, Robert
  1880 *The New Hebrides and Christian Missions: With a Sketch of the Labour
        Traffic.* London: James Nisbet.
Stoler, Anne Laura
  1991 Carnal Knowledge and Imperial Power: Gender, Race, and Morality
        in Colonial Asia. In *Gender at the Crossroads of Knowledge*, edited by
        Micaela di Leonardo, 51–101. Berkeley and Los Angeles: University of
        California Press.

Stone, Judith F
   1985 *The Search for Social Peace: Reform Legislation in France, 1890–1914.*
        New York: State University of New York Press.
Suckling, Lieutenant
   1873 Proceedings of HMS *Renard* in the New Hebrides, 4 September.
        Subenclosure 1: Despatches from the Governor of Victoria, no 16. In
        GBPP 1874.
Telegraph
   1892 Cutting from Brisbane *Telegraph* of 31 December 1892, an extract
        from the log of the British labor vessel *Foam.* Enclosed in letter of
        Sir H W Norman to Marquess of Ripon, 7 January 1893, with enclo-
        sures. In GBPP 1893–1894, no 39.
Thomas, Julian [Stanley James]
   1886 *Cannibals and Convicts: Notes of Personal Experiences in the Western
        Pacific.* London: Cassell.
   1887*a* In the South Seas. Series of articles by "The Vagabond" [Stanley
        James] in the *Age* (Melbourne), 2 July to 26 November.
   1887*b* Letter to High Commissioner of Western Pacific, 20 July. WPHC IC
        219/87.
Thompson, Ann-Gabrielle
   1982 John Higginson, 1839–1904: Patriot or Profiteer? PhD thesis, Uni-
        versity of Queensland, Brisbane.
Tinker, Hugh
   1974 *A New System of Slavery: The Export of Indian Labour Overseas, 1830–
        1920.* Oxford: Oxford University Press.
Town and Country
   1872–1887 *Town and Country: A Weekly Journal of Victorian Progress.*
        Melbourne.
Tribunal Correctionel
   1856–1896 Records of Judgments. Archives Territoriales de la Nouvelle
        Calédonie, Noumea.
Tribunal de Simple Police
   1881–1884 Tribunal de Simple Police. Thio, New Caledonia: Records of
        Judgments. Archives Territoriales de la Nouvelle Calédonie, Noumea.
Venus Inquiry
   1880 Report and Proceedings of the Inquiry into the Accusations against
        the *Venus* during the Immigration Voyage of 11 December 1879 to
        March of This Year. Noumea, 7 December. Archives d'Outre-Mer, NC
        carton 63.
Venus Trial
   1882 Notes of Evidence taken on the Trial of Walter Champion, Eu-
        gene Duret, and Marie-Ernst Perrot, of the *Venus,* for Kidnapping. In
        RNAS 16.
Vitte, Monseigneur Fernand, Bishop of New Caledonia
   1874 Rapport sur l'état de la religion Catholique dans le Vicariat Apos-
        tolique de la Nouvelle- Calédonie à Son Eminence le Cardinal Franchi,
        Préfet de la Sacra Congregatione di Propaganda Fide [SCPF], 4 Au-
        gust. Archives de l'Archevêché de Noumea. 24.5.7.

1875*a* Letter to SCPF, 25 March. Archives de l'Archevêché de Noumea. 24.5.12.

1875*b* Report to SCPF, 3 December. Archives de l'Archevêché de Noumea. 24.5.9.

1877 Letter to Cardinal Franchi, 20 May. Archives de l'Archevêché de Noumea. 24.5.14.

Walker, Vernon Lee

1885 Letter to his mother in Melbourne, from Noumea, 3 February. Manuscript in La Trobe Library, Melbourne. Copy in Rhodes House, Oxford.

Ward, John M

1948 *British Policy in the South Pacific.* Sydney: Australasian Publishing Company.

Wawn, William T

1870–1874 Amongst the South Sea Islands. Manuscript in Alexander Turnbull Library, Wellington.

1888–1900 Private logs of Cruises in the Pacific Islands, 1888–1900. Manuscript A1477 in Mitchell Library, Sydney.

1893 *The South Sea Islanders and the Queensland Labour Trade.* London: Swann & Sonnenschein.

Wecker, Government Agent E

1880 Extract from his journal on board the schooner *Winifred,* 22 July. Enclosure 3 in Courbet 1880*a*.

Wilkes, W

1912 Government Agent on Tanna to British Resident Commissioner for New Hebrides, 10 October. Enclosure in Mahaffy 1912*c*.

Wilson, Bishop Cecil

1903 Kidnapped: A True Story of 1903. *Southern Cross Log,* November, 83–86.

Wilson, Commodore J C

1880 Letter to British Consul in New Caledonia, 19 August. Enclosure 1 in Courbet 1880*a*.

1882 Report of Commodore Wilson on the labour trade in the Western Pacific [nd]. Enclosure 33, in Earl of Kimberley to Governors of the Australasian Colonies, 26 February. (Circular). In GBPP 1883.

Winslow, Donna

1990 Workers in New Caledonia to 1945. In *Labour in the South Pacific,* edited by Clive Moore, Jacqueline Leckie, and Doug Munro, 108–121. Townsville: James Cook University.

WPHC IC, Western Pacific High Commission Inwards Correspondence

1876–1925 Inwards Correspondence, General. Public Record Office, London. Microfilm in National Library of Australia, Canberra.

WPHC papers

1893–1898 H[er] B[ritannic] M[ajesty's] Consulate, Noumea, New Caledonia, 158. Various papers salvaged by Consul Dunlop in 1921 and relating to ships and consulate matters. Public Record Office, London. Microfilm in National Library of Australia, Canberra.

Index

Australia, 163, 164, 229. *See also* New
    South Wales; Queensland; Victoria
Australian Navigation Company, 163
Avenir, L' (newspaper), 211

Babai (Solomon Islander), 158
Babartanobe of Malakula, 88
Baguil (settler), 179
Bai of Santo, 85
Balade, 11–13
Ballande, André, 220
Ballande et Fils (merchant company),
    130, 142, 150, 172, 178, 198, 210;
    mines of, 70, 141
Ballière, Achille, 150
Bandler, Faith, 3, 8, 47
Banks Islands, 54, 71; as a source of la-
    bor, 5, 9. *See also* Gaua; Merelava;
    Vanua Lava
Barrau and Company (Maison Barrau),
    68, 162, 228
Baua of Epi, 37
"beach payment," 16, 18, 75, 77, 85, 122,
    235–236; in cash, 94; in firearms,
    60, 85, 122. *See also* "passage
    money"
Béchade, André de, 99, 100
bêche-de-mer trade, 15, 76, 132
Bel-Air nickel mine (Houailou), 38, 40
Bennett, Judith, 8, 235
Bérard, Louis Théodore, 13, 15, 208
Beriri of Santo, 98
Bernheim, Lucien, 57
Bice, Reverend Charles, 94
Bigant, Commander, 58, 59, 63, 64, 67,
    81, 82, 191, 224
Big-men: role of in the labor trade, 81,
    83, 85
Bili of Ambae, 168, 169
Bislama, 15, 25, 32, 54, 59, 105, 125,
    203; as lingua franca, 224. *See also*
    Pidgin
Blanchot, Barthélémy, 167
Blandeau, Councillor, 151, 172, 200
Bobtail Nag, 33
Bonite (French warship), 148
Boob of Ambrym, 38
Booth, Benjamin, 158
Bouléwara of Pentecost, 88
Bouloupari, 88, 158, 214
Bourail, 14
Bouscarel, François-Abel, 167
Bowie, Reverend F, 122

Bozérou, 171
Briault, Martial, 64, 65
Bridge, Captain Cyprian, 5
British consul: in Fiji, 29; in Noumea,
    36, 142, 193
Brock, John, 127
Brooke, Reverend Charles Hyde, 28
Bruat (French warship), 54, 64
Brun, Gratien, 139
Brunet, Charles, 99
Bulletin du Commerce (newspaper), 193
burial of laborers, 20, 195, 198, 202; cost
    of, 201; regulations on, 201

Cacon, 155
Calédonie, La (newspaper), 85, 142, 152,
    171, 193, 195, 211, 212, 222, 230
Calédonien (ship), 87
Campbell, F A, 7
Canala, 134, 158, 192; non-payment of
    workers at, 168, 171; plantation
    laborers at, 57, 111, 131, 132, 135,
    140, 168; recruits arriving at, 126,
    132; repatriates from, 22, 168
Caporn, William & Co, 201
Cariou, Marc, 99
Carter, Douglas, 34, 82, 126, 168, 169
Catholic church, 217, 227. *See also* Marist
    mission
cattle industry, 131, 137, 238
Chamber of Commerce, Noumea, 37, 48
Champion, Joseph, 44
Champion, Walter, 43, 44, 65, 158
Charley of Efaté, 97
Chassaniol (deputy administrator of the
    Marine Registry), 54–55
Chesterfield Islands, 134
Cheval, Hippolyte, 39
chiefs: role of, in labor trade, 81–83,
    85
child workers, 33, 89, 164, 193, 205, 208,
    234; age of, 116, 118, 119, 122;
    and the church, 218, 219; deaths
    among, 120, 184, 218, 219; food
    rations for, 148; how to recruit,
    122; occupations of, 121–122, 218;
    proportion of, 116, 119–122; term
    of indenture, 120; wages, 22, 167
Christianity: and Oceanian laborers,
    219, 220, 224; converts to, 7, 43, 87,
    88, 227; in the New Hebrides, 220.
    See also London Missionary Society;
    Marist mission; Melanesian Mis-

DOROTHY SHINEBERG holds a BA and PhD from Melbourne University and an MA from Smith College in Massachusetts, where she was a Teaching Fellow for two years. She taught Pacific Islands history (then called colonial history) at the Australian School of Pacific Administration as early as 1948 and introduced the first university course in the subject at Melbourne University in 1953. Moving to Canberra and the Australian National University in 1964, she became first a Research Fellow at the Institute of Advanced Studies and then, from 1971 to 1988, taught Pacific history in the history department. She is the author of *They Came for Sandalwood* (1967; the French edition appeared in 1973 as *Ils étaient venus chercher du santal*). She edited *The Trading Voyages of Andrew Cheyne* (1971) and has published numerous scholarly articles. She is presently a Visiting Fellow in the Division of Pacific and Asian History at the Australian National University.